AN INTRODUCTION TO POETRY

LOUIS SIMPSON
State University of New York,
Stony Brook

An Introduction to Poetry

SECOND EDITION

ST. MARTIN'S PRESS   NEW YORK

ACKNOWLEDGMENTS

LEBERT BETHUNE: "A Juju of My Own," Copyright © 1968 by Lebert Bethune. Re-
printed from *Black Fire*, edited by LeRoi Jones and Larry Neal, William Morrow
Co., Inc., New York, N.Y. Used with permission of the author and the Ronald Hobbs
Literary Agency.

ROBERT BLY: "Waking from Sleep," "Poem Against the British," "Summer, 1960,
Minnesota," and "Love Poem," from *Silence in the Snowy Fields*, published by
Wesleyan University Press, 1962. Copyright 1962. Reprinted by permission of the
author.

JONATHAN CAPE, LTD.: "Naming of Parts," from *A Map of Verona and Other Poems*
by Henry Reed. London: Jonathan Cape, Ltd. Reprinted by permission of the publisher.

CHILMARK PRESS, INC.: "Vergissmeinicht," from *Selected Poems* by Keith Douglas.
Copyright by Marie J. Douglas, 1964. Reprinted by permission of the publisher.

CITY LIGHTS BOOKS: "Howl," Part I, from *Howl and Other Poems* by Allen Ginsberg.
Copyright © 1956, 1959 by Allen Ginsberg. Reprinted by permission of City Lights
Books.

CORINTH BOOKS INC.: "Preface to a Twenty Volume Suicide Note" by LeRoi Jones.
New York: Totem Press in association with Corinth Books, 1961. Reprinted by
permission.

DODD, MEAD & CO.: "White Heliotrope" by Arthur Symons is reprinted from *Poems*
by Arthur Symons.

DOUBLEDAY & COMPANY, INC.: "Old Pond," "Fallen Petals Rise," and "Wild Geese,"
from *An Introduction to Haiku* by Harold G. Henderson. Copyright © 1956 by
Harold G. Henderson. Reprinted by permission of Doubleday & Company, Inc.

"Danny Deever," from *Rudyard Kipling's Verse: Definitive Edition*. Reprinted by
permission of Mrs. George Bambridge and Doubleday & Company, Inc.

"Night Journey," Copyright 1940 by Theodore Roethke; "My Papa's Waltz," Copy-
right 1942 by *Hearst* Magazines, Inc.; "Dolor," Copyright 1943 by Modern Poetry
Association Inc.; "Elegy for Jane," Copyright 1950 by Theodore Roethke; "The
Waking," Copyright 1953 by Theodore Roethke; and "The Rose," © 1963 by

PREFACE

In this new edition there is a larger selection of poems, with more poems by individual authors. There is also a considerable number of poems by men and women who are writing today. The introductory section on "The Art of Poetry" has been rewritten, and in general the text has been revised so that it will be more useful to students and teachers.

The emphasis, however, is on reading for enjoyment, for there is no understanding of poetry if we do not enjoy it. For this reason I have not given directions for reading the poems or lists of questions to be answered. Directions of this kind turn reading poetry into a dreary exercise, and though some readers may want them, many more do not. On the other hand, the book does offer considerable assistance in keeping with the main intention—to enable the reader to understand poetry for himself, not to tell him what it means. Without usurping the function of the reader or teacher, I have undertaken to explain the elements of poetry in sections on "The Art of Poetry" and "Reading the Poem." There is a straightforward explanation of "Meter, Rhyme, Stanza, and Sound," and a Glossary with numerous examples and cross-references to the poems. The poems in the anthology have footnotes explaining obscure words and allusions.

The poems are arranged in chronological order. Of course, this does not mean that they are to be read in that order. Some readers prefer to begin with contemporary poems that engage their interest immediately. A study of narrative poetry, for example, could begin with Gary Snyder's "Hay for the Horses," written a few years ago, move back in time to Robert Frost's "The Code," and further back to Gerard Manley Hopkins' "Felix Randal." A study of songs could begin with "Eleanor Rigby," then go to Robert Burns, and Shakespeare, and end with the anonymous lyrics at the beginning of the book.

Readers may want to study particular types or genres of poetry. The ballad . . . beginning with "Sir Patrick Spens," including literary ballads by Coleridge and Keats, and ending with a narrative song written in this century. The elegy . . . there are elegies by Tichborne, Donne, Milton, Dryden, Gray, Williams, Roethke, and Lowell. Other poems are elegiac, though they are not so called. Working from this anthology, a study could be made of the art of meditative poetry, or satiric verse. Readers may wish to concentrate on a certain aspect of technique. The study of a certain form of stanza, or a study of free verse, could be made in some depth.

There are poems about war by Byron, Whitman, Wilfred Owen, E. E. Cummings, Keith Douglas, and Denise Levertov. There are love poems from every age, expressing various attitudes. But I shall not make further suggestions of this kind, for it will be thought that poetry is to be read for its theme or subject matter and readers are to be continually comparing one poem with another. Anyone who reads the introductory sections will see that, in my opinion, the subject of a poem is only part of its effect. Nevertheless, understanding what a poem is about may be a sensible way to begin. Having understood the statement in the poem, the student may move toward understanding how the poet achieves his effects—that is, what the poetry itself consists of. And though comparisons may not prove anything, comparing two poems on the same theme may bring out the individual qualities of each author. In this anthology, Walt Whitman's meditations are immediately followed by Matthew Arnold's; the scenes the poems present are similar, but the thoughts are very different. To explore these differences would show something about both poets and the age in which they lived.

Since the first edition of this book was published my ideas about the nature of poetry have become clearer; I have read a great deal more and over a wider range. Therefore, in making this new edition I have felt freer to include poems I like, though they are off the beaten track—for example, John Clare's "The Badger" and John Davidson's "Thirty Bob a Week." In choosing poems by well-known authors, I have found aspects of their work that are not usually represented in anthologies. Some of the poems by Emily Dickinson that I have chosen show a colorful impressionism, unlike the witty or the funereal poetry she is usually represented by. The selections from the poetry of Wallace Stevens and William Carlos Williams are very much the product of an independent reconsideration of their work. The poems by thirty contemporary authors were selected after reading many books and listening to many poets read their own works aloud.

In one respect this edition is quite different from the first: there are more poems here that are fun. I had almost said "simply fun," but there is often more to such poems than meets the eye. It could be argued that T. S. Eliot's cat, Macavity, who becomes the more real the less he is actually there, demonstrates something in theology, or at least in logic; and that though Gregory Corso's poem on "Marriage" is funny, it is also social commentary.

In revising, I have taken into account the opinions of readers of the first edition, and I should like to thank them here for giving me the benefit of their experience with it in the classroom. In response to their suggestions, the section on "The Art of Poetry" has been rewritten, making it clearer and taking out the quotations. The section on "Reading the Poem" has been revised so that my readings of the poems show a line of development in the use of images through symbolism, imagism, and surrealism to the present.

The Glossary has been brought up to date; it now includes current items such as Concrete Poetry and Sound Poetry. Following the advice of readers, I have avoided making extracts from long poems. But on a few occasions it was necessary; not to represent Byron with passages from *Childe Harold* and *Don Juan* would be to misrepresent him; besides, these episodes are fairly complete in themselves.

There is a limit to what can be put in a book, and I trust that what is here will more than make up for what is not—that readers will be pleased to have eleven sonnets by Shakespeare, and three odes by Keats, including "Ode to Psyche," which is usually neglected. Some readers of this book will come across Robert Duncan or Sylvia Plath for the first time, and even readers who have read a good deal of contemporary poetry may not have read Carl Rakosi. There may be readers for whom my writing on "The Art of Poetry" will be useful; I hope so, for I have put nearly everything I know about poetry into these few pages.

CONTENTS

An Introduction
to Poetry

THE ART OF POETRY 1

READING THE POEM 13

METER, RHYME, STANZA, AND SOUND 34

An Anthology
of Poems

GEOFFREY CHAUCER   [1340?-1400]

FROM *The Canterbury Tales* 45

ANONYMOUS

I Sing of a Maiden 48
Adam Lay I-bowndyn 48
Who Wot Nowe That Ys Here 49
Sumer Is Icumen In 49
I Haue a Yong Suster 50
Sir Patrick Spens 50
Thomas the Rhymer 51
Edward, Edward 53

SIR THOMAS WYATT   [1503?-1542]

*The Lover Showeth How He Is Forsaken of Such
as He Sometime Enjoyed* 55

BARNABE GOOGE   [1540-1594]

Out of Sight, Out of Mind 55

SIR WALTER RALEGH   [1552?-1618]

   To His Son   56

EDMUND SPENSER   [1552?-1599]

   Epithalamion   56

SIR PHILIP SIDNEY   [1554-1586]

   31   With How Sad Steps   66

CHIDIOCK TICHBORNE   [1558-1586]

   Tichborne's Elegy   67

GEORGE PEELE   [1559-1596]

   Gently Dip   67
   A Sonnet   68

ROBERT SOUTHWELL   [1561-1595]

   The Burning Babe   68

SAMUEL DANIEL   [1562-1619]

   45   Care-Charmer Sleep   69

MICHAEL DRAYTON   [1563-1631]

   61   Since There's No Help   69

CHRISTOPHER MARLOWE   [1564-1593]

   The Passionate Shepherd to His Love   70

ANONYMOUS

   As You Came from the Holy Land of Walsingham   70
   Crabbed Age and Youth   72

WILLIAM SHAKESPEARE   [1564-1616]

   Under the Greenwood Tree   72
   Blow, Blow, Thou Winter Wind!   72
   It Was a Lover   73
   O Mistress Mine   74
   Take, O! Take   74
   Fear No More   74
   Full Fathom Five   75
   FROM *Sonnets*
      12   "When I do count the clock that tells the time"   75
      18   "Shall I compare thee to a summer's day?"   75

30   *"When to the sessions of sweet silent thought"*   76
65   *"Since brass, nor stone, nor earth, nor boundless sea"*   76
66   *"Tired with all these, for restful death I cry"*   77
73   *"That time of year thou mayst in me behold"*   77
87   *"Farewell! thou art too dear for my possessing"*   77
94   *"They that have power to hurt, and will do none"*   78
116   *"Let me not to the marriage of true minds"*   78
129   *"Th' expense of spirit in a waste of shame"*   79
130   *"My mistress' eyes are nothing like the sun"*   79

THOMAS CAMPION   [1567-1620]

Rose-Cheeked Laura   79

THOMAS DEKKER   [1570?-1632?]

Art Thou Poor   80

JOHN DONNE   [1572-1631]

The Good-morrow   81
Song   "Go and catch a falling star"   81
The Bait   82
A Valediction Forbidding Mourning   83
The Ecstasy   84
Elegie 9   The Autumnal   86
FROM *Holy Sonnets*
   7   *"At the round earth's imagin'd corners, blow"*   87
   13   *"What if this present were the world's last night?"*   87
   14   *"Batter my heart, three-person'd God; for you"*   88

BEN JONSON   [1572-1637]

Clerimont's Song   88
The Triumph of Charis   88
That Women Are but Men's Shadows   89

JOHN WEBSTER   [1580?-1638]

Cornelia's Song   90
Hark, Now Everything Is Still   90

ROBERT HERRICK   [1591-1674]

Delight in Disorder   91
To the Virgins, to Make Much of Time   91
To Daffodils   92
Upon Julia's Clothes   92
Grace for a Child   92

GEORGE HERBERT [1593-1633]

The Altar   93
Redemption   93
Easter Wings   94
Prayer (1)   94
Artillery   95
The Collar   95
The Pulley   96

THOMAS CAREW [1594?-1640?]

A Song *"Ask me no more where Jove bestows"*   97

JOHN MILTON [1608-1674]

How Soon Hath Time   98
Lycidas   98
On His Blindness   103

SIR JOHN SUCKLING [1609-1642]

Song *"Why so pale and wan, fond lover?"*   103

RICHARD LOVELACE [1618-1658]

To Lucasta, Going to the Wars   104
To Althea, from Prison   104

ANDREW MARVELL [1621-1678]

To His Coy Mistress   105
The Definition of Love   106
The Garden   107
An Horatian Ode Upon Cromwell's Return from Ireland   109

HENRY VAUGHAN [1622-1695]

The Retreat   112
They Are All Gone into the World of Light   113

JOHN DRYDEN [1631-1700]

To the Memory of Mr. Oldham   114
A Song for St. Cecilia's Day   115
All, All of a Piece   117

JONATHAN SWIFT [1667-1745]

A Description of the Morning   117

ALEXANDER POPE [1688-1744]

Epistle to Dr. Arbuthnot   118

SAMUEL JOHNSON [1709-1784]

    A Short Song of Congratulation   128
    On the Death of Dr. Robert Levet   129

THOMAS GRAY [1716-1771]

    Elegy   130

CHRISTOPHER SMART [1722-1771]

    FROM *Jubilate Agno*   133

WILLIAM BLAKE [1757-1827]

    FROM *Songs of Innocence*
        Introduction   135
        The Lamb   135
        Holy Thursday   136
    FROM *Songs of Experience*
        Introduction   136
        Earth's Answer   137
        The Clod and the Pebble   138
        Holy Thursday   138
        The Sick Rose   138
        The Tiger   139
        London   139
        Infant Sorrow   140
    FROM *Milton*   "*And did those feet in ancient time*"   140
    Never Seek to Tell Thy Love   140

ROBERT BURNS [1759-1796]

    Holy Willie's Prayer   141
    To a Mouse   144
    O Whistle, and I'll Come to You, My Lad   145
    O, My Luve Is Like a Red, Red Rose   145

WILLIAM WORDSWORTH [1770-1850]

    Lines Composed a Few Miles Above Tintern Abbey   146
    A Slumber Did My Spirit Seal   149
    Composed upon Westminster Bridge   150
    Resolution and Independence   150
    The Solitary Reaper   154

SAMUEL TAYLOR COLERIDGE [1772-1834]

    Kubla Khan   155
    The Rime of the Ancient Mariner   156

GEORGE GORDON, LORD BYRON   [1788-1824]

She Walks in Beauty   173
Prometheus   173
FROM *Childe Harold's Pilgrimage, Canto III*   175
FROM *Don Juan, Canto XI*   182

PERCY BYSSHE SHELLEY   [1792-1822]

Song to the Men of England   186
Similes for Two Political Characters of 1819   187
Ode to the West Wind   188
To a Skylark   190

JOHN CLARE   [1793-1864]

The Badger   193

JOHN KEATS   [1795-1821]

La Belle Dame sans Merci   194
Ode to Psyche   196
Ode to a Nightingale   197
Ode on a Grecian Urn   199
This Living Hand   201
Bright Star   201

ELIZABETH BARRETT BROWNING   [1806-1861]

43   How Do I Love Thee?   202

EDGAR ALLAN POE   [1809-1849]

To Helen   202

ALFRED, LORD TENNYSON   [1809-1892]

Mariana   203
Ulysses   205
Tears, Idle Tears   206
"Frater Ave Atque Vale"   207

ROBERT BROWNING   [1812-1889]

My Last Duchess   207
Meeting at Night   208
A Likeness   209
"De Gustibus——"   210

EDWARD LEAR   [1812-1888]

By Way of Preface   212

WALT WHITMAN [1819-1892]

There Was a Child Went Forth   213
FROM Starting from Paumanok   214
FROM Song of Myself   214
A Farm Picture   216
Beat! Beat! Drums!   216
Cavalry Crossing a Ford   217
An Army Corps on the March   217
FROM Marches Now the War Is Over   218
The Runner   218
The World Below the Brine   219
On the Beach, at Night   219

MATTHEW ARNOLD [1822-1888]

Dover Beach   220

EMILY DICKINSON [1830-1884]

Success Is Counted Sweetest   221
I Like a Look of Agony   222
The Soul Selects Her Own Society   222
After Great Pain, a Formal Feeling Comes   222
There's Been a Death, in the Opposite House   223
They Shut Me Up in Prose   223
The Way I Read a Letter's—This   224
The Name—of It—Is "Autumn"   224
Ah, Teneriffe!   225
A Drunkard Cannot Meet a Cork   225

LEWIS CARROLL [1832-1898]

The White Knight's Song   225
Jabberwocky   227

THOMAS HARDY [1840-1928]

Drummer Hodge   229
The Darkling Thrush   229
The Man He Killed   230
When I Set Out for Lyonnesse   231
"Ah, Are You Digging on My Grave?"   231
Afterwards   232

GERARD MANLEY HOPKINS [1844-1889]

The Starlight Night   233
The Windhover   233
Pied Beauty   234

Binsey Poplars 234
Felix Randal 235
Spring and Fall: To a Young Child 235
No Worst, There Is None 236
My Own Heart Let Me More Have Pity On 236

JOHN DAVIDSON [1857-1909]
Thirty Bob a Week 237

A. E. HOUSMAN [1859-1936]
On Forelands High in Heaven 239

RUDYARD KIPLING [1865-1936]
Danny Deever 240

ARTHUR SYMONS [1865-1945]
White Heliotrope 241

WILLIAM BUTLER YEATS [1865-1939]
The Lake Isle of Innisfree 242
Paudeen 242
Easter 1916 242
The Second Coming 244
Sailing to Byzantium 245
Byzantium 246
Meru 247
Lapis Lazuli 248
A Crazed Girl 249
Long-Legged Fly 249
Politics 250

ROBERT FROST [1875-1963]
Mending Wall 251
The Code 252
Stopping by Woods on a Snowy Evening 254
Design 255

EDWARD THOMAS [1878-1917]
The Gallows 255
Aspens 256

WALLACE STEVENS [1879-1955]
Hibiscus on the Sleeping Shores 257
Disillusionment of Ten O'Clock 257

Bantams in Pine-Woods   258
Peter Quince at the Clavier   258
Study of Two Pears   260
Mrs. Alfred Uruguay   261
The Plain Sense of Things   262
Song of Fixed Accord   262

WILLIAM CARLOS WILLIAMS [1883-1963]

Danse Russe   263
January Morning   263
To Elsie   266
Poem   268
This Is Just To Say   268
Iris   269
The Artist   269
The Sparrow   270

D. H. LAWRENCE [1885-1930]

The Song of a Man Who Has Come Through   273
Humming-bird   273
Kangaroo   274
To Women, As Far As I'm Concerned   276
Energetic Women   276
Volcanic Venus   276
It's No Good!   276
Bavarian Gentians   277

EZRA POUND [1885-   ]

The Study in Aesthetics   277
FROM Hugh Selwyn Mauberley   278
FROM Canto LXXXI   286

ROBINSON JEFFERS [1887-1962]

New Mexican Mountain   287
Love the Wild Swan   287

T. S. ELIOT [1888-1965]

The Love Song of J. Alfred Prufrock   288
Preludes   291
Gerontion   293
The Hollow Men   295
Macavity: The Mystery Cat   298

JOHN CROWE RANSOM [1888-   ]

Bells for John Whiteside's Daughter   299
Dog   299

HUGH MAC DIARMID [1892-   ]

The Bonnie Broukit Bairn   301
Crowdieknowe   301
FROM The Kind of Poetry I Want   301
Crystals Like Blood   303

WILFRED OWEN [1893-1918]

Insensibility   303
The Send-Off   305
Exposure   305
Disabled   306

E. E. CUMMINGS [1894-1963]

Portrait   308
Poem, or Beauty Hurts Mr. Vinal   308
my sweet old etcetera   309
somewhere i have never travelled, gladly beyond   310
a he as o   311
old age sticks   311

ALLEN TATE [1899-   ]

The Swimmers   312

HART CRANE [1899-1932]

For the Marriage of Faustus and Helen   314
FROM The Bridge
    To Brooklyn Bridge   318
    National Winter Garden   319

LANGSTON HUGHES [1902-1967]

Children's Rhymes   320
Night Funeral in Harlem   321
Harlem   322
Same in Blues   322

CARL RAKOSI [1903-   ]

Americana IX   323
Americana XV   Simplicity   324
Young Couples Strolling By   325

W. H. AUDEN [1907-   ]

On This Island   325
Musée des Beaux Arts   326
The Fall of Rome   327
Since   327

THEODORE ROETHKE [1908-1963]

Night Journey   329
My Papa's Waltz   329
Dolor   330
Elegy for Jane   330
The Waking   331
The Rose   331

DYLAN THOMAS [1914-1953]

The Force That Through the Green Fuse Drives the Flower   334
Fern Hill   335
Do Not Go Gentle into That Good Night   336

DUDLEY RANDALL [1914-   ]

Blackberry Sweet   337

HENRY REED [1914-   ]

Naming of Parts   337

DAVID IGNATOW [1914-   ]

Get the Gasworks   338

ROBERT LOWELL [1917-   ]

FROM Between the Porch and the Altar
    IV. At the Altar   339
Mr. Edwards and the Spider   339
Memories of West Street and Lepke   341
For the Union Dead   342

ROBERT DUNCAN [1919-   ]

Two Presentations   344

KEITH DOUGLAS [1920-1944]

Vergissmeinicht   347

RICHARD WILBUR [1921-   ]

The Beautiful Changes   347

Love Calls Us to the Things of This World   348
Piazza di Spagna, Early Morning   349

PHILIP LARKIN   [1922-　]

Within the Dream You Said   349
Night-Music   350
Mr. Bleaney   350
Wild Oats   351

JAMES DICKEY   [1923-　]

Listening to Foxhounds   352
Cherrylog Road   353

DENISE LEVERTOV   [1923-　]

February Evening in New York   355
In Mind   356
Advent 1966   357

LOUIS SIMPSON   [1923-　]

Frogs   357
The Inner Part   358
Simplicity   358

JOHN A. WILLIAMS   [1925-　]

Safari West   360

ALLEN GINSBERG   [1926-　]

FROM *Howl*   361

ROBERT CREELEY   [1926-　]

After Lorca   363
I Know a Man   364
Kore   364

ROBERT BLY   [1926-　]

Waking from Sleep   365
Poem Against the British   365
Summer, 1960, Minnesota   365
Love Poem   366

JAMES WRIGHT   [1927-　]

*Lying in a Hammock at William Duffy's Farm in Pine
Island, Minnesota*   366

Autumn Begins in Martins Ferry, Ohio 367
I Try to Waken and Greet the World Once Again 367

DONALD HALL [1928-   ]

An Airstrip in Essex, 1960 367
Gold 368

THOM GUNN [1929-   ]

My Sad Captains 368

TED HUGHES [1930-   ]

Crow's First Lesson 369
In Laughter 369
Crow's Last Stand 370
Truth Kills Everybody 371

GREGORY CORSO [1930-   ]

Marriage 371

GARY SNYDER [1930-   ]

Milton by Firelight 374
Hay for the Horses 375
Nansen 376
December 376
Looking At Pictures To Be Put Away 378

SYLVIA PLATH [1932-1963]

Morning Song 378
Daddy 379
The Bee Meeting 381

LEROI JONES [1934-   ]

Preface to a Twenty Volume Suicide Note 382

JACK ANDERSON [1935-   ]

The Invention of New Jersey 383

LUCILLE CLIFTON [1936-   ]

The 1st 385
Still 385
Good Times 385
Willie B (2) 386
Admonitions 386

DIANE WAKOSKI [1937-   ]
    The Ice Eagle   387

JIM HARRISON [1937-   ]
    Ghazals   389

LEBERT BETHUNE [1937-   ]
    A Juju of My Own   391

MICHAEL BENEDIKT [1937-   ]
    Clement Attlee   391

TONY HARRISON [1937-   ]
    Schwiegermutterlieder   392

JOHN LENNON [1940-   ] & PAUL McCARTNEY [1942-   ]
    Eleanor Rigby   394

BOB DYLAN [1941-   ]
    Desolation Row   395

NIKKI GIOVANNI [1943-   ]
    Knoxville, Tennessee   397

GLOSSARY   401

INDEX OF AUTHORS AND TITLES   465

AN INTRODUCTION TO POETRY

Metaphor

Poets make metaphors, figures of speech in which one thing is likened to or identified with another.[1]

Through metaphor, an idea may be translated into an image so that we perceive the idea through our senses, for it seems that we can hardly understand a thing unless we know what it looks like, or what it feels or sounds like.

Consider the famous soliloquy in which Hamlet is meditating on life and death:

> To be, or not to be: that is the question.
> Whether 'tis nobler in the mind to suffer
> The slings and arrows of outrageous fortune,
> Or to take arms against a sea of troubles,
> And by opposing end them?

In this speech, mental suffering is not merely compared to, it is translated into the picture of a man being shot at with stones and arrows. In the second metaphor, suffering is pictured as a man fighting against the waves. The metaphors have translated ideas into scene and drama. From these metaphors we get a more vivid impression than we would get from abstract words. Suppose Hamlet said:

> To be, or not to be: that is the question.
> Whether 'tis nobler in the mind to suffer
> The insults and misfortunes of our life,
> Or make a strenuous effort to resist,
> And by opposing end them?

How dull this is! Having no metaphorical power, the words do not affect our senses; they do not rouse the instincts that make us sympathize with what we think we see, hear, taste, or touch.

1 *Important:* there is also poetry without metaphors. I have begun with metaphorical writing because it is common. For a discussion of poetry without metaphors, see "Three Poems by Carl Rakosi," pp. 29–33.

It is not only people who write poems who think in metaphor—all people do, and in primitive times speech must have been vividly metaphorical, for people were naming the things around them. The first man who spoke of the "tooth of a plow" or the "foot of the mountain" had made a metaphor. He was identifying what he saw with himself, a part of his body. The first who said that "waves murmur" was a poet. To these people, the universe was filled with human characteristics and they were at home in it. They imagined that there were spirits in trees and rivers, and gods on the mountains, and that these behaved like human beings on a larger scale. The gods were much more powerful, but they spoke to men.

We no longer believe that the universe is an extension of ourselves; there are no longer spirits in trees and rivers that speak to human beings; but we still think in metaphors. And poets write metaphors—the greatest thing for a poet, said Aristotle, is to be a master of metaphor: "It is the one thing that cannot be learned from others; and it is also a sign of genius, since a good metaphor implies an intuitive perception of the similarity in dissimilars."

We want our experiences to have a unity and meaning, so we relate one thing to another through metaphor. "To primitive men and children, everything is infused with the same life. But we have lost the ability to perceive the unity of things."[2] Through poetry, however, we may regain this power. When poets write in metaphors, relating one thing to another, and all things to themselves, they give meaning to the world around them.

Rhythm[3]

Rhythm, repeated stress, is essential in poetry. We expect the stress to come again, and so we keep listening.

It is easy to see the pattern of rhythm when poetry is in meter, a regular pattern of stressed and unstressed syllables. The following lines are in meter:

> Since brass, nor stone, nor earth, nor boundless sea,
> But sad mortality o'er-sways their power,
> How with this rage shall beauty hold a plea,
> Whose action is no stronger than a flower?
>
> William Shakespeare, Sonnet 65

To see the pattern of meter, lines are divided into feet. A foot is a unit of stressed ($-$) and unstressed ($\smile$) syllables. The foot being used here is the

2 Owen Barfield, *Poetic Diction*, 1928.
3 See the Glossary for fuller explanations of technical terms, and also the section titled "Meter, Rhyme, Stanza, and Sound."

iamb—an unstressed syllable followed by a stressed (‿ —). The first line therefore may be scanned as follows:

Since bráss,/nŏr stóne,/nŏr eárth,/nŏr boúnd/lĕss séa/

The second line also is regular. In the third line, however, there is a substitution: at the start of the line a trochee is substituted for the iamb:

Hów wĭth

In any use of meter there will occasionally be substitutions where the need to accent syllables for meaning (the rhetorical accent) comes in conflict with the stress of the prevailing meter.

In this sonnet by Shakespeare, the iambic feet are moving like the thought, at a steady pace from one thing to another: "brass . . . earth . . . mortality . . . rage . . . beauty . . . flower." The meter is well-suited to the thought, which is meditative. Indeed, to some extent the meter *is* the thought, for a different meter would make for a different mood. Rhythm is not everything; there are other elements in poetry; but rhythm is essential.

In free verse, on the other hand, it is not easy to see the pattern of the rhythm, for it is irregular:

> Among the rain
> and lights
> I saw the figure 5
> in gold
> on a red
> firetruck
> moving
> tense
> unheeded
> to gong clangs
> siren howls
> and wheels rumbling
> through the dark city.

William Carlos Williams,
"The Great Figure"

This poem does not have a regular pattern of stressed and unstressed syllables. Yet there is a rhythm—of speech cadences, an irregular pattern of stressed and unstressed syllables such as we use in speaking. The measurable unit is not the foot but the phrase. In "The Great Figure" the phrase may have as many as six syllables or only one or two.

Among the rain	1st phrase
and lights	2nd "
I saw the figure 5	3rd "
in gold	4th "

In this poem each phrase is written as a separate line; this enables us to see the phrase. But in free verse there may be several phrases to the line, as in this line by Whitman:

$$\begin{array}{cccc} 1 & 2 & 3 & 4 \end{array}$$
Dumb swimmers there/ among the rocks—/ coral,/ gluten,/
$$\begin{array}{cccc} 5 & 6 & 7 & 8 \end{array}$$
grass,/ rushes—/ and the aliment/ of the swimmers/

Whitman's phrases could be written as separate lines, as Williams writes his; or Williams' poem could be written as one long line.

In some of his later poems Williams would arrange phrases in three steps across the page. The phrase, he said, was a "variable foot"; it was to be counted as a single stress. The three steps formed a kind of trimeter. If "The Great Figure" had been written later, it might have looked like this:

Among the rain
      and lights
            I saw the figure 5
  in gold
      on a red
        firetruck . . .

Free verse, as I have said, is written in the cadences of speech. To follow the cadences of the poet's speech, we must follow the movement of his thought, we must understand what he intends at every moment. Only in this way can we tell where the stress falls and where the phrase ends. Reading in a sing-song won't do. In reading "The Great Figure" we have to pay attention to exactly what is said, and seen, and heard: "the figure 5," the clanging gong, the rumbling wheels. We have to concentrate on these things as the man in the poem is concentrating.

Indeed, the objects in the poem seem to be compelling the observer to pay attention to them. They seem to be determining the language, the phrases, the rhythm. The rhythm of the poem depends upon what the poem is about—far more, it might be argued, than if the poem were in meter.

There are readers of poetry who find it difficult to read free verse. They want a poem to be written in meter—regular feet, and so many feet to the line. Also, they would like a regular pattern of rhymes. Free verse strikes them as unpoetic. What, they ask, makes it different from prose? One possible answer is that the difference is a matter of degree: in free verse there is a greater concentration of thought, selectivity in the use of words, intensity through the use of images. But though these are certainly qualities of free verse, they can also be found in prose. Then, perhaps, the difference is in rhythm. Perhaps rhythm plays a greater part in free verse than it does in prose.

So important is rhythm in poetry that in the first edition of this book I said that poetry was "thought expressed in rhythm," and that in poetry rhythm was essential to the meaning, while in prose it was not. Some readers objected, saying that there are passages of prose—"John Donne's Meditation XVII, for example"—in which rhythm is essential. They may have been right. In any case, as a poem consists of several elements, it is not possible to isolate one element and show that this is what poetry consists of; and we cannot say exactly what the difference is between poetry and prose, for they have several elements in common. Many people have tried to define poetry—there are eleven instances in the Glossary—but no definition seems conclusive. The reason for life in the poem, as in the human being, eludes analysis. This should not prevent us, however, from understanding how the parts work, separately and together.

Structure

Just as there is rhythm in the lines of a poem, there is a rhythm of the poem as a whole. This is evident where the poem is written in stanzas, groups of lines recurring in the same pattern:

> It is an ancient Mariner,
> And he stoppeth one of three.
> "By thy long gray beard and glittering eye,
> Now wherefore stopp'st thou me?
>
> "The Bridegroom's doors are opened wide,
> And I am next of kin,
> The guests are met, the feast is set:
> May'st hear the merry din."

The pattern here is of ballad stanzas, tetrameters and trimeters rhyming *a b c b*. (These terms are explained in the Glossary.)

Structure does not consist only of rhythmic patterns such as stanzas; there may be a pattern of symbols, or a structure of language. And there may be two or more structures in combination; indeed, as there are so many patterns in the use of words, syntax, plot, and symbolism, it would be hard to imagine a poem that had only a single, discernible structure.

Some twentieth-century poets have said that they are writing poetry without a structure, imitating a flow of experience, with no beginning, middle, or end. When we read some of these poems we really do have the impression of a mind moving freely:

> Three gas lamps lighted
> The boss has T.B.
> When you've finished we'll play backgammon
> A conductor who has a sore throat . . .
>
> Guillaume Apollinaire,
"Lundi Rue Christine"

But there is a structure in this poetry, though it is hidden. Everything that comes into the mind takes on a kind of structure; and though the poet may not be aware of it, everything that he writes gives back a pattern of his mind.

The poem by William Carlos Williams that we have seen, "The Great Figure," has the structure of a narrative: "I saw this, I heard that." Narrative poems and songs go back to the beginnings of history; it seems that men always wanted to sing a song or tell a story, and patterns of song and story were given to poetry from the start. But I shall not try to describe all the patterns that can be found in poems. This would be tedious and not in keeping with the purpose of this book. There is more to be learned from reading poems and discovering what is in the individual poem than from any amount of generalization. As an example, however, let us consider one passage of poetry in order to see the structure, and also the use of rhythm and images, the elements of poetry touched on so far.

The passage is taken from *The Prelude,* Wordsworth's autobiographical poem:

> So feeling comes in aid
> Of feeling, and diversity of strength
> Attends us, if but once we have been strong.
> Oh! mystery of man, from what a depth
> Proceed thy honours. I am lost, but see
> In simple childhood something of the base
> On which thy greatness stands; but this I feel,
> That from thyself it comes, that thou must give,
> Else never canst receive. The days gone by
> Return upon me almost from the dawn
> Of life: the hiding-places of man's power
> Open; I would approach them, but they close.
> I see by glimpses now; when age comes on,
> May scarcely see at all; and I would give,
> While yet we may, as far as words can give,
> Substance and life to what I feel, enshrining,
> Such is my hope, the spirit of the Past
> For future restoration.

In *The Prelude,* Wordsworth undertakes to trace "the growth of a poet's mind." The poem ranges from scene and incident to passages in which he attempts to describe the workings of his mind at certain times and explain how this contributed to his development as a poet. It is admirable to see how he manages to give passages of explanation a forward movement. When poets undertake to argue and explain they often fall into prose, but these lines have a deepening excitement.

How does Wordsworth accomplish this? Not by the weight of his ideas, though they are profound. The poetry comes of his skill in writing verse and of what Aristotle called mastery of metaphor. For at the center of this passage of explanation there is a powerful and original metaphor, the vision of the "hiding-places of man's power" opening and closing. This lifts the passage above the level of rational argument, toward a place where truths are seen in a flash. The image is vague, but so is a mystery; the poet is describing mysterious and awe-inspiring things, glimpsed only to be hidden again.

A vision can hardly be analyzed. The technique of verse is more understandable. When we scan the passage, we find that Wordsworth has broken the lines, unrhymed iambic pentameters (blank verse), into shorter units. Several of the lines are divided with a pause (caesura), and phrases run from the middle of a line to the middle of the next, running past the end of the pentameter as though there were an urgency, a thought too pressing to be contained within the five-foot measure:

> Oh! mystery of man,// from what a depth
> Proceed thy honours.// I am lost, but see
> In simple childhood// something of the base
> On which thy greatness stands;// but this I feel,
> That from thyself it comes,// that thou must give,
> Else never canst receive.// The days gone by . . .

This overriding of the line by the sentence makes the idea in the sentence seem irresistible. So the argument moves forward and carries us with it.

Toward the end Wordsworth makes parenthetical remarks. This is what he has to say: "I would give substance and life to what I feel, enshrining the spirit of the Past for future restoration." In the course of saying it, however, he makes these digressions: "While yet we may, as far as words can give . . . Such is my hope." These interruptions make us impatient to see to the end of the thought; we are not just drawn forward, we push forward to the end ourselves. The purpose of this delaying, keeping us in suspense, is to involve us more. Of course, a writer cannot digress too much, otherwise the reader may be confused or lose interest. Wordsworth has a lively sense of the drama of a sentence, what must be said right away and what may be delayed.

Moreover, there is an ingenious structure in the passage that we have not yet seen. By repeating a word, or by following a word with another that the first word has led us to expect, Wordsworth sets up a pattern of anticipation and reward. Then, suddenly, at the image of the "hiding-places," anticipation is disappointed: the "hiding-places" suddenly "close" rather than remain "open." This is a stroke of genius in sentence structure. Just as rhythm may contribute essentially to the effect of a poem, so may sentence structure. The syntax corresponds to, indeed helps to create, the idea:

                              feeling . . . feeling
                              strength . . . strong
                              give . . . receive
[but the hiding-places]   open . . . close
                              see by glimpses . . . scarcely see
[then, resoundingly, like the resolution of a Beethoven symphony]
                              give . . . give

When we consider the content of the passage, it is remarkable how many ideas have been put in a few lines. Much of Wordsworth's thinking is touched upon in this brief space. He states his belief that feeling is primary and that we develop by feeling, one feeling and thought leading to another. He affirms his faith in the dignity of man and asks the question he is frequently pondering: Where does man obtain his power to feel and think? He answers his own question, saying that man obtains the power from himself, by giving, whereupon something is given to him. He hints at mysteries we apprehend at certain moments from a contact with nature, and he describes the poet's task: by a process of recollection to recreate those moments in poems that will serve as a restorative.

These ideas, however, would not be as persuasive had Wordsworth not used rhythm, sentence structure, and words in ways that support the argument. And it needed more than philosophy, it required poetic genius, to see the hiding-places opening and closing. What were they? But we are left to wonder.

Language and Style

The following little poem has been remembered for hundreds of years:

> Western wind, when will thou blow
> The small rain down can rain?
> Christ, if my love were in my arms,
> And I in my bed again.

This is as simple and direct as the language a man might use in conversation. And if we look again at the passage from *The Prelude*, we see that though Wordsworth is philosophizing and speaking of difficult matters, he is for the most part using ordinary words. Poetry is the most expressive way of saying a thing, and sometimes plain words are best.

The language of some poetry, however, is difficult, for the poet is trying to convey a subtle or difficult idea. But still he is using the most efficient language that he can find. (Bad poets use vague words and difficult constructions when they don't have to; when they say something we feel that it could have been said better.)

Milton has sometimes been accused of using pompous words and writing Latin rather than English sentences. If this were all there was to Milton's style, then we would not be able to read him with pleasure. But when we examine a passage of his writing we are likely to find that the construction of a sentence, if it is peculiar, has a definite purpose. Putting the subject after the predicate, for example, may be an attempt to represent the order in which things are actually happening. Milton wants to make us see and feel, and therefore he changes the usual sentence order in which, all too often, words are used in a non-specific way and have lost their connection to the senses.

For the same reason Milton uses unusual words. In the following passage from *Paradise Lost*, Moloch, an angel who has been driven out of Heaven, is describing the battle in which the angels fell. He is arguing that as there is a kind of gravity that draws spirits upward, it will not be too hard for the fallen angels to fly up again:

> Who but felt of late
> When the fierce foe hung on our broken rear
> Insulting, and pursued us through the Deep,
> With what compulsion and laborious flight
> We sunk thus low?

Consider the words Milton is using, particularly "compulsion" and "laborious." The sound of these words is like the action they describe. In "compulsion" and "laborious," the plosives *p* and *b*, the following vowel sounds, and the ponderous length of the words give a sense of wings pushing back against a pressure that is forcing them downward, a pressure greater than the strength of wings but not irresistible.

Every true poet has a style of his own, a certain way of using language, figurative and rhetorical devices, tones and patterns of sound. Just as we can tell from a few bars of music that they were composed by Mozart, from a few lines of verse we can tell that they are by Gerard Manley Hopkins or by Robert Frost.

But as men live in communities their uses of language will have something in common. Though a poet has his own distinctive style, he owes something to the style of his time and place. Therefore we speak of the style of a period: Elizabethan, Augustan, Romantic, Victorian. In the early eighteenth century, Pope and Swift moved in elegant society. Though they were very different men, they both wrote wittily, with turns of speech that were fashionable in drawing-rooms. A hundred years later, after the French Revolution and the industrial revolution, poets were not so often in society and were given to taking long walks in the country and writing about nature. Wordsworth and Keats, who lived in this period, are closer to each other in their styles than they are to Pope and Swift.

At the beginning of the Romantic period, Wordsworth argued against the far-fetched words and euphemisms of verse in the late eighteenth century. He cited a passage from the Bible:

> Go to the Ant, thou sluggard, consider her ways, and be wise: which having no guide, overseer, or ruler, provideth her meat in the summer, and gathereth her food in the harvest.

Then he quoted Samuel Johnson's version of the passage:

> Turn on the prudent Ant thy heedless eyes,
> Observe her labors, Sluggard, and be wise;
> No stern command, no monitory voice,
> Prescribes her duties, or directs her choice.

This, Wordsworth said, was a hubbub of words, and indeed it does seem that the busy housekeeping little ant has been crushed under the weight of Doctor Johnson's attention.

In literary generations, writing swings like a pendulum from one style to another. Wordsworth's liking for simplicity enabled him to write lines of his own that have a Biblical grandeur:

> The silence that is in the starry sky,
> The sleep that is among the lonely hills . . .

However, later in the century Browning is anything but simple:

> While Paul looked archly on, pricked brow at whiles
> With the pen-point as to punish triumph there,
> And said "Count Guido, take your lawful wife
> Until death part you!"

The eccentricities of Gerard Manley Hopkins would have puzzled Wordsworth:

> In a flash, at a trumpet crash,
> I am all at once what Christ is, since he was what I am, and
> This Jack, joke, poor potsherd, patch, matchwood, immortal
>   diamond,
>   Is immortal diamond.

At the beginning of the present century, poets seemed again to be out of touch with common speech. The language of poems was vaguely romantic, but without the Romantics' power of thought. In reaction against this there was a swing toward a kind of "hardness," and about 1910 a group of poets who called themselves Imagists began to write a new kind of poem. The ideas of the Imagists have had an influence reaching far beyond the works they achieved at the time; prose writers as well as poets were affected—the novelist Ernest Hemingway as well as the poets T. S. Eliot and William Carlos Williams. The influence of the Imagists is still continuing today, and for this reason it is worth taking some time to look at their principles. These were described in the preface to an anthology, *Some Imagist Poets*, published in 1915:

> 1. To use the language of common speech, but to employ always the *exact* word, not the nearly exact, nor the merely decorative word.

> 2. To create new rhythms—as the expression of new moods—and not to copy old rhythms, which merely echo old moods. We do not insist upon "free-verse" as the only method of writing poetry. We fight for it as a principle of liberty. We believe that the individuality of a poet may often be better expressed in free-verse than in conventional forms. In poetry, a new cadence means a new idea.

> 3. To allow absolute freedom in the choice of subject. It is not good art to write badly about aeroplanes and automobiles; nor is it necessarily bad art to write about the past. We believe passionately in the artistic value of modern life, but we wish to point out that there is nothing so uninspiring nor so old-fashioned as an aeroplane of the year 1911.

> 4. To present an image (hence the name: "Imagist"). We are not a school of painters, but we believe that poetry should render particulars exactly and not deal in vague generalities, however magnificent and sonorous. It is for this reason that we oppose the cosmic poet, who seems to us to shirk the real difficulties of his art.

> 5. To produce poetry that is hard and clear, never blurred nor indefinite.

> 6. Finally, most of us believe that concentration is of the very essence of poetry.

It is in accordance with these principles that T. S. Eliot writes:

> They are rattling breakfast plates in basement kitchens,
> And along the trampled edges of the street
> I am aware of the damp souls of housemaids
> Sprouting despondently at area gates.

This is "hard and clear," but a generation later, in these lines by Dylan Thomas, the pendulum has swung the other way. Thomas is "cosmic":

> And I must enter again the round
> Zion of the water bead
> And the synagogue of the ear of corn

I have been speaking of changes in style as though they happened suddenly and to everyone at the same time. Literary history is a record of changes, like a map that enables us to see the main features of a country. But though this is useful, it is a limited and misleading way of looking at things. One literary movement does not necessarily come to an end when another starts; different ways of writing continue to be practised side by side.

There are writers who are not involved in the literary movements or fashions of their time; they seem to develop in isolation. It is not always the popular writer, or the poet of whom critics approve, who has the most important thing to say; indeed, the more original a poet is—Wordsworth and Whitman are instances—the slower he may be to gain wide acceptance.

There was a man who said that whenever a new book came out he read an old book instead. If that man had lived in the time of Shakespeare he would have ignored Shakespeare because he was new.

But these days it is not the new that is in danger of being neglected—it is the old. And why shouldn't it be? What is the use of tradition? Observed for its own sake, tradition is no use at all; there is no point in paying respect to something just because it is old. But tradition is not a museum—it is more like an assembly line. Tradition is what has been selected from the past because it is useful now; it is the life flowing through us from the past to the future. Tradition will drop a bad poem soon enough; no amount of arguing that a piece of writing has been respected for hundreds of years will recommend it to a new generation unless the writing has life in itself—vivid images, language, rhythm, a vital structure. Writing, like the human organism, must live in the present regardless of reasons if it is to live at all. The poems of Chaucer, Shakespeare, and Wordsworth are still living in the present. There are poems known today that will be forgotten in twenty years, and others at present unknown that will flow into the future.

READING THE POEM

In discussing the following poems I have used technical terms and references that may be unfamiliar to the reader. These words are explained in the Glossary.

When Icicles Hang by the Wall

When icicles hang by the wall,
    And Dick the shepherd blows his nail,
And Tom bears logs into the hall,
    And milk comes frozen home in pail,
When blood is nipped, and ways be foul,
Then nightly sings the staring owl,
        To-whit!
To-who!—a merry note,
While greasy Joan doth keel the pot.

When all aloud the wind doth blow,
    And coughing drowns the parson's saw,
And birds sit brooding in the snow,
    And Marian's nose looks red and raw,
When roasted crabs hiss in the bowl,
Then nightly sings the staring owl,
        To-whit!
To-who!—a merry note,
While greasy Joan doth keel the pot.

William Shakespeare,
Love's Labour's Lost, 1593-97

The origins of poetry are unknown, but I think there must always have been songs, and some songs are poetry. The words of this song by Shakespeare evoke a situation and mood, describing an English country scene in the winter. There is an intense selectivity of detail, a pleasure in everything, rising from the delight in his mind.

To a country-dweller today the scene would be almost as familiar as it was hundreds of years ago when Shakespeare was alive. The kitchen may be different, and milk may be delivered in bottles, but people still get red noses. A cold day can be exhilarating, and it is good to be warm inside when it is freezing out. It would be the same in China; a good poem can be understood by strangers and it may last for centuries.

There are, however, two or three places in the poem where the reader may have difficulty in understanding, due to changes in the use of words between Shakespeare's time and our own. Some difficulties will disappear when we look at the words carefully and think of all the possible meanings. The phrase "blows his nail," for instance, makes sense if we just think about it. The mind moves to "blows on his nail," and then to "blows on his finger-nail," whereupon the difficulty vanishes. Dick is blowing on the ends of his fingers to warm them. "Parson's saw" is a little more difficult. But what is it that parsons do in church? They make sermons. So "saw" probably means sermon. We cannot be certain of this, however, so we had better look in a dictionary. There we find that we are right: "A saying; discourse; speech. *Obs.*" Also, when we look up "crabs" we find that one of the meanings is: "*Brit.*—the wild form of the common apple." In the context, a description of an English countryside, "wild apples" is clearly the right meaning. These crabs are not crustaceans.

"Keel the pot" presents a serious obstacle. If I were to rely on my own ideas, my thinking would go like this: the bottom of a boat is called the keel, and Joan is described as greasy, so keeling the pot probably means greasing the bottom of the pot. A strange thing for her to do, but there it is. So I would settle the meaning of the line to my own satisfaction—and I would be mistaken. If, on the other hand, I went to a dictionary, I would find that one of the meanings given for "keel" is: "*Obs.* To cool (a hot or boiling liquid) by stirring, skimming, or pouring in something cold, in order to prevent it from boiling over; hence freq. in phr. *to keel the pot.*" A little further on I would find: "Shaks. L L L v.ii 930 While greasie Ione doth keele the pot."

The way to read, then, seems to be: use imagination and a dictionary.

"Greasy Joan" is unforgettable. Details such as this remind us, if ever we are inclined to doubt it, what a writer Shakespeare is. Many people think that poetry consists of high-flown, fanciful, euphemistic language. On the contrary, poets want to make their readers see and feel; therefore they say what they mean as exactly and vividly as possible. It is "officialese," the language bureaucrats speak, or the language used in politics or advertising, that is euphemistic. We know all too well the politician's speech that conceals his meaning in circumlocutions. Every day we are bombarded with language that tries to sell us something by calling it something else, or language which, out of a false sense of delicacy, tries to disguise plain functions.

But Shakespeare was happy with the word "greasy" because he liked Joan, greasy or not; he did not have to think of people as disinfected before he could put up with them. Having found this phrase he liked it so well that he used it twice, and it is the climax of his series of winter images—

icicles, frozen milk, muddy footpaths, Marian's nose, roast apples, the owl. The image of greasy Joan keeling the pot, right at the end, makes the whole poem stick in the mind.

The Sun Rising

Busy old fool, unruly sun,
    Why dost thou thus
Through windows and through curtains call on us?
Must to thy motions lovers' seasons run?
    Saucy, pedantic wretch, go chide
    Late schoolboys and sour 'prentices,
Go tell court huntsmen that the king will ride,
Call country ants to harvest offices.
Love, all alike, no season knows nor clime,
Nor hours, days, months, which are the rags of time.

    Thy beams, so reverend and strong
    Why shouldst thou think?
I could eclipse and cloud them with a wink,
But that I would not lose her sight so long.
    If her eyes have not blinded thine,
    Look, and tomorrow late tell me
Whether both th' Indias of spice and mine
Be where thou left'st them, or lie here with me;
Ask for those kings whom thou saw'st yesterday,
And thou shalt hear: All here in one bed lay.

    She's all states, and all princes I;
    Nothing else is.
Princes do but play us; compared to this,
All honor's mimic, all wealth alchemy.
    Thou, sun, art half as happy's we,
    In that the world's contracted thus;
    Thine age asks ease, and since thy duties be
    To warm the world, that's done in warming us.
Shine here to us, and thou art everywhere;
This bed thy center is, these walls thy sphere.

John Donne, 1633

In the twentieth century much has been written about Donne and the metaphysical poets. T. S. Eliot discovered in Donne's verse the "unified sensibility" that he was aiming at in his own lines. Donne was able to make sense of a variety of experiences at the same time; sense perception and reflection took place at once. Eliot, himself working out images that could render simultaneously thought, the smell of cabbage, and the clatter of typewriting, found Donne usable in a way that Milton and Dryden were not. Between their thoughts and feelings there were gaps.

Several critics—including, it seems, the later Eliot—have found fault with his first enthusiastic validation of Donne. In *The Monarch of Wit*, J. B. Leishman argues that Donne's main quality is not metaphysical thinking, nor does he have "unified sensibility." To the contrary, he is, like Hamlet, subject to fits and starts. He wants to be witty at any price, and is never happier than when developing an outrageous paradox. Donne's most striking characteristics, says Leishman, are wit, self-dramatization, and the use of the colloquial.

Certainly, the actor in Donne strikes us forcibly. He is always throwing himself into one role or another. He is John Donne pretending to be a cynic, or a Platonic lover, or a man terrified at the thought of death. He thinks best in dialogue. Even when he is not addressing another person or God, he carries on a dialogue with himself. The poems are a little theater, with curtain raisers:

> Busy old fool, unruly sun . . .
>
> For Godsake hold your tongue, and let me love . . .
>
> Batter my heart, three-personed God . . .

The poems have the scenery and furniture of stage sets: a bedroom into which the sun is shining, a sick room, an open grave, a panorama of the Last Judgment. A poem to his mistress suddenly lets in a view of Alps where a traveler, attacked by brigands, is stabbed and falling. This is the Donne of whom Sir Richard Baker said that after leaving Oxford he "lived at the *Inns of Court*, not dissolute, but very neat, a great visiter of ladies, a great frequenter of Plays, a great writer of conceited verses," and of whom it is reported that when he was dying he had his portrait painted in grave clothes and kept it beside his bed. This also is the man who ruined his chances of preferment by running off with Sir George More's daughter: "John Donne, Anne Donne, Un-done."

How serious is the drama? Donne seems in dead earnest, and then he is off on the scent of a pun or some wild comparison. In this he deserves the criticism Johnson makes of Shakespeare—he would throw away everything for a quibble. Does this mean Donne was not serious? I do not think so. Men of the Elizabethan age were serious in humorous ways. Hamlet was in earnest when he ran his sword through the arras and Polonius fell out, but at the same time Hamlet jested. This was barbarous to the age of Johnson, and must have seemed sheer fantasy to the Victorians. But in our century, which has seen violent extremes, peace and war, juxtaposed, and like the age of Donne sees new gulfs of science opening, Donne's taste for shock does not invalidate his seriousness.

To emphasize Donne's playfulness, J. B. Leishman says that he did not care what happened to his poems, once he wrote them. However, though Donne may have given the impression of tossing off his poems—a manner of acting that can be observed at any gathering of poets today—they are too well written to be jokes, and besides he knew there were copies in circulation and people were keeping them.

The sign of metaphysical poetry, as Johnson said, is a use of wild conceits, ransacking all fields of knowledge for comparisons. The technique has often been described: images are taken from science as well as nature, and the poet goes ranging over heaven and earth. But I do not think the purpose of the technique has been sufficiently underscored, and it is serious. The aim is not merely to astonish by showing how seemingly contradictory things can be yoked together. True, when Donne compares a flea to a marriage bed, something odd is happening for the sake of oddness. But when, as in "The Sun Rising," he brings into the bedroom of two lovers a vision of "both th' Indias of spice and mine," the leap does more than astonish, it joins two disparate areas of experience.

This is the real function of the metaphysical conceit: to join again the parts of a fractured world. In Donne's time, because of the new discoveries in astronomy, the earth is no longer at the center of the universe, no longer at the center of God's attention. Man is suddenly diminished. As Donne says, this new philosophy "calls all in doubt." On the earth itself, things are sliding off, east and west, as the explorers circumnavigate the globe. But the metaphysical conceit pulls the fractions together again; it draws the disordered parts back into order, the order of the poem and the mind. The man who controls the poem controls the world. Then, if the man is religious, God still orders the universe.

"The Sun Rising" is one of Donne's complimentary love poems. Here he is not proving that women are all untrue, nor is he engaged in a Platonic disquisition. The subject is clear: the centering, controlling power of love. A man and woman are in bed, and the sun looks in. The poet tells the sun to go about his business. There is a man-about-town's contemptuous reference to "country ants," a topical reference to King James' passion for hunting, and a picture of "Late schoolboys and sour 'prentices" which shows that morning scenes have not changed from that time to this. Then the theme of the poem is stated:

> Love, all alike, no season knows nor clime,
> Nor hours, days, months, which are the rags of time.

There follows a solipsism that has occurred to everyone, at one time or another: if you simply shut your eyes, reality goes away. Is reality in the perceiver or in the world perceived? This question, which has occupied some poets greatly—Wordsworth answered "half-and-half"—Donne solves, or rather evades, by tossing off a pretty compliment to the lady. He does not want to stop looking at her for as long as the wink of an eye. Then comes the advice to the sun which brings the Indies into the poem with a glimpse of potentates on their thrones. If the sun comes back tomorrow, he will have to confess that the lady is more beautiful than anything else in the world.

"She is all states." And by possessing her, the persona—Donne in one of his speaking roles—is "all princes." Everything but love is play-acting; honor and riches are poor imitations of the reality, love. Then, to polish off the poem, Donne has a happy conceit. The sun should be pleased to have them stay in bed, for the sun is old and tired, and here he can do his job all at once—warm the world by warming them. In the lovers' astronomy:

> This bed thy center is, these walls thy sphere.

(Donne is perfectly aware of the theory that the sun does not go round the world, but it appears to do so, and that is enough for a poem.)

Donne wrote "strong lines." Leishman speaks of the "colloquial vigor of the language, together with the absence of classical allusions, traditional ornaments, and, generally speaking, of anything obviously 'poetical'." However, I do not agree with his opinion that Donne was the first to introduce into lyrical verse "those natural speech-rhythms . . . that colloquial diction" which Shakespeare and his fellows introduced into dramatic verse. Wyatt had already done this, when he tuned his speech to the lute.

If we take Spenser as one extreme, with smoothness and softness:

> Sweete *Themmes* run softlie, till I end my Song

then Donne is the other. Spenser is all for smoothness and purity of effect; he uses classical allusions, ornaments, and Petrarchan conceits; he attaches his feelings to ideal things and so climbs the Platonic ladder. Donne's thoughts, on the other hand, are attracted to whatever he sees; he is fascinated with strange sights and ideas; his manner of speaking is informal, seeming at times abrupt. It is tempting to divide the poets of the early seventeenth century into two camps, those who followed Spenser and those who followed Donne. But this is too simple; poets do not fit neatly into categories. Also, among the poets—Donne, Vaughan, Crashaw, Herbert, and others—who are grouped together as metaphysicals, there is so much temperamental variety that perhaps their only resemblance is in the use of metaphysical conceits.

from *Absalom and Achitophel*

> Of these the false Achitophel was first;
> A name to all succeeding ages curst:
> For close designs and crooked counsels fit;
> Sagacious, bold, and turbulent of wit;
> Restless, unfixed in principles and place;
> In power unpleased, impatient of disgrace:
> A fiery soul, which, working out its way,
> Fretted the pigmy body to decay,
> And o'er-informed the tenement of clay.

A daring pilot in extremity;
Pleased with the danger, when the waves went high,
He sought the storms; but, for a calm unfit,
Would steer too nigh the sands, to boast his wit.
Great wits are sure to madness near allied,
And thin partitions do their bounds divide;
Else why should he, with wealth and honor blest,
Refuse his age the needful hours of rest?
Punish a body which he could not please;
Bankrupt of life, yet prodigal of ease?
And all to leave what with his toil he won,
To that unfeathered two-legged thing, a son;
Got, while his soul did huddled notions try,
And born a shapeless lump, like anarchy.
In friendship false, implacable in hate;
Resolved to ruin or to rule the State.
To compass this the triple bond he broke,
The pillars of the public safety shook;
And fitted Israel for a foreign yoke;
Then seized with fear, yet still affecting fame,
Usurped a patriot's all-atoning name.
So easy still it proves in factious times,
With public zeal to cancel private crimes.

John Dryden, 1681

Absalom and Achitophel is political satire in the form of an allegory. The satire is strong and biting. Dryden exhibits the despicable traits of his characters and holds them up to ridicule.

The poet pretends to be retelling the Biblical story of the revolt of Absalom and Achitophel again King David (2 Samuel, 14-18), but actually it is the story of the treason of the Duke of Monmouth and the Earl of Shaftesbury against King Charles II. They had plotted to secure the succession for Monmouth, Charles' illegitimate son, though rightfully it belonged to the Duke of York, the king's brother.

In Dryden's allegory Israel represents England; David is King Charles; Absalom is his son Monmouth; Achitophel is Shaftesbury. In the Bible story the illegitimate Absalom was the apple of his father's eye, and Charles dotes on Monmouth. Prudently Dryden avoids harsh criticism of Monmouth and throws all the blame on Shaftesbury, Lord Chancellor and leader of the Whig faction that plotted to cut out the Catholic Duke of York.

The poem is written in heroic couplets—iambic pentameter rhymed couplets, the lines end-stopped, the statement completed at the end of the second line. (Occasionally there is a third rhyming line, for variety.) The meter is fairly regular, except for an occasional trochaic opening to a line. The thought is organized by the regular meter and by rhyme, but it is especially the syntax that creates the special sense of the line.

In the portrait of Achitophel, the first two lines are very even iambic, with no caesuras. Moving relentlessly, they declare Dryden's point of view. In line 3 the cramped parallel structure of "close designs" and "crooked counsels" emphasizes Achitophel's secretive character; the inversion of the syntactical order suggests his crooked and inverted ways. The repetition of *p* in lines 5 and 6 ("*p*ower un*p*leased, im*p*atient of disgrace"), with its explosive quality, creates a tone of contempt. The zeugma in line 5, "principles" and "place" both depending on the word "unfixed," produces an ironic effect—Achitophel is as unsure of his footing as he is confused in his mind. The chiasmus in line 6 makes a cross structure:

As these nouns and adjectives cross over, so does Achitophel; perversely he hastens from honor to dishonor.

The lines linked by the triple rhyme "way," "decay," "clay" may be read in different ways. Achitophel's body was puny; his soul "fretted" it like the teeth of an animal; his soul "o'er-informed," over-filled his little body. Or Dryden may be using "fret" not in the sense of "gnaw," but to mean "fermentation" or "working" (heating and agitating), for it is a "fiery" soul that is "working out its way." In "o'er-inform'd" Dryden is playing on the scholastic notion of the soul as the "form" of the body. All these meanings are valid; they do not exclude each other; to the contrary, from different directions they reinforce the central argument.

Another image dominates the following lines. Achitophel is a pilot steering a ship, an eccentric pilot who welcomes storms but is incompetent in calm seas. In the line "Would steer too nigh the sands, to boast his wit," the syntactical inversion creates an anticlimax—just as Achitophel's grandiose, dangerous actions reveal small motives.

For Dryden, Achitophel's wit is close to madness; otherwise why should he "Refuse his age the needful hours of rest"? The word "age" has a double meaning. It means not only his "many years" but also his "times." The present age would like Achitophel to retire so that the body politic may rest. Instead, he is working himself to death, punishing both himself and the state, so that his son may inherit the fruits of his toil.

The son is an "unfeathered two-legged thing," an allusion to Plato's definition of man. The comparison becomes more ludicrous when we recall that Diogenes plucked the feathers of a cock and presented it as Plato's man. The heavy stress on the monosyllable "Got" and the caesura after the first syllable of the line, an unusual position, ironically emphasizes the word. It means not only "begot" but also "acquired," and his son is reduced to a thing acquired, like his other possessions, by hard work. The son is born a "shapeless lump," an image of formlessness and insignificance. He is further compared, in a simile, to anarchy, an abstract term. He is thus reduced from a thing to an abstraction, to nothingness.

Anticipating Dr. Johnson's remark that patriotism is the last refuge of scoundrels, Dryden goes on to knock this prop from under the figure he is demolishing. And this is not all, but perhaps it is enough to show what could be done by Dryden, and by Pope some years later, in the heroic couplet as a vehicle for satire. The couplet bites off a statement neatly in two lines; it has a logical movement, and with syntactical devices such as I have shown, lends itself to strokes of wit.

About forty years ago, Dryden was "rediscovered" by critics. T. S. Eliot said, "The effect of the portraits of Dryden is to transform the object into something greater." Quoting the lines

> A fiery soul, which, working out its way,
> Fretted the pigmy body to decay,
> And o'er-informed the tenement of clay

he commented: "These lines are not merely a magnificent tribute. They create the object which they contemplate." Dryden, he said, had great comic talent.

I think this is true. Dryden's portrait of Achitophel is entertaining; I am not sure that it improved anyone's morals. Writers of satire, men such as Dryden, Swift, and Pope, claimed that their purpose in writing was to improve morals and make the world a better place to live in. However, the world goes on much as it has, and satirists are remembered only because they are amusing.

Ode on Melancholy

> No, no, go not to Lethe, neither twist
>   Wolf's-bane, tight-rooted, for its poisonous wine;
> Nor suffer thy pale forehead to be kiss'd
>   By nightshade, ruby grape of Proserpine;
> Make not your rosary of yew-berries,
>   Nor let the beetle, nor the death-moth be
>   Your mournful Psyche, nor the downy owl
> A partner in your sorrow's mysteries;
>   For shade to shade will come too drowsily,
>   And drown the wakeful anguish of the soul.
>
> But when the melancholy fit shall fall
>   Sudden from heaven like a weeping cloud,
> That fosters the droop-headed flowers all,
>   And hides the green hill in an April shroud;
> Then glut thy sorrow on a morning rose,
>   Or on the rainbow of the salt sand-wave,
>   Or on the wealth of globed peonies;
> Or if thy mistress some rich anger shows,
>   Emprison her soft hand, and let her rave,
>   And feed deep, deep upon her peerless eyes.

She dwells with Beauty—Beauty that must die;
   And Joy, whose hand is ever at his lips
Bidding adieu; and aching Pleasure nigh,
   Turning to poison while the bee-mouth sips:
Ay, in the very temple of Delight
   Veil'd Melancholy has her sovran shrine,
     Though seen of none save him whose strenuous tongue
Can burst Joy's grape against his palate fine;
His soul shall taste the sadness of her might,
   And be among her cloudy trophies hung.

                         John Keats, 1819

Keats said that if English had to be "chained" in rhymes, he wished to discover complex, satisfying patterns of rhyme and sound. Also he wished to "load every rift with ore," by which he meant that poetry should be full of images and as sensuous as possible.

The first stanza is filled with images evoking death: Lethe, the river of forgetfulness that spirits cross on their way to the Underworld; wolf's-bane and nightshade, which are poisonous; Proserpine, queen of the Underworld; yew-berries, from the tree that grows in graveyards; the beetle, the death-moth, the owl, and shadows. Also there are sounds like a dirge accompanying a funeral: the *o* sounds with which the ode begins: "No, no, go not," "wolf's," "rooted," "poisonous"—and continues: "Proserpine," "rosary," "moth," "mournful," "downy owl," "your sorrow's," "come too drowsily," "drown," "soul."

In the second stanza, strong, fresh images of nature—rain, flowers, a green hill, a morning rose—oppose the dying mood. These are not merely pictures, they are images of taste and touch. The sand-wave is salt, the peonies are globed. The word "globed" fits the hand; we think that we are holding a flower, a round, globed peony, in the cup of the hand. A woman appears immediately after the peony, so that she is globed and we seem to touch her. She is in an angry mood, with streaks of rich color. As we are still thinking of weeping clouds, hills after showers, waves and peonies, the woman's anger seems a natural phenomenon and she herself is like nature.

"She dwells with Beauty." Some confusion may set in here. Does "She" refer to the mistress or to Melancholy? The difficulty exists only if we try to choose. "She" refers to both the woman and the mood, for in the keenest of pleasures, sexual intercourse, there is melancholy:

    in the very temple of Delight
    Veil'd Melancholy has her sovran shrine

And "Pleasure," a word that for Keats and his contemporaries in this context would have meant sexual intercourse, is "Turning to poison while the bee-mouth sips."

But who, for thinking of that, would refrain? If the lover is sad it is

22

because he has been happy—he has "burst Joy's grape against his palate fine." (In Keats, sexual intercourse is sometimes represented by images such as these, substituting food for sex. In "The Eve of St. Agnes," Porphyro heaps the table with "candied apple, quince, and plum, and gourd" and other delicacies, before waking Madeline.)

The argument of the ode runs as follows. "Do not try to escape from melancholy, for sadness and joy are two sides of the same coin. Instead, 'glut' your sorrow and study the results. The study of melancholy is a kind of pleasure." Keats is recommending a poet's receptivity to all kinds of experience, in the spirit of the letter to Woodhouse (see under *Poetry* in the Glossary) where he speaks of enjoying light and shade, foul or fair. The ode concludes with the idea that to be melancholy is a privilege. Some men seem possessed by melancholy; they have "cloudy" fates. These are men who have a heightened awareness of joy; they are the lovers of beauty.

This thought should be consoling, and to some extent it is, but the final image has a contrary effect.

> His soul shall taste the sadness of her might,
> And be among her cloudy trophies hung.

This is disturbing; it calls up the image of a hanged man. A frightening idea of sexual intercourse is surfacing here. Whether or not Keats consciously intended this effect, the image suggests that the lover is executed by the mistress he seeks. And the poet is consumed by beauty; a famous poet is a living man converted into a trophy. This is a sad distinction. Though Keats has resolved to be strong, he holds some resentment against fate and the nature he professes to love.

The Magi

> Now as at all times I can see in the mind's eye,
> In their stiff, painted clothes, the pale unsatisfied ones
> Appear and disappear in the blue depth of the sky
> With all their ancient faces like rain-beaten stones,
> And all their helms of silver hovering side by side,
> And all their eyes still fixed, hoping to find once more,
> Being by Calvary's turbulence unsatisfied,
> The uncontrollable mystery on the bestial floor.
>
> William Butler Yeats, 1914

A symbol is a thing that stands for something else. The cross is used to evoke Christianity, the rose to mean love, the sword to mean war. These are common symbols; their meanings have been fixed for centuries. But some symbols do not have easily recognizable meanings. The meaning of the symbol can be determined only from its context. In Yeats's poems "To the

Rose upon the Rood of Time" and "The Rose of the World," a rose is not simply love, or idealized woman, but an Irish peasant woman and the love of things of this world as well as spiritual love.

In the writings of the Symbolist school, which influenced Yeats strongly, symbols do not have explicit meanings. The Symbolists often seem to be hiding, rather than revealing, their meaning in symbols. This is not a perverse unwillingness to be understood; rather, it is an attempt to create a mystery, to make the poem infinitely suggestive. A mystery cannot be explained; it can only be suggested. To attach symbols to specific meanings would destroy the magic of poetry. "Evocation, allusion, suggestion," said Mallarmé, are the essence of poetry. The Symbolist "shuns the materials in nature, avoids any thought that might tend to arrange them too directly or precisely, and retains only the suggestiveness of things." The Symbolist poet "must establish a careful relationship between two images, from which a third element, clear and fusible, will be distilled and caught by our imagination." The poetry is in the spaces between the images, in the "shudder of the forest" rather than in the palpable wood of trees. The poetry is felt in silence after the words have stopped.

From his researches in the occult, his study of Blake's symbolism, and exposure to the Symbolist movement in France, Yeats derived symbols and arranged them in a system. He found correspondences among seasons, the ages of man, the elements, the points of the compass, and certain objects—sword, stone, spear, and cauldron. For example, the word "wave" or "dew" evokes the element of water. This is connected with autumn, evening, manhood, and the west. The west, as in the phrase "stepping westward," is the place of death. In later poems Yeats perfected symbols of his own. To know what he meant by sun, moon, tower, mask, tree, well, sphere, gyre, or dance, we must go to his poems and see what the words mean there.

Much modern writing is symbolist in method and writers invent their own symbolic systems, each different from the rest. There is really no such thing as modern poetry—there are only modern poets. To travel from Yeats to Pound we have to get a new visa. Each poet creates his own world, makes his own meanings, and rules in his own way.

> "When *I* use a word," Humpty Dumpty said, in rather a scornful tone, "it means just what I choose it to mean—neither more nor less."
> "The question is," said Alice, "whether you *can* make words mean so many different things."
> "The question is," said Humpty Dumpty, "which is to be master —that's all."

"The Magi" is not a long poem—but some great poems have only a few lines, and some epics are unreadable. Within its small space "The Magi" accomplishes much. Yeats takes a familiar symbol, the nursery picture of the

Wise Men following the star to Bethlehem, where Jesus was born. In Yeats's hands, the kindly figures turn into something quite different—faces hovering with obsessive, fanatical appetite. The faces are as remote from tenderness as stones, inhuman, filled with supernatural desire.

Also, the peaceful crib at Bethlehem and the cud-chewing oxen are changed. They are "bestial." The Christ child is remembered not as a harbinger of peace, but a cause of turbulence, the mob swarming around Calvary. It is not peace that these strange, un-Christian Magi desire, but the disorder and bloodshed of the world. The Crucifixion has not satisfied them. They want an even more passionate event. The conventional symbols of Christianity have been charged by Yeats and altered so that they symbolize urgent spiritual unrest, a hunger that will not be satisfied. This is not at all a Christian solution.

The poem has great intensity. The Magi have a wonderful lightness, appearing and disappearing in the sky. They share the impersonality of objects. They are moved by a rhythm from beyond nature. Their silver helmets are like gleams in a painting. Their clothes are painted. Everything is fixed in a design that shows the permanence of desire.

The River-Merchant's Wife: A Letter
(After Rihaku)

> While my hair was still cut straight across my forehead
> I played about the front gate, pulling flowers.
> You came by on bamboo stilts, playing horse,
> You walked about my seat, playing with blue plums.
> And we went on living in the village of Chokan:
> Two small people, without dislike or suspicion.
>
> At fourteen I married My Lord you.
> I never laughed, being bashful.
> Lowering my head, I looked at the wall.
> Called to, a thousand times, I never looked back.
>
> At fifteen I stopped scowling,
> I desired my dust to be mingled with yours
> Forever and forever and forever.
> Why should I climb the look out?
>
> At sixteen you departed,
> You went into far Ku-to-yen, by the river of swirling eddies,
> And you have been gone five months.
> The monkeys make sorrowful noise overhead.
>
> You dragged your feet when you went out.
> By the gate now, the moss is grown, the different mosses,
> Too deep to clear them away!
> The leaves fall early this autumn, in wind.
> The paired butterflies are already yellow with August

Over the grass in the West garden;
They hurt me. I grow older.
If you are coming down through the narrows of the river Kiang,
Please let me know beforehand,
And I will come out to meet you
      As far as Cho-fu-Sa.

Ezra Pound, 1915

This poem is a complaint, and if it had been written by a sentimental poet, say one of the worse imitators of Tennyson in the nineteenth century, it might be very sad indeed—a three-handkerchief movie, brimming with bathos. The poet would play on our heartstrings, the Hammond organ would moan, there would be a flitting of purple, violet, and pink, and we would walk out into the hard light of afternoon with a headache. Fortunately, neither Li Po nor Pound is sentimental. In his imitation of a poem by Li Po, the eighth-century Chinese poet whose name in Japanese—from which Pound was translating—is Rihaku, Pound keeps the delicate tone of the original.

A poem is many things, moving together, and what holds them together is tone, the poet's attitude toward the subject. The personality of the poet is the essential force in the poem. It is his humor or seriousness, his tenderness or callousness, that is being expressed. Or, more exactly, it is the mood that he has put on, that we feel—for, of course, when he is not writing the poem, he may have quite different feelings that have nothing to do with poetry.

The persona, the speaker of this dramatic monologue, does not utter her complaint directly; she implies and understates her feelings. Instead of talking about herself she tells us what she has experienced. Her world has been altered. She points to this and that, and we see how the appearances of things have changed. As we see through her eyes we become aware of her intelligence; we begin to wonder about the woman who is seeing all this. She begins to matter to us; the feelings of such a person are important.

Pound had learned from Ford Madox Ford how to write in easy, conversational phrases. From the French critic Rémy de Gourmont he learned how to "make it new" by writing in images. This is the characteristic technique of some Chinese poetry and the Japanese poems of seventeen syllables called haiku. In haiku, sadness may be represented by a fallen leaf, joy by a butterfly, and there are moments of experience that cannot be translated into abstract words such as sadness or joy—for instance, the sound of a frog jumping into a pond. The poem is a moment of perception conveyed to the reader through images.

In an Imagist poem, Pound said, "one is trying to record the precise instant when a thing outward and objective transforms itself, or darts into a thing inward and subjective."

Writing in images is not photography, not a mere listing of concrete details. There have been many "modern" poems of this kind, and they are as tedious as bad eighteenth-century didactic verse or Victorian effusions. The new poetry that Pound called for would give the reader, through a selection of significant details and appropriate movement of the line, an experience similar to that which the poet originally had. Writing a hundred years before Pound, Wordsworth formulated much the same theory of poetic composition in the preface to *Lyrical Ballads*.

It is not always clear what writers mean by image or symbol. But there is a difference. An image is the means by which a particular emotion is conveyed. The meaning of an image is determined by its context; in a sense, an image is the poem itself. A symbol, on the other hand, has connotations that range beyond the particular context, and these are more or less constant. Symbols may be carried from one place to another and still retain their value. But an image has only a moment of life.

An image may be symbolic, for the moment. In "The River-Merchant's Wife" the monkeys symbolize grief; the mosses that have grown next to the gate symbolize an accumulation of time. However, removed from these contexts, monkeys and mosses would not mean what they do here. In another poem they might have quite different connotations.

"The River-Merchant's Wife" is written in free verse; there is no regular meter. Most of the sentences are simple declaratives—subject, verb, object:

> The leaves fall early this autumn, in wind.

With the exception of the ending, no sentence is longer than one or two lines. This gives the poem an insistent, forward motion, as compelling as the motion imparted to metrical verse by a recurring foot. In another short line:

> They hurt me. I grow older.

there are two complete sentences balancing against each other, an antiphonal structure frequently used in the Hebrew psalms and the *Song of Solomon*. Repetition of sentence structure, or parallelism, used by Pound throughout this poem, is one of the main resources of free verse, giving the poem cohesion and a kind of rhythm. Instead of recurrence of feet and use of rhyme, there is the rhythm of a syntactical pattern.

Dreams

> But the light returns
> the pleasure of smoking
> The spider-fairy of the cinders in points of blue and red

is never content with her mansions of Mozart
The wound heals everything uses its ingenuity to make itself
recognized I speak and beneath your face the cone of shadow
turns which from the depths of the sea has called the pearls
the eyelids, the lips, inhale the day
the arena empties itself
one of the birds in flying away
did not think to forget the straw and the thread
hardly has a crowd thought it fit to stir
when the arrow flies
a star nothing but a star lost in the fur of the night

André Breton, *Du Rêve* (translated by Robert Duncan)

1920. The street has changed—there are automobiles, the women's skirts are shorter, the men wear straw hats. There is the sound of a phonograph playing a new kind of music, a foxtrot. Everything seems to be going a little quicker—the automobile, the phonograph. Everything but a man who passes slowly before the window, swinging on a crutch, a victim of the Great War.

What kind of poetry shall we read? Something that will talk about phonographs and automobiles, that is moving rapidly, like the age. Going where? Well, we don't know. But the important thing is to be moving, like the automobile. Just moving. Anything but standing still like a cripple. Or a man who is suffering from shell-shock, or a man who has been gassed.

We don't want the old pre-war ideas back again. We don't want the big guns. All those people in the nineteenth century who were so certain of their opinions, Victor Hugo and so on—what this came down to in the war was poison gas.

And now we know that we don't know anything.

"What is beautiful? What is ugly? What is great, strong, weak? What is Carpentier, Renan, Foch? Don't know. What is myself? Don't know. Don't know, don't know, don't know."

We are Dadaists. That is, we make jokes.

In Paris, after the war, a number of writers came from the capitals that had recently been at war and gathered together to make a common cause—fun of everything. It was hysterical high spirits. And the spectacle was called Dada. It wasn't a movement, but a reaction—against rhetoric, slogans, solemnity, against literature. As for poetry . . . the way to write a poem, said Tristan Tzara, was to "Take a newspaper, take scissors, choose an article, cut it out, then cut out each word, put them all in a bag, shake . . ."

Dadaism, it has been said often enough, was a wrecking enterprise, yet it did contribute to poetry—as perhaps everything that happens does contribute, including those movements that declare most fiercely that they are not literature. Indeed, it is possible that such movements contribute most to literature after all. Dadaism revealed the unconscious. Dadaism revived the joke, and God knows it was needed after the Great War. But, more important, Dadaism produced the surrealist image, some years before the Surrealists. In the Dadaist paintings of Max Ernst there were juxtaposed, seemingly by chance, and pasted to the surface, images that had no connection in the world we perceive. Ernst was attempting to create a new reality by contriving "the meeting of two distant realities on a plane foreign to them both."

We have seen that the symbol was an object taken from nature that evoked mysterious associations. Then came the image—also based on nature —a symbol without associations. The next step was the invention of the surrealist image. This differed from both the symbol of the Symbolists and the image of the Imagists in that the surrealist image did not represent nature— it was a dream. In Ezra Pound's little poem about faces seen in a station of the Metro—"petals on a wet, black bough"—the connection between the faces and blossoms is perfectly understandable according to the laws by which similes are made. Both faces and blossoms are yellow, white, or pink. They are both soft. They are both organic. Therefore, according to the habit of metaphor by which the human mind brings together things that have an element in common, faces and blossoms merge to create an image. But there is no connection we can find in nature to justify bringing together the following objects: "Funnels smoking with hyacinths and propelled by blue serpents." The image is purely invented. André Breton, who organized and led the Surrealist movement, said, "I am the plaything of no sensory power." Sense-perception and a natural relationship between one thing and another were no longer the basis of the image. The Surrealists were living in a dream.

Three Poems by Carl Rakosi, 1971

Americana XVII   A Reminder of William Carlos Williams

> How quickly the dandelions
> come up
>   after a rain.
> I picked them
>   all
> only yesterday.

The Medium IV   Sights

> I mean to penetrate the particular
> the way an owl waits

for a kangaroo rat
and the photomicrograph
beholds the hairy
pappus of a dandelion.

Americana XIII

Captain Patterson, the folks back home
would like to know how you feel
about your first kill.

We had just completed our mission
and were rolling out when we saw four MIG 17s
off our left wing.
They were headed toward us
so we jettisoned our tanks
and blew our afterburners
and climbed left.
The lead MIG started firing.
The fight was on.
I put our Phantom into a 70° dive.
One MIG crossed our canopy from right to left,
leaving the area at a good speed.
I was about to take off after him
When another MIG appeared at 10 o'clock high.
"That's our baby,"
I called to Doug.
"Let's get him on the radar."
He locked in
and for three miles we were in trail.
Then we closed in and fired the sidewinder
real smooth off our left wing.
For a long while it just trailed the MIG,
then delicately at about a thousand feet behind
it straightened out and sailed into his tailpipe.
Blew him into a brilliant fire ball.

It was a piece of cake.
We wish they'd come up
and say hello more often.

Fifty years ago American poetry and English poetry began diverging, and the gap has been widening ever since. To put it another way, American poets started in a new direction, passing through the Imagist movement and making a new start from that point. In England, on the other hand, Imagism had little influence; a few English poets imitated Eliot's *The*

Waste Land, and a few learned something from Ezra Pound—but that was all.[1]

After the Imagist movement, the American poets I am speaking of were much influenced by Pound's *Cantos.* There Pound seems to be telling everything that comes into his mind as it occurs to him. Episodes of history, legends, myths, anecdotes from the writer's life occur side by side—"Beer bottles on the statue's pediment!" The language is formal at times, at other times colloquial.

The emphasis is on facts. Pound makes lists of particulars; he excerpts from letters and documents, accounts of commercial and financial transactions, from the words of men who were making history. He ranges over Europe, America, and ancient China. The object is to transmit particular facts, not to express feelings in emotive language. There is little attempt to move the reader directly; instead, the reader is given data from which he may extrapolate the ideas Pound originally had. The *Cantos* are do-it-yourself poetry.

Besides learning from Pound, American poets learned from William Carlos Williams and the Objectivists, who carried Imagism into the 1930's. But the Objectivists wanted to eliminate "personality"—a point the Imagists had not insisted on. The Objectivists argued that poets should suppress their subjective feelings and let nature speak for itself. By nature they meant not just trees and flowers, but garbage cans as well. Williams wrote:

> Things, things unmentionable,
> the sink with the waste farina in it and
> lumps of rancid meat, milk-bottle tops: have
> here a tranquillity and loveliness

Poems were to be mirrors of actuality; an expression of personal opinion would be a distortion of the truth. In fact, truth was external to the human mind. The only ideas in poetry should be those the poet was forced to have by the nature of the material. In Williams' famous phrase—"No ideas but in things."

❋

So poetry may be written without metaphors.

I have said that poets make metaphors, that by relating one thing to another and to themselves poets find meaning in the world around them. So they do . . . many poets do. But there are others who don't. They don't compare or identify one thing with another, they try to say what a thing is in itself.

---

1 Basil Bunting has been the most assiduous follower of Pound in England. In Scotland there was MacDiarmid. See "The Kind of Poetry I Want," p. 301, where his debt to Pound is evident, especially in the emphasis on "facts."

This is seen in poems by Williams and the Objectivists and, above, in the poems by Carl Rakosi—who was one of the Objectivist group. The aim of this writing is to render a thing accurately, with attention to its shape, sound, texture, its essential . . . I was almost going to say "meaning," but this would have been exactly the habit of thinking that such poetry tries to avoid. The meaning of the poem is the thing itself. "No ideas but in things."

This seems a Japanese or Chinese way of looking at things, rather than Western. In the discussion of Pound's "River-Merchant's Wife," I mentioned the haiku about the frog jumping into water.

> Old pond:
>   frog jump in
>   water sound.

What is the sound of a frog jumping into water like? Like nothing else in the world. It is a "frog-jumping-into-water-sound." Similes and metaphors distract attention from the thing itself, distract from reality. We cannot see what is there, for thinking of some other thing. The Western poet tries to piece things together by finding "similarity in dissimilars" (Aristotle's description)—but in the process of comparison he is bound to find more *dis*-similars, fracturing experience into more parts.

The sixth-century Zen Buddhist hymn known as the *Hsinhsinming*, "The Believing Mind," says:

> No description by analogy is possible
> of this state where all relations have ceased.

Commenting on this, R. H. Blyth says:

> Metaphors and similes, parables and comparisons may be used to describe anything belonging to the relative, the intellectually dichotomized world, but even the simplest and commonest experience of reality, the touch of hot water, the smell of camphor, are incommunicable by such or any means.

Blyth goes on to talk of the Meaninglessness of Meaning, and of Absolute Value, trying to describe the indescribable. The point is, comparisons may be distracting; they may prevent us from concentrating upon what is actually there.

The point is, we can think without using metaphors, and poems are written without them.

I am not saying that the Objectivist poets, or William Carlos Williams, or the many poets who imitate Williams, never use a metaphor. No theory of writing can be practiced without swerving. The whole of the poem by Rakosi titled "Sights," for example, is an extended comparison, though there are no metaphors in the individual lines. But exceptions to a theory do not prevent it from having an effect, and this reduction in the use of metaphors has made a noticeable difference, producing an American poetry that keeps its eye on the object and its ears open, letting the subject speak for itself. Such poetry has, as Rakosi says elsewhere, an "honest presence."

Poets are "makers"; they know how poems are put together, and though they may not know the names for technical devices, they use them all the time. If we wish to discuss poetry, some knowledge of these things is necessary.

Meter

In English, meter is the pattern of stressed and unstressed syllables.

Prosodists distinguish between syllables with heavy and syllables with light stresses, but I shall not do so. Prosody, the "science" of poetical forms, is not an exact science, and if we attempt to make it so, it disappears. If we mark half-stresses, there is no reason that we should not mark quarter-stresses, and so on. But when we think we hear half- and quarter-stresses, we can be sure that other people do not hear them. At that point, either we must impose our own way of hearing upon others, which is impossible, or agree that it is up to the individual to say exactly how he hears the beat of verse. The only system we can agree upon is the division of meter into stressed and unstressed syllables.

As we read lines of verse, each stressed sound combines with one or two unstressed sounds. This combination is called a foot. In the following line I have separated the feet by putting a virgule (/) between them. I have marked each stressed syllable: ‒. Unstressed syllables are marked: ◡. (Quantities in Greek and Roman verse are also marked with these signs, but I am using them to mark stresses, not quantities):

      Ro̽man/tĭc Īre/land's dea̅d/ and go̅ne.

Here each foot consists of an unstressed syllable followed by a stressed. A foot of this kind is called an iamb, and verse in which such feet predominate is iambic. In the line above there are four feet. A line with four feet is called a tetrameter. Therefore, the complete description of the meter of the line above is iambic tetrameter.

Besides the stresses, or accents, of meter, there are rhetorical accents. Rhetorical accent is the emphasis given to a word because of its importance in the sentence. The meter of verse, the regular pattern of stressed and unstressed sounds, is sometimes wrenched by a rhetorical accent. It would be a rare poem that followed its meter exactly, without variation, and a poem like that would sound mechanical.

Though the poem by Yeats from which I have taken the line above is in iambic tetrameter—that is, most of the lines are in iambic tetrameter— there are places where the rhetorical accent wrenches the meter, substituting irregular feet and giving the line a more passionate, natural sound, as though a man were thinking and feeling:

> Wās ĭt/ fŏr thĭs/ thĕ wīld/ gēese spread
>
> Thĕ grāy/ wĭng ūp/ŏn ēv/ĕry tĭde;
>
> Fŏr thĭs/ thăt āll/ thăt blōod/ wăs shĕd,
>
> Fŏr thĭs/ Ēdwărd/ Fītzgĕr/ăld dīed,
>
> Ănd Rōb/ĕrt Ēmm/ĕt ănd/ Wōlfe Tŏne,
>
> Āll thăt/ dĕlīr/iŭm ŏf/ thĕ brăve?

I am not sure that Yeats would have stressed the sounds as I have done, for everyone reads in a different way, but I think he would have played as many variations, of one kind or another, upon the basic meter.

Meter is like waves of the sea, and rhetorical accents are like crosscurrents. The waves come on at a regular pace. They are crossed by the currents, and writhe, and seem to break. Then they resume their pace.

In English the basic feet are:

> the iamb (adjective, iambic) ⌣ —
> trochee (trochaic) — ⌣
> anapest (anapestic) ⌣ ⌣ —
> dactyl (dactylic) — ⌣ ⌣

Less common are:

> the spondee (spondaic) — —
> pyrrhus (pyrrhic) ⌣ ⌣
> amphibrach (amphibrachic) ⌣ — ⌣
> amphimacer (cretic) — ⌣ —

And there are other feet so rarely used that we do not need to know them.

Lines of verse are named for the number of feet they contain.

A line of one foot is a monometer
      two feet   dimeter
    three feet   trimeter
    four feet   tetrameter
    five feet   pentameter
    six feet   hexameter
  seven feet   heptameter
and so on.

Or else the line may be named for the number of syllables in it. A line of eight syllables is called octosyllabic; a line of ten syllables, decasyllabic.

Unrhymed iambic pentameter, the line in which Marlowe and Shakespeare wrote plays, is often called blank verse (not to be confused with free verse). The iambic hexameter is sometimes called an Alexandrine. In the following couplet, Pope shows the difference between a line of iambic pentameter and an Alexandrine:

Ă nēed/lĕss Āl/ĕxānd/rĭne ends/ hĭs sōng, (*iambic pentameter*)

Which,/ lĭke ă wound/ĕd snāke,// drāws ĭts/ slōw length/ ălōng.

                           (*iambic hexameter* or *Alexandrine*)

In this Alexandrine I have marked the caesura—that is, a "cutting" or pause in the line—with a double bar. Here the caesura is in the middle of the line, dividing it into two equal parts, each of which contains three feet. But a pause may occur anywhere in a line.

Here are other lines and meters. The first two examples are not very good poetry, but they are good enough for our purpose:

Whĕn thrēads/ căn māke   *iambic dimeter*
A heartstring shake,
Philosophy
Can scarce deny
Thĕ sōul/ cŏnsīsts/ ŏf hārm/ŏny̆.   *iambic tetrameter*

Nŏ, thĕ hēart/ thăt hăs trū/ly̆ lŏvĕd nēv/ĕr fŏrgēts,
                        anapestic tetrameter

Bŭt ăs trū/ly̆ lŏves ōn/ tŏ thĕ clōse,   *anapestic trimeter*
As the sunflower turns on her god when he sets,
The same look which she turned when he rose.

Long-ex/pected/ one and/ twenty,   *trochaic tetrameter*
Ling'ring year, at last is flown;
Pomp and pleasure, pride and plenty,
Great Sir John, are all your own.

Midnight has/ come, and the/ great Christ Church/ Bell
                                   dactylic tetrameter

And/ many a/ lesser bell/ sound through the/ room.

Though meter may reinforce the meaning of poetry, it cannot *be* the
meaning. Reading these lines by Tennyson, we may think we feel the gallop of horses:

Half a league, half a league,
   Half a league, onward,
All in the valley of Death
   Rode the six hundred.
"Forward the Light Brigade!
Charge for the guns!" he said.
Into the valley of Death
   Rode the six hundred.

But if we think we feel the pace of a cavalry charge, it is because the
words tell us it is a cavalry charge. The meter alone does not call up the
scene. A poet could write lines with the same meter but with different
words that would make us think of something entirely different. Once we
have a meaning, meter can support it; but without meaning, meter drifts
in a void.

In his *Life of Pope,* Samuel Johnson argues against the fallacy of thinking that meter alone can represent meaning. Johnson says that through
meter:

Motion . . . may be in some sort exemplified; and yet it may be
suspected that in such resemblances the mind often governs the
ear, and the sounds are estimated by their meaning.

He shows that Pope uses the same meter when describing a running girl,
and, in another place, a slow march. Pope himself says, "The sound must
seem an echo to the sense." But this is a far cry from saying that sound is
sense. Poetry has both meaning and meter, and in a good poem they are so
closely related that they seem one thing.

Though meter and sound cannot by themselves represent the subject,
frequently they represent the author's feelings about it—in Pope's phrase,
the sound echoes the sense. If the poet wishes to express a heroic mood, he

may choose a long, slowly moving line. To express lyrical feeling, he may write in short lines with tripping meters. But there are no standard correlations between lines and feelings. A long, slow line may be humorous, and a tripping line satirical.

There is no end to descriptions of meter. *Secondary stress* and *hovering accent,* and other kinds of rhythmic organization—*cadence* and *syllabic verse*—are described in the Glossary. We could go on talking about prosody, but it makes more sense, and it is certainly more enjoyable, to read poems than to try to think of all the kinds of poems there might possibly be.

Rhyme, Stanza, and Sound

Poems used to be called rhymes, and some people think that anything that rhymes is a poem. But, as Ben Jonson said, "A rhymer, and a poet, are two things." Poems are made with words that express thought and feeling; merely repeating sounds is not enough. Of course, many poets have written in rhyme—great poets use it, little poets depend on it. There may be a pleasure in the sound of rhyme even where sense is lacking:

> Lives of great men all remind us
>   We can make our lives sublime,
> And, departing, leave behind us
>   Footprints on the sands of time.
>
>   Longfellow, "A Psalm of Life"

Rhymes are memorable. And writers of light verse entertain us with their ingenuity in making rhymes:

> I'm very well acquainted too with matters mathematical,
> I understand equations, both the simple and quadratical,
> About binomial theorem I'm teeming with a lot of news,
> With many cheerful facts about the square of the hypotenuse.
>
>   W. S. Gilbert, "Major General's Song"

In the twentieth century, however, many poets have dispensed with rhyme in order to make new forms of verse.

Rhyme does not have a very long history. The ancient Greek, Hebrew, and Roman poets did not use rhyme. It was invented by monks in the Middle Ages as a memory aid; they found it easier to memorize chants if the ends of lines had the same sound. Then rhyme was taken up by Italian poets and their imitators, and by the time of Chaucer (c. 1340-1400) we find it ensconced in English.

In the history of verse, there has been a running quarrel between men such as Samuel Daniel (1562-1619), who *would* rhyme, and men such as Thomas Campion (c. 1567-1620), who *wouldn't*. Daniel defended rhyming on the ground that it was customary (though it was not customary with the ancients); Campion called rhyme, together with the English system of meter, a "vulgar and easie kind of Poesie." Milton, who had written several poems in rhyme, broke with it scornfully:

> rhyme being no necessary adjunct or true ornament of poem or good verse, in longer works especially, but the invention of a barbarous age, to set off wretched matter and lame meter.

The defenders of rhyme say that the sound is pleasing. Moreover, searching for rhymes makes the poet have thoughts he would not otherwise have had. Those who attack rhyme say that in searching for a rhyme the poet loses the thought he had to start with. As for sound, there are other, more subtle devices than the correspondence of terminal sounds. And besides, writing without rhyme is more *natural*. To this the defenders of rhyme reply that all art is artificial, and a poet is free to do as he likes.

In comparison with other languages, English does not have a large variety of rhyming words. This is evident if we read the poems of an English rhymer such as Pope, who is frequently compelled to use the same terminal words. Rhyme schemes that in other languages are easy—*terza rima,* for example—are hard to find rhymes for in English.

In scansion, rhymes are marked by placing the same letter of the alphabet after words that rhyme with each other. I have marked the following couplets from Pope's *The Rape of the Lock* in this manner:

The hungry Judges soon the Sentence sign,	*a*
And wretches hang that Jurymen may dine;	*a*
The Merchant from th'*Exchange* returns in Peace,	*b*
And the long Labors of the *Toilet* cease.	*b*

Actually, in this instance the letters *a a b b* are not needed to describe the lines, for the word "couplet" means two consecutive lines that rhyme with each other. But if we wish to describe other rhyme schemes, letters are useful. Here is a ballad stanza:

It is an ancient Mariner,	*a*
And he stoppeth one of three.	*b*
"By thy long gray beard and glittering eye,	*c*
Now wherefore stopp'st thou me?	*b*

We could describe this rhyme scheme simply by saying "a ballad stanza rhyming *a b c b.*" This would differentiate the stanza from others—for example, stanzas rhyming *a b a b.*

At the same time we could describe the meter by placing numbers after the letters to show the number of feet in each line: a^4 b^3 c^4 b^3.

A stanza is a group of lines forming a unit of a poem. It is recurrent, with a regular pattern of lines, meter, and rhyme—though the pattern may vary. Some of the stanza forms—quatrain, *rime royal, ottava rima,* Spenserian stanza, and so on—are described in the Glossary.

Before rhyme came into English, there was an entirely different system of sound-correspondence: by alliteration, the repetition of initial consonants or vowels in words placed close together. William Langland, a contemporary of Chaucer, wrote in this manner:

> In a somer seson whan soft was the sonne,
> I shope me in shroudes as I a shepe were,
> In habite as an heremite unholy of workes,
> Went wyde in this world wondres to here.

Piers Plowman

Though alliteration is no longer used as a system, in most poetry there is some alliteration:

> Now the old come out to look,
>   Winter past and winter's pains,
> How the sky in pool and brook
>   Glitters on the grassy plains.

A. E. Housman, "Spring Morning"

In this quatrain the initial consonant p occurs four times, and the g twice. (The initial consonant w occurs twice, in "Winter" and "winter's," but as it is the same word this is not alliteration but just repetition.)

Besides alliteration, in this quatrain there is another sound device: assonance, the repetition of vowel sounds within different words placed close together. "Past" and "pains" are assonant; so are "pool" and "brook."

On the other hand, if the main vowel sounds change but consonantal sounds recur, this is . . . consonance. The word "consonance" may be used also to mean line endings where the final consonants agree but the vowels that precede them differ.

> But cursed are dullards whom no cannon stu*n*s,
> That they should be as sto*nes.*

Wilfred Owen, "Insensibility"

And there is cacophony, a combination of discordant sounds:

> The ice was here, the ice was there,
> The ice was all around:
> It *cracked* and *growled,* and roared and howled,
> Like noises in a swound!

Coleridge,
The Rime of the Ancient Mariner

I have said that meter alone cannot convey meaning. Nor can onomatopoeia, the forming of words in imitation of sounds. In the following lines from Tennyson's *The Princess*, we may think that we hear, in the alliterative and consonant *m* sounds, and the assonant *o* and *u* sounds, the moaning of doves and humming of bees:

> The moan of doves in immemorial elms,
> And murmuring of innumerable bees

But without the nouns "doves" and "bees," these sounds would not conjure up doves and bees. We might be thinking of the ocean, or wind in the grass. In the "cracked" and "growled" of Coleridge's description we may think that we hear ice grinding and splitting, but without the word "ice" it might as well be breaking timber. Like meter, sound can reinforce meaning, but sounds alone are . . . Sound Poetry. See the entry in the Glossary.

Free Verse

Free verse—verse with an irregular metrical pattern—is an old form. The Hebrew psalms were written in lines that are more or less free; in the last century Whitman wrote free verse, and nowadays many poets write in this form. Free verse is not just prose broken into irregular lines. As Eliot said, no verse is free for the man who wants to do a good job—and free verse, to be written well, requires as much art as writing in regular meters. However, this has not been apparent to some people. Robert Frost said he would as soon play tennis without a net as try to write free verse. Even if we think that poetry is a game, there are games—jai alai, for example—that do not use a net, though they are not played in New England.

Free verse is discussed on pp. 3-5, in the reading of a poem by Williams and a line by Whitman. Also see Free Verse in the Glossary.

AN ANTHOLOGY OF POEMS

GEOFFREY CHAUCER [1340?–1400]

from The
Canterbury Tales

Whan that Aprill with his shoures° soote°	showers / sweet
The droghte of March hath perced to the roote,	
And bathed every veyne in swich licour°	such liquid
Of which vertu° engendred is the flour;	by power of which
Whan Zephirus eek° with his sweete breeth	also
Inspired hath in every holt° and heeth	wood
The tendre croppes, and the yonge sonne	
Hath in the Ram his halve cours yronne,°	run
And smale foweles° maken melodye,	birds
That slepen al the nyght with open ye°	eye
(So priketh hem° nature in hir	inspires them
corages°),	their hearts
Thanne longen° folk to goon on pilgrimages,	long
And palmeres° for to seken straunge strondes,°	pilgrims / shores
To ferne halwes,° kowthe° in sondry londes;	distant shrines / known
And specially from every shires ende	
Of Engelond to Caunterbury they wende,	
The hooly blisful martir[1] for to seke,	
That hem hath holpen° whan that they were seeke.°	helped / sick
Bifil° that in that seson on a day,	It befell
In Southwerk at the Tabard as I lay	
Redy to wenden° on my pilgrymage	go
To Caunterbury with ful devout corage,°	heart
At nyght was come into that hostelrye°	inn
Wel nyne and twenty in a compaignye,	
On sondry folk, by aventure yfalle°	by chance fallen
In felaweshipe, and pilgrimes were they alle,	
That toward Caunterbury wolden° ryde.	wanted to
The chambres and the stables weren wyde,	
And wel we weren esed° atte beste.	entertained
And shortly, whan the sonne was to reste,	
So hadde I spoken with hem everichon°	every one
That I was of hir felaweshipe anon,	
And made forward° erly for to ryse,	agreement
To take oure wey ther as I yow devyse.°	impart

◆

A Knyght ther was, and that a worthy man,	
That fro the tyme that he first bigan	
To riden out,° he loved chivalrie,	go on expeditions
Trouthe and honour, fredom and curteisie.	

1 Thomas à Beckett, Archbishop of Canterbury, murdered in 1170.

Ful worthy was he in his lordes werre,°   *war*
And therto hadde he riden, no man ferre,°   *farther*
As wel in cristendom as in hethenesse,°   *heathen lands*
And evere honoured for his worthynesse.
At Alisaundre° he was whan it was wonne.   *Alexandria*
Ful ofte tyme he hadde the bord bigonne°   *headed the table*
Aboven alle nacions in Pruce;°   *Prussia*
In Lettow° hadde he reysed° and in   *Lithuania / made a raid*
    Ruce,°   *Russia*
No Cristen man so ofte of his degree.°   *rank*
In Gernade° at the seege eek hadde he be   *Granada*
Of Algezir,° and riden in Belmarye.°   *Algeciras / Benmarin*
At Lyeys° was he and at Satalye,°   *Ayas / Attalia*
Whan they were wonne; and in the Grete See°   *Mediterranean Sea*
At many a noble armee° hadde he be.   *armed expedition*
At mortal batailles° hadde he been
    fiftene,   *tournaments fought to the death*
And foughten for oure feith at Tramyssene°   *Tlemcen*
In lystes° thries, and ay slayn his foo.   *tournaments*
This ilke worthy knyght hadde been also   *same*
Somtyme with the lord of Palatye°   *Palathia*
Agayn another hethen in Turkye.
And everemoore he hadde a sovereyn prys;°   *supreme reputation*
And though that he were worthy, he was wys,
And of his port° as meeke as is a mayde.   *demeanor*
He nevere yet no vileynye° ne sayde   *insult*
In al his lyf unto no maner wight.°   *person*
He was a verray, parfit gentil° knyght.   *true / perfect / noble*
But, for to tellen yow of his array,
His hors were goode, but he was nat gay.
Of fustian° he wered a gypon°   *thick cotton / tunic*
Al bismotered with his
    habergeon,°   *marked with rust from his coat of mail*
For he was late ycome from his viage,°   *expedition*
And wente for to doon his pilgrymage.

◆

A Clerk° ther was of   *ecclesiastical student*
    Oxenford° also,   *Oxford*
That unto logyk hadde longe ygo.
As leene was his hors as is a rake,
And he nas nat right fat, I undertake,
But looked holwe, and therto sobrely.
Ful thredbare was his overeste courtepy;°   *outer cloak*
For he hadde geten hym yet no benefice,
Ne was so worldly for to have office.°   *secular employment*
For hym was levere° have at his beddes heed   *would rather*
Twenty bookes, clad in blak or reed,

Of Aristotle[2] and his philosophie,
Than robes riche, or fithele,° or gay sautrie.°   *fiddle / psaltery*
But al be that he was a philosophre,
Yet hadde he but litel gold in cofre;[3]
But al that he myghte of his freendes hente,°   *obtain*
On bookes and on lernynge he it spente,
And bisily gan for the soules preye
Of hem that yaf hym wherwith to scoleye.°   *study*
Of studie took he moost cure° and moost heede.   *care*
Noght o word spak he moore than was neede,
And that was seyd in forme° and reverence,   *with decorum*
And short and quyk and ful of hy sentence;°   *thought*
Sownynge in° moral vertu was his speche,   *tending towards*
And gladly wolde he lerne and gladly teche.

◆

A good Wif was ther of biside° Bathe,   *near*
But she was somdel° deef, and that was scathe.°   *somewhat / a pity*
Of clooth-makyng she hadde swich an haunt,°   *skill*
She passed° hem of Ypres and of Gaunt.[4]   *surpassed*
In al the parisshe wif ne was ther noon
That to the offrynge° bifore hire sholde goon;   *offering of alms*
And if ther° dide, certeyn so wrooth was she,   *they*
That she was out of alle charitee.
Hir coverchiefs° ful fyne weren of ground;°   *kerchiefs / texture*
I dorste° swere they weyeden° ten pound   *dare / weighed*
That on a Sonday weren upon hir heed.
Hir hosen weren of fyn scarlet reed,
Ful streite yteyd,° and shoes ful moyste and newe.   *tied*
Boold was hir face, and fair, and reed of hewe.
She was a worthy womman al hir lyve:
Housbondes at chirche dore she hadde fyve,
Withouten° oother compaignye in youthe,—   *apart from*
But therof nedeth° nat to speke as nowthe.°   *need / now*
And thries hadde she been at Jerusalem;
She hadde passed many a straunge strem;
At Rome she hadde been, and at Boloigne,
In Galice at Seint-Jame, and at Coloigne.
She koude° muchel of wandrynge by the weye.   *knew*
Gat-tothed° was she, soothly for to seye.   *teeth wide apart*
Upon an amblere° esily she sat,   *slow horse*
Ywympled° wel, and on hir heed an hat   *veiled*
As brood as is a bokeler° or a targe;°   *buckler / shield*

2   famous Greek philosopher whose writings were particularly influential in
the Middle Ages.
3   a punning reference to the "philosopher's stone," which alchemists believed
would change base metals into gold.
4   Flemish towns famous for cloth-making.

A foot-mantel° aboute hir hipes large,   *skirt*
And on hir feet a paire of spores° sharpe.   *spurs*
In felaweshipe wel koude she laughe and carpe.°   *talk*
Of remedies of love she knew per chaunce,
For she koude° of that art the olde daunce.°   *knew / dance*

ANONYMOUS

I Sing
of a Maiden

I sing of a maiden
    That is makeles;°   *matchless, without a mate*
King of all kings
    To° her son she ches.°   *for / chose*

He came al so still
    There his mother was,
As dew in April
    That falleth on the grass.

He came al so still
    To his mother's bour,
As dew in April
    That falleth on the flour.

He came al so still
    There his mother lay,
As dew in April
    That falleth on the spray.

Mother and maiden
    Was never none but she;
Well may such a lady
    Goddes mother be.

Adam Lay I-bowndyn

Adam lay I-bowndyn,° bowndyn in a bond,   *bound*
forwe° thowsand wynter thowt he not to long;[1]   *four*
And al was for an appil, an appil that he tok,
As clerkis° fyndyn wretyn in here° book.   *clergy / their*

1 The Creation was thought to have taken place in 4004 B.C. From this to
the birth of Christ was four thousand years.

Ne hadde the appil take ben, the appil taken ben,
ne hadde neuer our lady a ben heuene qwen;[2]
Blyssid be the tyme that appil take was,
Ther-fore we mown° syngyn, "deo gracias!"[3]   *may*

Who Wot Nowe That Ys Here

Who wot° nowe that ys here,   *knows*
    Where he schall be anoder yere?
Anoder yere hit may betyde
This compeny to be full wyde,°   *far off*
And neuer on-odyr to abyde;
    Criste may send now sych a yere.

Another yere hit may befall
The lest° that is withyn this hall   *lowest*
To be more mastur then we all;
    Cryste may send now sych a yere.

This lordis that ben wonder grete,
They threton powre men for to bete;
Hyt lendith° lytull in hur° threte;   *there is / their*
    Cryste may send sich a yere.

Sumer Is Icumen In

Sumer is icumen in,
    Lhudé° sing cuccu;   *loud*
Groweth sed and bloweth° med°   *blossoms / meadow*
    And springth the wudé nu.°   *wood now*
        Sing cuccu!
Awé° bleteth after lomb,   *ewe*
    Lhouth° after calvé cu;°   *lows / cow*
Bulluc sterteth, bucké verteth;°   *breaks wind*
    Murie sing cuccu.
        Cuccu, cuccu,
    Wel singés thu, cuccu,
    Ne swik° thu naver nu.°   *stop / now*
Sing cuccu nu! Sing cuccu!
Sing cuccu! Sing cuccu nu!

2   Our Lady would never have been Queen of Heaven.
3   "thanks be to God."

I Haue
a Yong Suster

I haue a yong suster
 ffer be-yondyn the se,
many be the drowryis°   *love-tokens*
 that che sente me.

che sente me the cherye
 with-outyn ony ston,
& so che ded the dowe°   *dove*
 with-outyn ony bon.

sche sente me the brer°   *briar*
 with-outyn ony rinde,°   *branch*
sche bad me loue my lemman°   *sweetheart*
 with-oute longgyng.

how shuld ony cherye
 be with-oute ston?
& how shuld ony dowe
 ben with-oute bon?

how shuld ony brer
 ben with-oute rynde?
how shuld y loue myn lemman
 with-out longyng?

Quan° the cherye was a flour,   *when*
 than hadde it non ston.
quan the dowe was an ey,°   *egg*
 than hadde it non bon.

Quan the brer was on-bred,°   *unborn*
 than hadde it non rynd.
quan the maydyn hast that che louit,
 che is with-out longing.

Sir Patrick Spens

The king sits in Dumferling toune,
 Drinking the blude-reid wine:
"O whar will I get guid sailor,
 To sail this schip of mine?"

Up and spak an eldern knicht,
 Sat at the kings richt kne:
"Sir Patrick Spens is the best sailor
 That sails upon the se."

The king has written a braid° letter,   *broad*
    And signd it wi his hand,   10
And sent it to Sir Patrick Spens,
    Was walking on the sand.

The first line that Sir Patrick red,
    A loud lauch lauched he;
The next line that Sir Patrick red,
    The teir blinded his ee.°   *eye*

"O wha° is this has don this deid,   *who*
    This ill deid don to me,
To send me out this time o' the yeir,
    To sail upon the se!   20

"Mak haste, mak haste, my mirry men all,
    Our guid° schip sails the morne."   *good*
"O say na sae,° my master deir,   *so*
    For I feir a deadlie storme.

"Late late yestreen I saw the new moone,
    Wi the auld moone in hir arme,
And I feir, I feir, my deir master,
    That we will cum to harme."

O our Scots nobles wer richt laith°   *loath*
    To weet their cork-heild schoone;°   *cork-heeled shoes*
Bot lang owre° a' the play wer playd,   *before*
    Thair hats they swam aboone.°   *above*

O lang, lang may their ladies sit,
    Wi thair fans into their hand,
Or eir° they se Sir Patrick Spens   *before*
    Cum sailing to the land.

O lang, lang may the ladies stand
    Wi thair gold kems° in their hair,   *combs*
Waiting for thair ain deir lords,
    For they'll se thame na mair.   40

Haf owre,° haf owre to Abedour,   *half over*
    It's fiftie fadom deip,
And thair lies guid Sir Patrick Spens,
    Wi the Scots lords at his feit.

Thomas the Rhymer

True Thomas lay on Huntlie bank;
    A ferlie° he spied wi' his e'e;   *marvel*
And there he saw a ladye bright
    Come riding doun by Eildon Tree.

Her skirt was o' the grass-green silk,
  Her mantle o' the velvet fyne;
At ilka° tett° o' her horse's mane   *each / lock*
  Hung fifty siller bells and nine.

True Thomas he pu'd aff his cap,
  And louted° low doun on his knee: *bowed*
"Hail to thee, Mary, Queen of Heaven!   11
  For thy peer on earth could never be."

"O no, O no, Thomas," she said,
  "That name does not belang to me;
I'm but the Queen o' fair Elfland,
  That am hither come to visit thee.

"Harp and carp,° Thomas," she said;   *sing*
  "Harp and carp along wi' me;
And if ye dare to kiss my lips,
  Sure of your bodie I will be."   20

"Betide me weal, betide me woe,
  That weird° shall never daunten me."   *fate*
Syne° he has kissed her rosy lips,   *soon*
  All underneath the Eildon Tree.

"Now ye maun° go wi' me," she said,   *must*
  "True Thomas, ye maun go wi' me;
And ye maun serve me seven years,
  Thro' weal or woe as may chance to be."

She's mounted on her milk-white steed,
  She's ta'en true Thomas up behind;   30
And aye, whene'er her bridle rang,
  The steed gaed° swifter than the wind.   *went*

O they rade on, and farther on,
  The steed gaed swifter than the wind;
Until they reached a desert wide,
  And living land was left behind.

"Light down, light down now, true Thomas,
  And lean your head upon my knee;
Abide ye here a little space,
  And I will show you ferlies three.   40

"O see ye not yon narrow road,
  So thick beset wi' thorns and briars?
That is the Path of Righteousness,
  Though after it but few inquires.

"And see ye not yon braid,° braid road,   *broad*
  That lies across the lily leven?°   *white light*
That is the Path of Wickedness,
  Though some call it the Road to Heaven.

"And see ye not yon bonny road
　　That winds about the fernie brae?°　　　　　　　　　*hill*
That is the road to fair Elfland,　　　　　　　　　　　51
　　Where thou and I this night maun gae.

"But, Thomas, ye sall haud° your tongue,　　　　　　　　*hold*
　　Whatever ye may hear or see;
For speak ye word in Elfyn-land,
　　Ye'll ne'er win back to your ain countrie."

O they rade on, and farther on,
　　And they waded rivers abune° the knee;　　　　　　　*above*
And they saw neither sun nor moon,
　　But they heard the roaring of the sea.　　　　　　　　60

It was mirk,° mirk night, there was nae starlight,　　　　*dark*
　　They waded thro' red blude to the knee;
For a' the blude that's shed on the earth
　　Rins° through the springs o' that countrie.　　　　　　*runs*

Syne they came to a garden green,
　　And she pu'd an apple frae a tree:
"Take this for thy wages, true Thomas;
　　It will give thee the tongue that can never lee.°"　　　*lie*

"My tongue is my ain,°" true Thomas he said;　　　　　　*own*
　　"A gudely gift ye wad gie° to me!　　　　　　　　*would give*
I neither dought° to buy or sell　　　　　　　　　　*am able*
　　At fair or tryst° where I might be.　　　　　*appointed place*

"I dought neither speak to prince or peer,
　　Nor ask of grace from fair ladye!"
"Now haud° thy peace, Thomas," she said,　　　　　　　*hold*
　　"For as I say, so must it be."

He has gotten a coat of the even cloth,
　　And a pair o' shoon° of the velvet green;　　　　　　*shoes*
And till seven years were gane and past,
　　True Thomas on earth was never seen.　　　　　　　80

Edward, Edward

"Why does your brand° sae drop wi' blude,　　　　　　*sword*
　　Edward, Edward?
Why does your brand sae drop wi' blude,
　　And why sae sad gang ye, O?"—
"O I hae kill'd my hawk sae gude,
　　Mither, mither;
O I hae kill'd my hawk sae gude,
　　And I had nae mair but he, O."

"Your hawk's blude was never sae red,
    Edward, Edward;   10
Your hawk's blude was never sae red,
    My dear son, I tell thee, O."—
"O I hae kill'd my red-roan° steed,   *reddish-brown*
    Mither, mither;
O I hae kill'd my red-roan steed,
    That earst° was sae fair and free, O."   *previously*

"Your steed was auld, and ye hae got mair,°   *more*
    Edward, Edward;
Your steed was auld, and ye hae got mair;
    Some other dule° ye dree,° O."   *grief / suffer*
"O I hae kill'd my father dear,   21
    Mither, mither;
O I hae kill'd my father dear,
    Alas, and wae is me, O!"

"And whatten penance will ye dree° for that,   *undergo*
    Edward, Edward?
Whatten penance will ye dree for that?
    My dear son, now tell me, O."—
"I'll set my feet in yonder boat,
    Mither, mither;   30
I'll set my feet in yonder boat,
    And I'll fare over the sea, O."

"And what will ye do wi' your tow'rs and your ha',°   *hall*
    Edward, Edward?
And what will ye do wi' your tow'rs and your ha',
    That were sae fair to see, O?"
"I'll let them stand till they doun fa',°   *fall*
    Mither, mither;
I'll let them stand till they doun fa',
    For here never mair maun° I be, O."   *must*

"And what will ye leave to your bairns° and your wife, *children*
    Edward, Edward?
And what will ye leave to your bairns and your wife,
    When ye gang owre the sea, O?"—
"The warld's room: let them beg through life,
    Mither, mither;
The warld's room: let them beg through life;
    For them never mair will I see, O."

"And what will ye leave to your ain mither dear,
    Edward, Edward?   50
And what will ye leave to your ain mither dear,
    My dear son, now tell me, O?"—

"The curse of hell frae me sall ye bear,
    Mither, mither;
The curse of hell frae me sall ye bear:
    Sic° counsels ye gave to me, O!"   *such*

SIR THOMAS WYATT [1503?–1542]

The Lover Showeth
How He Is Forsaken
of Such as He Sometime Enjoyed

They flee from me that sometime did me seek,
    With naked foot stalking in my chamber.
I have seen them gentle, tame and meek,
    That now are wild and do not remember
    That sometime they put themselves in danger
        To take bread at my hand; and now they range
        Busily seeking with a continual change.

Thanked be fortune, it hath been otherwise
    Twenty times better; but once, in special,
In thin array, after a pleasant guise,
    When her loose gown from her shoulders did fall,
    And she me caught in her arms long and small,
        Therewith all sweetly did me kiss,
        And softly said: "Dear heart, how like you this?"

It was no dream; I lay broad waking:
    But all is turned thorough my gentleness
Into a strange fashion of forsaking;
    And I have leave to go of her goodness;
    And she also to use new-fangleness.
        But since that I so kindely[1] am served,
        I fain would know what she hath deserved.

BARNABE GOOGE [1540–1594]

Out of Sight,
Out of Mind

The oftener seen, the most I lust,
    The more I lust, the more I smart,
The more I smart, the more I trust,

1   naturally.

The more I trust, the heavier heart;
The heavy heart breeds mine unrest,
Thy absence, therefore, like I best.

The rarer seen, the less in mind,
    The less in mind, the lesser pain,
The lesser pain, less grief I find,
    The lesser grief, the greater gain,
The greater gain, the merrier I,
Therefore I wish thy sight to fly.

The further off, the more I joy,
    The more I joy, the happier life,
The happier life, less hurts annoy,
    The lesser hurts, pleasure most rife:
Such pleasures rife shall I obtain
When distance doth depart us twain.

SIR WALTER RALEGH   [1552?–1618]

To His Son

Three things there be that prosper all apace
And flourish, while they are asunder far;
But on a day they meet all in a place,
And when they meet, they one another mar.
And they be these: the wood, the weed, the wag.
The wood is that that makes the gallows tree;
The weed is that that strings the hangman's bag;
The wag, my pretty knave, betokens thee.
Now mark, dear boy: while these assemble not,
Green springs the tree, hemp grows, the wag is wild;
But when they meet, it makes the timber rot,
It frets the halter, and it chokes the child.
        God bless the child!

EDMUND SPENSER   [1552?–1599]

Epithalamion[1]

Ye learned sisters[2] which have oftentimes
Beene to me ayding, others to adorne:
Whom ye thought worthy of your gracefull rymes,
That even the greatest did not greatly scorne

1   a wedding song, celebrating Spenser's marriage to Elizabeth Boyle in 1594.
2   the Muses.

To heare theyr names sung in your simple layes,
But joyéd in theyr prayse.
And when ye list your owne mishaps to mourne,
Which death, or love, or fortunes wreck did rayse,
Your string could soone to sadder tenor turne,
And teach the woods and waters to lament 10
Your dolefull dreriment.
Now lay those sorrowfull complaints aside,
And having all your heads with girland crownd,
Helpe me mine owne loves prayses to resound,
Ne let the same of any be envide:
So Orpheus did for his owne bride,[3]
So I unto my selfe alone will sing,
The woods shall to me answer and my Eccho ring.

Early before the worlds light giving lampe,
His golden beame upon the hils doth spred, 20
Having disperst the nights unchearefull dampe,
Doe ye awake, and with fresh lustyhed
Go to the bowre of my belovéd love,
My truest turtle dove,
Bid her awake; for Hymen[4] is awake,
And long since ready forth his maske to move,
With his bright Tead[5] that flames with many a flake,
And many a bachelor to waite on him,
In theyr fresh garments trim.
Bid her awake therefore and soone her dight,[6] 30
For lo the wishéd day is come at last,
That shall for al the paynes and sorrowes past,
Pay to her usury of long delight:
And whylest she doth her dight,
Doe ye to her of joy and solace sing,
That all the woods may answer and your eccho ring.

Bring with you all the Nymphes that you can heare
Both of the rivers and the forrests greene:
And of the sea that neighbours to her neare,
Al with gay girlands goodly wel beseene. 40
And let them also with them bring in hand,
Another gay girland
For my fayre love of lillyes and of roses,
Bound truelove wize with a blew silke riband.
And let them make great store of bridale poses,
And let them eeke bring store of other flowers
To deck the bridale bowers.

3   Orpheus, on the death of his wife, Eurydice, descended to Hades and
charmed the god of the underworld with his song so that she was released.
4   god of marriage.
5   a torch used in Roman wedding ceremonies.
6   dress.

And let the ground whereas her foot shall tread,
For feare the stones her tender foot should wrong
Be strewed with fragrant flowers all along, 50
And diapred lyke the discolored mead.[7]
Which done, doe at her chamber dore awayt,
For she will waken strayt,
The whiles doe ye this song unto her sing,
The woods shall to you answer and your Eccho ring.

Ye Nymphes of Mulla[8] which with carefull heed,
The silver scaly trouts doe tend full well,
And greedy pikes which use therein to feed,
(Those trouts and pikes all others doo excell)
And ye likewise which keepe the rushy lake, 60
Where none doo fishes take,
Bynd up the locks the which hang scatterd light,
And in his waters which your mirror make,
Behold your faces as the christall bright,
That when you come whereas my love doth lie,
No blemish she may spie.
And eke ye lightfoot mayds which keepe the deere,
That on the hoary mountayne use to towre,
And the wylde wolves which seeke them to devoure,
With your steele darts doo chace from comming neer 70
Be also present heere,
To helpe to decke her and to help to sing,
That all the woods may answer and your eccho ring.

Wake, now my love, awake; for it is time,
The Rosy Morne long since left Tithones bed,[9]
All ready to her silver coche to clyme,
And Phoebus[10] gins to shew his glorious hed.
Hark how the cheerefull birds do chaunt theyr laies
And carroll of loves praise.
The merry Larke hir mattins sings aloft, 80
The thrush replyes, the Mavis descant playes,
The Ouzell shrills, the Ruddock warbles soft,[11]
So goodly all agree with sweet consent,
To this dayes merriment.
Ah my deere love why doe ye sleepe thus long,
When meeter were that ye should now awake,
T' awayt the comming of your joyous make,[12]
And hearken to the birds lovelearnéd song,
The deawy leaves among.

7 diversified like the many-colored meadow.
8 a river near Spenser's home in Ireland.
9 Tithonus' wife, the dawn goddess Aurora ("Rosy Morne"), obtained immortality for him but not eternal youth.
10 Apollo, the sun god, also god of music and the arts.
11 Mavis, Ouzell, and Ruddock are birds.
12 mate.

For they of joy and pleasance to you sing,   90
That all the woods them answer and theyr eccho ring.

My love is now awake out of her dreame,
And her fayre eyes like stars that dimméd were
With darksome cloud, now shew theyr goodly beams
More bright then Hesperus[13] his head doth rere.
Come now ye damzels, daughters of delight,
Helpe quickly her to dight,
But first come ye fayre houres which were begot
In Joves sweet paradice, of Day and Night,
Which doe the seasons of the yeare allot,   100
And al that ever in this world is fayre
Doe make and still repayre.
And ye three handmayds of the Cyprian Queene,[14]
The which doe still adorne her beauties pride,
Helpe to addorne my beautifullest bride:
And as ye her array, still throw betweene
Some graces to be seene,
And as ye use to Venus, to her sing,
The whiles the woods shal answer and your eccho ring.

Now is my love all ready forth to come,   110
Let all the virgins therefore well awayt,
And ye fresh boyes that tend upon her groome
Prepare your selves; for he is comming strayt.
Set all your things in seemely good aray
Fit for so joyfull day,
The joyfulst day that ever sunne did see.
Faire Sun, shew forth thy favourable ray,
And let thy lifull[15] heat not fervent be
For feare of burning her sunshyny face,
Her beauty to disgrace.   120
O fayrest Phoebus, father of the Muse,
If ever I did honour thee aright,
Or sing the thing, that mote thy mind delight,
Doe not thy servants simple boone refuse,
But let this day let this one day be myne,
Let all the rest be thine.
Then I thy soverayne prayses loud wil sing,
That all the woods shal answer and theyr eccho ring.

Harke how the Minstrels gin to shrill aloud
Their merry Musick that resounds from far,   130
The pipe, the tabor, and the trembling Croud,[16]
That well agree withouten breach or jar.

13   evening star.
14   Venus, to whom a temple on Cyprus was dedicated.
15   vital.
16   violin.

But most of all the Damzels doe delite,
When they their tymbrels smyte,
And thereunto doe daunce and carrol sweet,
That all the sences they doe ravish quite,
The whyles the boyes run up and down the street,
Crying aloud with strong confuséd noyce,
As if it were one voyce.
Hymen iô Hymen, Hymen they do shout,   140
That even to the heavens theyr shouting shrill
Doth reach, and all the firmament doth fill,
To which the people standing all about,
As in approvance doe thereto applaud
And loud advaunce her laud,
And evermore they *Hymen Hymen* sing,
That al the woods them answer and theyr eccho ring.

Loe where she comes along with portly pace
Lyke Phoebe[17] from her chamber of the East,
Arysing forth to run her mighty race,   150
Clad all in white, that seemes a virgin best.
So well it her beseemes that ye would weene
Some angell she had beene.
Her long loose yellow locks lyke golden wyre,
Sprinckled with perle, and perling flowres a tweene,
Doe lyke a golden mantle her attyre,
And being crownéd with a girland greene,
Seeme lyke some mayden Queene.
Her modest eyes abashéd to behold
So many gazers, as on her do stare,   160
Upon the lowly ground affixéd are.
Ne dare lift up her countenance too bold,
But blush to heare her prayses sung so loud,
So farre from being proud.
Nathlesse doe ye still loud her prayses sing.
That all the woods may answer and your eccho ring.

Tell me ye merchants daughters did ye see
So fayre a creature in your towne before,
So sweet, so lovely, and so mild as she,
Adornd with beautyes grace and vertues store,   170
Her goodly eyes lyke Saphyres shining bright,
Her forehead yvory white,
Her cheekes lyke apples which the sun hath rudded,
Her lips lyke cherryes charming men to byte,
Her brest lyke to a bowle of creame uncrudded,
Her paps lyke lyllies budded,
Her snowie necke lyke to a marble towre,
And all her body like a pallace fayre,

17   Diana, goddess of the moon; also called Cinthia (*l.* 374).

Ascending uppe with many a stately stayre,
To honors seat and chastities sweet bowre.   180
Why stand ye still ye virgins in amaze,
Upon her so to gaze,
Whiles ye forget your former lay to sing,
To which the woods did answer and your eccho ring.

But if ye saw that which no eyes can see,
The inward beauty of her lively spright,[18]
Garnisht with heavenly guifts of high degree,
Much more then would ye wonder at that sight,
And stand astonisht lyke to those which red
Medusaes mazeful hed.[19]   190
There dwels sweet love and constant chastity,
Unspotted fayth and comely womanhood,
Regard of honour and mild modesty,
There vertue raynes as Queene in royal throne,
And giveth lawes alone.
The which the base affections doe obay,
And yeeld theyr services unto her will,
Ne thought of thing uncomely ever may
Thereto approch to tempt her mind to ill.
Had ye once seene these her celestial threasures,   200
And unrevealéd pleasures,
Then would ye wonder and her prayses sing,
That al the woods should answer and your eccho ring.

Open the temple gates unto my love,
Open them wide that she may enter in,
And all the postes adorne as doth behove,
And all the pillours deck with girlands trim,
For to recyve this Saynt with honour dew,
That commeth in to you.
With trembling steps and humble reverence,   210
She commeth in, before th' almighties vew,
Of her ye virgins learne obedience,
When so ye come into those holy places,
To humble your proud faces:
Bring her up to th' high altar, that she may
The sacred ceremonies there partake,
The which do endlesse matrimony make,
And let the roring Organs loudly play
The praises of the Lord in lively notes,
The whiles with hollow throates,   220
The Choristers the joyous Antheme sing,
That al the woods may answere and their eccho ring.

18   soul.
19   Medusa had serpents instead of hair, and those who saw ("red") her were
turned to stone.

Behold whiles she before the altar stands
Hearing the holy priest that to her speakes
And blesseth her with his two happy hands,
How the red roses flush up in her cheekes,
And the pure snow with goodly vermill stayne,
Like crimsin dyde in grayne,
That even th' Angels which continually,
About the sacred Altare doe remaine,   230
Forget their service and about her fly,
Ofte peeping in her face that seemes more fayre,
The more they on it stare.
But her sad eyes still fastened on the ground,
Are governéd with goodly modesty,
That suffers not one looke to glaunce awry,
Which may let in a little thought unsownd.
Why blush ye love to give to me your hand,
The pledge of all our band?
Sing ye sweet Angels, Alleluya sing,   240
That all the woods may answere and your eccho ring.

Now al is done; bring home the bride againe,
Bring home the triumph of our victory,
Bring home with you the glory of her gaine,
With joyance bring her and with jollity.
Never had man more joyfull day then this,
Whom heaven would heape with blis.
Make feast therefore now all this live long day,
This day for ever to me holy is,
Poure out the wine without restraint or stay,   250
Poure not by cups, but by the belly full,
Poure out to all that wull,
And sprinkle all the postes and wals with wine,
That they may sweat, and drunken be withall.
Crowne ye God Bacchus[20] with a coronall,
And Hymen also crowne with wreathes of vine,
And let the Graces daunce unto the rest;
For they can doo it best:
The whiles the maydens doe theyr carroll sing,
To which the woods shal answer and theyr eccho ring.   260

Ring ye the bels, ye yong men of the towne,
And leave your wonted labors for this day:
This day is holy; doe ye write it downe,
That ye for ever it remember may.
This day the sunne is in his chiefest hight,
With Barnaby[21] the bright,
From whence declining daily by degrees,

20   god of wine and festivity.
21   the wedding took place on June 11, St. Barnabas' day.

62

He somewhat loseth of his heat and light,
When once the Crab[22] behind his back he sees.
But for this time it ill ordainéd was,   270
To chose the longest day in all the yeare,
And shortest night, when longest fitter weare:
Yet never day so long, but late would passe.
Ring ye the bels, to make it weare away,
And bonefiers make all day,
And daunce about them, and about them sing:
That all the woods may answer, and your eccho ring.

Ah when will this long weary day have end,
And lende me leave to come unto my love?
How slowly do the houres theyr numbers spend?   280
How slowly does sad Time his feathers move?
Hast thee O fayrest Planet to thy home
Within the Westerne fome:
Thy tyred steedes long since have need of rest.
Long though it be, at last I see it gloome,
And the bright evening star with golden creast
Appeare out of the East.
Fayre childe of beauty, glorious lampe of love
That all the host of heaven in rankes doost lead,
And guydest lovers through the nightés dread,   290
How chearefully thou lookest from above,
And seems to laugh atweene thy twinkling light
As joying in the sight
Of these glad many which for joy doe sing,
That all the woods them answer and their eccho ring.

Now ceasse ye damsels your delights forepast;
Enough is it, that all the day was youres:
Now day is doen, and night is nighing fast:
Now bring the Bryde into the brydall boures.
Now night is come, now soone her disaray,   300
And in her bed her lay;
Lay her in lillies and in violets,
And silken courteins over her display,
And odourd sheetes, and Arras coverlets.
Behold how goodly my faire love does ly
In proud humility;
Like unto Maia;[23] when as Jove her tooke,
In Tempe, lying on the flowry gras,
Twixt sleepe and wake, after she weary was,
With bathing in the Acidalian brooke.   310
Now it is night, ye damsels may be gon,
And leave my love alone,

22 a sign of the zodiac, which the sun enters in June.
23 mother of Mercury by Jove.

And leave likewise your former lay to sing:
The woods no more shal answere, nor your eccho ring.

Now welcome night, thou night so long expected,
That long daies labour doest at last defray,
And all my cares, which cruell love collected,
Hast sumd in one, and cancelléd for aye:
Spread thy broad wing over my love and me,
That no man may us see,   320
And in thy sable mantle us enwrap,
From feare of perrill and foule horror free.
Let no false treason seeke us to entrap,
Nor any dread disquiet once annoy
The safety of our joy:
But let the night be calme and quietsome,
Without tempestuous storms or sad afray:
Lyke as when Jove with fayre Alcmena[24] lay,
When he begot the great Tirynthian groome:
Or lyke as when he with thy selfe did lie,   330
And begot Majesty.
And let the mayds and yongmen cease to sing:
Ne let the woods them answer, nor theyr eccho ring.

Let no lamenting cryes, nor dolefull teares,
Be heard all night within nor yet without:
Ne let false whispers, breeding hidden feares,
Breake gentle sleepe with misconceivéd dout.
Let no deluding dreames, nor dreadful sights
Make sudden sad affrights;
Ne let housefyres, nor lightnings helpelesse harmes,   340
Ne let the Pouke, nor other evill sprights,
Ne let mischivous witches with theyr charmes,
Ne let hob Goblins, names whose sence we see not,
Fray us with things that be not.
Let not the shriech Oule, nor the Storke be heard:
Nor the night Raven that still deadly yels,
Nor damnéd ghosts cald up with mighty spels,
Nor griesly vultures make us once affeard:
Ne let th' unpleasant Quyre of Frogs still croking
Make us to wish theyr choking.   350
Let none of these theyr drery accents sing;
Ne let the woods them answer, nor theyr eccho ring.

But let stil Silence trew night watches keepe,
That sacred peace may in assurance rayne,
And tymely sleep, when it is tyme to sleepe,
May poure his limbs forth on your pleasant playne,
The whiles an hundred little wingéd loves,

24 mother, by Jove, of Hercules, the "great Tirynthian groome."

64

Like divers fethered doves,
Shall fly and flutter round about your bed,
And in the secret darke, that none reproves,   360
Their prety stealthes shal worke, and snares shal spread
To filch away sweet snatches of delight,
Conceald through covert night.
Ye sonnes of Venus, play your sports at will,
For greedy pleasure, carelesse of your toyes,
Thinks more upon her paradise of joyes,
Then what ye do, albe it good or ill.
All night therefore attend your merry play,
For it will soone be day:
Now none doth hinder you, that say or sing,   370
Ne will the woods now answer, nor your Eccho ring.

Who is the same, which at my window peepes?
Or whose is that faire face, that shines so bright,
Is it not Cinthia, she that never sleepes,
But walkes about high heaven al the night?
O fayrest goddesse, do thou not envy
My love with me to spy:
For thou likewise didst love, though now unthought.
And for a fleece of woll, which privily,
The Latmian shephard[25] once unto thee brought,   380
His pleasures with thee wrought.
Therefore to us be favorable now;
And sith of wemens labours thou hast charge,
And generation goodly dost enlarge,
Encline thy will t' effect our wishfull vow,
And the chast wombe informe with timely seed,
That may our comfort breed:
Till which we cease our hopefull hap to sing,
Ne let the woods us answere, nor our Eccho ring.

And thou great Juno, which with awful might   390
The lawes of wedlock still dost patronize,
And the religion of the faith first plight
With sacred rites hast taught to solemnize:
And eeke for comfort often calléd art
Of women in their smart,
Eternally bind thou this lovely band,
And all thy blessings unto us impart.
And thou glad Genius,[26] in whose gentle hand,
The bridale bowre and geniall bed remaine,
Without blemish or staine,   400
And the sweet pleasures of theyr loves delight

25   The goddess of the moon fell in love with the shepherd Endymion while he was sleeping on Mt. Latmus.
26   god of reproduction.

With secret ayde doest succour and supply,
Till they bring forth the fruitfull progeny,
Send us the timely fruit of this same night.
And thou fayre Hebe,[27] and thou Hymen free,
Grant that it may so be.
Til which we cease your further prayse to sing,
Ne any woods shal answer, nor your Eccho ring.

And ye high heavens, the temple of the gods,
In which a thousand torches flaming bright   410
Doe burne, that to us wretched earthly clods,
In dreadful darknesse lend desired light;
And all ye powers which in the same remayne,
More then we men can fayne,
Poure out your blessing on us plentiously,
And happy influence upon us raine,
That we may raise a large posterity,
Which from the earth, which they may long possesse,
With lasting happinesse,
Up to your haughty pallaces may mount,   420
And for the guerdon of theyr glorious merit
May heavenly tabernacles there inherit,
Of blessed Saints for to increase the count.
So let us rest, sweet love, in hope of this,
And cease till then our tymely joyes to sing,
The woods no more us answer, nor our eccho ring.

Song made in lieu of many ornaments,
With which my love should duly have bene dect,
Which cutting off through hasty accidents,
Ye would not stay your dew time to expect,   430
But promist both to recompens,
Be unto her a goodly ornament,
And for short time an endlesse moniment.

SIR PHILIP SIDNEY [1554–1586]

31 With How Sad Steps

With how sad steps, Oh Moon, thou clim'st the skies!
How silently, and with how wan a face!
What, may it be that even in heavenly place
That busy archer his sharp arrows tries?
Sure, if that long-with-love-acquainted eyes

27   the goddess of youth and cupbearer to Jove. She became the wife of
Hercules after he was deified.

Can judge of love, thou feel'st a lover's case,
I read it in thy looks; thy languished grace,
To me, that feel the like, thy state descries.
Then, even of fellowship, Oh Moon, tell me,
Is constant love deemed there but want of wit?
Are beauties there as proud as here they be?
Do they above love to be loved, and yet
Those lovers scorn whom that love doth possess?
Do they call virtue there ungratefulness?

CHIDIOCK TICHBORNE [1558–1586]

Tichborne's Elegy

Written with His Own Hand in the Tower Before His Execution

My prime of youth is but a frost of cares,
My feast of joy is but a dish of pain,
My crop of corn is but a field of tares,
And all my good is but vain hope of gain;
The day is past, and yet I saw no sun,
And now I live, and now my life is done.

My tale was heard and yet it was not told,
My fruit is fallen and yet my leaves are green,
My youth is spent and yet I am not old,
I saw the world and yet I was not seen;
My thread is cut and yet it is not spun,
And now I live, and now my life is done.

I sought my death and found it in my womb,
I looked for life and saw it was a shade,
I trod the earth and knew it was my tomb,
And now I die, and now I was but made;
My glass is full, and now my glass is run,
And now I live, and now my life is done.

GEORGE PEELE [1559–1596]

Gently Dip

Gently dip, but not too deep;
For fear you make the golden beard to weep.
Fair maiden white and red,
Comb me smooth, and stroke my head:
And thou shalt have some cockle bread.

Gently dip, but not too deep,
For fear thou make the golden beard to weep.
Fair maiden white and red,
Comb me smooth, and stroke my head;
And every hair, a sheaf shall be,
And every sheaf a golden tree.

A Sonnet

His golden locks time hath to silver turned;
O time too swift, O swiftness never ceasing!
His youth gainst time and age hath ever spurned,
But spurned in vain; youth waneth by increasing.
    Beauty, strength, youth, are flowers but fading seen,
    Duty, faith, love are roots and ever green.

His helmet now shall make a hive for bees,
And, lovers' sonnets turned to holy psalms,
A man at arms must now serve on his knees,
And feed on prayers, which are age his alms.
    But though from court to cottage he depart,
    His saint is sure of his unspotted heart.

And when he saddest sits in homely cell,
He'll teach his swains this carol for a song,
Blessed be the hearts that wish my sovereign well,
Cursed be the souls that think her any wrong.
    Goddess, allow this agéd man his right,
    To be your bedesman now, that was your knight.

ROBERT SOUTHWELL [1561–1595]

The Burning Babe

As I in hoary winter's night stood shivering in the snow,
Surprised I was with sudden heat, which made my heart to glow;
And lifting up a fearful eye to view what fire was near,
A pretty babe all burning bright, did in the air appear,
Who scorched with excessive heat, such floods of tears did shed,
As though his floods should quench his flames which with his tears
      were fed;
"Alas!" quoth he, "but newly born, in fiery heats I fry,
Yet none approach to warm their hearts or feel my fire but I!
My faultless breast the furnace is, the fuel wounding thorns,
Love is the fire, and sighs the smoke, the ashes shame and scorns;
The fuel justice layeth on, and mercy blows the coals,

The metal in this furnace wrought are men's defiled souls,
For which, as now on fire I am to work them to their good,
So will I melt into a bath to wash them in my blood."
With this he vanished out of sight, and swiftly shrank away,
And straight I called unto mind that it was Christmas day.

SAMUEL DANIEL [1562–1619]

45   Care-Charmer Sleep

Care-charmer sleep, son of the sable night,
Brother to death, in silent darkness born,
Relieve my languish and restore the light;
With dark forgetting of my cares, return.
And let the day be time enough to mourn
The shipwreck of my ill-adventured youth;
Let waking eyes suffice to wail their scorn
Without the torment of the night's untruth.
Cease, dreams, th' imagery of our day desires,
To model forth the passions of the morrow;
Never let rising sun approve you liars,
To add more grief to aggravate my sorrow.
Still let me sleep, embracing clouds in vain,
And never wake to feel the day's disdain.

MICHAEL DRAYTON [1563–1631]

61   Since There's
No Help

Since there's no help, come let us kiss and part;
Nay, I have done, you get no more of me;
And I am glad, yea, glad with all my heart,
That thus so cleanly I myself can free.
Shake hands for ever, cancel all our vows,
And when we meet at any time again,
Be it not seen in either of our brows
That we one jot of former love retain.
Now at the last gasp of love's latest breath,
When, his pulse failing, passion speechless lies,
When faith is kneeling by his bed of death,
And innocence is closing up his eyes,
Now if thou wouldst, when all have given him over,
From death to life thou might'st him yet recover.

CHRISTOPHER MARLOWE [1564–1593]

The Passionate Shepherd
to His Love

Come live with me, and be my love,
And we will all the pleasures prove,
That valleys, groves, hills and fields,
Woods, or steepy mountains yields.

And we will sit upon the rocks,
Seeing the shepherds feed their flocks,
By shallow rivers, to whose falls,
Melodious birds sing madrigals.

And I will make thee beds of roses,
And a thousand fragrant posies,
A cap of flowers, and a kirtle[1]
Embroidered all with leaves of myrtle;

A gown made of the finest wool,
Which from our pretty lambs we pull,
Fair-linéd slippers for the cold,
With buckles of the purest gold;

A belt of straw and ivy buds
With coral clasps and amber studs:
And if these pleasures may thee move,
Come live with me, and be my love.

The shepherd swains shall dance and sing,
For thy delight each May morning:
If these delights thy mind may move,
Then live with me, and be my love.

ANONYMOUS

As You Came
from the Holy Land
of Walsingham

As you came from the holy land
    Of Walsingham,
Met you not with my true love,
    By the way as you came?

1   skirt.

70

"How should I know your true love
    That have met many a one
As I came from the holy land,
    That have come, that have gone?"

She is neither white nor brown,
    But as the heavens fair;
There is none hath her form so divine,
    On the earth, in the air.

"Such a one did I meet, good sir,
    With angel-like face,
Who like a nymph, like a queen did appear
    In her gait, in her grace."

She hath left me here alone,
    All alone unknown,
Who sometime loved me as her life,
    And called me her own.

"What is the cause she hath left thee alone,
    And a new way doth take,
That sometime did thee love as herself,
    And her joy did thee make?"

I have loved her all my youth,
    But now am old as you see;
Love liketh not the falling fruit,
    Nor the withered tree.

For love is a careless child,
    And forgets promise past;
He is blind, he is deaf, when he list,
    And in faith never fast.

His desire is fickle found,
    And a trustless joy;
He is won with a world of despair,
    And is lost with a toy.

Such is the love of womenkind,
    Or the word, love, abused,
Under which many childish desires
    And conceits are excused.

But love, it is a durable fire
    In the mind ever burning,
Never sick, never dead, never cold,
    From itself never turning.

Crabbed Age
and Youth

Crabbed age and youth cannot live together:
Youth is full of pleasance, age is full of care;
Youth like summer morn, age like winter weather;
Youth like summer brave, age like winter bare.
Youth is full of sport, age's breath is short;
Youth is nimble, age is lame;
Youth is hot and bold, age is weak and cold;
Youth is wild, and age is tame.
Age, I do abhor thee, youth, I do adore thee;
Oh! my love, my love is young:
Age, I do defy thee: Oh! sweet shepherd, hie thee,
For methinks thou stay'st too long.

WILLIAM SHAKESPEARE [1564–1616]

Under the
Greenwood Tree

Under the greenwood tree
Who loves to lie with me,
And turn his merry note
Unto the sweet bird's throat,
Come hither, come hither, come hither:
　　Here shall he see
　　No enemy
But winter and rough weather.

Who doth ambition shun
And loves to lie i' the sun,
Seeking the food he eats
And pleased with what he gets,
Come hither, come hither, come hither:
　　Here shall he see
　　No enemy
But winter and rough weather.
(*As You Like It*)

Blow, Blow,
Thou Winter Wind!

Blow, blow, thou winter wind!
Thou art not so unkind
As man's ingratitude;

Thy tooth is not so keen
Because thou art not seen,
Although thy breath be rude.
Heigh ho! sing heigh ho! unto the green holly:
Most friendship is feigning, most loving mere folly:
Then, heigh ho! the holly!
This life is most jolly.

Freeze, freeze, thou bitter sky,
Thou dost not bite so nigh
As benefits forgot:
Though thou the waters warp,
Thy sting is not so sharp
As friend remembered not.
Heigh ho! sing heigh ho! unto the green holly:
Most friendship is feigning, most loving mere folly:
Then, heigh ho! the holly!
This life is most jolly.

(As You Like It)

It Was a Lover

It was a lover and his lass,
   With a hey, and a ho, and a hey nonino!
That o'er the green corn-field did pass,
   In spring time, the only pretty ring time,
When birds do sing, hey ding a ding, ding;
   Sweet lovers love the spring.

Between the acres of the rye,
   With a hey, and a ho, and a hey nonino!
Those pretty country folks would lie,
   In spring time, the only pretty ring time,
When birds do sing, hey ding a ding, ding;
   Sweet lovers love the spring.

This carol they began that hour,
   With a hey, and a ho, and a hey nonino!
How that a life was but a flower
   In spring time, the only pretty ring time,
When birds do sing, hey ding a ding, ding;
   Sweet lovers love the spring.

And therefore take the present time,
   With a hey, and a ho, and a hey nonino!
For love is crownéd with the prime
   In spring time, the only pretty ring time,
When birds do sing, hey ding a ding, ding;
   Sweet lovers love the spring.

(As You Like It)

O Mistress Mine

O mistress mine, where are you roaming?
O stay and hear; your true love's coming,
    That can sing both high and low.
Trip no further, pretty sweeting;
Journeys end in lovers' meeting,
    Every wise man's son doth know.

What is love? 'Tis not hereafter;
Present mirth hath present laughter;
    What's to come is still unsure.
In delay there lies no plenty;
Then come kiss me, sweet and twenty;
    Youth's a stuff will not endure.
                                        (*Twelfth Night*)

Take, O! Take

Take, O! take those lips away,
    That so sweetly were forsworn,
And those eyes, the break of day,
    Lights that do mislead the morn;
But my kisses bring again, bring again,
Seals of love, but sealed in vain, sealed in vain.
                                        (*Measure for Measure*)

Fear No More

Fear no more the heat o' the sun
    Nor the furious winter's rages;
Thou thy worldly task hast done,
    Home art gone and ta'en thy wages.
Golden lads and girls all must,
As chimney-sweepers, come to dust.

Fear no more the frown o' the great,
    Thou art past the tyrant's stroke;
Care no more to clothe and eat;
    To thee the reed is as the oak.
The scepter, learning, physic, must
All follow this, and come to dust.

Fear no more the lightning-flash,
    Nor the all-dreaded thunder-stone:
Fear not slander, censure rash;

Thou hast finished joy and moan.
All lovers young, all lovers must
Consign to thee, and come to dust.
                    (*Cymbeline*)

Full Fathom Five

Full fathom five thy father lies;
    Of his bones are coral made;
Those are pearls, that were his eyes;
    Nothing of him that doth fade
But doth suffer a sea-change
Into something rich and strange.
Sea-nymphs hourly ring his knell.
    Ding-dong!
Hark, now I hear them
    Ding dong, bell!
                    (*The Tempest*)

from Sonnets

12

When I do count the clock that tells the time,
And see the brave day sunk in hideous night,
When I behold the violet past prime,
And sable curls all silvered o'er with white:
When lofty trees I see barren of leaves,
Which erst[1] from heat did canopy the herd
And summer's green all girded up in sheaves
Borne on the bier with white and bristly beard:
Then of thy beauty do I question make
That thou among the wastes of time must go,
Since sweets and beauties do themselves forsake,
And die as fast as they see others grow,
    And nothing 'gainst Time's scythe can make defence
    Save breed[2] to brave him, when he takes thee hence.

1   formerly.
2   offspring.

18

Shall I compare thee to a summer's day?
Thou art more lovely and more temperate.
Rough winds do shake the darling buds of May,
And summer's lease hath all too short a date.
Sometime too hot the eye of heaven shines,

And often is his gold complexion dimmed;
And every fair from fair sometime declines,
By chance, or nature's changing course, untrimmed;
But thy eternal summer shall not fade
Nor lose possession of that fair thou ow'st,[1]
Nor shall Death brag thou wand'rest in his shade
When in eternal lines to time thou grow'st.
   So long as men can breathe or eyes can see,
   So long lives this, and this gives life to thee.

1   beauty you possess.

30

When to the sessions[1] of sweet silent thought
I summon up remembrance of things past,
I sigh the lack of many a thing I sought
And with old woes new wail my dear time's waste.
Then can I drown an eye (unused to flow)
For precious friends hid in death's dateless night,
And weep afresh love's long since canceled woe,
And moan th' expense[2] of many a vanished sight.
Then can I grieve at grievances foregone,
And heavily from woe to woe tell o'er
The sad account of fore-bemoanéd moan,
Which I new pay as if not paid before.
   But if the while I think on thee, dear friend,
   All losses are restored and sorrows end.

1   sittings of a court of justice.
2   loss.

65

Since brass, nor stone, nor earth, nor boundless sea,
But sad mortality o'ersways their power,
How with this rage shall beauty hold a plea,
Whose action is no stronger than a flower?
O how shall summer's honey breath hold out,
Against the wrackful[1] siege of batt'ring days,
When rocks impregnable are not so stout,
Nor gates of steel so strong but time decays?
O fearful meditation, where alack,
Shall Time's best jewel from Time's chest lie hid?
Or what strong hand can hold his swift foot back,
Or who his spoil of beauty can forbid?
   O none, unless this miracle have might,
   That in black ink my love may still shine bright.

1   destructive.

66

Tired with all these, for restful death I cry:
As, to behold desert[1] a beggar born,
And needy nothing trimmed in jollity,[2]
And purest faith unhappily forsworn,
And gilded honor shamefully misplaced,
And maiden virtue rudely strumpeted,
And right perfection wrongfully disgraced,
And strength by limping sway disabled,
And art made tongue-tied by authority,
And folly (doctor-like) controlling skill,
And simple truth miscalled simplicity,[3]
And captive good attending captain ill.
    Tired with all these, from these would I be gone,
    Save that, to die, I leave my love alone.

1   merit.
2   emptiness clothed in finery.
3   ignorance, silliness.

73

That time of year thou mayst in me behold
When yellow leaves, or none, or few, do hang
Upon those boughs which shake against the cold,
Bare ruined choirs where late the sweet birds sang.
In me thou see'st the twilight of such day
As after sunset fadeth in the West,
Which by-and-by black night doth take away,
Death's second self, that seals up all in rest.
In me thou see'st the glowing of such fire
That on the ashes of his youth doth lie,
As the deathbed whereon it must expire,
Consumed with that which it was nourished by.
    This thou perceiv'st, which makes thy love more strong,
    To love that well which thou must leave ere long.

87

Farewell! thou art too dear[1] for my possessing,
And like enough thou know'st thy estimate,[2]
The charter[3] of thy worth gives thee releasing:
My bonds in thee are all determinate.[4]
For how do I hold thee but by thy granting,
And for that riches where is my deserving?
The cause of this fair gift in me is wanting,
And so my patent[5] back again is swerving.[6]

1   precious.
2   value.
3   contract.
4   limited.
5   grant of a monopoly.
6   returning.

Thy self thou gav'st, thy own worth then not knowing,
Or me to whom thou gav'st it, else mistaking,
So thy great gift upon misprision[7] growing,
Comes home again, on better judgment making.
    Thus have I had thee as a dream doth flatter,
    In sleep a king, but waking no such matter.

7   contempt, undervaluing.

94

They that have power to hurt, and will do none,
That do not do the thing, they most do show,[1]
Who moving others, are themselves as stone,
Unmovéd, cold, and to temptation slow:
They rightly do inherit heaven's graces,
And husband nature's riches from expense,[2]
They are the lords and owners of their faces,
Others, but stewards[3] of their excellence:
The summer's flower is to the summer sweet,
Though to it self, it only live and die,
But if that flower with base infection meet,
The basest weed outbraves his dignity:
    For sweetest things turn sourest by their deeds,
    Lilies that fester, smell far worse than weeds.

1   seem capable of doing.
2   expenditure.
3   A steward manages property on behalf of the owner.

116

Let me not to the marriage of true minds
Admit impediments, love is not love
Which alters when it alteration finds,
Or bends with the remover to remove.[1]
O no, it is an ever-fixéd mark[2]
That looks on tempests and is never shaken;
It is the star[3] to every wand'ring bark,[4]
Whose worth's unknown, although his height be taken.
Love's not Time's fool, though rosy lips and cheeks
Within his bending sickle's compass come,
Love alters not with his brief hours and weeks,
But bears it out[5] even to the edge of doom:
    If this be error and upon me proved,
    I never writ, nor no man ever loved.

1   "Remove" was used both in a transitive and an intransitive sense—to move
someone or something, or to go from one place to another.
2   beacon.
3   the North Star, a navigational aid.
4   ship.
5   endures.

129

Th' expense[1] of spirit in a waste of shame
Is lust in action, and till action, lust
Is perjured, murd'rous, bloody, full of blame,
Savage, extreme, rude,[2] cruel, not to trust,
Enjoyed no sooner but despised straight,
Past reason hunted, and no sooner had
Past reason hated as a swallowed bait,
On purpose laid to make the taker mad.
Mad in pursuit and in possession so,
Had, having, and in quest, to have extreme,
A bliss in proof[3] and proved, a very woe,
Before a joy proposed behind a dream.
    All this the world well knows yet none knows well,
    To shun the heaven that leads men to this hell.

1   expenditure.
2   brutal.
3   while being experienced.

130

My mistress' eyes are nothing like the sun,
Coral is far more red, than her lips red,
If snow be white, why then her breasts are dun:
If hairs be wires, black wires grow on her head:
I have seen roses damasked,[1] red and white,
But no such roses see I in her cheeks,
And in some perfumes is there more delight,
Than in the breath that from my mistress reeks.[2]
I love to hear her speak, yet well I know,
That music hath a far more pleasing sound:
I grant I never saw a goddess go,
My mistress when she walks treads on the ground.
    And yet by heaven I think my love as rare,
    As any she belied with false compare.

1   arranged in ornamental patterns.
2   is exhaled.

THOMAS CAMPION   [1567–1620]

Rose-Cheeked Laura

Rose-cheeked Laura, come,
Sing thou smoothly with thy beauty's
Silent music, either other
    Sweetly gracing.

Lonely forms do flow
From concent divinely franéd;
Heav'n is music, and thy beauty's
      Birth is heavenly.

These dull notes we sing
Discords need for helps to grace them;
Only beauty purely loving
      Knows no discord,

But still moves delight,
Like clear springs renewed by flowing,
Ever perfect, ever in them-
      Selves eternal.

THOMAS DEKKER[1]   [1570?–1632?]

Art Thou Poor

Art thou poor, yet hast thou golden slumbers?
      O sweet content!
Art thou rich, yet is thy mind perplexed?
      O punishment!
Dost thou laugh to see how fools are vexed
To add to golden numbers, golden numbers?
O sweet content! O sweet content!
      Work apace, apace, apace, apace;
      Honest labor bears a lovely face;
   Then hey nonny nonny, hey nonny nonny!

Canst drink the waters of the crisped[2] spring?
      O sweet content!
Swim'st thou in wealth, yet sink'st in thine own tears?
      O punishment!
Then he that patiently want's burden bears
No burden bears, but is a king, a king!
O sweet content! O sweet content!
      Work apace, apace, apace, apace;
      Honest labor bears a lovely face;
   Then hey nonny nonny, hey nonny nonny!

1   This poem may have been written by Dekker's co-author, Henry Chettle.
2   rippling.

80

JOHN DONNE [1572–1631]

The Good-morrow

I wonder by my troth, what thou and I
Did, till we lov'd? were we not wean'd till then?
But suck'd on country pleasures, childishly?
Or snorted[1] we in the seven sleepers' den?[2]
'Twas so; but[3] this, all pleasures fancies be.
If ever any beauty I did see,
Which I desir'd, and got, 'twas but a dream of thee.

And now good-morrow to our waking souls,
Which watch not one another out of fear;
For love all love of other sights controls,
And makes one little room an everywhere.
Let sea-discoverers to new worlds have gone,
Let maps to other, worlds on worlds have shown,
Let us possess one world, each hath one, and is one.

My face in thine eye, thine in mine appears,
And true plain hearts do in the faces rest;
Where can we find two better hemispheres
Without sharp North, without declining West?[4]
What ever dies, was not mixt equally;[5]
If our two loves be one, or thou and I
Love so alike that none do slacken, none can die.

Song

Go and catch a falling star,
    Get with child a mandrake root,
Tell me where all past years are,
    Or who cleft the devil's foot;
Teach me to hear mermaids singing,
Or to keep off envy's stinging,
            And find
            What wind
Serves to advance an honest mind.

If thou be'st born to strange sights,
    Things invisible to see,

1   snored.
2   It is said that during the persecution of Decius (250 A.D.) seven Christian
soldiers were walled up in a cave, where they slept for 200 years.
3   except for.
4   A hemisphere is half the globe, containing the points of the compass, e.g.,
the cold North, and the West where the sun goes down.
5   This refers to the idea that death or corruption was due to a disproportionate
mixture of opposing elements.

Ride ten thousand days and nights
    Till age snow white hairs on thee;
Thou, when thou return'st, wilt tell me
All strange wonders that befell thee,
        And swear
        No where
Lives a woman true, and fair.

If thou find'st one, let me know;
    Such a pilgrimage were sweet.
Yet do not; I would not go,
    Though at next door we might meet.
Though she were true when you met her,
And last, till you write your letter,
        Yet she
        Will be
False, ere I come, to two, or three.

The Bait

Come live with me, and be my love,[1]
And we will some new pleasures prove
Of golden sands, and crystal brooks,
With silken lines, and silver hooks.

There will the river whispering run
Warm'd by thy eyes, more than the Sun.
And there th' enamour'd fish will stay,
Begging themselves they may betray.

When thou wilt swim in that live bath,
Each fish, which every channel hath,
Will amorously to thee swim,
Gladder to catch thee, than thou him.

If thou, to be so seen, be'st loth,
By Sun, or Moon, thou dark'nest both,
And if myself have leave to see,
I need not their light, having thee.

Let others freeze with angling reeds,
And cut their legs, with shells and weeds,
Or treacherously poor fish beset,
With strangling snare, or windowy net:

Let coarse bold hands, from slimy nest
The bedded fish in banks out-wrest,[2]

1   Compare Marlowe's "The Passionate Shepherd to His Love."
2   drag out.

Or curious[3] traitors, sleeve-silk[4] flies
Bewitch poor fishes' wand'ring eyes.

For thee, thou need'st no such deceit,
For thou thyself art thine own bait;
That fish, that is not catch'd thereby,
Alas, is wiser far than I.

3   beautifully made.
4   "Sleeve-silk" is a kind of silk which
can be divided into fine filaments.

A Valediction
Forbidding Mourning

As virtuous men pass mildly away,
    And whisper to their souls to go,
Whilst some of their sad friends do say,
    The breath goes now, and some say, No:

So let us melt, and make no noise,
    No tear-floods, nor sigh-tempests move;
'Twere profanation of our joys
    To tell the laity our love.

Moving of th' earth brings harms and fears,
    Men reckon what it did, and meant;   10
But trepidation of the spheres,[1]
    Though greater far, is innocent.

Dull sublunary[2] lovers' love
    (Whose soul is sense) cannot admit
Absence, because it doth remove
    Those things which elemented it.

But we by a love so much refined
    That ourselves know not what it is,
Inter-assuréd of the mind,
    Care less eyes, lips and hands to miss.   20

Our two souls therefore, which are one,
    Though I must go, endure not yet
A breach, but an expansion,
    Like gold to airy thinness beat.

If they be two, they are two so
    As still twin compasses are two;
Thy soul, the fixed foot, makes no show
    To move, but doth, if th' other do.

1   a reference to the theory that attempted to explain oscillation of heavenly
bodies while still maintaining the belief in a stationary earth.
2   under the moon, earthly, and therefore subject to mutability.

And though it in the center sit,
    Yet, when the other far doth roam,   30
It leans, and hearkens after it,
    And grows erect, as that comes home.

Such wilt thou be to me, who must,
    Like th' other foot, obliquely run;
Thy firmness makes my circle just,
    And makes me end where I begun.

The Ecstasy[1]

Where, like a pillow on a bed,
    A pregnant bank swell'd up, to rest
The violet's reclining head,
    Sat we two, one another's best.
Our hands were firmly cemented[2]
    With a fast balm,[3] which thence did spring,
Our eye-beams twisted, and did thread
    Our eyes, upon one double string;
So t' intergraft our hands, as yet
    Was all the means to make us one,   10
And pictures in our eyes to get
    Was all our propagation.
As 'twixt two equal Armies, Fate
    Suspends uncertain victory,
Our souls, (which to advance their state,
    Were gone out,) hung 'twixt her, and me.
And whilst our souls negotiate there,
    We like sepulchral statues lay;
All day, the same our postures were,
    And we said nothing, all the day.   20
If any, so by love refin'd,
    That he soul's language understood,
And by good love were grown all mind,
    Within convenient distance stood,
He (though he knew not which soul spake,
    Because both meant, both spake the same)
Might thence a new concoction[4] take,
    And part far purer than he came.
This Ecstasy doth unperplex
    (We said) and tell us what we love,   30
We see by this, it was not sex,

1 Ecstasy is the state in which the soul escapes from the body to achieve a vision of God, or the Absolute.
2 joined.
3 moisture.
4 a process used in refining metals.

We see, we saw not what did move:
But as all several souls contain
　　Mixture of things, they know not what,
Love these mix'd souls doth mix again,
　　And makes both one, each this and that.
A single violet transplant,
　　The strength, the colour, and the size,
(All which before was poor, and scant,)
　　Redoubles still, and multiplies.

40

When love, with one another so
　　Interinanimates two souls,
That abler soul, which thence doth flow,
　　Defects of loneliness[5] controls.
We then, who are this new soul, know,
　　Of what we are compos'd, and made,
For, th' Atomies of which we grow,
　　Are souls, whom no change can invade.
But O alas, so long, so far
　　Our bodies why do we forbear?[6]

50

They are ours, though they are not we, We are
　　The intelligences, they the spheres.[7]
We owe them thanks, because they thus,
　　Did us, to us, at first convey,
Yielded their forces, sense, to us,
　　Nor are dross to us, but allay.
On man heaven's influence works not so,
　　But that it first imprints the air,
So soul into the soul may flow,
　　Though it to body first repair.

60

As our blood labours to beget
　　Spirits, as like souls as it can,
Because such fingers need to knit
　　That subtle knot, which makes us man:
So must pure lovers' souls descend
　　T' affections, and to faculties,
Which sense may reach and apprehend,
　　Else a great Prince in prison lies.
To our bodies turn we then, that so
　　Weak men on love reveal'd may look;

70

Love's mysteries in souls do grow,
　　But yet the body is his book,
And if some lover, such as we,
　　Have heard this dialogue of one,
Let him still mark us, he shall see
　　Small change, when we're to bodies gone.

5　separateness.
6　avoid.
7　In astronomy the heavenly bodies were thought of as attached to moving
spheres.

Elegie 9
The Autumnal

No spring, nor summer beauty hath such grace,
    As I have seen in one autumnal face.
Young beauties force our love, and that's a rape,
    This doth but counsel, yet you cannot 'scape.
If t'were a shame to love, here t'were no shame,
    Affection here takes reverence's name.
Were her first years the Golden Age; that's true,
    But now she's gold oft tried, and ever new.
That was her torrid and inflaming time,
    This is her tolerable tropic clime.   10
Fair eyes, who asks more heat than comes from hence,
    He in a fever wishes pestilence.
Call not these wrinkles, graves; if graves they were,
    They were love's graves; for else he is no where.
Yet lies not love dead here, but here doth sit
    Vowed to this trench, like an anchorite.
And here, till hers, which must be his death, come,
    He doth not dig a grave, but build a tomb.
Here dwells he, though he sojourn every where,
    In progress,[1] yet his standing house is here.   20
Here, where still evening is; not noon, nor night,
    Where no voluptuousness, yet all delight.
In all her words, unto all hearers fit,
    You may at revels, you at counsel, sit.
This is love's timber, youth his under-wood;
    There he, as wine in June, enrages blood,
Which then comes seasonabliest, when our taste
    And appetite to other things, is past.
Xerxes strange Lydian love, the platan tree,[2]
    Was loved for age, none being so large as she,   30
Or else because, being young, nature did bless
    Her youth with age's glory, barrenness.
If we love things long sought, age is a thing
    Which we are fifty years in compassing.
If transitory things, which soon decay,
    Age must be loveliest at the latest day.
But name not winter faces, whose skin's slack;
    Lank, as an unthrift's purse; but a soul's sack;
Whose eyes seek light within, for all here's shade;
    Whose mouths are holes, rather worn out, than made,   40
Whose every tooth to a several place is gone,
    To vex their souls at resurrection;

1   state journey of royalty.
2   Xerxes the Great was smitten by the plane-tree's beauty and had it decorated
with gold.

Name not these living deaths-heads unto me,
    For these, not ancient, but antique be.
I hate extremes; yet I had rather stay
    With tombs than cradles, to wear out a day.
Since such love's natural lation³ is, may still
    My love descend, and journey down the hill,
Not panting after growing beauties, so,
    I shall ebb out with them, who homeward go.   50

from Holy Sonnets

7

At the round earth's imagin'd corners, blow
Your trumpets, Angels, and arise, arise
From death, you numberless infinities
Of souls, and to your scatter'd bodies go,
All whom the flood did, and fire shall o'erthrow,
All whom war, dearth, age, agues, tyrannies,
Despair, law, chance, hath slain, and you whose eyes,
Shall behold God, and never taste death's woe.
But let them sleep, Lord, and me mourn a space,
For, if above all these, my sins abound,
'Tis late to ask abundance of Thy grace,
When we are there; here on this lowly ground,
Teach me how to repent; for that's as good
As if Thou hadst seal'd my pardon, with Thy blood.

13

What if this present were the world's last night?
Mark in my heart, O Soul, where thou dost dwell,
The picture of Christ crucified, and tell
Whether that countenance can thee affright,
Tears in His eyes quench the amazing light,
Blood fills His frowns, which from His pierc'd head fell.
And can that tongue adjudge thee unto hell,
Which pray'd forgiveness for His foes' fierce spite?
No, no; but as in my idolatry
I said to all my profane mistresses,
Beauty, of pity, foulness only is
A sign of rigour: so I say to thee,
To wicked spirits are horrid shapes assign'd,
This beauteous form assures a piteous mind.

3   motion (astrology).

14

Batter my heart, three-person'd God; for you
As yet but knock, breathe, shine, and seek to mend;
That I may rise, and stand, o'erthrow me, and bend
Your force, to break, blow, burn, and make me new.
I, like an usurp'd town, to another due,
Labour to admit you, but Oh, to no end,
Reason your viceroy in me, me should defend,
But is captiv'd, and proves weak or untrue.
Yet dearly I love you, and would be loved fain,
But am betroth'd unto your enemy:
Divorce me, untie, or break that knot again,
Take me to you, imprison me, for I
Except you enthral me, never shall be free,
Nor ever chaste, except you ravish me.

BEN JONSON [1572–1637]

Clerimont's Song

Still[1] to be neat, still to be dressed
As you were going to a feast:
Still to be powdered, still perfumed:
Lady, it is to be presumed,
Though art's hid causes are not found,
All is not sweet, all is not sound.

Give me a look, give me a face
That makes simplicity a grace;
Robes loosely flowing, hair as free:
Such sweet neglect more taketh me,
Than all the adulteries of art,
That strike mine eyes, but not my heart.

The Triumph
of Charis

See the chariot at hand here of Love,
    Wherein my lady rideth!
Each that draws is a swan or a dove,
    And well the car Love guideth.

1   always.

As she goes, all hearts do duty
    Unto her beauty;
And enamored do wish, so they might
    But enjoy such a sight,
That they still were to run by her side,
Through swords, through seas, whither she would ride.   10

Do but look on her eyes, they do light
    All that Love's world compriseth!
Do but look on her hair, it is bright
    As Love's star when it riseth!
Do but mark, her forehead's smoother
    Than words that soothe her;
And from her arched brows such a grace
    Sheds itself through the face,
As alone there triumphs to the life
All the gain, all the good of the elements' strife.   20

Have you seen but a bright lily grow
    Before rude hands have touched it?
Have you marked but the fall of the snow
    Before the soil hath smutched it?
Have you felt the wool o' the beaver,
    Or swan's down ever?
Or have smelt o' the bud o' the brier,
    Or the nard[1] i' the fire?
Or have tasted the bag o' the bee?
Oh so white, oh so soft, oh so sweet is she!   30

That Women Are but Men's Shadows

Follow a shadow, it still flies you,
    Seem to fly it, it will pursue:
So court a mistress, she denies you;
    Let her alone, she will court you.
Say, are not women truly, then,
    Styled but the shadows of us men?

At morn and even shades are longest;
    At noon they are or short, or none:
So men at weakest, they are strongest,
    But grant us perfect, they're not known.
Say, are not women truly then
    Styled but the shadows of us men?

1   a sweet-smelling ointment.

JOHN WEBSTER [1580?–1638]

Cornelia's Song

Call for the robin-redbreast, and the wren,
Since o'er shady groves they hover.
And with leaves and flowers do cover
The friendless bodies of unburied men.
Call unto his funeral dole
The ant, the field-mouse, and the mole,
To rear him hillocks that shall keep him warm,
And, when gay tombs are robbed, sustain no harm;
But keep the wolf far thence, that's foe to men,
For with his nails he'll dig them up again.

(The White Devil)

Hark, Now
Everything Is Still

Hark, now everything is still;
The screech-owl and the whistler shrill
Call upon our dame aloud,
And bid her quickly don her shroud;
Much you had of land and rent,
Your length in clay's now competent.
A long war disturbed your mind;
Here your perfect peace is signed.
Of what is 't fools make such vain keeping?
Sin their conception, their birth weeping,
Their life a general mist of error,
Their death a hideous storm of terror.
Strew your hair with powders sweet,
Don clean linen, bathe your feet,
And, the foul fiend more to check,
A crucifix let bless your neck;
'Tis now full tide, 'tween night and day,
End your groan and come away.

(The Duchess of Malfi)

ROBERT HERRICK [1591–1674]

Delight
in Disorder

A sweet disorder in the dress
Kindles in clothes a wantonness:
A lawn about the shoulders thrown
Into a fine distraction:
An erring lace, which here and there
Enthrals the crimson stomacher:[1]
A cuff neglectful, and thereby
Ribbands to flow confusedly:
A winning wave (deserving note)
In the tempestuous petticoat:
A careless shoe-string, in whose tie
I see a wild civility:
Do more bewitch me than when art
Is too precise in every part.

To the Virgins,
to Make Much
of Time

Gather ye rosebuds while ye may:
    Old Time is still a-flying,
And this same flower that smiles to-day
    Tomorrow will be dying.

The glorious lamp of heaven, the sun,
    The higher he's a-getting,
The sooner will his race be run,
    And nearer he's to setting.

That age is best which is the first,
    When youth and blood are warmer;
But, being spent, the worse, and worst
    Times, still succeed the former.

Then be not coy, but use your time,
    And while ye may, go marry:
For having lost but once your prime,
    You may for ever tarry.

1   bodice.

To Daffodils

Fair daffodils, we weep to see
   You haste away so soon:
As yet the early rising sun
   Has not attained his noon.
     Stay, stay,
   Until the hasting day
     Has run
   But to the Evensong;
And, having prayed together, we
   Will go with you along.

We have short time to stay, as you,
   We have as short a spring;
As quick a growth to meet decay,
   As you, or any thing.
     We die,
   As your hours do, and dry
     Away,
   Like to the summer's rain;
Or as the pearls of morning's dew
   Ne'er to be found again.

Upon
Julia's Clothes

Whenas in silks my Julia goes,
Then, then, methinks how sweetly flows
The liquefaction of her clothes.

Next, when I cast mine eyes, and see
That brave vibration, each way free,
O, how that glittering taketh me!

Grace
for a Child

Here a little child I stand,
Heaving[1] up my either hand:
Cold as paddocks[2] though they be,
Here I lift them up to Thee,
For a benison to fall
On our meat, and on us all. Amen.

1   raising.
2   toads.

GEORGE HERBERT [1593–1633]

The Altar

A broken A L T A R, Lord, thy servant rears,
Made of a heart, and cemented with tears:
  Whose parts are as thy hand did frame;
  No workman's tool hath touched the same.
           A   H E A R T   alone
           Is   such   a   stone,
           As   nothing   but
           Thy power doth cut.
           Wherefore each part
           Of my hard heart
           Meets in this frame,
           To praise thy Name:
  That, if I chance to hold my peace,
  These stones to praise thee may not cease.
O let thy blessed S A C R I F I C E be mine,
And sanctify this A L T A R to be thine.

Redemption

Having been tenant long to a rich Lord,
  Not thriving, I resolved to be bold,
  And make a suit unto him, to afford
A new small-rented lease, and cancel th' old.
In heaven at his manor I him sought:
  They told me there, that he was lately gone
  About some land, which he had dearly bought
Long since on earth, to take possession.
I straight returned, and knowing his great birth,
  Sought him accordingly in great resorts;
  In cities, theaters, gardens, parks, and courts:
At length I heard a ragged noise and mirth
  Of thieves and murderers: there I him espied,
  Who straight, *Your suit is granted*, said, and died.

Easter Wings

Lord, who createdst man in wealth and store,
   Though foolishly he lost the same,
      Decaying more and more,
         Till he became
           Most poor;
           With Thee
        O let me rise
     As   larks,   harmoniously,
   And sing this day Thy victories:
Then shall the fall further the flight in me.[1]

My   tender   age   in   sorrow   did   begin:
   And still with sicknesses and shame
      Thou did'st so punish sin,
         That I became
           Most thin.
           With Thee
        Let me combine
     And feel this day Thy victory;
   For, if I imp[2] my wing on Thine,
Affliction shall advance the flight in me.

Prayer (1)

Prayer the Churches banquet, Angels age,
   Gods breath in man returning to his birth,
   The soul in paraphrase, heart in pilgrimage,
The Christian plummet sounding heaven and earth;
Engine against th' Almighty, sinners tower,
   Reversed thunder, Christ-side-piercing spear,
   The six-days' world transposing in an hour,
A kind of tune, which all things hear and fear;
Softness, and peace, and joy, and love, and bliss,
   Exalted Manna, gladness of the best,
   Heaven in ordinary, man well dressed,
The milky way, the bird of Paradise,
   Church-bells beyond the stars heard, the souls blood,
   The land of spices; something understood.

1   a reference to the doctrine of "felix culpa," happy fault, in which Adam's
fall was thought of as "happy," for had there not been a fall there would not
have been the promise of Redemption. See the anonymous song, "Adam Lay
I-bowndyn":
     Ne hadde the appil take ben, the appil taken ben,
     ne hadde neuer our lady a ben heuene qwen;
     Blyssid be the tyme that appil take was . . .
2   engraft feathers on a damaged wing to restore the ability to fly.

Artillery

As I one evening sat before my cell,
Me thoughts a star did shoot into my lap.
I rose, and shook my clothes, as knowing well,
That from small fires comes oft no small mishap.
    When suddenly I heard one say,
    Do as thou usest, disobey,
    Expel good motions[1] *from thy breast,*
Which have the face of fire, but end in rest.

I, who had heard of music in the spheres,
But not of speech in stars, began to muse: 10
But turning to my God, whose ministers
The stars and all things are; If I refuse,
    Dread Lord, said I, so oft my good;
    Then I refuse not ev'n with blood
    To wash away my stubborn thought:
For I will do or suffer what I ought.

But I have also stars and shooters[2] too,
Born where thy servants both artilleries use.
My tears and prayers night and day do woo,
And work up to thee; yet thou dost refuse.   20
    Not but I am (I must say still)
    Much more obliged to do thy will,
    Then thou to grant mine: but because
Thy promise now hath ev'n set thee thy laws.

Then we are shooters both, and thou dost deign
To enter combat with us, and contest
With thine own clay. But I would parley fain:
Shun not my arrows, and behold my breast.
    Yet if thou shunnest, I am thine:
    I must be so, if I am mine.   30
    There is no articling[3] with thee:
I am but finite, yet thine infinitely.

1   impulses.
2   shooting stars.
3   bargaining.

The Collar

    I struck the board,[1] and cried, No more.
        I will abroad.
    What? shall I ever sigh and pine?
    My lines and life are free; free as the road,
      Loose as the wind, as large as store.[2]

1   table.
2   abundance.

Shall I be still in suit?
Have I no harvest but a thorn
To let me blood, and not restore
What I have lost with cordial fruit?
                    Sure there was wine   10
Before my sighs did dry it: there was corn
    Before my tears did drown it.
    Is the year only lost to me?
        Have I no bays³ to crown it?
No flowers, no garlands gay? all blasted?
            All wasted?
    Not so, my heart: but there is fruit,
            And thou hast hands.
    Recover all thy sigh-blown age
On double pleasures: leave thy cold dispute   20
Of what is fit and not; forsake thy cage,
            Thy rope of sands,
    Which petty thoughts have made, and made to thee
    Good cable, to enforce and draw,
            And be thy law,
    While thou didst wink and would not see.
            Away; take heed:
            I will abroad.
Call in thy death's-head there: tie up thy fears.
            He that forbears   30
        To suit and serve his need,
            Deserves his load.
But as I raved and grew more fierce and wild
            At every word,
Methought I heard one calling, *Child*;
        And I replied, *My Lord.*

3   laurel wreath, symbol of honor.

The Pulley

            When God at first made man,
Having a glass of blessings standing by,
"Let us," said He, "pour on him all we can:
Let the world's riches, which dispersed lie,
            Contract into a span."¹

            So Strength first made a way;
Then Beauty flowed, then Wisdom, Honor, Pleasure:
When almost all was out, God made a stay,
Perceiving that alone of all His treasure
            Rest in the bottom lay.

1   a small space.

"For if I should," said He,
"Bestow this jewel also on My creature,
He would adore My gifts instead of Me,
And rest in Nature, not the God of Nature:
So both should losers be.

"Yet let him keep the rest,
But keep them with repining restlessness:
Let him be rich and weary, that at least,
If goodness lead him not, yet weariness
May toss him to My breast."

THOMAS CAREW [1594?–1640?]

A Song

Ask me no more where Jove bestows,
When June is past, the fading rose;
For in your beauty's orient deep
These flowers, as in their causes, sleep.

Ask me no more whither do stray
The golden atoms of the day;
For, in pure love, heaven did prepare
Those powders to enrich your hair.

Ask me no more whither doth haste
The nightingale, when May is past;
For in your sweet dividing throat
She winters, and keeps warm her note.

Ask me no more where those stars light
That downwards fall in dead of night;
For in your eyes they sit, and there
Fixed become, as in their sphere.

Ask me no more if east or west
The phoenix[1] builds her spicy nest;
For unto you at last she flies,
And in your fragrant bosom dies.

1   a mythical Egyptian bird believed to live for five hundred years, to consume
itself in flames, and to rise from its own ashes.

JOHN MILTON [1608–1674]

How Soon
Hath Time

How soon hath Time, the subtle thief of youth,
   Stol'n on his wing my three and twentieth year!
   My hasting days fly on with full career,
   But my late spring no bud or blossom shew'th.
Perhaps my semblance might deceive the truth,
   That I to manhood am arrived so near,[1]
   And inward ripeness doth much less appear,
   That some more timely-happy spirits indu'th.
Yet be it less or more, or soon or slow,
   It shall be still in strictest measure ev'n,
   To that same lot, however mean or high,
Towards which Time leads me, and the will of heav'n;
   All is, if I have grace to use it so,
   As ever in my great task Master's eye.

1   a reference to Milton's youthful appearance. He was
known at Cambridge as "The Lady of Christ's" (College).

Lycidas

Yet once more, O ye laurels, and once more,
Ye myrtles brown, with ivy never sere,
I come to pluck your berries harsh and crude,
And with forced fingers rude
Shatter your leaves before the mellowing year.
Bitter constraint and sad occasion dear
Compels me to disturb your season due:
For Lycidas[1] is dead, dead ere his prime,
Young Lycidas, and hath not left his peer.
Who would not sing for Lycidas? he knew   10
Himself to sing, and build the lofty rhyme.
He must not float upon his watery bier
Unwept, and welter[2] to the parching wind,
Without the meed[3] of some melodious tear.
   Begin then, Sisters[4] of the sacred well
That from beneath the seat of Jove doth spring;
Begin, and somewhat loudly sweep the string;
Hence with denial vain and coy excuse:

1   a pastoral name for Edward King, a fellow student of Milton at Cambridge,
who drowned in the Irish seas in 1637.
2   toss about.
3   gift.
4   the Muses.

So may some gentle Muse
With lucky words favor *my* destined urn;   20
And as he passes, turn
And bid fair peace be to my sable shroud.
    For we were nursed upon the self-same hill,
Fed the same flock by fountain, shade, and rill.
Together both, ere the high lawns appeared
Under the opening eye-lids of the Morn,
We drove a-field, and both together heard
What time the gray-fly winds her sultry horn,
Battening our flocks with the fresh dews of night;
Oft till the star, that rose at evening bright,   30
Toward heaven's descent had sloped his westering wheel.
Meanwhile the rural ditties were not mute;
Tempered to the oaten flute,
Rough Satyrs danced, and Fauns with cloven heel
From the glad sound would not be absent long;
And old Damoetas⁵ loved to hear our song.
    But, O! the heavy change, now thou art gone,
Now thou art gone, and never must return!
Thee, Shepherd, thee the woods and desert caves,
With wild thyme and the gadding vine o'ergrown,   40
And all their echoes, mourn:
The willows and the hazel copses green
Shall now no more be seen
Fanning their joyous leaves to thy soft lays.
As killing as the canker to the rose,
Or taint-worm to the weanling herds that graze,
Or frost to flowers, that their gay wardrobe wear
When first the white-thorn blows;
Such, Lycidas, thy loss to shepherd's ear.
    Where were ye, Nymphs, when the remorseless deep   50
Closed o'er the head of your loved Lycidas?
For neither were ye playing on the steep
Where your old bards, the famous Druids, lie,
Nor on the shaggy top of Mona high,
Nor yet where Deva⁶ spreads her wizard stream.
Ay me! I fondly dream
"Had ye been there,"—for what could that have done?
What could the Muse herself that Orpheus bore,⁷
The Muse herself, for her enchanting son,
Whom universal nature did lament,   60
When by the rout that made the hideous roar

5   probably a Cambridge tutor.
6   Deva is a river in Wales; Mona, an island off Wales where the Druids,
poets and priests of the ancient Celtic religion, celebrated their rites.
7   Orpheus was the son of Calliope, the muse of epic poetry. He was torn to
pieces by the Thracian woman.

His gory visage down the stream was sent,
Down the swift Hebrus to the Lesbian[8] shore?
   Alas! what boots it with uncessant care
To tend the homely, slighted, shepherd's trade
And strictly meditate the thankless Muse?
Were it not better done, as others use,
To sport with Amaryllis in the shade,
Or with the tangles of Neaera's[9] hair?
Fame is the spur that the clear spirit doth raise   70
(That last infirmity of noble mind)
To scorn delights, and live laborious days;
But the fair guerdon when we hope to find,
And think to burst out into sudden blaze,
Comes the blind Fury[10] with the abhorred shears
And slits the thin-spun life. "But not the praise,"
Phoebus[11] replied, and touched my trembling ears:
"Fame is no plant that grows on mortal soil,
Nor in the glistering foil
Set off to the world, nor in broad rumor lies: 80
But lives and spreads aloft by those pure eyes
And perfect witness of all-judging Jove;
As he pronounces lastly on each deed,
Of so much fame in heaven expect thy meed."
   O fountain Arethuse, and thou honored flood,
Smooth-sliding Mincius,[12] crowned with vocal reeds,
That strain I heard was of a higher mood.
But now my oat proceeds,
And listens to the herald of the sea
That came in Neptune's plea;   90
He asked the waves, and asked the felon winds,
What hard mishap hath doomed this gentle swain?
And questioned every gust of rugged wings
That blows from off each beaked promontory:
They knew not of his story;
And sage Hippotades[13] their answer brings,
That not a blast was from his dungeon strayed;
The air was calm, and on the level brine
Sleek Panope[14] with all her sisters played.
It was that fatal and perfidious bark,   100
Built in the eclipse, and rigged with curses dark,
That sunk so low that sacred head of thine.

8   Orpheus' head was thrown into the Hebrus river, and floated to the island
Lesbos.
9   Amaryllis and Neaera are pastoral maidens.
10   Atropos, one of the three Fates, who cuts the thread of life.
11   Apollo, god of poetry.
12   Arethuse and Mincius are a fountain and river associated with pastoral
poetry.
13   Aeolus, god of winds.
14   a sea nymph.

Next Camus,[15] reverend sire, went footing slow,
His mantle hairy, and his bonnet sedge,
Inwrought with figures dim, and on the edge
Like to that sanguine flower[16] inscribed with woe.
"Ah! who hath reft," quoth he, "my dearest pledge?"
Last came, and last did go
The Pilot of the Galilean lake;
Two massy keys[17] he bore of metals twain   110
(The golden opes, the iron shuts amain);
He shook his mitred[18] locks, and stern bespake:
"How well could I have spared for thee, young swain,
Enow of such, as for their bellies' sake
Creep and intrude and climb into the fold!
Of other care they little reckoning make
Than how to scramble at the shearers' feast,
And shove away the worthy bidden guest.
Blind mouths! that scarce themselves know how to hold
A sheep-hook, or have learned aught else the least   120
That to the faithful herdman's art belongs!
What recks it them? What need they? They are sped;
And when they list, their lean and flashy songs
Grate on their scrannel pipes of wretched straw;
The hungry sheep look up, and are not fed,
But, swoll'n with wind and the rank mist they draw,
Rot inwardly, and foul contagion spread:
Besides what the grim wolf with privy paw
Daily devours apace, and nothing said:
—But that two-handed engine at the door   130
Stands ready to smite once, and smite no more."
    Return, Alpheus;[19] the dread voice is past
That shrunk thy streams; return, Sicilian Muse,
And call the vales, and bid them hither cast
Their bells and flowerets of a thousand hues.
Ye valleys low, where the mild whispers use
Of shades, and wanton winds, and gushing brooks
On whose fresh lap the swart star[20] sparely looks;
Throw hither all your quaint enameled eyes
That on the green turf suck the honeyed showers,   140
And purple all the ground with vernal flowers.
Bring the rathe primrose that forsaken dies,
The tufted crow-toe, and pale jessamine,
The white pink, and the pansy freaked with jet,

15   personification of the River Cam, Cambridge.
16   the hyacinth, which sprang from the blood of Hyacinthus, a young boy
loved and accidentally killed by Apollo.
17   keys of the kingdom of heaven given to St. Peter (the "Pilot") by Christ.
18   miter: bishop's headdress.
19   river god in love with Arethusa.
20   Sirius, the Dog Star, whose rising in the late summer brings heat which
may burn the landscape.

The glowing violet,
The musk-rose, and the well-attired woodbine,
With cowslips wan that hang the pensive head,
And every flower that sad embroidery wears;
Bid amaranthus[21] all his beauty shed,
And daffadillies fill their cups with tears   150
To strew the laureate hearse where Lycid lies.
For so to interpose a little ease,
Let our frail thoughts dally with false surmise.
Ay me! whilst thee the shores and sounding seas
Wash far away, where'er thy bones are hurled;
Whether beyond the stormy Hebrides
Where thou, perhaps, under the whelming tide,
Visit'st the bottom of the monstrous world;
Or whether thou, to our moist vows denied,
Sleep'st by the fable of Bellerus old,   160
Where the great Vision of the guarded mount[22]
Looks toward Namancos and Bayona's hold.[23]
Look homeward, Angel, now, and melt with ruth:
And, O ye dolphins, waft the hapless youth!
    Weep no more, woeful shepherds, weep no more,
For Lycidas, your sorrow, is not dead,
Sunk though he be beneath the watery floor;
So sinks the day-star in the ocean bed,
And yet anon repairs his drooping head,
And tricks his beams, and with new-spangled ore   170
Flames in the forehead of the morning sky:
So Lycidas sunk low, but mounted high
Through the dear might of Him that walked the waves;
Where, other groves and other streams along,
With nectar pure his oozy locks he laves,
And hears the unexpressive nuptial song
In the blest kingdoms meek of joy and love.
There entertain him all the saints above
In solemn troops, and sweet societies,
That sing, and singing in their glory move,   180
And wipe the tears for ever from his eyes.
Now, Lycidas, the shepherds weep no more;
Henceforth thou art the Genius of the shore
In thy large recompense, and shalt be good
To all that wander in that perilous flood.
    Thus sang the uncouth swain to the oaks and rills,
While the still morn went out with sandals gray;
He touched the tender stops of various quills,

21 an imaginary flower that never fades.
22 Bellerus is a legendary hero after whom the Romans named a part of
Cornwall, where there is a mountain guarded by the archangel Michael.
23 a Spanish fortification in Namancos, a mountainous region on the northwest
coast of Spain.

With eager thought warbling his Doric[24] lay:
And now the sun had stretched out all the hills, 190
And now was dropt into the western bay.
At last he rose, and twitched his mantle blue:
Tomorrow to fresh woods, and pastures new.

24   the dialect in which Greek pastorals were written.

On His Blindness

When I consider how my light is spent
Ere half my days in this dark world and wide,
And that one talent[1] which is death to hide
Lodged with me useless, though my soul more bent
To serve therewith my Maker, and present
My true account, lest He returning chide,
"Doth God exact day-labor, light denied?"
I fondly[2] ask. But Patience, to prevent
That murmur, soon replies, "God doth not need
Either man's work or his own gifts. Who best
Bear His mild yoke, they serve Him best. His state
Is kingly: thousands at His bidding speed,
And post o'er land and ocean without rest;
They also serve who only stand and wait."

SIR JOHN SUCKLING [1609–1642]

Song

Why so pale and wan, fond lover?
    Prithee why so pale?
Will, when looking well can't move her,
    Looking ill prevail?
    Prithee why so pale?

Why so dull and mute, young sinner?
    Prithee why so mute?
Will, when speaking well can't win her,
    Saying nothing do 't?
    Prithee why so mute?

1   refers to the parable of the servants to whom various talents (weights of
gold) were entrusted. The man who received only one talent neglected it and
deserved the reproach of his master (Matt., xxv. 14-30).
2   foolishly.

Quit, quit, for shame; this will not move,
　　This cannot take her;
If of herself she will not love,
　　Nothing can make her:
　　The devil take her!

RICHARD LOVELACE　[1618–1658]

To Lucasta,
Going to
the Wars

Tell me not, Sweet, I am unkind
　　That from the nunnery
Of thy chaste breast and quiet mind
　　To war and arms I fly.

True, a new mistress now I chase,
　　The first foe in the field;
And with a stronger faith embrace
　　A sword, a horse, a shield.

Yet this inconstancy is such
　　As you too shall adore;
I could not love thee, Dear, so much,
　　Loved I not Honor more.

To Althea,
from Prison[1]

When Love with unconfined wings
　　Hovers within my gates,
And my divine Althea brings
　　To whisper at the grates;
When I lie tangled in her hair,
　　And fetter'd to her eye,
The gods that wanton in the air
　　Know no such liberty.

When flowing cups run swiftly round
　　With no allaying Thames,   10
Our careless heads with roses bound,
　　Our hearts with loyal flames;

1　Lovelace was imprisoned for a while in 1642 for political reasons.

When thirsty grief in wine we steep,
  When healths and draughts go free,
Fishes that tipple in the deep
  Know no such liberty.

When, like committed² linnets, I
  With shriller throat shall sing
The sweetness, mercy, majesty,
  And glories of my king;   20
When I shall voice aloud how good
  He is, how great should be;
Enlarged winds that curl the flood
  Know no such liberty.

Stone walls do not a prison make,
  Nor iron bars a cage;
Minds innocent and quiet take
  That for an hermitage;
If I have freedom in my love,
  And in my soul am free,   30
Angels alone that soar above
  Enjoy such liberty.

2   imprisoned.

ANDREW MARVELL [1621–1678]

To His
Coy Mistress

Had we but world enough, and time,
This coyness, lady, were no crime.
We would sit down, and think which way
To walk, and pass our long love's day.
Thou by the Indian Ganges' side
Should'st rubies find: I by the tide
Of Humber¹ would complain. I would
Love you ten years before the Flood,
And you should, if you please, refuse
Till the conversion of the Jews.   10
My vegetable love should grow
Vaster than empires, and more slow.
An hundred years should go to praise
Thine eyes, and on thy forehead gaze:
Two hundred to adore each breast:
But thirty thousand to the rest;

1   river flowing by Hull, where Marvell lived.

An age at least to every part,
And the last age should show your heart.
For, lady, you deserve this state,
Nor would I love at lower rate.

But at my back I always hear
Time's wingéd chariot hurrying near:
And yonder all before us lie
Deserts of vast eternity.
Thy beauty shall no more be found;
Nor, in thy marble vault, shall sound
My echoing song: then worms shall try
That long-preserved virginity,
And your quaint honor turn to dust,
And into ashes all my lust.

The grave's a fine and private place,
But none, I think, do there embrace.

Now, therefore, while the youthful hue
Sits on thy skin like morning dew,
And while thy willing soul transpires
At every pore with instant fires,
Now let us sport us while we may;
And now, like amorous birds of prey,
Rather at once our Time devour,
Than languish in his slow-chapt² power.

Let us roll all our strength and all
Our sweetness up into one ball,
And tear our pleasures with rough strife
Thorough the iron gates of life.
Thus, though we cannot make our sun
Stand still, yet we will make him run.

2   slow-devouring.

The Definition of Love

My love is of a birth as rare
As 'tis for object¹ strange and high;
It was begotten by despair
Upon impossibility.

Magnanimous despair alone
Could show me so divine a thing,
Where feeble hope could ne'er have flown,
But vainly flapped its tinsel wing.

1   in the philosophical sense of *objectum*, a thing thrown before the mind.

And yet I quickly might arrive
Where my extended soul is fixed,
But fate does iron wedges drive,
And always crowds itself betwixt.

For fate with jealous eye does see
Two perfect loves, nor lets them close;[2]
Their union would her ruin be,
And her tyrannic power depose.

And therefore her decrees of steel
Us as the distant poles have placed,
Though love's whole world on us doth wheel,
Not by themselves to be embraced;

Unless the giddy heaven fall,
And earth some new convulsion tear,
And, us to join, the world should all
Be cramped into a planisphere.[3]

As lines, so loves, oblique may well
Themselves in every angle greet;
But ours so truly parallel,
Though infinite, can never meet.

Therefore the love which us doth bind,
But fate so enviously debars,
Is the conjunction of the mind,
And opposition[4] of the stars.

10

20

30

The Garden

How vainly men themselves amaze
To win the palm, the oak, or bays;
And their uncessant labors see
Crowned from some single herb or tree,
Whose short and narrow verged shade
Does prudently their toils upbraid;
While all flow'rs and all trees do close
To weave the garlands of repose.

Fair Quiet, have I found thee here,
And Innocence, thy sister dear?
Mistaken long, I sought you then
In busy companies of men.

10

2   unite.
3   a sphere represented on a plane.
4   "Conjunction" is the astronomical term for the apparent proximity of two
planets or stars; "opposition" is the relative position of two heavenly bodies
when exactly opposite each other as seen from the earth's surface.

Your sacred plants, if here below,
Only among the plants will grow.
Society is all but rude
To this delicious solitude.

No white nor red was ever seen
So am'rous as this lovely green.
Fond lovers, cruel as their flame,
Cut in these trees their mistress' name.   20
Little, alas, they know, or heed,
How far these beauties hers exceed!
Fair trees! where s'eer your barks I wound,
No name shall but your own be found.

When we have run our passions' heat,
Love hither makes his best retreat.
The gods, that mortal beauty chase,
Still in a tree did end their race.
Apollo hunted Daphne so,
Only that she might laurel grow.   30
And Pan did after Syrinx speed
Not as a nymph, but for a reed.[1]

What wond'rous life in this I lead!
Ripe apples drop about my head;
The luscious clusters of the vine
Upon my mouth do crush their wine;
The nectarine, and curious[2] peach
Into my hands themselves do reach;
Stumbling on melons, as I pass,
Ensnared with flow'rs, I fall on grass.   40

Meanwhile the mind from pleasure less
Withdraws into its happiness:
The mind, that Ocean where each kind
Does straight its own resemblance find;[3]
Yet it creates, transcending these,
Far other worlds, and other seas;
Annihilating all that's made
To a green thought in a green shade.

Here at the fountain's sliding foot,
Or at some fruit-tree's mossy root,   50
Casting the body's vest aside,

1   Daphne was a river-god's daughter. Pursued by Apollo, she changed into a
laurel tree to escape him. Syrinx, in order to escape from Pan, turned into a
reed; Pan made his pipes from the reed.
2   exquisite.
3   an allusion to the idea that all land animals had a counterpart in the sea.

My soul into the boughs does glide;
There, like a bird, it sits and sings,
Then whets,[4] and combs its silver wings,
And, till prepared for longer flight,
Waves in its plumes the various light.

Such was that happy Garden-state[5]
While man there walked without a mate;
After a place so pure, and sweet,
What other help could yet be meet!   60
But 'twas beyond a mortal's share
To wander solitary there:
Two Paradises 'twere in one
To live in Paradise alone.

How well the skilful Gard'ner drew
Of flow'rs and herbs this dial new;[6]
Where, from above, the milder sun
Does from a fragrant Zodiac[7] run;
And, as it works, th ' industrious bee
Computes its time as well as we.   70
How could such sweet and wholesome hours
Be reckoned, but with herbs and flow'rs!

4   preens.
5   the Garden of Eden.
6   A "flower dial" was a bed made up of flowers
opening at different times, which formed a clock.
7   an imaginary belt in the sky which contained the planets.

An Horatian Ode
Upon Cromwell's Return from Ireland[1]

The forward youth that would appear
Must now forsake his Muses dear,
    Nor in the shadows sing
    His numbers languishing.

'Tis time to leave the books in dust,
And oil the unused armor's rust,
    Removing from the wall
    The corslet of the hall.

So restless Cromwell could not cease
In the inglorious arts of peace,   10
    But through adventurous war
    Urged his active star:

1   Oliver Cromwell (1599–1658) was responsible for the execution of King
Charles I and became Lord Protector of England during its only period of
republican rule. This poem was written after his suppression of mutiny in
Ireland, following the king's execution, and before his march against Scotland
where Charles II had been proclaimed king.

And, like the three-fork'd lightning, first
Breaking the clouds where it was nursed,
 Did thorough his own side
 His fiery way divide.

For 'tis all one to courage high,
The emulous, or enemy;
 And with such, to enclose
 Is more than to oppose.   20

Then burning through the air he went,
And palaces and temples rent:
 And Caesar's[2] head at last
 Did through his laurels blast.[3]

'Tis madness to resist or blame
The force of angry Heaven's flame;
 And, if we would speak true,
 Much to the man is due,

Who, from his private gardens, where
He lived reserved and austere,   30
 As if his highest plot
 To plant the bergamot,[4]

Could by industrious valor climb
To ruin the great work of time,
 And cast the Kingdom old
 Into another mould.

Though Justice against Fate complain,
And plead the ancient rights in vain:
 But those do hold or break
 As men are strong or weak: 40

Nature, that hateth emptiness,
Allows of penetration[5] less,
 And therefore must make room
 Where greater spirits come.

What field of all the Civil Wars,
Where his were not the deepest scars?
 And Hampton[6] shows what part
 He had of wiser art:

Where, twining subtle fears with hope,
He wove a net of such a scope   50
 That Charles himself might chase
 To Carisbrook's narrow case:

2 Charles I.
3 Laurels were believed to be lightning-proof. They were traditionally worn by
emperors.
4 a kind of pear.
5 occupation of space by two bodies at the same time.
6 In 1647, Charles I fled from Hampton Court to Carisbrooke Castle in
the Isle of Wight. It was rumored at the time that Cromwell had engineered this.

That thence the Royal Actor borne
The tragic scaffold might adorn;
  While round the armed bands
  Did clap their bloody hands.

He nothing common did or mean
Upon that memorable scene,
  But with his keener eye
  The axe's edge did try: 60

Nor called the Gods, with vulgar spite,
To vindicate his helpless Right,[7]
  But bowed his comely head
  Down, as upon a bed.

This was that memorable hour
Which first assured the forced power.
  So when they did design
  The Capitol's first line,

A bleeding Head, where they begun,
Did fright the architects to run;   70
  And yet in that the State
  Foresaw its happy fate.[8]

And now the Irish are ashamed
To see themselves in one year tamed:
  So much can one man do,
  That does both act and know.

They can affirm his praises best,
And have, though overcome, confessed
  How good he is, how just,
  And fit for highest trust;   80

Nor yet grown stiffer with command,
But still in the Republic's hand:
  How fit he is to sway[9]
  That can so well obey.

He to the Commons' feet presents
A Kingdom, for his first year's rents,
  And, what he may, forbears
  His fame, to make it theirs;

And has his sword and spoils ungirt,
To lay them at the public's skirt.   90
  So when the falcon high
  Falls heavy from the sky,

7 Divine Right, the doctrine that kings derived their authority directly from
God and were therefore responsible to Him alone.
8 When foundations were dug for the Capitol temple in Rome, a human head
was found intact. This was considered a good omen for the city's future.
9 rule.

She, having killed, no more does search
But on the next green bow[10] to perch,
 Where, when he first does lure,
 The falconer has her sure.

What may not then our Isle presume
While victory his crest does plume!
 What may not others fear
 If thus he crown each year!   100

A Caesar he, ere long, to Gaul,
To Italy an Hannibal,[11]
 And to all States not free
 Shall climacteric be.[12]

The Pict no shelter now shall find
Within his particolor'd mind,[13]
 But, from this valour, sad
 Shrink underneath the plaid.[14]

Happy if in the tufted brake
The English hunter him mistake,   110
 Nor lay his hounds in near
 The Caledonian[15] deer.

But thou, the War's and Fortune's son,
March indefatigably on:
 And for the last effect
 Still keep thy sword erect:

Besides the force it has to fright
The spirits of the shady night,[16]
 The same arts that did gain
 A power must it maintain.   120

HENRY VAUGHAN [1622–1695]

The Retreat

Happy those early days! when I
Shined in my angel-infancy.
Before I understood this place
Appointed for my second race,

10 bough.
11 Julius Caesar, the Roman dictator, conquered Gaul (France) in his most famous campaign. Hannibal was a Carthaginian general who occupied Italy for some years.
12 make a climax.
13 a pun on the derivation of the word "Pict," meaning "painted." The Picts were a Scottish tribe.
14 a Scottish cloak.
15 Scottish.
16 an allusion to the cross-hilt of the sword, which had the power to avert demons and witches.

Or taught my soul to fancy aught
But a white, celestial thought;
When yet I had not walked above
A mile or two from my first love,
And looking back, at that short space
Could see a glimpse of his bright face;   10
When on some gilded cloud or flower
My gazing soul would dwell an hour,
And in those weaker glories spy
Some shadows of eternity;
Before I taught my tongue to wound
My conscience with a sinful sound,
Or had the black art to dispense
A several[1] sin to every sense,
But felt through all this fleshly dress
Bright shoots of everlastingness.   20
   Oh, how I long to travel back,
And tread again that ancient track!
That I might once more reach that plain,
Where first I left my glorious train;
From whence the enlightened spirit sees
That shady city of palm trees;[2]
But ah! my soul with too much stay
Is drunk, and staggers in the way.
Some men a forward motion love,
But I by backward steps would move;   30
And when this dust falls to the urn,
In that state I came, return.

They Are All Gone into the World of Light

They are all gone into the world of light!
       And I alone sit ling'ring here;
Their very memory is fair and bright,
       And my sad thoughts doth clear.

It glows and glitters in my cloudy breast,
       Like stars upon some gloomy grove,
Or those faint beams in which this hill is dressed,
       After the sun's remove.

I see them walking in an air of glory,
       Whose light doth trample on my days: 10

1   different.
2   as Moses was permitted a vision of the Promised Land, "the valley of
Jericho, the city of palm trees" (Deut., xxxiv. 3).

My days, which are at best but dull and hoary,
    Mere glimmering and decays.

O holy Hope! and high Humility,
    High as the heavens above!
These are your walks, and you have showed them me,
    To kindle my cold love.

Dear, beauteous Death! the jewel of the just,
    Shining nowhere, but in the dark;
What mysteries do lie beyond thy dust,
    Could man outlook that mark! 20

He that hath found some fledged bird's nest, may know
    At first sight if the bird be flown;
But what fair well or grove he sings in now,
    That is to him unknown.

And yet, as angels in some brighter dreams
    Call to the soul when man doth sleep,
So some strange thoughts transcend our wonted themes,
    And into glory peep.

If a star were confin'd into a tomb,
    Her captive flames must needs burn there; 30
But when the hand that locked her up, gives room,
    She'll shine through all the sphere.

O Father of eternal life, and all
    Created glories under Thee!
Resume Thy spirit from this world of thrall
    Into true liberty.

Either disperse these mists, which blot and fill
    My perspective,[1] still, as they pass:
Or else remove me hence unto that hill
    Where I shall need no glass. 40

1   telescope.

JOHN DRYDEN [1631–1700]

To the Memory
of Mr. Oldham[1]

Fare well, too little and too lately known,
Whom I began to think and call my own:
For sure our souls were near allied, and thine
Cast in the same poetic mold with mine.

1   John Oldham, a satiric poet, died at the age of 30.

One common note on either lyre did strike,
And knaves and fools we both abhorred alike.
To the same goal did both our studies drive:
The last set out the soonest did arrive.
Thus Nisus[2] fell upon the slippery place,
Whilst his young friend performed and won the race.
O early ripe! to thy abundant store
What could advancing age have added more?
It might (what nature never gives the young)
Have taught the numbers of thy native tongue.
But satire needs not those, and wit will shine
Through the harsh cadence of a rugged line.
A noble error, and but seldom made,
When poets are by too much force betrayed.
Thy gen'rous fruits, though gathered ere their prime,
Still showed a quickness; and maturing time
But mellows what we write to the dull sweets of rhyme.
Once more, hail, and farewell! farewell, thou young,
But ah! too short, Marcellus[3] of our tongue!
Thy brows with ivy and with laurels bound;
But fate and gloomy night encompass thee around.

2 In Virgil's *Aeneid,* V. 315–39, Nisus slipped in the
blood of a slain steer but tripped the runner-up and thus
helped his friend Euryalus win the race.
3   nephew and heir to the emperor Augustus. He died at
the age of 20.

A Song
for St. Cecilia's Day[1]

1

From harmony, from heavenly harmony
    This universal frame began:
    When Nature underneath a heap
      Of jarring atoms lay,
    And could not heave her head,
The tuneful voice was heard from high:
    "Arise, ye more than dead."
Then cold, and hot, and moist, and dry,
In order to their stations leap,
    And Music's power obey.   10
From harmony, from heavenly harmony
    This universal frame began:
    From harmony to harmony
Through all the compass of the notes it ran,
The diapason closing full in man.

1   St. Cecilia is the patron saint of music.

2

What passion cannot Music raise and quell!
    When Jubal[2] struck the corded shell,
    His listening brethren stood around,
    And, wondering, on their faces fell
    To worship that celestial sound 20
Less than a god they thought there could not dwell
    Within the hollow of that shell
    That spoke so sweetly and so well.
What passion cannot Music raise and quell!

3

    The trumpet's loud clangor
      Excites us to arms,
    With shrill notes of anger,
      And mortal alarms.
    The double double double beat
      Of the thundering drum 30
Cries: "Hark! the foes come;
Charge, charge, 'tis too late to retreat."

4

    The soft complaining flute
    In dying notes discovers
    The woes of hopeless lovers,
Whose dirge is whispered by the warbling lute.

5

    Sharp violins proclaim
Their jealous pangs, and desperation,
Fury, frantic indignation,
Depth of pains, and height of passion, 40
    For the fair, disdainful dame.

6

    But O! what art can teach,
    What human voice can reach,
The sacred organ's praise?
    Notes inspiring holy love,
Notes that wing their heavenly ways
    To mend the choirs above.

7

Orpheus could lead the savage race;
And trees unrooted left their place,
    Sequacious of the lyre; 50
But bright Cecilia raised the wonder higher:

2   a descendant of Cain and "father of all those who play the lyre and pipe" (Genesis, iv. 21).

When to her organ vocal breath was given,
An angel heard, and straight appeared,
    Mistaking earth for heaven.

GRAND CHORUS

As from the power of sacred lays
    The spheres began to move,
And sung the great Creator's praise
    To all the blest above;
So, when the last and dreadful hour
This crumbling pageant shall devour,   60
The trumpet shall be heard on high,
The dead shall live, the living die,
And Music shall untune the sky.

All, All of a Piece

All, all of a piece throughout;
Thy chase had a beast in view,
Thy wars brought nothing about,
Thy lovers were all untrue;
'Tis well an old age is out
And time to begin a new.

JONATHAN SWIFT   [1667–1745]

A Description of the Morning

Now hardly here and there an hackney coach
Appearing, showed the ruddy morn's approach.
Now Betty from her master's bed had flown,
And softly stole to discompose her own;
The slipshod 'prentice from his master's door
Had pared the dirt, and sprinkled round the floor.
Now Moll had whirled her mop with dextrous airs,
Prepared to scrub the entry and the stairs.
The youth with broomy stumps began to trace
The kennel's edge,[1] where wheels had worn the place.
The small-coal man was heard with cadence deep,
Till drowned in shriller notes of chimney sweep:
Duns at his lordship's gate began to meet;

1   edge of the gutter.

And brickdust Moll had screamed through half the street.
The turnkey now his flock returning sees,
Duly let out a-nights to steal for fees:
The watchful bailiffs take their silent stands,
And schoolboys lag with satchels in their hands.

ALEXANDER POPE [1688–1744]

Epistle to
Dr. Arbuthnot[1]

Advertisement TO THE FIRST PUBLICATION OF THIS EPISTLE

This paper is a sort of bill of complaint, begun many years since, and
drawn up by snatches, as the several occasions offered. I had no
thoughts of publishing it, till it pleased some persons of rank and fortune (the authors of *Verses to the Imitator of Horace,* and of an
Epistle to a Doctor of Divinity from a Nobleman at Hampton Court)
to attack, in a very extraordinary manner, not only my writings (of
which, being public, the public is judge) but my person, morals, and
family, whereof, to those who know me not, a truer information may
be requisite. Being divided between the necessity to say something of
myself, and my own laziness to undertake so awkward a task, I
thought it the shortest way to put the last hand to this Epistle. If it
have anything pleasing, it will be that by which I am most desirous
to please, the truth and the sentiment; and if anything offensive, it
will be only to those I am least sorry to offend, the vicious or the
ungenerous.

Many will know their own pictures in it, there being not a cir-
cumstance but what is true; but I have, for the most part, spared their
names, and they may escape being laughed at, if they please.

I would have some of them know, it was owing to the request of
the learned and candid friend to whom it is inscribed, that I make not
as free use of theirs as they have done of mine. However, I shall have
this advantage, and honor, on my side, that whereas, by their proceed-
ing, any abuse may be directed at any man, no injury can possibly be
done by mine, since a nameless character can never be found out, but
by its truth and likeness.

P. Shut, shut the door, good John! (fatigued, I said),
Tie up the knocker, say I'm sick, I'm dead.
The Dog Star[2] rages! nay 'tis past a doubt

1 John Arbuthnot was a close and faithful friend of Pope, and, like Pope
and Swift, a member of the "Scriblerus Club," which produced satiric verse and
prose. Arbuthnot was Queen Anne's favorite physician.
2 Sirius, which is prominent in the heavens in late summer. In ancient Rome
this was the customary time for rehearsing poetry.

All Bedlam, or Parnassus,[3] is let out:
Fire in each eye, and papers in each hand,
They rave, recite, and madden round the land.

    What walls can guard me, or what shades can hide?
They pierce my thickets, through my grot they glide,
By land, by water, they renew the charge,
They stop the chariot, and they board the barge.   10
No place is sacred, not the church is free;
Even Sunday shines no Sabbath day to me:
Then from the Mint[4] walks forth the man of rhyme,
Happy to catch me just at dinner time.

    Is there a parson, much bemused in beer,
A maudlin poetess, a rhyming peer,
A clerk foredoomed his father's soul to cross,
Who pens a stanza when he should engross?
Is there who, locked from ink and paper, scrawls
With desperate charcoal round his darkened walls?   20
All fly to Twit'nam,[5] and in humble strain
Apply to me to keep them mad or vain.
Arthur,[6] whose giddy son neglects the laws,
Imputes to me and my damned works the cause:
Poor Cornus[7] sees his frantic wife elope,
And curses wit, and poetry, and Pope.

    Friend to my life (which did not you prolong,
The world had wanted many an idle song)
What drop or nostrum can this plague remove?
Or which must end me, a fool's wrath or love?   30
A dire dilemma! either way I'm sped,
If foes, they write, if friends, they read me dead.
Seized and tied down to judge, how wretched I!
Who can't be silent, and who will not lie.
To laugh were want of goodness and of grace,
And to be grave exceeds all power of face.
I sit with sad civility, I read
With honest anguish and an aching head,
And drop at last, but in unwilling ears,
This saving counsel, "Keep your piece nine years."   40

    "Nine years!" cries he, who high in Drury Lane,[8]
Lulled by soft zephyrs through the broken pane,
Rhymes ere he wakes, and prints before term[9] ends

3 Bedlam is the oldest English insane asylum; Parnassus is a mountain sacred
to Apollo and the Muses.
4 a sanctuary for insolvent debtors.
5 Pope's home, Twickenham, a suburb of London.
6 Arthur Moore's son James, who adopted the name Smythe, wrote a
comedy in which he incorporated some unpublished verses by Pope,
with Pope's permission. The permission was later withdrawn, but
Moore Smythe refused to take out the verses.
7 "horn," caricatural name for cuckold.
8 London street and theater district.
9 "Terms" were judicial sessions, with which the publishing "seasons" were
synchronized.

Obliged by hunger and request of friends:
"The piece, you think, is incorrect? why, take it,
I'm all submission, what you'd have it, make it."

　　Three things another's modest wishes bound,
My friendship, and a prologue, and ten pound.
　　Pitholeon[10] sends to me: "You know his Grace,
I want a patron; ask him for a place."　　　　　　　　　　　　50
Pitholeon libeled me—"but here's a letter
Informs you, sir, 'twas when he knew no better.
Dare you refuse him? Curll[11] invites to dine,
He'll write a *Journal*, or he'll turn Divine."
Bless me! a packet.—" 'Tis a stranger sues,
A virgin tragedy, an orphan Muse."
If I dislike it, "Furies, death, and rage!"
If I approve, "Commend it to the stage."
There (thank my stars) my whole commission ends,
The players and I are, luckily, no friends.　　　　　　　　　　60
Fired that the house reject him, " 'Sdeath, I'll print it,
And shame the fools—Your interest, sir, with Lintot!"
Lintot, dull rogue, will think your price too much.
"Not, sir, if you revise it, and retouch."
All my demurs but double his attacks;
At last he whispers, "Do; and we go snacks."
Glad of a quarrel, straight I clap the door,
"Sir, let me see your works and you no more."
　　'Tis sung, when Midas' ears began to spring
(Midas, a sacred person and a king),　　　　　　　　　　　　70
His very minister who spied them first,
(Some say his queen) was forced to speak, or burst.[12]
And is not mine, my friend, a sorer case,
When every coxcomb perks them in my face?
　　A. Good friend, forbear! you deal in dangerous things.
I'd never name queens, ministers, or kings;
Keep close to ears, and those let asses prick;
'Tis nothing——P. Nothing? if they bite and kick?
Out with it, *Dunciad!*[13] let the secret pass,
That secret to each fool, that he's an ass:　　　　　　　　　　80
The truth once told (and wherefore should we lie?)
The queen of Midas slept, and so may I.
　　You think this cruel? take it for a rule,
No creature smarts so little as a fool.
Let peals of laughter, Codrus[14]! round thee break,
Thou unconcerned canst hear the mighty crack.

10　"A foolish poet at Rhodes who pretended much to Greek" (Pope).
11　Edmund Curll and Bernard Lintot (who is mentioned in the following lines) were booksellers.
12　Midas, king of Phrygia, judged a musical contest between Pan and Apollo; when Midas favored Pan, Apollo changed Midas' ears into those of an ass.
13　Pope's mock heroic poem celebrating the triumph of dullness.
14　a poet ridiculed by Virgil and Juvenal.

Pit, box, and gallery in convulsions hurled,
Thou stand'st unshook amidst a bursting world.
Who shames a scribbler? break one cobweb through,
He spins the slight, self-pleasing thread anew: 90
Destroy his fib or sophistry, in vain;
The creature's at his dirty work again,
Throned in the center of his thin designs,
Proud of a vast extent of flimsy lines.
Whom have I hurt? has poet yet or peer
Lost the arched eyebrow or Parnassian sneer?
And has not Colley still his lord and whore?
His butchers Henley? his freemasons Moore?
Does not one table Bavius still admit?
Still to one bishop Philips seem a wit?   100
Still Sappho[15]——A. Hold! for God's sake—you'll offend.
No names—be calm—learn prudence of a friend.
I too could write, and I am twice as tall;
But foes like these!——P. One flatterer's worse than all.
Of all mad creatures, if the learn'd are right,
It is the slaver kills, and not the bite.
A fool quite angry is quite innocent:
Alas! 'Tis ten times worse when they repent.
    One dedicates in high heroic prose,
And ridicules beyond a hundred foes;   110
One from all Grub Street[16] will my fame defend,
And, more abusive, calls himself my friend.
This prints my letters, that expects a bribe,
And others roar aloud, "Subscribe, subscribe!"
    There are, who to my person pay their court:
I cough like Horace, and, though lean, am short;
Ammon's great son[17] one shoulder had too high,
Such Ovid's nose, and "Sir! you have an eye—"
Go on, obliging creatures, make me see
All that disgraced my betters met in me.   120
Say for my comfort, languishing in bed,
"Just so immortal Maro[18] held his head":
And when I die, be sure you let me know
Great Homer died three thousand years ago.
    Why did I write? what sin to me unknown
Dipped me in ink, my parents', or my own?
As yet a child, nor yet a fool to fame,
I lisped in numbers, for the numbers came.

15   Colley Cibber was a contemporary poet laureate; Henley preached on the
uses of the butcher's calling; Bavius was an enemy of the Roman poet Virgil;
Philips, a rival of Pope and secretary to an Irish archbishop. Sappho was a
Greek poetess of the seventh century B.C.; the reference is to Lady Mary
Wortley Montagu.
16   satiric name for Fleet Street, the publishing center of London.
17   Alexander the Great.
18   Virgil.

I left no calling for this idle trade,
No duty broke, no father disobeyed.   130
The Muse but served to ease some friend, not wife,
To help me through this long disease, my life,
To second, Arbuthnot! thy art and care,
And teach the being you preserved, to bear.
    A. But why then publish? P. Granville the polite,
And knowing Walsh, would tell me I could write;
Well-natured Garth inflamed with early praise,
And Congreve loved, and Swift endured my lays;
The courtly Talbot, Somers, Sheffield, read;
Even mitered Rochester would nod the head,   140
And St. John's self (great Dryden's friends before)
With open arms received one poet more.[19]
Happy my studies, when by these approved!
Happier their author, when by these beloved!
From these the world will judge of men and books,
Not from the Burnets, Oldmixons, and Cookes.[20]
    Soft were my numbers; who could take offense
While pure description held the place of sense?
Like gentle Fanny's[21] was my flowery theme,
A painted mistress, or a purling stream.   150
Yet then did Gildon draw his venal quill;
I wished the man a dinner, and sat still.
Yet then did Dennis[22] rave in furious fret;
I never answered, I was not in debt.
If want provoked, or madness made them print,
I waged no war with Bedlam or the Mint.
    Did some more sober critic come abroad?
If wrong, I smiled; if right, I kissed the rod.
Pains, reading, study are their just pretense,
And all they want is spirit, taste, and sense.   160
Commas and points they set exactly right,
And 'twere a sin to rob them of their mite.
Yet ne'er one sprig of laurel graced these ribalds,
From slashing Bentley down to piddling Tibbalds.[23]
Each wight who reads not, and but scans and spells,
Each word-catcher that lives on syllables,
Even such small critics some regard may claim,
Preserved in Milton's or in Shakespeare's name.
Pretty! in amber to observe the forms
Of hairs, or straws, or dirt, or grubs, or worms!   170

19 Granville, Walsh, Garth, poets, and Congreve, the playwright, were
contemporary with Pope; and Talbot, Somers, Sheffield, the Bishop of Rochester,
and Henry St. John were statesmen and patrons of the arts.
20 "Authors of secret and scandalous history" (Pope).
21 reference to a poem by Thomas Parnell.
22 authors who had censured some of Pope's poetry.
23 Bentley had meddled with the text of Milton's *Paradise Lost;* Tibbald with
Shakespeare's plays.

The things, we know, are neither rich nor rare,
But wonder how the devil they got there.
   Were others angry? I excused them too;
Well might they rage; I gave them but their due.
A man's true merit 'tis not hard to find;
But each man's secret standard in his mind,
That casting weight pride adds to emptiness,
This, who can gratify? for who can guess?
The bard whom pilfered pastorals renown,
Who turns a Persian tale for half a crown,   180
Just writes to make his barrenness appear,
And strains from hard-bound brains eight lines a year:
He, who still wanting, though he lives on theft,
Steals much, spends little, yet has nothing left;
And he who now to sense, now nonsense leaning,
Means not, but blunders round about a meaning:
And he whose fustian's so sublimely bad,
It is not poetry, but prose run mad:
All these, my modest satire bade translate,
And owned that nine such poets made a Tate.[24]   190
How did they fume, and stamp, and roar, and chafe!
And swear, not Addison[25] himself was safe.
   Peace to all such! but were there one whose fires
True Genius kindles, and fair Fame inspires;
Blessed with each talent and each art to please,
And born to write, converse, and live with ease:
Should such a man, too fond to rule alone,
Bear, like the Turk, no brother near the throne;
View him with scornful, yet with jealous eyes,
And hate for arts that caused himself to rise;   200
Damn with faint praise, assent with civil leer,
And without sneering, teach the rest to sneer;
Willing to wound, and yet afraid to strike,
Just hint a fault, and hesitate dislike;
Alike reserved to blame or to commend,
A timorous foe, and a suspicious friend;
Dreading even fools; by flatterers besieged,
And so obliging that he ne'er obliged;
Like Cato, give his little senate laws,
And sit attentive to his own applause;   210
While wits and Templars every sentence raise,
And wonder with a foolish face of praise—
Who but must laugh, if such a man there be?
Who would not weep, if Atticus were he?
   What though my name stood rubric on the walls

24   an inferior British poet who became poet laureate.
25   Joseph Addison, to whom Pope gives the name Atticus, was the author of a
tragedy, *Cato*, but more important, reformed English taste and manners through
his articles in *The Tatler* and *The Spectator*.

Or plastered posts, with claps, in capitals?
Or smoking forth, a hundred hawkers' load,
On wings of winds came flying all abroad?
I sought no homage from the race that write;
I kept, like Asian monarchs, from their sight: 220
Poems I heeded (now berhymed so long)
No more than thou, great George![26] a birthday song.
I ne'er with wits or witlings passed my days
To spread about the itch of verse and praise;
Nor like a puppy daggled through the town
To fetch and carry sing-song up and down;
Nor at rehearsals sweat, and mouthed, and cried,
With handkerchief and orange at my side;
But sick of fops, and poetry, and prate,
To Bufo left the whole Castalian state.[27]   230
    Proud as Apollo on his forkéd hill,
Sat full-blown Bufo, puffed by every quill;
Fed with soft dedication all day long,
Horace and he went hand in hand in song.
His library (where busts of poets dead
And a true Pindar stood without a head)
Received of wits an undistinguished race,
Who first his judgment asked, and then a place:
Much they extolled his pictures, much his seat,
And flattered every day, and some days eat: 240
Till grown more frugal in his riper days,
He paid some bards with port, and some with praise;
To some a dry rehearsal was assigned,
And others (harder still) he paid in kind.
Dryden alone (what wonder?) came not nigh;
Dryden alone escaped this judging eye:
But still the great have kindness in reserve;
He helped to bury whom he helped to starve.
    May some choice patron bless each gray goose quill!
May every Bavius have his Bufo still!   250
So when a statesman wants a day's defense,
Or Envy holds a whole week's war with Sense,
Or simple Pride for flattery makes demands,
May dunce by dunce be whistled off my hands!
Blessed be the great! for those they take away,
And those they left me—for they left me Gay;[28]
Left me to see neglected genius bloom,
Neglected die, and tell it on his tomb;
Of all thy blameless life the sole return

26   George II, King of England, 1727–1760.
27   Bufo, caricatural name for a patron; Castalia, a spring on Mt. Parnassus,
sacred to Apollo and the Muses, and hence a source of poetic inspiration.
28   John Gay, close friend of Pope and author of the *Beggar's Opera*, had a
monument erected to him by the Duke of Queensberry.

My verse, and Queensberry weeping o'er thy urn!   260
Oh, let me live my own, and die so too!
("To live and die is all I have to do")
Maintain a poet's dignity and ease,
And see what friends, and read what books I please;
Above a patron, though I condescend
Sometimes to call a minister my friend.
I was not born for courts or great affairs;
I pay my debts, believe, and say my prayers,
Can sleep without a poem in my head,
Nor know if Dennis be alive or dead.   270
    Why am I asked what next shall see the light?
Heavens! was I born for nothing but to write?
Has life no joys for me? or (to be grave)
Have I no friend to serve, no soul to save?
"I found him close with Swift"—"Indeed? no doubt"
Cries prating Balbus, "something will come out."
'Tis all in vain, deny it as I will.
"No, such a genius never can lie still,"
And then for mine obligingly mistakes
The first lampoon Sir Will or Bubo makes.[29]   280
Poor guiltless I! and can I choose but smile,
When every coxcomb knows me by my style?
    Cursed be the verse, how well soe'er it flow,
That tends to make one worthy man my foe,
Give Virtue scandal, Innocence a fear,
Or from the soft-eyed virgin steal a tear!
But he who hurts a harmless neighbor's peace,
Insults fallen worth, or Beauty in distress,
Who loves a lie, lame Slander helps about,
Who writes a libel, or who copies out: 290
That fop whose pride affects a patron's name,
Yet absent, wounds an author's honest fame;
Who can your merit selfishly approve,
And show the sense of it without the love;
Who has the vanity to call you friend,
Yet wants the honor, injured, to defend;
Who tells whate'er you think, whate'er you say,
And, if he lie not, must at least betray:
Who to the dean and silver bell can swear,
And sees at Cannons what was never there:[30]   300
Who reads but with a lust to misapply,
Make satire a lampoon, and fiction, lie:
A lash like mine no honest man shall dread,
But all such babbling blockheads in his stead.

29 Sir William Yonge and Bubb Dodington, Whig politicians and patrons of the
arts.
30 Pope's enemies unjustly accused him of satirizing the estate of the Duke of
Chandos at Cannons.

Let Sporus[31] tremble——A. What? that thing of silk,
Sporus, that mere white curd of ass's milk?
Satire or sense, alas! can Sporus feel?
Who breaks a butterfly upon a wheel?
    P. Yet let me flap this bug with gilded wings,
This painted child of dirt, that stinks and stings;   310
Whose buzz the witty and the fair annoys,
Yet wit ne'er tastes, and beauty ne'er enjoys;
So well-bred spaniels civilly delight
In mumbling of the game they dare not bite.
Eternal smiles his emptiness betray,
As shallow streams run dimpling all the way.
Whether in florid impotence he speaks,
And, as the prompter breathes, the puppet squeaks;
Or at the ear of Eve, familiar toad,
Half froth, half venom, spits himself abroad,   320
In puns, or politics, or tales, or lies,
Or spite, or smut, or rhymes, or blasphemies.
His wit all seesaw between *that* and *this*,
Now high, now low, now master up, now miss,
And he himself one vile antithesis.
Amphibious thing! that acting either part,
The trifling head or the corrupted heart,
Fop at the toilet, flatterer at the board,
Now trips a lady, and now struts a lord.
Eve's tempter thus the rabbins[32] have expressed,   330
A cherub's face, a reptile all the rest;
Beauty that shocks you, parts that none will trust,
Wit that can creep, and pride that licks the dust.
    Not Fortune's worshiper, nor Fashion's fool,
Not Lucre's madman, nor Ambition's tool,
Not proud, nor servile, be one poet's praise,
That if he pleased, he pleased by manly ways:
That flattery, even to kings, he held a shame,
And thought a lie in verse or prose the same:
That not in fancy's maze he wandered long,   340
But stooped to truth, and moralized his song:
That not for fame, but Virtue's better end,
He stood the furious foe, the timid friend,
The damning critic, half approving wit,
The coxcomb hit, or fearing to be hit;
Laughed at the loss of friends he never had,
The dull, the proud, the wicked, and the mad;
The distant threats of vengeance on his head,
The blow unfelt, the tear he never shed;
The tale revived, the lie so oft o'erthrown,   350

31   name for Lord Hervey, who had collaborated with Lady Mary Wortley
Montagu in attacks on Pope.
32   rabbis, Jewish theologians and scholars.

The imputed trash, and dullness not his own;
The morals blackened when the writings 'scape,
The libeled person, and the pictured shape;[33]
Abuse on all he loved, or loved him, spread,
A friend in exile, or a father dead;
The whisper, that to greatness still too near,
Perhaps yet vibrates on his Sovereign's ear—
Welcome for thee, Fair Virtue! all the past!
For thee, fair Virtue! welcome even the last!
    A. But why insult the poor, affront the great?   360
P. A knave's a knave to me in every state:
Alike my scorn, if he succeed or fail,
Sporus at court, or Japhet[34] in a jail,
A hireling scribbler, or a hireling peer,
Knight of the post corrupt, or of the shire,
If on a pillory, or near a throne,
He gain his prince's ear, or lose his own.
    Yet soft by nature, more a dupe than wit,
Sappho can tell you how this man was bit:
This dreaded satirist Dennis will confess   370
Foe to his pride, but friend to his distress:
So humble, he has knocked at Tibbald's door,
Has drunk with Cibber, nay, has rhymed for Moore.
Full ten years slandered, did he once reply?
Three thousand suns went down on Welsted's lie.[35]
To please a mistress one aspersed his life;
He lashed him not, but let her be his wife.
Let Budgell charge low Grub Street on his quill,
And write whate'er he pleased, except his will,
Let the two Curlls of town and court,[36] abuse   380
His father, mother, body, soul, and muse.
Yet why? that father held it for a rule,
It was a sin to call our neighbor fool;
That harmless mother thought no wife a whore:
Hear this, and spare his family, James Moore!
Unspotted names, and memorable long,
If there be force in virtue, or in song.
    Of gentle blood (part shed in honor's cause,
While yet in Britain honor had applause)
Each parent sprung——A. What fortune, pray?——P. Their own,   390
And better got than Bestia's[37] from the throne.
Born to no pride, inheriting no strife,

33   Hervey ridiculed Pope's deformed back by an illustration in a book he
published.
34   Japhet Crook, a forger.
35   "This man had the impudence to tell in print that Mr. P. had occasioned
a Lady's death, and to name a person he never heard of" (Pope).
36   Budgell, poet and miscellaneous writer, was thought to have forged a will
in order to obtain property; the two Curlls are the bookseller and Hervey.
37   a Roman consul who was bribed to make a dishonorable peace.

Nor marrying discord in a noble wife,
Stranger to civil and religious rage,
The good man walked innoxious through his age.
No courts he saw, no suits would ever try,
Nor dared an oath, nor hazarded a lie.
Unlearn'd, he knew no schoolman's subtle art,
No language but the language of the heart.
By nature honest, by experience wise,   400
Healthy by temperance, and by exercise;
His life, though long, to sickness passed unknown,
His death was instant, and without a groan.
Oh, grant me thus to live, and thus to die!
Who sprung from kings shall know less joy than I.
   O friend! may each domestic bliss be thine!
Be no unpleasing melancholy mine:
Me, let the tender office long engage,
To rock the cradle of reposing Age,
With lenient arts extend a mother's breath,   410
Make Languor smile, and smooth the bed of Death,
Explore the thought, explain the asking eye,
And keep a while one parent from the sky!
On cares like these if length of days attend,
May Heaven, to bless those days, preserve my friend,
Preserve him social, cheerful, and serene,
And just as rich as when he served a Queen!
A. Whether that blessing be denied or given,
Thus far was right—the rest belongs to Heaven.

SAMUEL JOHNSON [1709–1784]

A Short Song
of Congratulation

Long-expected one and twenty,
Lingering year, at last is flown;
Pomp and pleasure, pride and plenty,
Great Sir John,[1] are all your own.

Loosen'd from the minor's tether,
Free to mortgage or to sell,
Wild as wind, and light as feather,
Bid the slaves of thrift farewell.

Call the Bettys, Kates, and Jennys,
Every name that laughs at care,

1 The poem is addressed to the nephew of Henry Thrale, whose wife was a
friend of Johnson.

Lavish of your grandsire's guineas,
Show the spirit of an heir.

All that prey on vice and folly
Joy to see their quarry fly,
Here the gamester light and jolly,
There the lender grave and sly.

Wealth, Sir John, was made to wander,
Let it wander as it will:
See the jockey, see the pander,
Bid them come, and take their fill.

When the bonny blade carouses,
Pockets full, and spirits high,
What are acres? What are houses?
Only dirt, or wet or dry.

If the guardian or the mother
Tell the woes of wilful waste,
Scorn their counsel and their pother,
You can hang or drown at last.

On the Death of Dr. Robert Levet[1]

Condemn'd to hope's delusive mine,
    As on we toil from day to day,
By sudden blasts, or slow decline,
    Our social comforts drop away.

Well tried through many a varying year,
    See LEVET to the grave descend;
Officious,[2] innocent, sincere,
    Of ev'ry friendless name the friend.

Yet still he fills affection's eye,
    Obscurely wise, and coarsely kind;   10
Nor, letter'd arrogance, deny
    Thy praise to merit unrefin'd.

When fainting nature call'd for aid,
    And hov'ring death prepar'd the blow,
His vig'rous remedy display'd
    The power of art without the show.

In misery's darkest caverns known,
    His useful care was ever nigh,

1   Levet, a humble doctor, was a member of Johnson's household of poor
dependents.
2   kind.

Where hopeless anguish pour'd his groan,
  And lonely want retir'd to die.   20

No summons mock'd by chill delay,
  No petty gain disdain'd by pride,
The modest wants of ev'ry day
  The toil of ev'ry day supplied.

His virtues walk'd their narrow round,
  Nor made a pause, nor left a void;
And sure th'Eternal Master found
  The single talent well employed.[3]

The busy day, the peaceful night,
  Unfelt, uncounted, glided by;   30
His frame was firm, his powers were bright,
  Tho' now his eightieth year was nigh.

Then with no throbbing fiery pain,
  No cold gradations of decay,
Death broke at once the vital chain,
  And free'd his soul the nearest way.

THOMAS GRAY [1716–1771]

Elegy
Written in a Country Churchyard

The curfew tolls the knell of parting day,
  The lowing herd wind slowly o'er the lea,
The plowman homeward plods his weary way,
  And leaves the world to darkness and to me.

Now fades the glimmering landscape on the sight,
  And all the air a solemn stillness holds,
Save where the beetle wheels his droning flight,
  And drowsy tinklings lull the distant folds;

Save that from yonder ivy-mantled tower
  The moping owl does to the moon complain   10
Of such, as wandering near her secret bower,
  Molest her ancient solitary reign.

Beneath those rugged elms, that yew-tree's shade,
  Where heaves the turf in many a mouldering heap,
Each in his narrow cell for ever laid,
  The rude forefathers of the hamlet sleep.

3 a reference to the parable of the talents (Matt., xxv, 14–30). The servant
who multiplied the talent (a sum of money) left in his care was praised by
the master; the servant who merely hid the talent safely was blamed.

The breezy call of incense-breathing Morn,
    The swallow twittering from the straw-built shed,
The cock's shrill clarion, or the echoing horn,
    No more shall rouse them from their lowly bed.   20

For them no more the blazing hearth shall burn,
    Or busy housewife ply her evening care:
No children run to lisp their sire's return,
    Or climb his knees the envied kiss to share.

Oft did the harvest to their sickle yield,
    Their furrow oft the stubborn glebe[1] has broke;
How jocund did they drive their team afield!
    How bowed the woods beneath their sturdy stroke!

Let not Ambition mock their useful toil,
    Their homely joys, and destiny obscure;   30
Nor Grandeur hear with a disdainful smile
    The short and simple annals of the poor.

The boast of heraldry, the pomp of power,
    And all that beauty, all that wealth e'er gave,
Awaits alike the inevitable hour.
    The paths of glory lead but to the grave.

Nor you, ye proud, impute to these the fault,
    If Memory o'er their tomb no trophies raise,
Where through the long-drawn aisle and fretted vault
    The pealing anthem swells the note of praise.   40

Can storied urn or animated bust
    Back to its mansion call the fleeting breath?
Can honor's voice provoke the silent dust,
    Or flattery sooth the dull cold ear of death?

Perhaps in this neglected spot is laid
    Some heart once pregnant with celestial fire;
Hands, that the rod of empire might have swayed,
    Or waked to ecstasy the living lyre.

But Knowledge to their eyes her ample page
    Rich with the spoils of time did ne'er unroll;   50
Chill Penury repressed their noble rage,
    And froze the genial current of the soul.

Full many a gem of purest ray serene,
    The dark unfathomed caves of ocean bear:
Full many a flower is born to blush unseen,
    And waste its sweetness on the desert air.

Some village Hampden,[2] that with dauntless breast
    The little Tyrant of his fields withstood;

1   soil.
2   John Hampden opposed Charles I's taxes, which were unconstitutionally
imposed.

Some mute inglorious Milton here may rest,
    Some Cromwell guiltless of his country's blood.   60

The applause of listening senates to command,
    The threats of pain and ruin to despise,
To scatter plenty o'er a smiling land,
    And read their history in a nation's eyes,

Their lot forbade: nor circumscribed alone
    Their growing virtues, but their crimes confined;
Forbade to wade through slaughter to a throne,
    And shut the gates of mercy on mankind,

The struggling pangs of conscious truth to hide,
    To quench the blushes of ingenuous shame,   70
Or heap the shrine of Luxury and Pride
    With incense kindled at the Muse's flame.

Far from the madding crowd's ignoble strife,
    Their sober wishes never learned to stray;
Along the cool sequestered vale of life
    They kept the noiseless tenor of their way.

Yet even these bones from insult to protect,
    Some frail memorial still erected nigh,
With uncouth rhymes and shapeless sculpture decked,
    Implores the passing tribute of a sigh.   80

Their name, their years, spelt by the unlettered muse,
    The place of fame and elegy supply:
And many a holy text around she strews,
    That teach the rustic moralist to die.

For who to dumb Forgetfulness a prey,
    This pleasing anxious being e'er resigned,
Left the warm precincts of the cheerful day,
    Nor cast one longing lingering look behind?

On some fond breast the parting soul relies,
    Some pious drops the closing eye requires;   90
Ev'n from the tomb the voice of Nature cries,
    Ev'n in our ashes live their wonted fires.

For thee, who mindful of the unhonored dead
    Dost in these lines their artless tale relate,
If chance, by lonely contemplation led,
    Some kindred spirit shall inquire thy fate,

Haply some hoary-headed swain may say,
    "Oft have we seen him at the peep of dawn
Brushing with hasty steps the dews away
    To meet the sun upon the upland lawn.   100

"There at the foot of yonder nodding beech
    That wreathes its old fantastic roots so high,

His listless length at noontide would he stretch,
　And pore upon the brook that babbles by.

"Hard by yon wood, now smiling as in scorn,
　Muttering his wayward fancies he would rove,
Now drooping, woeful wan, like one forlorn,
　Or crazed with care, or crossed in hopeless love.

"One morn I missed him on the customed hill,
　Along the heath and near his favorite tree;　　　　　　110
Another came; nor yet beside the rill,
　Nor up the lawn, nor at the wood was he;

"The next with dirges due in sad array
　Slow through the church-way path we saw him borne.
Approach and read (for thou can'st read) the lay,
　Graved on the stone beneath yon agéd thorn."

THE EPITAPH

Here rests his head upon the lap of earth
　A youth to fortune and to fame unknown.
Fair Science frowned not on his humble birth,
　And Melancholy marked him for her own.　　　　　　120

Large was his bounty, and his soul sincere,
　Heaven did a recompense as largely send:
He gave to Misery all he had, a tear,
　He gained from Heaven ('twas all he wished) a friend.

No farther seek his merits to disclose,
　Or draw his frailties from their dread abode,
(There they alike in trembling hope repose)
　The bosom of his Father and his God.

CHRISTOPHER SMART [1722–1771]

from Jubilate Agno[1]

For I bless the PRINCE of PEACE and pray that all the guns may be
　　nail'd up, save such are for the rejoicing days.
For I have abstained from the blood of the grape and that even at
　　the Lord's table.
For I have glorified God in GREEK and LATIN, the consecrated lan-
　　guages spoken by the Lord on earth.
For I meditate the peace of Europe amongst family bickerings and
　　domestic jars.

1　These lines are taken from a fragment of manuscript. Each line beginning
with the word "For" is in some manner a response to a line beginning with
"Let." But, as W. H. Bond has said, Smart "intended the 'Let' and 'For'
sections to be physically distinct." Therefore, I have felt justified in omitting
the corresponding "Let" passage—which is much inferior.

For the HOST is in the WEST—The Lord make us thankful unto salvation.

For I preach the very GOSPEL of CHRIST without comment & with this weapon shall I slay envy.

For I bless God in the rising generation, which is on my side.

For I have translated in the charity, which makes things better & I shall be translated[2] myself at the last.

For he that walked upon the sea, hath prepared the floods with the Gospel of peace.

For the merciful man is merciful to his beast, and to the trees that give them shelter. 10

For he hath turned the shadow of death into the morning, the Lord is his name.

For I am come home again, but there is nobody to kill the calf or to play the musick.[3]

For the hour of my felicity, like the womb of Sarah,[4] shall come at the latter end.

For I shou'd have avail'd myself of waggery,[5] had not malice been multitudinous.

For there are still serpents that can speak—God bless my head, my heart & my heel.

For I bless God that I am of the same seed with Ehud, Mutius Scaevola and Colonel Draper.[6]

For the word of God is a sword on my side—no matter what other weapon a stick or a straw.

For I have adventured myself in the name of the Lord, and he hath mark'd me for his own.

For I bless God for the Postmaster general & all conveyancers of letters under his care especially Allen & Shevlock.[7]

For my grounds in New Canaan shall infinitely compensate for the flats & maynes of Staindrop Moor.[8] 20

For the praise of God can give to a mute fish the notes of a nightingale.

For I have seen the White Raven & Thomas Hall of Willingham & am myself a greater curiosity than both.[9]

For I look up to heaven which is my prospect to escape envy by surmounting it.

For if Pharaoh had known Joseph,[10] he would have blessed God & me for the illumination of the people.

---

2 transformed, conveyed to heaven.
3 a reference to the parable of the Prodigal Son (Luke xv., 11–32).
4 Sarah, wife of Abraham, conceived in old age.
5 joking.
6 Ehud delivered the Israelites by killing the King of Moab; Mutius Scaevola delivered the Romans from tyranny by attempted murder of Porsena. Colonel Draper was a soldier and patron of Smart.
7 Ralph Allen began a system of cross-country posts. George Shevlock was Secretary to the Postmaster General.
8 Staindrop Moor lay adjacent to Raby Castle, the seat of the Vane family. Smart's father had been the Vanes' steward. Maynes: a wide expanse.
9 Albino ravens were displayed as curiosities. Thomas Hall was a "gigantic boy," a freak who died young.
10 The story of Joseph is told in Genesis, xxxvii-l.

For I pray God to bless improvements in gardening till London be a
    city of palm-trees.

For I pray to give his grace to the poor of England, that Charity be
    not offended & that benevolence may increase.

For in my nature I quested for beauty, but God, God hath sent me to
    sea for pearls.

For there is a blessing from the STONE of JESUS[11] which is founded
    upon hell to the precious jewell on the right hand of God.

For the nightly Visitor is at the window of the impenitent, while I
    sing a psalm of my own composing.

For there is a note added to the scale, which the Lord hath made
    fuller, stronger & more glorious.   30

WILLIAM BLAKE [1757–1827]

from Songs of Innocence

Introduction

Piping down the valleys wild,
Piping songs of pleasant glee,
On a cloud I saw a child,
And he laughing said to me:

"Pipe a song about a Lamb!"
So I piped with merry cheer.
"Piper, pipe that song again";
So I piped: he wept to hear.

"Drop thy pipe, thy happy pipe;
Sing thy songs of happy cheer":
So I sung the same again,
While he wept with joy to hear.

"Piper, sit thee down and write
In a book that all may read."
So he vanished from my sight,
And I plucked a hollow reed,

And I made a rural pen,
And I stained the water clear,
And I wrote my happy songs
Every child may joy to hear.

The Lamb

Dost thou know who made thee?
Little Lamb, who made thee?

11   the White Stone of the Apocalypse (Revelations II., 17).

Gave thee life, and bid thee feed
By the stream and o'er the mead;
Gave thee clothing of delight,
Softest clothing, woolly, bright;
Gave thee such a tender voice,
Making all the vales rejoice?
    Little Lamb, who made thee?
    Dost thou know who made thee?

    Little Lamb, I'll tell thee,
    Little Lamb, I'll tell thee:
He is calléd by thy name,
For he calls himself a Lamb.
He is meek, and he is mild;
He became a little child.
I a child, and thou a lamb,
We are calléd by his name.
    Little Lamb, God bless thee!
    Little Lamb, God bless thee!

Holy Thursday

'Twas on a Holy Thursday, their innocent faces clean,
The children walking two and two, in red and blue and green,
Gray-headed beadles walked before, with wands as white as snow,
Till into the high dome of Paul's[1] they like Thames' waters flow.

O what a multitude they seemed, these flowers of London town!
Seated in companies they sit with radiance all their own.
The hum of multitudes was there, but multitudes of lambs,
Thousands of little boys and girls raising their innocent hands.

Now like a mighty wind they raise to heaven the voice of song,
Or like harmonious thunderings the seats of Heavens among.
Beneath them sit the aged men, wise guardians of the poor;
Then cherish pity, lest you drive an angel from your door.

from Songs of Experience

Introduction

Hear the voice of the Bard!
Who Present, Past, and Future sees;
Whose ears have heard
The Holy Word
That walked among the ancient trees,

1 St. Paul's Cathedral in London.

Calling the lapséd Soul,
And weeping in the evening dew;
That might control
The starry pole,
And fallen, fallen light renew!

"O Earth, O Earth, return!
Arise from out the dewy grass;
Night is worn,
And the morn
Rises from the slumberous mass.

"Turn away no more;
Why wilt thou turn away?
The starry floor,
The watery shore,
Is given thee till the break of day."

Earth's Answer

Earth raised up her head
From the darkness dread and drear.
Her light fled,
Stony dread!
And her locks covered with gray despair.

"Prisoned on watery shore,
Starry Jealousy does keep my den:
Cold and hoar,
Weeping o'er,
I hear the Father of the ancient men.

"Selfish Father of men!
Cruel, jealous, selfish fear!
Can delight,
Chained in night,
The virgins of youth and morning bear?

"Does spring hide its joy
When buds and blossoms grow?
Does the sower
Sow by night,
Or the plowman in darkness plow?

"Break this heavy chain
That does freeze my bones around.
Selfish! vain!
Eternal bane!
That free Love with bondage bound."

The Clod
and the Pebble

"Love seeketh not Itself to please,
Nor for itself hath any care,
But for another gives its ease,
And builds a Heaven in Hell's despair."

So sang a little Clod of Clay
Trodden with the cattle's feet,
But a Pebble of the brook
Warbled out these meters meet:

"Love seeketh only Self to please,
To bind another to Its delight,
Joys in another's loss of ease,
And builds a Hell in Heaven's despite."

Holy Thursday

Is this a holy thing to see
In a rich and fruitful land,
Babes reduced to misery,
Fed with cold and usurous hand?

Is that trembling cry a song?
Can it be a song of joy?
And so many children poor?
It is a land of poverty!

And their sun does never shine,
And their fields are bleak and bare,
And their ways are filled with thorns:
It is eternal winter there.

For where'er the sun does shine,
And where'er the rain does fall,
Babe can never hunger there,
Nor poverty the mind appall.

The Sick Rose

O Rose, thou art sick!
The invisible worm
That flies in the night,
In the howling storm,

Has found out thy bed
Of crimson joy:
And his dark secret love
Does thy life destroy.

The Tiger

Tiger! Tiger! burning bright
In the forests of the night,
What immortal hand or eye
Could frame thy fearful symmetry?

In what distant deeps or skies
Burnt the fire of thine eyes?
On what wings dare he aspire?[1]
What the hand dare seize the fire?

And what shoulder, and what art,
Could twist the sinews of thy heart?
And when thy heart began to beat,
What dread hand? and what dread feet?

What the hammer? what the chain?
In what furnace was thy brain?
What the anvil? what dread grasp
Dare its deadly terrors clasp?

When the stars threw down their spears,[2]
And watered heaven with their tears,
Did he smile his work to see?
Did he who made the Lamb make thee?

Tiger! Tiger! burning bright
In the forests of the night,
What immortal hand or eye
Dare frame thy fearful symmetry?

1 fly upward.
2 allusion to the fallen angels who
rebelled against heaven.

London

I wander through each chartered[1] street,
Near where the chartered Thames does flow,
And mark in every face I meet
Marks of weakness, marks of woe.

In every cry of every Man,
In every Infant's cry of fear,
In every voice, in every ban,
The mind-forged manacles I hear.

How the Chimney-sweeper's cry
Every blackening Church appalls;

1 to charter: originally, to grant privileges or concede rights; in commercial
usage, to let or to hire by contract.

And the hapless Soldier's sigh
Runs in blood down Palace walls.

But most through midnight streets I hear
How the youthful Harlot's curse
Blasts the new born Infant's tear,
And blights with plagues the Marriage hearse.

Infant Sorrow

My mother groaned! my father wept.
Into the dangerous world I leapt:
Helpless, naked, piping loud:
Like a fiend hid in a cloud.

Struggling in my father's hands,
Striving against my swaddling bands,
Bound and weary I thought best
To sulk upon my mother's breast.

from Milton

And did those feet in ancient time
Walk upon England's mountains green?
And was the holy Lamb of God
On England's pleasant pastures seen?

And did the Countenance Divine
Shine forth upon our clouded hills?
And was Jerusalem builded here
Among these dark Satanic Mills?

Bring me my Bow of burning gold!
Bring me my Arrows of desire!
Bring me my Spear! O clouds unfold!
Bring me my Chariot of fire!

I will not cease from Mental Fight,
Nor shall my Sword sleep in my hand,
Till we have built Jerusalem
In England's green and pleasant Land.

Never Seek
to Tell Thy Love

Never seek to tell thy love,
Love that never told can be;
For the gentle wind does move
Silently, invisibly.

I told my love, I told my love,
I told her all my heart;
Trembling, cold, in ghastly fears,
Ah! she doth depart.

Soon as she was gone from me,
A traveler came by,
Silently, invisibly:
He took her with a sigh.

ROBERT BURNS [1759–1796]

Holy Willie's Prayer

And send the godly in a pet to pray—POPE.

ARGUMENT

Holy Willie was a rather oldish bachelor elder, in the parish of Mauch-line, and much and justly famed for that polemical chattering which ends in tippling orthodoxy, and for that spiritualized bawdry which refines to liquorish devotion. In a sessional process with a gentleman in Mauchline—a Mr. Gavin Hamilton—Holy Willie and his priest, Father Auld, after full hearing in the Presbytery of Ayr, came off but second best, owing partly to the oratorical powers of Mr. Robert Aiken, Mr. Hamilton's counsel; but chiefly to Mr. Hamilton's being one of the most irreproachable and truly respectable characters in the country. On losing his process, the muse overheard him at his devotions as follows—

O Thou, wha in the Heavens dost dwell,
Wha, as it pleases best Thysel',
Sends ane to heaven and ten to hell,
   A' for Thy glory,
And no for ony guid or ill
   They've done afore Thee!

I bless and praise Thy matchless might,
Whan thousands Thou has left in night,
That I am here afore Thy sight,
   For gifts an' grace   10
A burnin' an' a shinin' light,
   To a' this place.

What was I, or my generation,
That I should get sic° exaltation?   *such*
I, wha deserve most just damnation,
   For broken laws,
Sax° thousand years 'fore my creation,   *six*
   Thro' Adam's cause.

When frae° my mither's womb I fell,   *from*
Thou might hae plunged me in Hell,   20
To gnash my gums, to weep and wail,
            In burnin' lakes,
Where damnéd devils roar and yell,
            Chained to their stakes;

Yet I am here a chosen sample,
To show Thy grace is great and ample;
I'm here a pillar in Thy temple,
            Strong as a rock,
A guide, a buckler, an example
            To a' Thy flock.   30

O Lord, Thou kens° what zeal I bear,   *knows*
When drinkers drink, and swearers swear,
And singin' there and dancin' here,
            Wi' great an' sma':
For I am keepit by thy fear
            Free frae them a'.

But yet, O Lord! confess I must
At times I'm fashed° wi' fleshly lust;   *plagued*
An' sometimes too, in warldly trust,
            Vile self gets in;   40
But Thou remembers we are dust,
            Defiled in sin.

O Lord! yestreen, Thou kens, wi' Meg—
Thy pardon I sincerely beg—
O! may't ne'er be a livin' plague
            To my dishonor,
An' I'll ne'er lift a lawless leg
            Again upon her.

Besides I farther maun° allow,   *must*
Wi' Lizzie's lass, three times I trow°—   *believe*
But, Lord, that Friday I was fou,°   *drunk*
            When I cam near her,
Or else Thou kens Thy servant true
            Wad never steer° her.   *touch*

May be Thou lets this fleshly thorn
Beset Thy servant e'en and morn
Lest he owre high and proud should turn,
            That he's sae gifted;
If sae, Thy hand maun e'en be borne,
            Until Thou lift it.   60

Lord, bless Thy chosen in this place,
For here Thou hast a chosen race;
But God confound their stubborn face,
      An' blast their name,
Wha bring Thy elders to disgrace
      An' public shame.

Lord, mind Gawn Hamilton's deserts,
He drinks, an' swears, an' plays at cartes,
Yet has sae mony takin' arts
      Wi' grit an' sma',   70
Frae God's ain priest the people's hearts
      He steals awa'.

An' when we chastened him therefor,
Thou kens how he bred sic a splore°   *disturbance*
As set the warld in a roar
      O' laughin' at us;
Curse Thou his basket and his store,
      Kail° and potatoes.   *cabbage*

Lord, hear my earnest cry an' pray'r,   80
Against that Presbyt'ry o' Ayr;
Thy strong right hand, Lord, make it bare
      Upo' their heads;
Lord, weigh it down, an' dinna spare,
      For their misdeeds.

O Lord my God, that glib-tongued Aiken,
My very heart and flesh are quakin',
To think how I sat sweatin', shakin,'
      An' pissed wi' dread,
While Auld wi' hingin' lip gaed sneakin',
      An' hid his head.   90

Lord, in the day o' vengeance try him;
Lord, visit them wha did employ him,
And pass not in Thy mercy by them,
      Nor hear their prayer:
But, for Thy people's sake, destroy them,
      And dinna spare.

But, Lord, remember me and mine
Wi' mercies temp'ral and divine,
That I for gear an' grace may shine
      Excelled by nane,   100
And a' the glory shall be Thine,
      Amen, Amen!

To a Mouse
On Turning Her Up in Her Nest, with the Plough, November, 1785

Wee, sleeket,° cowran, tim'rous beastie,   *smooth*
O, what a panic 's in thy breastie!
Thou need na start awa sae hasty,
        Wi' bickering brattle!°   *scurrying hurry*
I wad be laith° to rin an' chase thee,   *loath*
        Wi' murd'ring pattle!°   *spade*

I'm truly sorry Man's dominion
Has broken Nature's social union,
An' justifies that ill opinion,
        Which makes thee startle,   10
At me, thy poor, earth-born companion,
        An' fellow-mortal!

I doubt na, whyles,° but thou may thieve;   *now and then*
What then? poor beastie, thou maun° live!   *must*
A daimen-icker in a thrave°   *occasional ear of corn in a sheaf*
        'S a sma' request:
I'll get a blessin wi' the lave,°   *remainder*
        An' never miss 't!

Thy wee-bit housie, too, in ruin!
It's silly wa's the win's are strewin!   20
An' naething, now, to big° a new ane,   *build*
        O' foggage° green!   *grass*
An' bleak December's winds ensuin,
        Baith snell° an' keen!   *bitter*

Thou saw the fields laid bare an' wast,
An' weary Winter comin fast,
An' cozie here, beneath the blast,
        Thou thought to dwell,
Till crash! the cruel coulter° past   *plough-blade*
        Out thro' thy cell.   30

That wee-bit heap o' leaves an' stibble,
Has cost thee monie a weary nibble!
Now thou 's turn'd out, for a' thy trouble,
        But° house or hald,   *without*
To thole° the Winter's sleety dribble,   *endure*
        An' cranreuch° cauld!   *hoar-frost*

But Mousie, thou art no thy-lane,°   *alone*
In proving foresight may be vain:
The best laid schemes o' Mice an' Men,
        Gang aft agley,°   *often go wrong*
An' lea'e us nought but grief an' pain,   41
        For promis'd joy!

Still, thou art blest, compar'd wi' me!
The present only toucheth thee:
But Och! I backward cast my e'e,
         On prospects drear!
An' forward, tho' I canna see,
         I guess an' fear!

O Whistle, and I'll Come to You, My Lad

O whistle, and I'll come to you, my lad;
O whistle, and I'll come to you, my lad:
Tho' father and mither and a' should gae mad,
O whistle, and I'll come to you, my lad.

But warily tent,° when ye come to court me,   *heed*
And come na unless the back-yett° be a-jee°;   *gate / ajar*
Syne up the back-stile, and let naebody see,
And come as ye were na comin' to me.
And come as ye were na comin' to me.

At kirk,° or at market, whene'er ye meet me,   *church*
Gang° by me as tho' that ye car'd na a flee: *go*
But steal me a blink o' your bonnie black e'e,
Yet look as ye were na lookin' at me.
Yet look as ye were na lookin' at me.

Aye vow and protest that ye care na for me,
And whiles° ye may lightly my beauty a wee°;   *sometimes / little*
But court na anither, tho' jokin' ye be,
For fear that she wyle your fancy frae me.
For fear that she wyle your fancy frae me.

O, My Luve Is Like a Red, Red Rose

O, my luve is like a red, red rose,
    That's newly sprung in June.
O, my luve is like the melodie,
    That's sweetly played in tune.

As fair art thou, my bonnie lass,
    So deep in luve am I,
And I will luve thee still, my dear,
    Till a' the seas gang dry.

Till a' the seas gang dry, my dear,
    And the rocks melt wi' the sun!
And I will luve thee still, my dear,
    While the sands o' life shall run.

And fare thee weel, my only luve,
    And fare thee weel a while!
And I will come again, my luve,
    Though it were ten thousand mile!

WILLIAM WORDSWORTH   [1770–1850]

Lines Composed a Few Miles Above Tintern Abbey

Five years have passed; five summers, with the length
Of five long winters! and again I hear
These waters, rolling from their mountain-springs
With a soft inland murmur. Once again
Do I behold these steep and lofty cliffs,
That on a wild secluded scene impress
Thoughts of more deep seclusion; and connect
The landscape with the quiet of the sky.
The day is come when I again repose
Here, under this dark sycamore, and view   10
These plots of cotttage ground, these orchard tufts,
Which at this season, with their unripe fruits,
Are clad in one green hue, and lose themselves
'Mid groves and copses. Once again I see
These hedgerows, hardly hedgerows, little lines
Of sportive wood run wild; these pastoral farms,
Green to the very door; and wreaths of smoke
Sent up, in silence, from among the trees!
With some uncertain notice, as might seem
Of vagrant dwellers in the houseless woods,   20
Or of some Hermit's cave, where by his fire
The Hermit sits alone.

                These beauteous forms,
Through a long absence, have not been to me
As is a landscape to a blind man's eye;
But oft, in lonely rooms, and 'mid the din
Of towns and cities, I have owed to them,
In hours of weariness, sensations sweet,
Felt in the blood, and felt along the heart;
And passing even into my purer mind,
With tranquil restoration—feelings too   30

Of unremembered pleasure; such, perhaps,
As have no slight or trivial influence
On that best portion of a good man's life,
His little, nameless, unremembered, acts
Of kindness and of love. Nor less, I trust,
To them I may have owed another gift,
Of aspect more sublime; that blessed mood,
In which the burthen of the mystery,
In which the heavy and the weary weight
Of all this unintelligible world,   40
Is lightened—that serene and blessed mood,
In which the affections gently lead us on—
Until, the breath of this corporeal frame
And even the motion of our human blood
Almost suspended, we are laid asleep
In body, and become a living soul;
While with an eye made quiet by the power
Of harmony, and the deep power of joy,
We see into the life of things.

                            If this
Be but a vain belief, yet, oh! how oft—   50
In darkness and amid the many shapes
Of joyless daylight; when the fretful stir
Unprofitable, and the fever of the world,
Have hung upon the beatings of my heart—
How oft, in spirit, have I turned to thee,
O sylvan Wye! thou wanderer through the woods,
How often has my spirit turned to thee!

    And now, with gleams of half-extinguished thought,
With many recognitions dim and faint,
And somewhat of a sad perplexity,   60
The picture of the mind revives again;
While here I stand, not only with the sense
Of present pleasure, but with pleasing thoughts
That in this moment there is life and food
For future years. And so I dare to hope,
Though changed, no doubt, from what I was when first
I came among these hills; when like a roe
I bounded o'er the mountains, by the sides
Of the deep rivers, and the lonely streams,
Wherever nature led—more like a man   70
Flying from something that he dreads than one
Who sought the thing he loved. For nature then
(The coarser pleasures of my boyish days,
And their glad animal movements all gone by)
To me was all in all.—I cannot paint
What then I was. The sounding cataract

Haunted me like a passion; the tall rock,
The mountain, and the deep and gloomy wood,
Their colors and their forms, were then to me
An appetite; a feeling and a love,   80
That had no need of a remoter charm,
By thought supplied, nor any interest
Unborrowed from the eye.—That time is past,
And all its aching joys are now no more,
And all its dizzy raptures. Not for this
Faint I, nor mourn nor murmur; other gifts
Have followed; for such loss, I would believe,
Abundant recompense. For I have learned
To look on nature, not as in the hour
Of thoughtless youth; but hearing often times   90
The still, sad music of humanity,
Nor harsh nor grating, though of ample power
To chasten and subdue. And I have felt
A presence that disturbs me with the joy
Of elevated thoughts; a sense sublime
Of something far more deeply interfused,
Whose dwelling is the light of setting suns,
And the round ocean and the living air,
And the blue sky, and in the mind of man:
A motion and a spirit, that impels   100
All thinking things, all objects of all thought,
And rolls through all things. Therefore am I still
A lover of the meadows and the woods,
And mountains; and of all that we behold
From this green earth; of all the mighty world
Of eye, and ear—both what they half create,
And what perceive; well pleased to recognize
In nature and the language of the sense
The anchor of my purest thoughts, the nurse,
The guide, the guardian of my heart, and soul   110
Of all my moral being.

                    Nor perchance,
If I were not thus taught, should I the more
Suffer my genial spirits to decay:
For thou art with me here upon the banks
Of this fair river; thou my dearest Friend,[1]
My dear, dear Friend; and in thy voice I catch
The language of my former heart, and read
My former pleasures in the shooting lights
Of thy wild eyes. Oh! yet a little while
May I behold in thee what I was once,   120
My dear, dear Sister! and this prayer I make,
Knowing that Nature never did betray
The heart that loved her; 'tis her privilege,

1   his sister Dorothy.

Through all the years of this our life, to lead
From joy to joy: for she can so inform
The mind that is within us, so impress
With quietness and beauty, and so feed
With lofty thoughts, that neither evil tongues,
Rash judgments, nor the sneers of selfish men,
Nor greetings where no kindness is, nor all 130
The dreary intercourse of daily life,
Shall e'er prevail against us, or disturb
Our cheerful faith, that all which we behold
Is full of blessings. Therefore let the moon
Shine on thee in thy solitary walk;
And let the misty mountain winds be free
To blow against thee: and, in after years,
When these wild ecstasies shall be matured
Into a sober pleasure; when thy mind
Shall be a mansion for all lovely forms, 140
Thy memory be as a dwelling place
For all sweet sounds and harmonies; oh! then,
If solitude, or fear, or pain, or grief
Should be thy portion, with what healing thoughts
Of tender joy wilt thou remember me,
And these my exhortations! Nor, perchance—
If I should be where I no more can hear
Thy voice, nor catch from thy wild eyes these gleams
Of past existence—wilt thou then forget
That on the banks of this delightful stream 150
We stood together; and that I, so long
A worshiper of Nature, hither came
Unwearied in that service; rather say
With warmer love—oh! with far deeper zeal
Of holier love. Nor wilt thou then forget,
That after many wanderings, many years
Of absence, these steep woods and lofty cliffs,
And this green pastoral landscape, were to me
More dear, both for themselves and for thy sake!

A Slumber
Did My Spirit Seal

A slumber did my spirit seal;
    I had no human fears;
She seemed a thing that could not feel
    The touch of earthly years.

No motion has she now, no force;
    She neither hears nor sees;
Rolled round in earth's diurnal course,
    With rocks, and stones, and trees.

Composed upon
Westminster Bridge

Earth has not anything to show more fair:
Dull would he be of soul who could pass by
A sight so touching in its majesty:
This city now doth, like a garment, wear
The beauty of the morning: silent, bare,
Ships, towers, domes, theaters, and temples lie
Open unto the fields, and to the sky;
All bright and glittering in the smokeless air.
Never did sun more beautifully steep
In his first splendor, valley, rock, or hill;
Ne'er saw I, never felt, a calm so deep!
The river glideth at his own sweet will:
Dear God! the very houses seem asleep;
And all that mighty heart is lying still!

Resolution
and Independence

1

There was a roaring in the wind all night;
The rain came heavily and fell in floods;
But now the sun is rising calm and bright;
The birds are singing in the distant woods;
Over his own sweet voice the Stock-dove broods;
The Jay makes answer as the Magpie chatters;
And all the air is filled with pleasant noise of waters.

2

All things that love the sun are out of doors;
The sky rejoices in the morning's birth;
The grass is bright with rain-drops;—on the moors   10
The hare is running races in her mirth;
And with her feet she from the plashy earth
Raises a mist; that, glittering in the sun,
Runs with her all the way, wherever she doth run.

3

I was a Traveller then upon the moor;
I saw the hare that raced about with joy;
I heard the woods and distant waters roar;
Or heard them not, as happy as a boy:
The pleasant season did my heart employ:
My old remembrances went from me wholly;   20
And all the ways of men, so vain and melancholy.

4

But, as it sometimes chanceth, from the might
Of joy in minds that can no further go,
As high as we have mounted in delight
In our dejection do we sink as low;
To me that morning did it happen so;
And fears and fancies thick upon me came;
Dim sadness—and blind thoughts, I knew not, nor could name.

5

I heard the sky-lark warbling in the sky;
And I bethought me of the playful hare: 30
Even such a happy Child of earth am I;
Even as these blissful creatures do I fare;
Far from the world I walk, and from all care;
But there may come another day to me—
Solitude, pain of heart, distress, and poverty.

6

My whole life I have lived in pleasant thought,
As if life's business were a summer mood;
As if all needful things would come unsought
To genial faith, still rich in genial good;
But how can He expect that others should   40
Build for him, sow for him, and at his call
Love him, who for himself will take no heed at all?

7

I thought of Chatterton, the marvellous Boy,[1]
The sleepless Soul that perished in his pride;
Of Him who walked in glory and in joy[2]
Following his plough, along the mountain-side:
By our own spirits are we deified:
We Poets in our youth begin in gladness;
But thereof come in the end despondency and madness.

8

Now, whether it were by peculiar grace,   50
A leading from above, a something given,
Yet it befell that, in this lonely place,
When I with these untoward thoughts had striven,
Beside a pool bare to the eye of heaven
I saw a Man before me unawares:
The oldest man he seemed that ever wore grey hairs.

1   Thomas Chatterton (1752–1770) killed himself by taking arsenic.
2   Robert Burns (1759–1796), who tried to make a living at farming, but
succumbed to poverty and illness.

9

As a huge stone is sometimes seen to lie
Couched on the bald top of an eminence;
Wonder to all who do the same espy,
By what means it could thither come, and whence;   60
So that it seems a thing endued with sense:
Like a sea-beast crawled forth, that on a shelf
Of rock or sand reposeth, there to sun itself;

10

Such seemed this Man, not all alive nor dead,
Nor all asleep—in his extreme old age:
His body was bent double, feet and head
Coming together in life's pilgrimage;
As if some dire constraint of pain, or rage
Of sickness felt by him in times long past,
A more than human weight upon his frame had cast.   70

11

Himself he propped, limbs, body, and pale face,
Upon a long grey staff of shaven wood:
And, still as I drew near with gentle pace,
Upon the margin of that moorish flood
Motionless as a cloud the old Man stood,
That heareth not the loud winds when they call;
And moveth all together, if it move at all.

12

At length, himself unsettling, he the pond
Stirred with his staff, and fixedly did look
Upon the muddy water, which he conned,[3]   80
As if he had been reading in a book:
And now a stranger's privilege I took;
And, drawing to his side, to him did say,
"This morning gives us promise of a glorious day."

13

A gentle answer did the old Man make,
In courteous speech which forth he slowly drew:
And him with further words I thus bespake,
"What occupation do you there pursue?
This is a lonesome place for one like you."
Ere he replied, a flash of mild surprise   90
Broke from the sable orbs of his yet-vivid eyes.

14

His words came feebly, from a feeble chest,
But each in solemn order followed each,

3   studied.

With something of a lofty utterance drest—
Choice word and measured phrase, above the reach
Of ordinary men; a stately speech;
Such as grave Livers do in Scotland use,
Religious men, who give to God and man their dues.

15
He told, that to these waters he had come
To gather leeches,[4] being old and poor: 100
Employment hazardous and wearisome!
And he had many hardships to endure:
From pond to pond he roamed, from moor to moor;
Housing, with God's good help, by choice or chance;
And in this way he gained an honest maintenance.

16
The old Man still stood talking by my side;
But now his voice to me was like a stream
Scarce heard; nor word from word could I divide;
And the whole body of the Man did seem
Like one whom I had met with in a dream;   110
Or like a man from some far region sent,
To give me human strength, by apt admonishment.

17
My former thoughts returned: the fear that kills;
And hope that is unwilling to be fed;
Cold, pain, and labor, and all fleshly ills;
And mighty Poets in their misery dead.
—Perplexed, and longing to be comforted,
My question eagerly did I renew,
"How is it that you live, and what is it you do?"

18
He with a smile did then his words repeat;   120
And said that, gathering leeches, far and wide
He travelled; stirring thus about his feet
The waters of the pools where they abide.
"Once I could meet with them on every side;
But they have dwindled long by slow decay;
Yet still I persevere, and find them where I may."

19
While he was talking thus, the lonely place,
The old Man's shape, and speech—all troubled me:
In my mind's eye I seemed to see him pace
About the weary moors continually,   130
Wandering about alone and silently.

4 Leeches were used in medical treatment, for drawing blood.

While I these thoughts within myself pursued,
He, having made a pause, the same discourse renewed.

20

And soon with this he other matter blended,
Cheerfully uttered, with demeanor kind,
But stately in the main; and when he ended,
I could have laughed myself to scorn to find
In that decrepit Man so firm a mind.
"God," said I, "be my help and stay secure;
I'll think of the Leech-gatherer on the lonely moor!"   140

The Solitary Reaper

Behold her, single in the field,
Yon solitary Highland lass!
Reaping and singing by herself;
Stop here, or gently pass!
Alone she cuts and binds the grain,
And sings a melancholy strain;
O listen! for the vale profound
Is overflowing with the sound.

No nightingale did ever chaunt
More welcome notes to weary bands   10
Of travelers in some shady haunt,
Among Arabian sands:
A voice so thrilling ne'er was heard
In springtime from the cuckoo-bird,
Breaking the silence of the seas
Among the farthest Hebrides.

Will no one tell me what she sings?—
Perhaps the plaintive numbers flow
For old, unhappy, far-off things,
And battles long ago: 20
Or is it some more humble lay,
Familiar matter of today?
Some natural sorrow, loss, or pain,
That has been, and may be again?

Whate'er the theme, the maiden sang
As if her song could have no ending;
I saw her singing at her work,
And o'er the sickle bending;—
I listened, motionless and still;
And, as I mounted up the hill   30
The music in my heart I bore,
Long after it was heard no more.

SAMUEL TAYLOR COLERIDGE [1772–1834]

Kubla Khan

In Xanadu did Kubla Khan[1]
   A stately pleasure dome decree:
Where Alph, the sacred river, ran
Through caverns measureless to man
   Down to a sunless sea.
So twice five miles of fertile ground
With walls and towers were girdled round:
And here were gardens bright with sinuous rills,
Where blossomed many an incense-bearing tree,
And here were forests ancient as the hills,   10
Enfolding sunny spots of greenery.

But oh! that deep romantic chasm which slanted
Down the green hill athwart a cedarn cover!
A savage place; as holy and enchanted
As e'er beneath a waning moon was haunted
By woman wailing for her demon lover!
And from this chasm, with ceaseless turmoil seething,
As if this earth in fast thick pants were breathing,
A mighty fountain momently was forced,
Amid whose swift half-intermitted burst   20
Huge fragments vaulted like rebounding hail,
Or chaffy grain beneath the thresher's flail:
And 'mid these dancing rocks at once and ever
It flung up momently the sacred river.
Five miles meandering with a mazy motion
Through wood and dale the sacred river ran,
Then reached the caverns measureless to man,
And sank in tumult to a lifeless ocean:
And 'mid this tumult Kubla heard from far
Ancestral voices prophesying war!   30

      The shadow of the dome of pleasure
      Floated midway on the waves;
      Where was heard the mingled measure
      From the fountain and the caves.
It was a miracle of rare device,
A sunny pleasure dome with caves of ice!

      A damsel with a dulcimer
      In a vision once I saw:
      It was an Abyssinian maid,
      And on her dulcimer she played,   40

1   Kubla Khan founded the Mongol empire in the thirteenth century. Xanadu,
Alph, and Mount Abora are modifications of exotic geographical names that
Coleridge read of in books of travel and exploration.

Singing of Mount Abora.
Could I revive within me
Her symphony and song,
   To such a deep delight 'twould win me,
That with music loud and long,
I would build that dome in air,
That sunny dome! those caves of ice!
And all who heard should see them there,
And all should cry, Beware! Beware!
His flashing eyes, his floating hair!   50
Weave a circle round him thrice,
And close your eyes with holy dread,
For he on honey-dew hath fed,
And drunk the milk of Paradise.

The Rime of
the Ancient Mariner

IN SEVEN PARTS

Facile credo, plures esse Naturas invisibiles quam visibiles in rerum universitate. Sed horum omnium familiam quis nobis enarrabit? et gradus et cognationes et discrimina et singulorum munera? Quid agunt? quae loca habitant? Harum rerum notitiam semper ambivit ingenium humanum, nunquam attigit. Juvat, interea, non diffiteor, quandoque in animo, tanquam in tabula, majoris et melioris mundi imaginem contemplari: ne mens assuefacta hodiernae vitae minutiis se contrahat nimis, et tota subsidat in pusillas cogitationes. Sed veritati interea in vigilandum est, modusque servandus, ut certa ab incertis, diem a nocte, distinguamus.

—*T. Burnet*, Archæol. Phil. *P. 68.*

[I readily believe that there are more invisible than visible beings in the universe. But who will tell us the family, the ranks, the relationships, the differences, the respective functions of all these beings? What do they do? Where do they dwell? The human mind has circled around this knowledge, but has never reached it. Still, it is pleasant, I have no doubt, to contemplate sometimes in one's mind, as in a picture, the image of a bigger and better world; lest the mind, accustomed to the details of daily life, be too narrowed and settle down entirely on trifling thoughts. Meanwhile, however, we must be on the lookout for truth and observe restraint, in order that we may distinguish the certain from the uncertain, day from night.]

ARGUMENT

How a Ship having passed the Line was driven by storms to the cold Country towards the South Pole; and how from thence she made her course to the tropical Latitude of the Great Pacific Ocean; and of the strange things that befell: and in what manner the Ancyent Marinere came back to his own Country.

PART I

An ancient
Mariner meeteth
three Gallants
bidden to a
wedding-feast,
and detaineth
one.

It is an ancient Mariner,
And he stoppeth one of three.
"By thy long gray beard and glittering eye,
Now wherefore stopp'st thou me?

The Bridegroom's doors are opened wide,
And I am next of kin;
The guests are met, the feast is set:
May'st hear the merry din."

He holds him with his skinny hand,
"There was a ship," quoth he.   10
"Hold off! unhand me, graybeard loon!"
Eftsoons[1] his hand dropped he.

The Wedding
Guest is
spellbound by the
eye of the old
seafaring man,
and constrained
to hear his tale.

He holds him with his glittering eye—
The Wedding Guest stood still,
And listens like a three years' child:
The Mariner hath his will.

The Wedding Guest sat on a stone:
He cannot choose but hear;
And thus spake on that ancient man,
The bright-eyed Mariner.   20

The Mariner tells
how the ship sailed
southward with
a good wind and
fair weather, till
it reached the
line.[2]

"The ship was cheered, the harbor cleared,
Merrily did we drop
Below the kirk, below the hill,
Below the lighthouse top.

The Sun came up upon the left,
Out of the sea came he!
And he shone bright, and on the right
Went down into the sea.

Higher and higher every day,
Till over the mast at noon—"   30
The Wedding Guest here beat his breast,
For he heard the loud bassoon.

The Wedding
Guest heareth
the bridal music;
but the Mariner
continueth his
tale.

The bride hath paced into the hall,
Red as a rose is she;
Nodding their heads before her goes
The merry minstrelsy.

1   at once.
2   equator.

The Wedding Guest he beat his breast,
Yet he cannot choose but hear;
And thus spake on that ancient man,
The bright-eyed Mariner.   40

The ship driven by a storm towards the south pole.

"And now the STORM-BLAST came, and he
Was tyrannous and strong:
He struck with his o'ertaking wings,
And chased us south along.

With sloping masts and dipping prow,
As who pursued with yell and blow
Still treads the shadow of his foe,
And forward bends his head,
The ship drove fast, loud roared the blast,
And southward aye we fled.   50

And now there came both mist and snow,
And it grew wondrous cold:
And ice, mast-high, came floating by,
As green as emerald.

The land of ice, and of fearful sounds where no living thing was to be seen.

And through the drifts the snowy clifts
Did send a dismal sheen:
Nor shapes of men nor beasts we ken—
The ice was all between.

The ice was here, the ice was there,
The ice was all around: 60
It cracked and growled, and roared and howled,
Like noises in a swound!

Till a great sea-bird, called the Albatross, came through the snow-fog, and was received with great joy and hospitality.

At length did cross an Albatross,
Thorough the fog it came;
As if it had been a Christian soul,
We hailed it in God's name.

It ate the food it ne'er had eat,
And round and round it flew.
The ice did split with a thunder-fit;
The helmsman steered us through!   70

And lo! the Albatross proveth a bird of good omen, and followeth the ship as it returned northward through fog and floating ice.

And a good south wind sprung up behind;
The Albatross did follow,
And every day, for food or play,
Came to the mariner's hollo!

In mist or cloud, on mast or shroud,[3]
It perched for vespers nine;

3   rope extending from masthead to the side of the ship.

Whiles all the night, through fog-smoke white,
Glimmered the white Moon-shine."

*The ancient
Mariner
inhospitably
killeth the pious
bird of good
omen.*

"God save thee, ancient Mariner!
From the fiends, that plague thee thus!—
Why look'st thou so?"—With my cross-bow
I shot the ALBATROSS.

80

PART II

The Sun now rose upon the right:
Out of the sea came he,
Still hid in mist, and on the left
Went down into the sea.

And the good south wind still blew behind,
But no sweet bird did follow,
Nor any day for food or play
Came to the mariners' hollo!

90

*His shipmates
cry out against
the ancient
Mariner, for
killing the bird
of good luck.*

And I had done a hellish thing,
And it would work 'em woe:
For all averred, I had killed the bird
That made the breeze to blow.
Ah wretch! said they, the bird to slay,
That made the breeze to blow!

*But when the
fog cleared off,
they justify the
same, and thus
make themselves
accomplices in
the crime.*

Nor dim nor red, like God's own head,
The glorious Sun uprist:
Then all averred, I had killed the bird
That brought the fog and mist.
'Twas right, said they, such birds to slay,
That bring the fog and mist.

100

*The fair breeze
continues; the
ship enters the
Pacific Ocean,
and sails north-
ward, even till
it reaches the
Line.*

*The ship hath
been suddenly
becalmed.*

The fair breeze blew, the white foam flew,
The furrow followed free;
We were the first that ever burst
Into that silent sea.

Down dropped the breeze, the sails dropped down,
'Twas sad as sad could be;
And we did speak only to break
The silence of the sea!

110

All in a hot and copper sky,
The bloody Sun, at noon,
Right up above the mast did stand,
No bigger than the Moon.

Day after day, day after day,
We stuck, nor breath nor motion;
As idle as a painted ship
Upon a painted ocean.

And the Albatross begins to be avenged.

Water, water, every where
And all the boards did shrink;   120
Water, water, every where,
Nor any drop to drink.

The very deep did rot: O Christ!
That ever this should be!
Yea, slimy things did crawl with legs
Upon the slimy sea.

About, about, in reel and rout
The death-fires[4] danced at night;
The water, like a witch's oils,
Burned green, and blue and white.   130

A Spirit had followed them; one of the invisible inhabitants of this planet, neither departed souls nor angels; concerning whom the learned Jew, Josephus, and the Platonic Constantinopolitan, Michael Psellus, may be consulted.

And some in dreams assuréd were
Of the Spirit that plagued us so;
Nine fathom deep he had followed us
From the land of mist and snow.

And every tongue, through utter drought,
Was withered at the root;
We could not speak, no more than if
We had been choked with soot.

They are very numerous, and there is no climate or element without one or more.

Ah! well a-day! what evil looks
Had I from old and young!   140
Instead of the cross, the Albatross
About my neck was hung.

The shipmates, in their sore distress, would fain throw the whole guilt on the ancient Mariner: in sign whereof they hang the dead sea-bird round his neck.

PART III

There passed a weary time. Each throat
Was parched, and glazed each eye.
A weary time! a weary time!
How glazed each weary eye,
When looking westward, I beheld
A something in the sky.

The ancient Mariner beholdeth a sign in the element afar off.

At first it seemed a little speck,
And then it seemed a mist;   150

4   phosphorescent light on the ship's rigging, an omen of disaster to sailors.

160

It moved and moved, and took at last
A certain shape, I wist.[5]

A speck, a mist, a shape, I wist!
And still it neared and neared:
As if it dodged a water-sprite,
It plunged and tacked and veered.

*At its nearer
approach, it
seemeth him
to be a ship;
and at a dear
ransom he freeth
his speech from
the bonds of
thirst.*

With throats unslaked, with black lips baked,
We could nor laugh nor wail;
Through utter drought all dumb we stood!
I bit my arm, I sucked the blood,   160
And cried, A sail! a sail!

A flash of joy;

With throats unslaked, with black lips baked,
Agape they heard me call:
Gramercy! they for joy did grin,
And all at once their breath drew in,
As they were drinking all.

*And horror
follows. For
can it be a ship
that comes
onward without
wind or tide?*

See! see! (I cried) she tacks no more!
Hither to work us weal;
Without a breeze, without a tide,
She steadies with upright keel!   170

The western wave was all aflame.
The day was well nigh done!
Almost upon the western wave
Rested the broad bright Sun;
When that strange shape drove suddenly
Betwixt us and the Sun.

*It seemeth
him but the
skeleton of a
ship.*

And straight the Sun was flecked with bars,
(Heaven's Mother send us grace!)
As if through a dungeon-grate he peered
With broad and burning face.   180

*And its ribs are
seen as bars on
the face of the
setting Sun.*

Alas! (thought I, and my heart beat loud)
How fast she nears and nears!
Are those *her* sails that glance in the Sun,
Like restless gossameres?

*The Specter
Woman and her
Deathmate, and
no other on
board the
skeleton ship.*

Are those *her* ribs through which the Sun
Did peer, as through a grate?
And is that Woman all her crew?
Is that a DEATH? and are there two?
Is DEATH that woman's mate?

5   knew.

Like vessel,
like crew!

Her lips were red, *her* looks were free,
Her locks were yellow as gold:

Death and
Life-in-Death
have diced for
the ship's
crew, and she
(the latter)
winneth the
ancient
Mariner.

Her skin was as white as leprosy,
The Night-mare LIFE-IN-DEATH was she,
Who thicks man's blood with cold.

The naked hulk alongside came,
And the twain were casting dice;
"The game is done! I've won! I've won!"
Quoth she, and whistles thrice.

No twilight
within the
courts of the
Sun.

The Sun's rim dips; the stars rush out:
At one stride comes the dark;
With far-heard whisper, o'er the sea,
Off shot the specter bark.

At the rising
of the Moon,

We listened and looked sideways up!
Fear at my heart, as at a cup,
My life-blood seemed to sip!
The stars were dim, and thick the night,
The steersman's face by his lamp gleamed white;
From the sails the dew did drip—
Till clomb above the eastern bar
The hornéd Moon, with one bright star
Within the nether tip.

One after one, by the star-dogged Moon,[6]
Too quick for groan or sigh,
Each turned his face with a ghastly pang,
And cursed me with his eye.

His shipmates
drop down dead.

Four times fifty living men,
(And I heard nor sigh nor groan)
With heavy thump, a lifeless lump,
They dropped down one by one.

But Life-in-Death
begins her work
on the ancient
Mariner.

The souls did from their bodies fly,—
They fled to bliss or woe!
And every soul, it passed me by,
Like the whizz of my cross-bow!

PART IV

The Wedding
Guest feareth
that a Spirit is
talking to him;

"I fear thee, ancient Mariner!
I fear thy skinny hand!
And thou art long, and lank, and brown,
As is the ribbed sea-sand.

6 an omen of evil when a star "dogs the moon."

I fear thee and thy glittering eye,
And thy skinny hand, so brown."—
Fear not, fear not, thou Wedding Guest!   230
This body dropped not down.

Alone, alone, all, all alone,
Alone on a wide wide sea!
And never a saint took pity on
My soul in agony.

The many men, so beautiful!
And they all dead did lie:
And a thousand thousand slimy things
Lived on; and so did I.

I looked upon the rotting sea,   240
And drew my eyes away;
I looked upon the rotting deck,
And there the dead men lay.

I looked to heaven, and tried to pray;
But or ever a prayer had gushed,
A wicked whisper came, and made
My heart as dry as dust.

I closed my lids, and kept them close,
And the balls like pulses beat;
For the sky and the sea, and the sea and the sky   250
Lay like a load on my weary eye,
And the dead were at my feet.

The cold sweat melted from their limbs,
Nor rot nor reek did they:
The look with which they looked on me
Had never passed away.

An orphan's curse would drag to hell
A spirit from on high;
But oh! more horrible than that
Is the curse in a dead man's eye!   260
Seven days, seven nights, I saw that curse,
And yet I could not die.

The moving Moon went up the sky,
And no where did abide:
Softly she was going up,
And a star or two beside—

Her beams bemocked the sultry main,
Like April hoar-frost spread;

and is their appointed rest, and their native country and their own natural homes, which they enter unannounced, as lords that are certainly expected and yet there is a silent joy at their arrival.

But where the ship's huge shadow lay,
The charméd water burnt alway   270
A still and awful red.

Beyond the shadow of the ship,
I watched the water-snakes:
They moved in tracks of shining white,
And when they reared, the elfish light
Fell off in hoary flakes.

By the light of the Moon he beholdeth God's creatures of the great calm.

Within the shadow of the ship
I watched their rich attire:
Blue, glossy green, and velvet black,
They coiled and swam; and every track   280
Was a flash of golden fire.

Their beauty and their happiness.

O happy living things! no tongue
Their beauty might declare:
A spring of love gushed from my heart,

He blesseth them in his heart.

And I blessed them unaware:
Sure my kind saint took pity on me,
And I blessed them unaware.

The spell begins to break.

The self-same moment I could pray;
And from my neck so free
The Albatross fell off, and sank   290
Like lead into the sea.

PART V

Oh sleep! it is a gentle thing,
Beloved from pole to pole!
To Mary Queen the praise be given!
She sent the gentle sleep from Heaven,
That slid into my soul.

By grace of the holy Mother, the ancient Mariner is refreshed with rain.

The silly[7] buckets on the deck,
That had so long remained,
I dreamt that they were filled with dew;
And when I awoke, it rained.   300

My lips were wet, my throat was cold,
My garments all were dank;
Sure I had drunken in my dreams,
And still my body drank.

7   useless (because empty).

I moved, and could not feel my limbs:
I was so light—almost
I thought that I had died in sleep,
And was a blesséd ghost.

*He heareth
sounds and seeth
strange sights
and commotions
in the sky and
the element.*

And soon I heard a roaring wind:
It did not come anear;   310
But with its sound it shook the sails,
That were so thin and sere.

The upper air burst into life!
And a hundred fire-flags sheen,[8]
To and fro they were hurried about!
And to and fro, and in and out,
The wan stars danced between.

And the coming wind did roar more loud,
And the sails did sigh like sedge;
And the rain poured down from one black cloud;   320
The Moon was at its edge.

The thick black cloud was cleft, and still
The Moon was at its side:
Like waters shot from some high crag,
The lightning fell with never a jag,
A river steep and wide.

*The bodies of
the ship's crew
are inspired and
the ship moves
on;*

The loud wind never reached the ship,
Yet now the ship moved on!
Beneath the lightning and the Moon
The dead men gave a groan.   330

They groaned, they stirred, they all uprose,
Nor spake, nor moved their eyes;
It had been strange, even in a dream,
To have seen those dead men rise.

The helmsman steered, the ship moved on;
Yet never a breeze up-blew;
The mariners all 'gan work the ropes,
Where they were wont to do;
They raised their limbs like lifeless tools—
We were a ghastly crew.   340

The body of my brother's son
Stood by me, knee to knee:
The body and I pulled at one rope,
But he said nought to me.

8   gleaming.

"I fear thee, ancient Mariner!"
Be calm, thou Wedding Guest!
'Twas not those souls that fled in pain,
Which to their corses came again,
But a troop of spirits blessed:

But not by the souls of the men, nor by demons of earth or middle air, but by a blessed troop of angelic spirits, sent down by the invocation of the guardian saint.

For when it dawned—they dropped their arms,   350
And clustered round the mast;
Sweet sounds rose slowly through their mouths,
And from their bodies passed.

Around, around, flew each sweet sound,
Then darted to the Sun;
Slowly the sounds came back again,
Now mixed, now one by one.

Sometimes adropping from the sky
I heard the skylark sing;
Sometimes all little birds that are,   360
How they seemed to fill the sea and air
With their sweet jargoning!

And now 'twas like all instruments,
Now like a lonely flute;
And now it is an angel's song,
That makes the heavens be mute.

It ceased; yet still the sails made on
A pleasant noise till noon,
A noise like of a hidden brook
In the leafy month of June,   370
That to the sleeping woods all night
Singeth a quiet tune.

Till noon we quietly sailed on,
Yet never a breeze did breathe:
Slowly and smoothly went the ship,
Moved onward from beneath.

The lonesome Spirit from the south pole carries on the ship as far as the Line, in obedience to the angelic troop, but still requireth vengeance.

Under the keel nine fathom deep,
From the land of mist and snow,
The spirit slid: and it was he
That made the ship to go.   380
The sails at noon left off their tune,
And the ship stood still also.

The Sun, right up above the mast,
Had fixed her to the ocean:
But in a minute she 'gan stir,

166

With a short uneasy motion—
Backwards and forwards half her length
With a short uneasy motion.

Then like a pawing horse let go,
She made a sudden bound: 390
It flung the blood into my head,
And I fell down in a swound.

How long in that same fit I lay,
I have not to declare;
But ere my living life returned,
I heard and in my soul discerned
Two voices in the air.

"Is it he?" quoth one, "Is this the man?
By him who died on cross,
With his cruel bow he laid full low   400
The harmless Albatross.

The spirit who bideth by himself
In the land of mist and snow,
He loved the bird that loved the man
Who shot him with his bow."

The other was a softer voice,
As soft as honey dew:
Quoth he, "The man hath penance done,
And penance more will do."

PART VI

First Voice
"But tell me, tell me! speak again,   410
Thy soft response renewing—
What makes that ship drive on so fast?
What is the ocean doing?"

Second Voice
"Still as a slave before his lord,
The ocean hath no blast;
His great bright eye most silently
Up to the Moon is cast—

If he may know which way to go;
For she guides him smooth or grim.
See, brother, see! how graciously   420
She looketh down on him."

First Voice
"But why drives on that ship so fast,
Without or wave or wind?"

Second Voice
"The air is cut away before,
And closes from behind.

Fly, brother, fly! more high, more high!
Or we shall be belated:
For slow and slow that ship will go,
When the Mariner's trance is abated."

I woke, and we were sailing on   430
As in a gentle weather:
'Twas night, calm night, the moon was high;
The dead men stood together.

All stood together on the deck,
For a charnel-dungeon fitter:
All fixed on me their stony eyes,
That in the Moon did glitter.

The pang, the curse, with which they died,
Had never passed away:
I could not draw my eyes from theirs,   440
Nor turn them up to pray.

And now this spell was snapped: once more
I viewed the ocean green,
And looked far forth, yet little saw
Of what had else been seen—

Like one, that on a lonesome road
Doth walk in fear and dread,
And having once turned round walks on,
And turns no more his head;
Because he knows, a frightful fiend   450
Doth close behind him tread.

But soon there breathed a wind on me,
Nor sound nor motion made:
Its path was not upon the sea,
In ripple or in shade.

It raised my hair, it fanned my cheek
Like a meadow-gale of spring—
It mingled strangely with my fears,
Yet it felt like a welcoming.

The Mariner hath been cast into a trance; for the angelic power causeth the vessel to drive northward faster than human life could endure.

The supernatural motion is retarded; the Mariner awakes, and his penance begins anew.

The curse is finally expiated.

Swiftly, swiftly flew the ship,   460
Yet she sailed softly too:
Sweetly, sweetly blew the breeze—
On me alone it blew.

*And the ancient
Mariner
beholdeth his
native country.*

Oh! dream of joy! is this indeed
The lighthouse top I see?
Is this the hill? is this the kirk?
Is this mine own countree?

We drifted o'er the harbor-bar,
And I with sobs did pray—
O let me be awake, my God!   470
Or let me sleep alway.

The harbor-bay was clear as glass,
So smoothly it was strewn!
And on the bay the moonlight lay,
And the shadow of the Moon.

The rock shone bright, the kirk no less,
That stands above the rock:
The moonlight steeped in silentness
The steady weathercock.

*The angelic
spirits leave the
dead bodies,*

And the bay was white with silent light,   480
Till rising from the same,
Full many shapes, that shadows were,
In crimson colors came.

*And appear in
their own forms
of light.*

A little distance from the prow
Those crimson shadows were:
I turned my eyes upon the deck—
Oh, Christ! what saw I there!

Each corse lay flat, lifeless and flat,
And, by the holy rood!
A man all light, a seraph-man,   490
On every corse there stood.

This seraph-band, each waved his hand:
It was a heavenly sight!
They stood as signals to the land,
Each one a lovely light;

This seraph-band, each waved his hand,
No voice did they impart—
No voice; but oh! the silence sank
Like music on my heart.

But soon I heard the dash of oars,   500
I heard the Pilot's cheer;
My head was turned perforce away
And I saw a boat appear.

The Pilot and the Pilot's boy,
I heard them coming fast:
Dear Lord in Heaven! it was a joy
The dead men could not blast.

I saw a third—I heard his voice:
It is the Hermit good!
He singeth loud his godly hymns   510
That he makes in the wood.
He'll shrieve my soul, he'll wash away
The Albatross's blood.

PART VII

The Hermit of the Wood, This Hermit good lives in that wood
Which slopes down to the sea.
How loudly his sweet voice he rears!
He loves to talk with marineres
That come from a far countree.

He kneels at morn, and noon, and eve—
He hath a cushion plump: 520
It is the moss that wholly hides
The rotted old oak-stump.

The skiff-boat neared: I heard them talk,
"Why, this is strange, I trow!
Where are those lights so many and fair,
That signal made but now?"

Approacheth the ship with wonder. "Strange, by my faith!" the Hermit said—
"And they answered not our cheer!
The planks looked warped! and see those sails,
How thin they are and sere!   530
I never saw aught like to them,
Unless perchance it were

Brown skeletons of leaves that lag
My forest-brook along;
When the ivy-tod⁹ is heavy with snow,
And the owlet whoops to the wolf below,
That eats the she-wolf's young."

9   ivy bush.

170

"Dear Lord! it hath a fiendish look—"
(The Pilot made reply)
"I am a-feared"—"Push on, push on!"   540
Said the Hermit cheerily.

The boat came closer to the ship,
But I nor spake nor stirred;
The boat came close beneath the ship,
And straight a sound was heard.

Under the water it rumbled on,
Still louder and more dread:
It reached the ship, it split the bay;
The ship went down like lead.

Stunned by that loud and dreadful sound,   550
Which sky and ocean smote,
Like one that hath been seven days drowned
My body lay afloat;
But swift as dreams, myself I found
Within the Pilot's boat.

Upon the whirl, where sank the ship,
The boat spun round and round;
And all was still, save that the hill
Was telling of the sound.

I moved my lips—the Pilot shrieked   560
And fell down in a fit;
The holy Hermit raised his eyes,
And prayed where he did sit.

I took the oars: the Pilot's boy,
Who now doth crazy go,
Laughed loud and long, and all the while
His eyes went to and fro.
"Ha! ha!" quoth he, "full plain I see,
The Devil knows how to row."

And now, all in my own countree,   570
I stood on the firm land!
The Hermit stepped forth from the boat,
And scarcely he could stand.

"O shrieve me, shrieve[10] me, holy man!"
The Hermit crossed his brow.
"Say quick," quoth he, "I bid thee say—
What manner of man art thou?"

Forthwith this frame of mine was wrenched
With a woeful agony,

10   shrive: hear confession and grant absolution.

Which forced me to begin my tale;   580
And then it left me free.

Since then, at an uncertain hour,
That agony returns:
And till my ghastly tale is told,
This heart within me burns.

I pass, like night, from land to land;
I have strange power of speech;
That moment that his face I see,
I know the man that must hear me:
To him my tale I teach.   590

What loud uproar bursts from that door!
The wedding guests are there:
But in the garden bower the bride
And bride-maids singing are:
And hark the little vesper bell,
Which biddeth me to prayer!

O Wedding Guest! this soul hath been
Alone on a wide wide sea:
So lonely 'twas, that God himself
Scarce seeméd there to be.   600

O sweeter than the marriage feast,
'Tis sweeter far to me,
To walk together to the kirk
With a goodly company!—

To walk together to the kirk,
And all together pray,
While each to his great Father bends,
Old men, and babes, and loving friends
And youth and maidens gay!

Farewell, farewell! but this I tell   610
To thee, thou Wedding Guest!
He prayeth well, who loveth well
Both man and bird and beast.

He prayeth best, who loveth best
All things both great and small;
For the dear God who loveth us,
He made and loveth all.

The Mariner, whose eye is bright,
Whose beard with age is hoar,

Is gone: and now the Wedding Guest
Turned from the bridegroom's door.

He went like one that hath been stunned,
And is of sense forlorn:
A sadder and a wiser man,
He rose the morrow morn.

GEORGE GORDON, LORD BYRON   [1788–1824]

She Walks in Beauty

She walks in Beauty, like the night
    Of cloudless climes and starry skies;
And all that's best of dark and bright
    Meet in her aspect and her eyes:
Thus mellowed to that tender light
    Which Heaven to gaudy day denies.

One shade the more, one ray the less,
    Had half impaired the nameless grace
Which waves in every raven tress,
    Or softly lightens o'er her face;
Where thoughts serenely sweet express,
    How pure, how dear their dwelling-place.

And on that cheek, and o'er that brow,
    So soft, so calm, yet eloquent,
The smiles that win, the tints that glow,
    But tell of days in goodness spent,
A mind at peace with all below,
    A heart whose love is innocent!

Prometheus[1]

1

Titan! to whose immortal eyes
    The sufferings of mortality,
    Seen in their sad reality,
Were not as things that gods despise;
What was thy pity's recompense?

1   in Greek mythology a Titan—one of the race of giants. Prometheus was
employed by Zeus, ruler of the gods, to make men out of mud and water.
Out of pity for men's suffering Prometheus stole fire from heaven and brought
it to earth. For this he was punished by Zeus who had him chained to
Mt. Caucasus where an eagle fed on his liver.

A silent suffering, and intense;
The rock, the vulture, and the chain,
All that the proud can feel of pain,
The agony they do not show,
The suffocating sense of woe,   10
 Which speaks but in its loneliness,
And then is jealous lest the sky
Should have a listener, nor will sigh
 Until its voice is echoless.

   2
Titan! to thee the strife was given
 Between the suffering and the will,
 Which torture where they cannot kill;
And the inexorable Heaven,
And the deaf tyranny of Fate,
The ruling principle of Hate,   20
Which for its pleasure doth create
The things it may annihilate,
Refused thee even the boon to die:
The wretched gift Eternity
Was thine—and thou hast borne it well.
All that the Thunderer[2] wrung from thee
Was but the menace which flung back
On him the torments of thy rack;
The fate thou didst so well foresee,
But would not to appease him tell;   30
And in thy Silence was his Sentence,
And in his Soul a vain repentance,
And evil dread so ill dissembled,
That in his hand the lightnings trembled.

   3
Thy Godlike crime was to be kind,
 To render with thy precepts less
 The sum of human wretchedness,
And strengthen Man with his own mind;
But baffled as thou wert from high,
Still in thy patient energy,   40
In the endurance, and repulse
 Of thine impenetrable Spirit,
Which Earth and Heaven could not convulse,
 A mighty lesson we inherit:
 Thou art a symbol and a sign
  To Mortals of their fate and force;
 Like thee, Man is in part divine,
  A troubled stream from a pure source;
 And Man in portions can foresee

2   Zeus.

174

His own funereal destiny;
His wretchedness, and his resistance,
And his sad unallied existence:
To which his Spirit may oppose
Itself—an equal to all woes—
   And a firm will, and a deep sense,
Which even in torture can descry
   Its own concentered recompense,
Triumphant where it dares defy,
And making Death a Victory.

from Childe Harold's Pilgrimage, Canto III

17

Stop!—for thy tread is on an Empire's dust![1]
   An Earthquake's spoil is sepulchred below!
   Is the spot marked with no colossal bust?
   Nor column trophied for triumphal show?
   None; but *the moral's truth* tells simpler so.—
   As the ground was before, thus let it be;—   150
   How that red rain hath made the harvest grow!
   And is this all the world has gained by thee,
Thou first and last of Fields! king-making Victory?

18

And Harold stands upon this place of skulls,
   The grave of France, the deadly Waterloo![2]
   How in an hour the Power which gave annuls
   Its gifts, transferring fame as fleeting too!—
   In "pride of place" here last the Eagle[3] flew,
   Then tore with bloody talon the rent plain,
   Pierced by the shaft of banded nations through;   160
   Ambition's life and labours all were vain—
He wears the shattered links of the World's broken chain.

19

Fit retribution! Gaul[4] may champ the bit
   And foam in fetters;—but is Earth more free?

1   The third canto of *Childe Harold's Pilgrimage* was published on November 18, 1816. The battle of Waterloo had been fought on June 18, 1815. In this canto Byron brings his hero to the battlefield, twelve miles south of Brussels; here Byron is addressing both Childe Harold and the reader.
2   At Waterloo the combined armies of Britain and Prussia defeated the French army of Napoleon. The victory was "king-making" in that it restored the Bourbons to the throne of France. Napoleon was banished to St. Helena.
3   The Old Guard, Napoleon's elite battalions, carried standards topped with bronze eagles.
4   Frenchmen.

Did nations combat to make *One* submit?
Or league to teach all Kings true Sovereignty?
What! shall reviving Thraldom again be
The patched-up Idol of enlightened days?
Shall we, who struck the Lion down, shall we
Pay the Wolf homage? proffering lowly gaze   170
And servile knees to Thrones? No! *prove* before ye praise!

20

If not, o'er one fallen Despot boast no more!
In vain fair cheeks were furrowed with hot tears
For Europe's flowers long rooted up before
The trampler of her vineyards; in vain, years
Of death, depopulation, bondage, fears,
Have all been borne, and broken by the accord
Of roused-up millions: all that most endears
Glory, is when the myrtle wreathes a Sword,
Such as Harmodius[5] drew on Athens' tyrant Lord.   180

21

There was a sound of revelry by night,[6]
And Belgium's Capital had gathered then
Her Beauty and her Chivalry—and bright
The lamps shone o'er fair women and brave men;
A thousand hearts beat happily; and when
Music arose with its voluptuous swell,
Soft eyes looked love to eyes which spake again,
And all went merry as a marriage bell;
But hush! hark! a deep sound strikes like a rising knell!

22

Did ye not hear it?—No—'twas but the Wind,   190
Or the car rattling o'er the stony street;
On with the dance! let joy be unconfined;
No sleep till morn, when Youth and Pleasure meet
To chase the glowing Hours with flying feet—
But hark!—that heavy sound breaks in once more,
As if the clouds its echo would repeat;
And nearer—clearer—deadlier than before!
Arm! Arm! it is—it is—the cannon's opening roar!

23

Within a windowed niche of that high hall
Sate Brunswick's fated Chieftain;[7] he did hear   200

5   an Athenian youth, executed in 514 B.C. after assassinating the tyrant
Hipparchus. Hipparchus had insulted Harmodius' sister.
6   On the night of June 15 the Duchess of Richmond gave a ball in Brussels,
attended by officers of the Allied armies. This was on the eve of the battle of
Quatre Bras, which preceded the battle of Waterloo.
7   Frederick William, Duke of Brunswick and nephew of George III, was
killed in the front lines at the battle of Quatre Bras.

That sound the first amidst the festival,
And caught its tone with Death's prophetic ear;
And when they smiled because he deemed it near,
His heart more truly knew that peal too well
Which stretched his father on a bloody bier,[8]
And roused the vengeance blood alone could quell;
He rushed into the field, and, foremost fighting, fell.

24

Ah! then and there was hurrying to and fro—
And gathering tears, and tremblings of distress,
And cheeks all pale, which but an hour ago   210
Blushed at the praise of their own loveliness—
And there were sudden partings, such as press
The life from out young hearts, and choking sighs
Which ne'er might be repeated; who could guess
If ever more should meet those mutual eyes,
Since upon night so sweet such awful morn could rise!

25

And there was mounting in hot haste—the steed,
The mustering squadron, and the clattering car,
Went pouring forward with impetuous speed,
And swiftly forming in the ranks of war—   220
And the deep thunder peal on peal afar;
And near, the beat of the alarming drum
Roused up the soldier ere the Morning Star;
While thronged the citizens with terror dumb,
Or whispering, with white lips—"The foe! They come! they come!"

26

And wild and high the "Cameron's Gathering" rose!
The war-note of Lochiel,[9] which Albyn's[10] hills
Have heard, and heard, too, have her Saxon foes:—
How in the noon of night that pibroch thrills,
Savage and shrill! But with the breath which fills   230
Their mountain-pipe, so fill the mountaineers
With the fierce native daring which instils
The stirring memory of a thousand years,
And Evan's—Donald's[11] fame rings in each clansman's ears!

27

And Ardennes[12] waves above them her green leaves,
Dewy with Nature's tear-drops, as they pass—

8   The Duke of Brunswick's father had been killed at Auerbach in 1806,
fighting against the army of the French Empire.
9   head of the Clan Cameron.
10   Albion, Roman name for Britain, meaning "the white land"—a reference to
the white cliffs.
11   heroes of the clan.
12   forest in Belgium.

Grieving, if aught inanimate e'er grieves,
  Over the unreturning brave,—alas!
  Ere evening to be trodden like the grass
  Which now beneath them, but above shall grow   240
  In its next verdure, when this fiery mass
  Of living Valor, rolling on the foe
And burning with high Hope, shall moulder cold and low.

28

Last noon beheld them full of lusty life;—
  Last eve in Beauty's circle proudly gay;
  The Midnight brought the signal-sound of strife,
  The Morn the marshalling in arms,—the Day
  Battle's magnificently-stern array!
  The thunder-clouds close o'er it, which when rent
  The earth is covered thick with other clay   250
  Which her own clay shall cover, heaped and pent,
Rider and horse,—friend,—foe,—in one red burial blent!

♦

68

Lake Leman[13] woos me with its crystal face,
  The mirror where the stars and mountains view
  The stillness of their aspect in each trace
  Its clear depth yields of their far height and hue:
  There is too much of Man here, to look through
  With a fit mind the might which I behold;
  But soon in me shall Loneliness renew   610
  Thoughts hid, but not less cherished than of old,
Ere mingling with the herd had penned me in their fold.

69

To fly from, need not be to hate, mankind:
  All are not fit with them to stir and toil,
  Nor is it discontent to keep the mind
  Deep in its fountain, lest it overboil
  In the hot throng, where we become the spoil
  Of our infection, till too late and long
  We may deplore and struggle with the coil,   620
  In wretched interchange of wrong for wrong
Midst a contentious world, striving where none are strong.

70

There, in a moment, we may plunge our years
  In fatal penitence, and in the blight
  Of our own Soul turn all our blood to tears,
  And color things to come with hues of Night;
  The race of life becomes a hopeless flight

13   Lake Geneva.

To those that walk in darkness: on the sea
The boldest steer but where their ports invite—
But there are wanderers o'er Eternity
Whose bark drives on and on, and anchored ne'er shall be.   630

71

Is it not better, then, to be alone,
    And love Earth only for its earthly sake?
    By the blue rushing of the arrowy Rhone,
    Or the pure bosom of its nursing Lake,[14]
    Which feeds it as a mother who doth make
    A fair but froward infant her own care,
    Kissing its cries away as these awake;—
    Is it not better thus our lives to wear,
Than join the crushing crowd, doomed to inflict or bear?

72

I live not in myself, but I become   640
    Portion of that around me; and to me
    High mountains are a feeling, but the hum
    Of human cities torture: I can see
    Nothing to loathe in Nature, save to be
    A link reluctant in a fleshly chain,
    Classed among creatures, when the soul can flee,
    And with the sky—the peak—the heaving plain
Of Ocean, or the stars, mingle—and not in vain.

73

And thus I am absorbed, and this is life:—
    I look upon the peopled desert past,   650
    As on a place of agony and strife,
    Where, for some sin, to Sorrow I was cast,
    To act and suffer, but remount at last
    With a fresh pinion; which I feel to spring,
    Though young, yet waxing vigorous as the Blast
    Which it would cope with, on delighted wing,
Spurning the clay-cold bonds which round our being cling.

74

And when, at length, the mind shall be all free
    From what it hates in this degraded form,
    Reft of its carnal life, save what shall be   660
    Existent happier in the fly and worm,—
    When Elements to Elements conform,
    And dust is as it should be, shall I not
    Feel all I see less dazzling but more warm?
    The bodiless thought? the Spirit of each spot?
Of which, even now, I share at times the immortal lot?

14   Lake Geneva is the source of the Rhone River.

75

Are not the mountains, waves, and skies, a part
  Of me and of my Soul, as I of them?
  Is not the love of these deep in my heart
  With a pure passion? should I not contemn   670
  All objects, if compared with these? and stem
  A tide of suffering, rather than forego
  Such feelings for the hard and worldly phlegm
  Of those whose eyes are only turned below,
Gazing upon the ground, with thoughts which dare not glow?

76

But this is not my theme; and I return
  To that which is immediate, and require
  Those who find contemplation in the urn,
  To look on One, whose dust was once all fire,—
  A native of the land where I respire   680
  The clear air for a while—a passing guest,
  Where he became a being,—whose desire
  Was to be glorious; 'twas a foolish quest,
The which to gain and keep, he sacrificed all rest.

77

Here the self-torturing sophist, wild Rousseau,[15]
  The apostle of Affliction, he who threw
  Enchantment over Passion, and from Woe
  Wrung overwhelming eloquence, first drew
  The breath which made him wretched; yet he knew
  How to make Madness beautiful, and cast   690
  O'er erring deeds and thoughts, a heavenly hue
  Of words, like sunbeams, dazzling as they past
The eyes, which o'er them shed tears feelingly and fast.

78

His love was Passion's essence—as a tree
  On fire by lightning; with ethereal flame
  Kindled he was, and blasted; for to be
  Thus, and enamored, were in him the same.
  But his was not the love of living dame,
  Nor of the dead who rise upon our dreams,

15   Jean Jacques Rousseau, French writer (1712–1778), was born at Geneva
in Switzerland. Rousseau has been called the "father of Romanticism" and
"one of the greatest of the 'universal geniuses' in eighteenth-century French
literature." Through his demands for social justice he influenced men's thinking
in the years leading up to the French Revolution. Through his novel, *La
Nouvelle Héloïse,* and other writings in which the rights of the individual are
stressed and the wrongs of society are exposed and in which nature is praised
as the source of all that is good in human character, Rousseau made way for
the Romantic movement. His writings influenced the revolutionary leader
Robespierre, the philosopher Kant, the political writer Tom Paine, and the
poets Schiller, Wordsworth, and Byron. In his last years Rousseau became
suspicious of everyone and lived in poverty and isolation.

But of ideal Beauty, which became   700
  In him existence, and o'erflowing teems
Along his burning page, distempered though it seems.

79

This breathed itself to life in Julie,[16] *this*
  Invested her with all that's wild and sweet;
  This hallowed, too, the memorable kiss
  Which every morn his fevered lip would greet,
  From hers,[17] who but with friendship his would meet;
  But to that gentle touch, through brain and breast
  Flashed the thrilled Spirit's love-devouring heat;
  In that absorbing sigh perchance more blest   710
Than vulgar minds may be with all they seek possest.

80

His life was one long war with self-sought foes,
  Or friends by him self-banished; for his mind
  Had grown Suspicion's sanctuary, and chose,
  For its own cruel sacrifice, the kind,
  'Gainst whom he raged with fury strange and blind.
  But he was phrensied,—wherefore, who may know?
  Since cause might be which Skill could never find;
  But he was phrensied by disease or woe,
To that worst pitch of all, which wears a reasoning show.   720

81

For then he was inspired, and from him came,
  As from the Pythian's mystic cave of yore,[18]
  Those oracles which set the world in flame,
  Nor ceased to burn till kingdoms were no more:
  Did he not this for France? which lay before
  Bowed to the inborn tyranny of years?
  Broken and trembling to the yoke she bore,
  Till by the voice of him and his compeers,
Roused up to too much wrath which follows o'ergrown fears?

82

They made themselves a fearful monument!   730
  The wreck of old opinions—things which grew,
  Breathed from the birth of Time: the veil they rent,
  And what behind it lay, all earth shall view.

16   the heroine of Rousseau's novel, *Julie, ou la nouvelle Héloise* (1761). The
hero of the novel, Saint Preux, Julie's tutor, is drawn chiefly from Rousseau
himself.
17   Comtesse d'Houdetot. Rousseau fell in love with her, but she remained
faithful to a previous lover. As Byron says, Julie in the novel is modeled on the
countess.
18   a cave at Delphi, Greece, presided over by a priestess who gave oracles.
As it was guarded by the serpent Pythos, it was called the Pythian cave.

But good with ill they also overthrew,
Leaving but ruins, wherewith to rebuild
Upon the same foundation, and renew
Dungeons and thrones, which the same hour refilled,
As heretofore, because Ambition was self-willed.

83

But this will not endure, nor be endured!
Mankind have felt their strength, and made it felt.   740
They might have used it better, but, allured
By their new vigor, sternly have they dealt
On one another; Pity ceased to melt
With her once natural charities. But they,
Who in Oppression's darkness caved had dwelt,
They were not eagles, nourished with the day;
What marvel then, at times, if they mistook their prey?

84

What deep wounds ever closed without a scar?
The heart's bleed longest, and but heal to wear
That which disfigures it; and they who war   750
With their own hopes, and have been vanquished, bear
Silence, but not submission: in his lair
Fixed Passion holds his breath, until the hour
Which shall atone for years; none need despair:
It came—it cometh—and will come,—the power
To punish or forgive—in *one* we shall be slower.

85

Clear, placid Leman! thy contrasted lake,
With the wild world I dwelt in, is a thing
Which warns me, with its stillness, to forsake
Earth's troubled waters for a purer spring.   760
This quiet sail is as a noiseless wing
To waft me from distraction; once I loved
Torn Ocean's roar, but thy soft murmuring
Sounds sweet as if a Sister's voice reproved,
That I with stern delights should e'er have been so moved.

from Don Juan,
Canto XI

7

To our theme.[1]—The man who has stood on the Acropolis,
And looked down over Attica; or he   50
Who has sailed where picturesque Constantinople is,
Or seen Timbuctoo, or hath taken tea

1 Byron's hero, Juan, is approaching London for the first time. Juan was born
in Spain. He has been shipwrecked in Greece, sold as a slave to the Turks, has

In small-eyed China's crockery-ware metropolis,
　　Or sat amidst the bricks of Nineveh,
May not think much of London's first appearance—
But ask him what he thinks of it a year hence!

8

Don Juan had got out on Shooter's Hill;
　　Sunset the time, the place the same declivity
Which looks along that vale of Good and Ill
　　Where London streets ferment in full activity,　　　　　60
While everything around was calm and still,
　　Except the creak of wheels, which on their pivot he
Heard,—and that bee-like, bubbling, busy hum
Of cities, that boil over with their scum:—

9

I say, Don Juan, wrapped in contemplation,
　　Walked on behind his carriage, o'er the summit,
And lost in wonder of so great a nation,
　　Gave way to 't, since he could not overcome it.
"And here," he cried, "is Freedom's chosen station;
　　Here peals the People's voice, nor can entomb it　　　　　70
Racks—prisons—inquisitions; Resurrection
Awaits it, each new meeting or election.

10

"Here are chaste wives, pure lives; here people pay
　　But what they please; and if that things be dear,
'T is only that they love to throw away
　　Their cash, to show how much they have a-year.
Here laws are all inviolate—none lay
　　Traps for the traveller—every highway 's clear—
Here"—he was interrupted by a knife,
With—"Damn your eyes! your money or your life!"—　　　　　80

11

These free-born sounds proceeded from four pads
　　In ambush laid, who had perceived him loiter
Behind his carriage; and, like handy lads,
　　Had seized the lucky hour to reconnoitre,
In which the heedless gentleman who gads
　　Upon the road, unless he prove a fighter,
May find himself within that isle of riches
Exposed to lose his life as well as breeches.

---

taken part in the siege of Ismail, and lived at the court of Catherine the Great of Russia, where he was one of the queen's favorites. He is now being sent by Catherine on a diplomatic mission to England, to negotiate a treaty.

12

Juan, who did not understand a word
  Of English, save their shibboleth, "God damn!"   90
And even that he had so rarely heard,
  He sometimes thought 't was only their "Salām,"
Or "God be with you!"—and 't is not absurd
  To think so,—for half English as I am
(To my misfortune), never can I say
I heard them wish "God with you," save that way;—

13

Juan yet quickly understood their gesture,
  And being somewhat choleric and sudden,
Drew forth a pocket pistol from his vesture,
  And fired it into one assailant's pudding—   100
Who fell, as rolls an ox o'er in his pasture,
  And roared out, as he writhed his native mud in,
Unto his nearest follower or henchman,
"Oh Jack! I 'm floored by that 'ere bloody Frenchman!"

14

On which Jack and his train set off at speed,
  And Juan's suite, late scattered at a distance,
Came up, all marvelling at such a deed,
  And offering, as usual, late assistance.
Juan, who saw the moon's late minion bleed
  As if his veins would pour out his existence,   110
Stood calling out for bandages and lint,
And wished he had been less hasty with his flint.

15

"Perhaps," thought he, "it is the country's wont
  To welcome foreigners in this way: now
I recollect some innkeepers who don't
  Differ, except in robbing with a bow,
In lieu of a bare blade and brazen front—
  But what is to be done? I can't allow
The fellow to lie groaning on the road:
So take him up—I 'll help you with the load."   120

16

But ere they could perform this pious duty,
  The dying man cried, "Hold! I've got my gruel!
Oh! for a glass of *max!*[2] We've missed our booty;
  Let me die where I am!" And as the fuel
Of Life shrunk in his heart, and thick and sooty
  The drops fell from his death-wound, and he drew ill

2 gin.

His breath,—he from his swelling throat untied
A kerchief, crying, "Give Sal that!"—and died.

                    17
The cravat stained with bloody drops fell down
    Before Don Juan's feet: he could not tell   130
Exactly why it was before him thrown,
    Nor what the meaning of the man's farewell.
Poor Tom was once a kiddy upon town,
    A thorough varmint, and a *real* swell,
Full flash, all fancy,³ until fairly diddled,
His pockets first and then his body riddled.

                    18
Don Juan, having done the best he could
    In all the circumstances of the case,
As soon as "Crowner's quest"⁴ allowed, pursued
    His travels to the capital apace;—   140
Esteeming it a little hard he should
    In twelve hours' time, and very little space,
Have been obliged to slay a free-born native
In self-defence: this made him meditative.

                    19
He from the world had cut off a great man,
    Who in his time had made heroic bustle.
Who in a row like Tom could lead the van,
    Booze in the ken, or at the spellken hustle?
Who queer a flat? Who (spite of Bow-street's ban)
    On the high toby-spice so flash the muzzle?   150
Who on a lark with black-eyed Sal (his blowing),
So prime—so swell—so nutty—and so knowing?⁵

                    20
But Tom's no more—and so no more of Tom.
    Heroes must die; and by God's blessing 't is
Not long before the most of them go home.
    Hail! Thamis, hail! Upon thy verge it is
That Juan's chariot, rolling like a drum
    In thunder, holds the way it can't well miss,
Through Kennington and all the other "tons,"
Which make us wish ourselves in town at once;—   160

3 flash: knowing . . . fancy: a sport.
4 coroner's inquest.
5 ken: thieves' lodging house . . . spellken: a play house . . . queer a flat: cheat
a simpleton . . . Bow street: the first London police were stationed in Bow
Street . . . high toby-spice: robbery on horseback . . . flash the muzzle: show
off the face, swagger . . . blowing (or blowen): piece . . . nutty: amorous,
fascinating.

21

Through Groves, so called as being void of trees,
    (Like *lucus* from *no* light); through prospects named
Mount Pleasant, as containing nought to please,
    Nor much to climb; through little boxes framed
Of bricks, to let the dust in at your ease,
    With "To be let," upon their doors proclaimed;
Through "Rows" most modestly called "Paradise,"[6]
Which Eve might quit without much sacrifice;—

22

Through coaches, drays, choked turnpikes, and a whirl
    Of wheels, and roar of voices, and confusion;   170
Here taverns wooing to a pint of "purl,"
    There mails fast flying off like a delusion;
There barbers' blocks with periwigs in curl
    In windows; here the lamplighter's infusion
Slowly distilled into the glimmering glass
(For in those days we had not got to gas—);

23

Through this, and much, and more, is the approach
    Of travellers to mighty Babylon:
Whether they come by horse, or chaise, or coach,
    With slight exceptions, all the ways seem one.   180
I could say more, but do not choose to encroach
    Upon the Guide-book's privilege. The Sun
Had set some time, and night was on the ridge
Of twilight, as the party crossed the bridge.

PERCY BYSSHE SHELLEY   [1792–1822]

Song to the Men of England

Men of England, wherefore plough
For the lords who lay ye low?
Wherefore weave with toil and care
The rich robes your tyrants wear?

Wherefore feed, and clothe, and save,
From the cradle to the grave,
Those ungrateful drones who would
Drain your sweat—nay, drink your blood?

6   Juan has driven by Pleasant Row and Paradise Row on the way from
Kennington to Westminster Bridge.

Wherefore, Bees of England, forge
Many a weapon, chain, and scourge,
That these stingless drones may spoil
The forced produce of your toil?

Have ye leisure, comfort, calm,
Shelter, food, love's gentle balm?
Or what is it ye buy so dear
With your pain and with your fear?

The seed ye sow, another reaps;
The wealth ye find, another keeps;
The robes ye weave, another wears;
The arms ye forge, another bears.

Sow seed—but let no tyrant reap;
Find wealth—let no impostor heap;
Weave robes—let not the idle wear;
Forge arms—in your defense to bear.

Shrink to your cellars, holes, and cells;
In halls ye deck another dwells.
Why shake the chains ye wrought? Ye see
The steel ye tempered glance on ye.

With plough and spade, and hoe and loom,
Trace your grave, and build your tomb,
And weave your winding-sheet, till fair
England be your sepulcher.

Similes for Two Political Characters of 1819[1]

1

As from an ancestral oak
  Two empty ravens sound their clarion,
Yell by yell, and croak by croak,
When they scent the noonday smoke
    Of fresh human carrion:—

2

As two gibbering night-birds flit
  From their bowers of deadly yew
Through the night to frighten it,
When the moon is in a fit,
    And the stars are none, or few:—

1 This poem was subtitled "To S — th and C — gh," i.e., Lord Sidmouth and Lord Castlereagh, two prominent politicians who were hated because of their repressive policies.

3

As a shark and dog-fish wait
   Under an Atlantic isle,
For the negro-ship, whose freight
Is the theme of their debate,
    Wrinkling their red gills the while—

4

Are ye, two vultures sick for battle,
   Two scorpions under one wet stone,
Two bloodless wolves whose dry throats rattle,
Two crows perched on the murrained[2] cattle,
    Two vipers tangled into one.

2   Murrain is cattle plague.

Ode to the West Wind

1

O wild West Wind, thou breath of Autumn's being,
Thou, from whose unseen presence the leaves dead
Are driven, like ghosts from an enchanter fleeing,

Yellow, and black, and pale, and hectic red,
Pestilence-stricken multitudes: O thou,
Who chariotest to their dark wintry bed

The wingéd seeds, where they lie cold and low,
Each like a corpse within its grave, until
Thine azure sister of the Spring shall blow

Her clarion o'er the dreaming earth, and fill   10
(Driving sweet buds like flocks to feed in air)
With living hues and odors plain and hill:

Wild Spirit, which art moving everywhere;
Destroyer and preserver; hear, oh, hear!

2

Thou on whose stream, mid the steep sky's commotion,
Loose clouds like earth's decaying leaves are shed,
Shook from the tangled boughs of Heaven and Ocean,

Angels of rain and lightning: there are spread
On the blue surface of thine aery surge,
Like the bright hair uplifted from the head   20

Of some fierce Maenad,[1] even from the dim verge
Of the horizon to the zenith's height,
The locks of the approaching storm. Thou dirge

1   a female attendant of Bacchus, the god of wine.

Of the dying year, to which this closing night
Will be the dome of a vast sepulcher,
Vaulted with all thy congregated might

Of vapors, from whose solid atmosphere
Black rain, and fire, and hail will burst: oh, hear!

3

Thou who didst waken from his summer dreams
The blue Mediterranean, where he lay,   30
Lulled by the coil of his crystálline streams,

Beside a pumice isle in Baiae's bay,[2]
And saw in sleep old palaces and towers
Quivering within the wave's intenser day,

All overgrown with azure moss and flowers
So sweet, the sense faints picturing them! Thou
For whose path the Atlantic's level powers

Cleave themselves into chasms, while far below
The sea-blooms and the oozy woods which wear
The sapless foliage of the ocean, know   40

Thy voice, and suddenly grow gray with fear,
And tremble and despoil themselves: oh, hear!

4

If I were a dead leaf thou mightest bear;
If I were a swift cloud to fly with thee;
A wave to pant beneath thy power, and share

The impulse of thy strength, only less free
Than thou, O uncontrollable! If even
I were as in my boyhood, and could be

The comrade of thy wanderings over Heaven
As then, when to outstrip thy skiey speed   50
Scarce seemed a vision; I would ne'er have striven

As thus with thee in prayer in my sore need.
Oh, lift me as a wave, a leaf, a cloud!
I fall upon the thorns of life! I bleed!

A heavy weight of hours has chained and bowed
One too like thee; tameless, and swift, and proud.

5

Make me thy lyre, even as the forest is:
What if my leaves are falling like its own!
The tumult of thy mighty harmonies

2   near Naples, the site of the palaces of Julius Caesar, Pompey, and Nero.

Will take from both a deep, autumnal tone,   60
Sweet though in sadness. Be thou, Spirit fierce,
My spirit! Be thou me, impetuous one!

Drive my dead thoughts over the universe
Like withered leaves to quicken a new birth!
And, by the incantation of this verse,

Scatter, as from an unextinguished hearth
Ashes and sparks, my words among mankind!
Be through my lips to unawakened earth

The trumpet of a prophecy! O, Wind,
If Winter comes, can Spring be far behind?   70

To a Skylark

Hail to thee, blithe Spirit!
    Bird thou never wert,
That from Heaven, or near it,
    Pourest thy full heart
In profuse strains of unpremeditated art.

Higher still and higher
    From the earth thou springest
Like a cloud of fire;
    The blue deep thou wingest,
And singing still dost soar, and soaring ever singest.   10

In the golden lightning
    Of the sunken sun,
O'er which clouds are bright'ning,
    Thou dost float and run;
Like an unbodied joy whose race is just begun.

The pale purple even
    Melts around thy flight;
Like a star of Heaven,
    In the broad daylight
Thou art unseen, but yet I hear thy shrill delight,   20

Keen as are the arrows
    Of that silver sphere,
Whose intense lamp narrows
    In the white dawn clear
Until we hardly see—we feel that it is there.

All the earth and air
    With thy voice is loud,

As, when night is bare,
    From one lonely cloud
The moon rains out her beams, and Heaven is overflowed.   30

What thou art we know not;
    What is most like thee?
From rainbow clouds there flow not
    Drops so bright to see
As from thy presence showers a rain of melody.

Like a Poet hidden
    In the light of thought,
Singing hymns unbidden,
    Till the world is wrought
To sympathy with hopes and fears it heeded not: 40

Like a high-born maiden
    In a palace-tower,
Soothing her love-laden
    Soul in secret hour
With music sweet as love, which overflows her bower:

Like a glow-worm golden
    In a dell of dew,
Scattering unbeholden
    Its aereal hue
Among the flowers and grass, which screen it from the view!   50

Like a rose embowered
    In its own green leaves,
By warm winds deflowered,
    Till the scent it gives
Makes faint with too much sweet those heavy-wingéd thieves:

Sound of vernal showers
    On the twinkling grass,
Rain-awakened flowers,
    All that ever was
Joyous, and clear, and fresh, thy music doth surpass: 60

Teach us, Sprite or Bird,
    What sweet thoughts are thine:
I have never heard
    Praise of love or wine
That panted forth a flood of rapture so divine.

Chorus Hymeneal,[1]
    Or triumphal chant,

1   marriage song.

Matched with thine would be all
   But an empty vaunt,
A thing wherein we feel there is some hidden want.   70

What objects are the fountains
   Of thy happy strain?
What fields, or waves, or mountains?
   What shapes of sky or plain?
What love of thine own kind? what ignorance of pain?

With thy clear keen joyance
   Languor cannot be:
Shadow of annoyance
   Never came near thee:
Thou lovest—but ne'er knew love's sad satiety.   80

Waking or asleep,
   Thou of death must deem
Things more true and deep
   Than we mortals dream,
Or how could thy notes flow in such a crystal stream?

We look before and after,
   And pine for what is not:
Our sincerest laughter
   With some pain is fraught;
Our sweetest songs are those that tell of saddest thought.   90

Yet if we could scorn
   Hate, and pride, and fear;
If we were things born
   Not to shed a tear,
I know not how thy joy we ever should come near.

Better than all measures
   Of delightful sound,
Better than all treasures
   That in books are found,
Thy skill to poet were, thou scorner of the ground!   100

Teach me half the gladness
   That thy brain must know,
Such harmonious madness
   From my lips would flow
The world should listen then—as I am listening now.

JOHN CLARE [1793–1864]

The Badger

The badger grunting on his woodland track
With shaggy hide and sharp nose scrowed[1] with black
Roots in the bushes and the woods and makes
A great hugh[2] burrow in the ferns and brakes[3]
With nose on ground he runs a awkard pace
And anything will beat him in the race
The shepherds dog will run him to his den
Followed and hooted by the dogs and men
The woodman when the hunting comes about
Go round at night to stop the foxes out[4]   10
And hurrying through the bushes ferns and brakes
Nor sees the many hol[e]s the badger makes
And often through the bushes to the chin
Breaks the old holes and tumbles headlong in

When midnight comes a host of dogs and men
Go out and track the badger to his den
And put a sack within the hole and lye
Till the old grunting badger passes bye
He comes and hears they let the strongest loose
The old fox hears the noise and drops the goose   20
The poacher shoots and hurrys from the cry
And the old hare half wounded buzzes bye
They get a forked stick to bear him down
And clapt[5] the dogs and bore him to the town
And bait him all the day with many dogs
And laugh and shout and fright the scampering hogs
He runs along and bites at all he meets
They shout and hollo down the noisey streets

He turns about to face the loud uproar
And drives the rebels to their very doors   30
The frequent stone is hurled where ere they go
When badgers fight and every ones a foe
The dogs are clapt and urged to join the fray
The badger turns and drives them all away
Though scarcly half as big dimute[6] and small
He fights with dogs for hours and beats them all
The heavy mastiff savage in the fray

1 marked in lines.
2 Clare's spelling of "huge." Clare did not believe in conventional spelling or
punctuation. This text follows his manuscript.
3 thickets.
4 block up the lairs.
5 placed in position.
6 a variant of "diminute," meaning diminished.

Lies down and licks his feet and turns away
The bull dog knows his match and waxes cold
The badger grins and never leaves his hold   40
He drive[s] the crowd and follows at their heels
And bites them through the drunkard swears and reels

The frighted women takes the boys away
The blackguard laughs and hurrys on the fray
He tries to reach the woods a awkard race
But sticks and cudgels quickly stop the chace
He turns agen and drives the noisey crowd
And beats the many dogs in noises loud
He drives away and beats them every one
And then they loose them all and set them on   50
He falls as dead and kicked by boys and men
Then starts and grins and drives the crowd agen
Till kicked and torn and beaten out he lies
And leaves his hold and cackles groans and dies

Some keep a baited badger tame as hog
And tame him till he follows like the dog
They urge him on like dogs and show fair play
He beats and scarcely wounded goes away
Lapt up as if asleep he scorns to fly
And siezes any dog that ventures nigh   60
Clapt like a dog he never bites the men
But worrys dogs and hurrys to his den
They let him out and turn a harrow down
And there he fights the host of all the town
He licks the patting hand and trys to play
And never trys to bite or run away
And runs away from noise in hollow trees
Burnt by the boys to get a swarm of bees

JOHN KEATS [1795–1821]

La Belle Dame
sans Merci[1]

O what can ail thee, knight at arms,
  Alone and palely loitering?
The sedge has withered from the lake,
  And no birds sing.

O what can ail thee, knight at arms,
  So haggard and so woebegone?

1 The Beautiful Lady Without Pity.

194

The squirrel's granary is full,
    And the harvest's done.

I see a lily on thy brow
    With anguish moist and fever dew,   10
And on thy cheeks a fading rose
    Fast withereth too.

I met a lady in the meads,
    Full beautiful, a faery's child:
Her hair was long, her foot was light,
    And her eyes were wild.

I made a garland for her head,
    And bracelets too, and fragrant zone;[2]
She looked at me as she did love,
    And made sweet moan.   20

I set her on my pacing steed,
    And nothing else saw all day long;
For sidelong would she bend and sing
    A faery's song.

She found me roots of relish sweet,
    And honey wild, and manna dew,
And sure in language strange she said,
    "I love thee true!"

She took me to her elfin grot,
    And there she wept and sighed full sore;   30
And there I shut her wild, wild eyes
    With kisses four.

And there she lulléd me asleep,
    And there I dreamed—Ah! woe betide!
The latest dream I ever dreamed
    On the cold hill side.

I saw pale kings, and princes too,
    Pale warriors, death-pale were they all;
Who cried—"La Belle Dame Sans Merci
    Hath thee in thrall!"   40

I saw their starved lips in the gloam,
    With horrid warning gapéd wide,
And I awoke and found me here,
    On the cold hill's side.

And this is why I sojourn here,
    Alone and palely loitering,
Though the sedge is withered from the lake,
    And no birds sing.

2   belt.

Ode to Psyche[1]

O Goddess! hear these tuneless numbers, wrung
   By sweet enforcement and remembrance dear,
And pardon that thy secrets should be sung
   Even into thine own soft-conched[2] ear:
Surely I dreamt to-day, or did I see
   The winged Psyche with awaken'd eyes?
I wander'd in a forest thoughtlessly,
   And, on the sudden, fainting with surprise,
Saw two fair creatures, couched side by side
   In deepest grass, beneath the whisp'ring roof   10
   Of leaves and trembled blossoms, where there ran
      A brooklet, scarce espied:
'Mid hush'd, cool-rooted flowers, fragrant-eyed,
   Blue, silver-white, and budded Tyrian,[3]
They lay calm-breathing on the bedded grass;
   Their arms embraced, and their pinions too;
   Their lips touch'd not, but had not bade adieu,
As if disjoined by soft-handed slumber,
And ready still past kisses to outnumber
   At tender eye-dawn of aurorean love: 20
      The winged boy I knew;
But who wast thou, O happy, happy dove?
      His Psyche true!

O latest born and loveliest vision far
   Of all Olympus'[4] faded hierarchy!
Fairer than Phœbe's sapphire-region'd star,[5]
   Or Vesper,[6] amorous glow-worm of the sky;
Fairer than these, though temple thou hast none,
     Nor altar heap'd with flowers;
Nor virgin-choir to make delicious moan   30
     Upon the midnight hours;
No voice, no lute, no pipe, no incense sweet
   From chain-swung censer teeming;
No shrine, no grove, no oracle, no heat
   Of pale-mouth'd prophet dreaming.

O brightest! though too late for antique vows,
   Too, too late for the fond believing lyre,
When holy were the haunted forest boughs,
   Holy the air, the water, and the fire;

1   Psyche was a nymph who married Cupid, god of love ("the winged boy").
In later mythology the word came to signify the soul.
2   shell-like.
3   purple.
4   a mountain where the Greek gods lived.
5   Phoebe is another name for Diana, goddess of the moon.
6   the evening star.

Yet even in these days so far retir'd   40
   From happy pieties, thy lucent fans,[7]
   Fluttering among the faint Olympians,
I see, and sing, by my own eyes inspired.
So let me be thy choir, and make a moan
     Upon the midnight hours;
Thy voice, thy lute, thy pipe, thy incense sweet
   From swinged censer teeming;
Thy shrine, thy grove, thy oracle, thy heat
   Of pale-mouth'd prophet dreaming.

Yes, I will be thy priest, and build a fane   50
   In some untrodden region of my mind,
Where branched thoughts, new grown with pleasant pain,
   Instead of pines shall murmur in the wind:
Far, far around shall those dark-cluster'd trees
   Fledge the wild-ridged mountains steep by steep;
And there by zephyrs, streams, and birds, and bees,
   The moss-lain Dryads[8] shall be lull'd to sleep;
And in the midst of this wide quietness
A rosy sanctuary will I dress
With the wreath'd trellis of a working brain,   60
   With buds, and bells, and stars without a name,
With all the gardener Fancy e'er could feign,
   Who breeding flowers, will never breed the same:
And there shall be for thee all soft delight
   That shadowy thought can win,
A bright torch, and a casement ope at night,
   To let the warm Love in!

7 wings.
8 wood nymphs.

Ode to a Nightingale

1
My heart aches, and a drowsy numbness pains
   My sense, as though of hemlock I had drunk
Or emptied some dull opiate to the drains
   One minute past, and Lethe-wards[1] had sunk:
'Tis not through envy of thy happy lot,
   But being too happy in thine happiness,—
        That thou, light-winged Dryad[2] of the trees,
          In some melodious plot
Of beechen green, and shadows numberless,
      Singest of summer in full-throated ease.   10

1 Lethe is the river of forgetfulness.
2 wood nymph.

2

O, for a draught of vintage! that hath been
  Cooled a long age in the deep-delved earth,
Tasting of Flora[3] and the country green,
  Dance, and Provençal song, and sunburnt mirth!
O for a beaker full of the warm South,
  Full of the true, the blushful Hippocrene,[4]
    With beaded bubbles winking at the brim,
      And purple-stained mouth;
  That I might drink, and leave the world unseen,
    And with thee fade away into the forest dim: 20

3

Fade far away, dissolve, and quite forget
  What thou among the leaves hast never known,
The weariness, the fever, and the fret
  Here, where men sit and hear each other groan;
Where palsy shakes a few, sad, last gray hairs,
  Where youth grows pale, and specter-thin, and dies;
    Where but to think is to be full of sorrow
      And leaden-eyed despairs,
  Where Beauty cannot keep her lustrous eyes,
    Or new Love pine at them beyond tomorrow.   30

4

Away! away! for I will fly to thee,
  Not charioted by Bacchus[5] and his pards,
But on the viewless wings of Poesy,
  Though the dull brain perplexes and retards:
Already with thee! tender is the night,
  And haply the Queen-Moon is on her throne,
    Clustered around by all her starry Fays;[6]
      But here there is no light,
Save what from heaven is with the breezes blown
    Through verdurous glooms and winding mossy ways.   40

5

I cannot see what flowers are at my feet,
  Nor what soft incense hangs upon the boughs,
But, in embalmed darkness, guess each sweet
  Wherewith the seasonable month endows
The grass, the thicket, and the fruit-tree wild;
  White hawthorn, and the pastoral eglantine;
    Fast fading violets covered up in leaves;
      And mid-May's eldest child,

3   goddess of flowers.
4   a spring sacred to the Muses.
5   god of wine.
6   fairies.

The coming musk-rose, full of dewy wine,
    The murmurous haunt of flies on summer eves.   50

6

Darkling I listen; and, for many a time
    I have been half in love with easeful Death,
Called him soft names in many a muséd rhyme,
    To take into the air my quiet breath;
Now more than ever seems it rich to die,
    To cease upon the midnight with no pain,
        While thou art pouring forth thy soul abroad
            In such an ecstasy!
Still wouldst thou sing, and I have ears in vain—
    To thy high requiem become a sod.   60

7

Thou wast not born for death, immortal Bird!
    No hungry generations tread thee down;
The voice I hear this passing night was heard
    In ancient days by emperor and clown:
Perhaps the self-same song that found a path
    Through the sad heart of Ruth,[7] when, sick for home,
        She stood in tears amid the alien corn;
            The same that oft-times hath
Charmed magic casements, opening on the foam
    Of perilous seas, in faery lands forlorn.   70

8

Forlorn! the very word is like a bell
    To toll me back from thee to my sole self!
Adieu! the fancy cannot cheat so well
    As she is famed to do, deceiving elf.
Adieu! adieu! thy plaintive anthem fades
    Past the near meadows, over the still stream,
        Up the hill-side; and now 'tis buried deep
            In the next valley-glades:
Was it a vision, or a waking dream?
    Fled is that music:—Do I wake or sleep?   80

Ode on a Grecian Urn

1

Thou still unravished bride of quietness,
    Thou foster child of silence and slow time,

7   After her husband's death, Ruth left her native land and lived in Palestine
with her mother-in-law Naomi. See the Book of Ruth in the Old Testament.

Sylvan historian, who canst thus express
 A flowery tale more sweetly than our rhyme:
What leaf-fringed legend haunts about thy shape
 Of deities or mortals, or of both,
  In Tempe or the dales of Arcady?[1]
 What men or gods are these? What maidens loth?
What mad pursuit? What struggle to escape?
  What pipes and timbrels? What wild ecstasy? 10

2

Heard melodies are sweet, but those unheard
 Are sweeter; therefore, ye soft pipes, play on;
Not to the sensual ear, but, more endeared,
 Pipe to the spirit ditties of no tone:
Fair youth, beneath the trees, thou canst not leave
 Thy song, nor ever can those trees be bare;
 Bold Lover, never, never canst thou kiss,
Though winning near the goal—yet, do not grieve;
 She cannot fade, though thou hast not thy bliss,
  For ever wilt thou love, and she be fair! 20

3

Ah, happy, happy boughs! that cannot shed
 Your leaves, nor ever bid the Spring adieu;
And, happy melodist, unwearied,
 For ever piping songs for ever new;
More happy love! more happy, happy love!
 For ever warm and still to be enjoyed,
  For ever panting, and for ever young,
All breathing human passion far above,
 That leaves a heart high-sorrowful and cloyed,
  A burning forehead, and a parching tongue. 30

4

Who are these coming to the sacrifice?
 To what green altar, O mysterious priest,
Lead'st thou that heifer lowing at the skies,
 And all her silken flanks with garlands drest?
What little town by river or sea shore,
 Or mountain-built with peaceful citadel,
  Is emptied of this folk, this pious morn?
And, little town, thy streets for evermore
 Will silent be; and not a soul to tell
  Why thou art desolate, can e'er return. 40

1 Tempe is a valley sacred to Apollo, god of music and poetry. Arcady is a
region in Greece frequently presented as an idyllic pastoral scene.

5

O Attic[2] shape! Fair attitude! with brede[3]
　Of marble men and maidens overwrought,
With forest branches and the trodden weed;
　Thou, silent form, dost tease us out of thought
As doth eternity: Cold Pastoral!
　When old age shall this generation waste,
　　Thou shalt remain, in midst of other woe
Than ours, a friend to man, to whom thou say'st,
　"Beauty is truth, truth beauty,"—that is all
　　Ye know on earth, and all ye need to know.　　　　50

2　belonging to Attica, or ancient Athens, and connoting elegance.
3　embroidery.

This Living Hand

This living hand, now warm and capable
Of earnest grasping, would, if it were cold
And in the icy silence of the tomb,
So haunt thy days and chill thy dreaming nights
That thou wouldst wish thine own heart dry of blood
So in my veins red life might stream again,
And thou be conscience-calm'd—see here it is—
I hold it towards you.

Bright Star

Bright star, would I were steadfast as thou art—
Not in lone splendor hung aloft the night,
And watching, with eternal lids apart,
Like nature's patient sleepless Eremite,[1]
The moving waters at their priestlike task
Of pure ablution round earth's human shores,
Or gazing on the new soft fallen mask
Of snow upon the mountains and the moors:
No—yet still steadfast, still unchangeable,
Pillowed upon my fair love's ripening breast
To feel for ever its soft fall and swell,
Awake for ever in a sweet unrest;
Still, still to hear her tender-taken breath,
And so live ever—or else swoon to death.

1　hermit.

ELIZABETH BARRETT BROWNING [1806–1861]

43 How Do I Love Thee?

How do I love thee? Let me count the ways.
I love thee to the depth and breadth and height
My soul can reach, when feeling out of sight
For the ends of Being and ideal Grace.
I love thee to the level of every day's
Most quiet need, by sun and candle light.
I love thee freely, as men strive for right;
I love thee purely, as they turn from praise.
I love thee with the passion put to use
In my old griefs, and with my childhood's faith.
I love thee with a love I seemed to lose
With my lost saints!—I love thee with the breath,
Smiles, tears, of all my life—and, if God choose,
I shall but love thee better after death.

EDGAR ALLAN POE [1809–1849]

To Helen[1]

Helen, thy beauty is to me
    Like those Nicean[2] barks of yore
That gently, o'er a perfumed sea,
    The weary way-worn wanderer bore
    To his own native shore.

On desperate seas long wont to roam,
    Thy hyacinth hair, thy classic face,
Thy Naiad[3] airs have brought me home
    To the glory that was Greece,
And the grandeur that was Rome.

Lo, in yon brilliant window-niche
    How statue-like I see thee stand,
    The agate lamp within thy hand,
Ah! Psyche,[4] from the regions which
    Are holy land!

1   Helen of Troy.
2   pertaining to Nicaea, an ancient city in Asia Minor.
3   water nymph.
4   a beautiful princess with whom Cupid fell in love.

Mariana[1]

Mariana in the moated grange (Measure for Measure)

With blackest moss the flower-plots
  Were thickly crusted, one and all:
The rusted nails fell from the knots
  That held the pear to the gable-wall.
The broken sheds looked sad and strange:
  Unlifted was the clinking latch;
  Weeded and worn the ancient thatch
Upon the lonely moated grange.
    She only said, "My life is dreary,
      He cometh not," she said;   10
    She said, "I am aweary, aweary,
      I would that I were dead!"

Her tears fell with the dews at even;
  Her tears fell ere the dews were dried;
She could not look on the sweet heaven,
  Either at morn or eventide.
After the flitting of the bats,
  When thickest dark did trance the sky,
  She drew her casement-curtain by,
And glanced athwart the glooming flats.   20
    She only said, "The night is dreary,
      He cometh not," she said;
    She said, "I am aweary, aweary,
      I would that I were dead!"

Upon the middle of the night,
  Waking she heard the night-fowl crow:
The cock sung out an hour ere light:
  From the dark fen the oxen's low
Came to her: without hope of change,
  In sleep she seemed to walk forlorn,   30
  Till cold winds woke the gray-eyed morn
About the lonely moated grange.
    She only said, "The day is dreary,
      He cometh not," she said;
    She said, "I am aweary, aweary,
      I would that I were dead!"

About a stone-cast from the wall
  A sluice with blackened waters slept,

1 Mariana, a character in Shakespeare's *Measure for Measure,* had been jilted
by Angelo and lived in great unhappiness in the "moated grange." A grange is
an isolated farmhouse.

And o'er it many, round and small,
    The clustered marish²-mosses crept.   40
Hard by a poplar shook alway,
    All silver-green with gnarlèd bark:
For leagues no other tree did mark
The level waste, the rounding gray.
        She only said, "My life is dreary,
          He cometh not," she said;
        She said, "I am aweary, aweary,
          I would that I were dead!"

And ever when the moon was low,
    And the shrill winds were up and away,   50
In the white curtain, to and fro,
    She saw the gusty shadow sway.
But when the moon was very low,
    And wild winds bound within their cell,
    The shadow of the poplar fell
Upon her bed, across her brow.
        She only said, "The night is dreary,
          He cometh not," she said;
        She said, "I am aweary, aweary,
          I would that I were dead!"   60

All day within the dreamy house,
    The doors upon their hinges creaked;
The blue fly sung in the pane; the mouse
    Behind the mouldering wainscot shrieked,
Or from the crevice peered about.
    Old faces glimmered through the doors,
    Old footsteps trod the upper floors,
Old voices called her from without.
        She only said, "My life is dreary,
          He cometh not," she said;   70
        She said, "I am aweary, aweary,
          I would that I were dead!"

The sparrow's chirrup on the roof,
    The slow clock ticking, and the sound
Which to the wooing wind aloof
    The poplar made, did all confound
Her sense; but most she loathed the hour
    When the thick-moted sunbeam lay
    Athwart the chambers, and the day
Was sloping toward his western bower.   80
        Then, said she, "I am very dreary,
          He will not come," she said;
        She wept, "I am aweary, aweary,
          Oh God, that I were dead!"

2   marsh.

Ulysses

It little profits that an idle king,
By this still hearth, among these barren crags,
Matched with an aged wife, I mete and dole
Unequal laws unto a savage race,
That hoard, and sleep, and feed, and know not me.
I cannot rest from travel: I will drink
Life to the lees: all times I have enjoyed
Greatly, have suffered greatly, both with those
That loved me, and alone; on shore, and when
Through scudding drifts the rainy Hyades[1]   10
Vext the dim sea. I am become a name;
For always roaming with a hungry heart
Much have I seen and known: cities of men
And manners, climates, councils, governments,
Myself not least, but honored of them all,—
And drunk delight of battle with my peers,
Far on the ringing plains of windy Troy.
I am a part of all that I have met;
Yet all experience is an arch wherethrough
Gleams that untraveled world, whose margin fades   20
For ever and for ever when I move.
How dull it is to pause, to make an end,
To rust unburnished, not to shine in use!
As though to breathe were life. Life piled on life
Were all too little, and of one to me
Little remains: but every hour is saved
From that eternal silence, something more,
A bringer of new things; and vile it were
For some three suns to store and hoard myself,
And this gray spirit yearning in desire   30
To follow knowledge, like a sinking star,
Beyond the utmost bound of human thought.

    This is my son, mine own Telemachus,
To whom I leave the scepter and the isle—
Well-loved of me, discerning to fulfill
This labor, by slow prudence to make mild
A rugged people, and through soft degrees
Subdue them to the useful and the good.
Most blameless is he, centered in the sphere
Of common duties, decent not to fail   40
In offices of tenderness, and pay
Meet adoration to my household gods,
When I am gone. He works his work, I mine.

    There lies the port: the vessel puffs her sail:
There gloom the dark broad seas. My mariners,
Souls that have toiled, and wrought, and thought with me—
That ever with a frolic welcome took

1   a group of stars believed to bring rain.

The thunder and the sunshine, and opposed
Free hearts, free foreheads—you and I are old;
Old age hath yet his honor and his toil; 50
Death closes all: but something ere the end,
Some work of noble note, may yet be done,
Not unbecoming men that strove with Gods.
The lights begin to twinkle from the rocks:
The long day wanes: the slow moon climbs: the deep
Moans round with many voices. Come, my friends,
'Tis not too late to seek a newer world.
Push off, and sitting well in order smite
The sounding furrows; for my purpose holds
To sail beyond the sunset, and the baths 60
Of all the western stars, until I die.
It may be that the gulfs will wash us down:
It may be we shall touch the Happy Isles,[2]
And see the great Achilles, whom we knew.
Though much is taken, much abides; and though
We are not now that strength which in old days
Moved earth and heaven, that which we are, we are,—
One equal temper of heroic hearts,
Made weak by time and fate, but strong in will
To strive, to seek, to find, and not to yield. 70

Tears, Idle Tears

Tears, idle tears, I know not what they mean,
Tears from the depth of some divine despair
Rise in the heart, and gather to the eyes,
In looking on the happy autumn-fields,
And thinking of the days that are no more.

Fresh as the first beam glittering on a sail,
That brings our friends up from the underworld,
Sad as the last which reddens over one
That sinks with all we love below the verge;
So sad, so fresh, the days that are no more.

Ah, sad and strange as in dark summer dawns
The earliest pipe of half-awakened birds
To dying ears, when unto dying eyes
The casement slowly grows a glimmering square;
So sad, so strange, the days that are no more.

Dear as remembered kisses after death,
And sweet as those by hopeless fancy feigned
On lips that are for others; deep as love,
Deep as first love, and wild with all regret;
O Death in Life, the days that are no more!

2   the home of the blessed after death.

"Frater Ave Atque Vale"[1]

Row us out from Desenzano, to your Sirmione[2] row!
So they rowed, and there we landed—"O venusta Sirmio!"[3]
There to me through all the groves of olive in the summer glow,
There beneath the Roman ruin where the purple flowers grow,
Came that "Ave atque Vale" of the poet's hopeless woe,
Tenderest of Roman poets nineteen hundred years ago,
"Frater Ave atque Vale"—as we wandered to and fro
Gazing at the Lydian[4] laughter of the Garda Lake below
Sweet Catullus's all-but-island, olive-silvery Sirmio!

ROBERT BROWNING [1812–1889]

My Last Duchess

Ferrara

That's my last Duchess painted on the wall,
Looking as if she were alive. I call
That piece a wonder, now: Frà Pandolf's hands
Worked busily a day, and there she stands.
Will't please you sit and look at her? I said
"Frà Pandolf" by design, for never read
Strangers like you that pictured countenance,
The depth and passion of its earnest glance,
But to myself they turned (since none puts by
The curtain I have drawn for you, but I)   10
And seemed as they would ask me, if they durst,
How such a glance came there; so, not the first
Are you to turn and ask thus. Sir, 'twas not
Her husband's presence only, called that spot
Of joy into the Duchess' cheek; perhaps
Frà Pandolf chanced to say, "Her mantle laps
Over my lady's wrist too much," or "Paint
Must never hope to reproduce the faint
Half-flush that dies along her throat": such stuff
Was courtesy, she thought, and cause enough   20
For calling up that spot of joy. She had
A heart—how shall I say?—too soon made glad,

1   "Brother, Hail and Farewell," a quotation from Catullus, a Latin poet of
the first century B.C. Catullus' poem is a last farewell to his brother.
2   Desenzano is a town on Lake Garda in northern Italy. Sirmione, known as
Sirmio in antiquity, is the peninsula on Lake Garda where the villa of Catullus
once stood.
3   "O beautiful Sirmio," a quotation from Catullus.
4   The Etruscans, who lived near Lake Garda, were believed to have come from
Lydia in Asia Minor.

Too easily impressed: she liked whate'er
She looked on, and her looks went everywhere.
Sir, 'twas all one! My favor at her breast,
The dropping of the daylight in the West,
The bough of cherries some officious fool
Broke in the orchard for her, the white mule
She rode with round the terrace—all and each
Would draw from her alike the approving speech,   30
Or blush, at least. She thanked men,—good! but thanked
Somehow—I know not how—as if she ranked
My gift of a nine-hundred-years-old name
With anybody's gift. Who'd stoop to blame
This sort of trifling? Even had you skill
In speech—(which I have not)—to make your will
Quite clear to such an one, and say, "Just this
Or that in you disgusts me; here you miss,
Or there exceed the mark"—and if she let
Herself be lessoned so, nor plainly set   40
Her wits to yours, forsooth, and made excuse,
—E'en then would be some stooping; and I choose
Never to stoop. Oh sir, she smiled, no doubt,
Whene'er I passed her; but who passed without
Much the same smile? This grew; I gave commands;
Then all smiles stopped together. There she stands
As if alive. Will't please you rise? We'll meet
The company below, then. I repeat,
The Count your master's known munificence
Is ample warrant that no just pretence   50
Of mine for dowry will be disallowed;
Though his fair daughter's self, as I avowed
At starting, is my object. Nay, we'll go
Together down, sir. Notice Neptune, though,
Taming a sea-horse, thought a rarity,
Which Claus of Innsbruck cast in bronze for me!

Meeting at Night

The gray sea and the long black land;
And the yellow half-moon large and low;
And the startled little waves that leap
In fiery ringlets from their sleep,
As I gain the cove with pushing prow,
And quench its speed i' the slushy sand.

Then a mile of warm sea-scented beach;
Three fields to cross till a farm appears;
A tap at the pane, the quick sharp scratch

And blue spurt of a lighted match,
And a voice less loud, through its joys and fears,
Than the two hearts beating each to each!

A Likeness

Some people hang portraits up
In a room where they dine or sup:
And the wife clinks tea things under,
And her cousin, he stirs his cup,
Asks, "Who was the lady, I wonder?"
" 'Tis a daub John bought at a sale,"
Quoth the wife—looks black as thunder:
"What a shade beneath her nose!
Snuff-taking, I suppose—"
Adds the cousin, while John's corns ail.   10

Or else, there's no wife in the case,
But the portrait's queen of the place,
Alone mid the other spoils
Of youth—masks, gloves and foils,
And pipe sticks, rose, cherry tree, jasmine,
And the long whip, the tandem-lasher,
And the cast from a fist ("not, alas! mine,
But my master's, the Tipton Slasher")
And the cards where pistol balls mark ace,
And a satin shoe used for cigar case,   20
And the chamois horns ("shot in the Chablais")
And prints—Rarey drumming on Cruiser,
And Sayers, our champion, the bruiser,
And the little edition of Rabelais:
Where a friend, with both hands in his pockets,
May saunter up close to examine it,
And remark a good deal of Jane Lamb in it,
"But the eyes are half out of their sockets;
That hair's not so bad, where the gloss is,
But they've made the girl's nose a proboscis: 30
Jane Lamb, that we danced with at Vichy!
What, is not she Jane? Then, who is she?"

All that I own is a print,
An etching, a mezzotint;
'Tis a study, a fancy, a fiction,
Yet a fact (take my conviction)
Because it has more than a hint
Of a certain face, I never
Saw elsewhere touch or trace of

In women I've seen the face of: 40
Just an etching, and, so far, clever.

I keep my prints, an imbroglio,
Fifty in one portfolio.
When somebody tries my claret,
We turn round chairs to the fire,
Chirp over days in a garret,
Chuckle o'er increase of salary,
Taste the good fruits of our leisure,
Talk about pencil and lyre,
And the National Portrait Gallery: 50
Then I exhibit my treasure.
After we've turned over twenty,
And the debt of wonder my crony owes
Is paid to my Marc Antonios,
He stops me—"*Festina lentè!*[1]
What's that sweet thing there, the etching?"
How my waistcoat-strings want stretching,
How my cheeks grow red as tomatoes,
How my heart leaps! But hearts, after leaps, ache.

"By the by, you must take, for a keepsake, 60
That other, you praised, of Volpato's."

The fool! would he try a flight further and say
He never saw, never before to-day,
What was able to take his breath away,
A face to lose youth for, to occupy age
With the dream of, meet death with—why, I'll not engage
But that, half in a rapture and half in a rage,
I should toss him the thing's self—" 'Tis only a duplicate,
A thing of no value! Take it, I supplicate!"

1   "Make haste slowly."

"*De Gustibus* ——"[1]

1

Your ghost will walk, you lover of trees,
    (If our loves remain)
    In an English lane,
By a cornfield-side a-flutter with poppies.
Hark, those two in the hazel coppice—

1   The full quotation is "De gustibus et de coloribus non est disputandum,"
a Latin proverb meaning "There is no arguing over tastes and colors."

A boy and a girl, if the good fates please,
    Making love, say,—
    The happier they!
Draw yourself up from the light of the moon,
And let them pass, as they will too soon,   10
    With the bean-flowers' boon,
    And the blackbird's tune,
    And May, and June!

2

What I love best in all the world
Is a castle, precipice-encurled,
In a gash of the wind-grieved Apennine.[2]
Or look for me, old fellow of mine,
(If I get my head from out the mouth
O' the grave, and loose my spirit's bands,
And come again to the land of lands)—   20
In a sea-side house to the farther South,
Where the baked cicala[3] dies of drouth,
And one sharp tree—'tis a cypress—stands,
By the many hundred years red-rusted,
Rough iron-spiked, ripe fruit-o'ercrusted,
My sentinel to guard the sands
To the water's edge. For, what expands
Before the house, but the great opaque
Blue breadth of sea without a break?
While, in the house, for ever crumbles   30
Some fragment of the frescoed walls,
From blisters where a scorpion sprawls.
A girl bare-footed brings, and tumbles
Down on the pavement, green-flesh melons,
And says there 's news to-day—the king
Was shot at, touched in the liver-wing,[4]
Goes with his Bourbon arm in a sling:
—She hopes they have not caught the felons.
Italy, my Italy!
Queen Mary's saying serves for me—   40
    (When fortune's malice
    Lost her—Calais)—
Open my heart and you will see
Graved inside of it, "Italy."
Such lovers old are I and she:
So it always was, so shall ever be!

2   The Apennines are mountains in Italy.
3   The cicala, or cicada, is a large chirping insect common in southern Europe.
4   the right wing of a bird, i.e., the one which encloses the liver.

EDWARD LEAR   [1812–1888]

By Way
of Preface

"How pleasant to know Mr. Lear!"
   Who has written such volumes of stuff!
Some think him ill-tempered and queer,
   But a few think him pleasant enough.

His mind is concrete and fastidious,
   His nose is remarkably big;
His visage is more or less hideous,
   His beard it resembles a wig.

He has ears, and two eyes, and ten fingers,
   Leastways if you reckon two thumbs;   10
Long ago he was one of the singers,
   But now he is one of the dumbs.

He sits in a beautiful parlor,
   With hundreds of books on the wall;
He drinks a great deal of Marsala,[1]
   But never gets tipsy at all.

He has many friends, laymen and clerical,
   Old Foss is the name of his cat;
His body is perfectly spherical,
   He weareth a runcible[2] hat.   20

When he walks in a waterproof white,
   The children run after him so!
Calling out, "He's come out in his night-
   gown, that crazy old Englishman, oh!"

He weeps by the side of the ocean,
   He weeps on the top of the hill;
He purchases pancakes and lotion,
   And chocolate shrimps from the mill.

He reads but he cannot speak Spanish,
   He cannot abide ginger-beer: 30
Ere the days of his pilgrimage vanish,
   How pleasant to know Mr. Lear!

1   a kind of Italian white wine.
2   a nonsense word invented by Lear.

WALT WHITMAN [1819–1892]

There Was a
Child Went Forth

There was a child went forth every day,
And the first object he look'd upon, that object he became,
And that object became part of him for the day or a certain part of the
    day,
Or for many years or stretching cycles of years.

The early lilacs became part of this child,
And grass and white and red morning-glories, and white and red
    clover, and the song of the phœbe-bird,
And the Third-month lambs and the sow's pink-faint litter, and the
    mare's foal and the cow's calf,
And the noisy brood of the barnyard or by the mire of the pond-side,
And the fish suspending themselves so curiously below there, and the
    beautiful curious liquid,
And the water-plants with their graceful flat heads, all became part of
    him.   10

The field-sprouts of Fourth-month and Fifth-month became part of
    him,
Winter-grain sprouts and those of the light-yellow corn, and the escu-
    lent roots of the garden,
And the apple-trees cover'd with blossoms and the fruit afterward, and
    wood-berries, and the commonest weeds by the road,
And the old drunkard staggering home from the outhouse of the tavern
    whence he had lately risen,
And the schoolmistress that pass'd on her way to the school,
And the friendly boys that pass'd, and the quarrelsome boys,
And the tidy and fresh-cheek'd girls, and the barefoot negro boy and
    girl,
And all the changes of city and country wherever he went.

His own parents, he that had father'd him and she that had conceiv'd
    him in her womb and birth'd him,
They gave this child more of themselves than that,   20
They gave him afterward every day, they became part of him.

The mother at home quietly placing the dishes on the supper-table,
The mother with mild words, clean her cap and gown, a wholesome
    odor falling off her person and clothes as she walks by,
The father, strong, self-sufficient, manly, mean, anger'd, unjust,
The blow, the quick loud word, the tight bargain, the crafty lure,
The family usages, the language, the company, the furniture, the
    yearning and swelling heart,

Affection that will not be gainsay'd, the sense of what is real, the
    thought if after all it should prove unreal,
The doubts of day-time and the doubts of night-time, the curious
    whether and how,
Whether that which appears so is so, or is it all flashes and specks?
Men and women crowding fast in the streets, if they are not flashes
    and specks what are they?   30
The streets themselves and the façades of houses, and goods in the
    windows,
Vehicles, teams, the heavy-plank'd wharves, the huge crossing at the
    ferries,
The village on the highland seen from afar at sunset, the river
    between,
Shadows, aureola and mist, the light falling on roofs and gables of
    white or brown two miles off,
The schooner near by sleepily dropping down the tide, the little boat
    slack-tow'd astern,
The hurrying tumbling waves, quick-broken crests, slapping,
The strata of color'd clouds, the long bar of maroon-tint away solitary
    by itself, the spread of purity it lies motionless in,
The horizon's edge, the flying sea-crow, the fragrance of salt marsh
    and shore mud,
These became part of that child who went forth every day, and who
    now goes, and will always go forth every day.

from Starting from Paumanok

Dead poets, philosophs, priests,
Martyrs, artists, inventors, governments long since,
Language-shapers, on other shores,
Nations once powerful, now reduced, withdrawn, or desolate,
I dare not proceed till I respectfully credit what you have left, wafted
    hither:
I have perused it—own it is admirable, (moving awhile among it;)
Think nothing can ever be greater—nothing can ever deserve more
    than it deserves;
Regarding it all intently a long while—then dismissing it,
I stand in my place, with my own day, here.

from Song of Myself

Trippers and askers surround me;
People I meet—the effect upon me of my early life, or the ward and
    city I live in, or the nation,
The latest dates, discoveries, inventions, societies, authors old and
    new,   60

My dinner, dress, associates, looks, compliments, dues,
The real or fancied indifference of some man or woman I love,
The sickness of one of my folks, or of myself, or ill-doing, or loss or
    lack of money, or depressions or exaltations;
Battles, the horrors of fratricidal war, the fever of doubtful news, the
    fitful events;
These come to me days and nights, and go from me again,
But they are not the Me myself.

Apart from the pulling and hauling stands what I am;
Stands amused, complacent, compassionating, idle, unitary;
Looks down, is erect, or bends an arm on an impalpable certain rest,
Looking with side-curved head, curious what will come next;   70
Both in and out of the game, and watching and wondering at it.

◆

I believe a leaf of grass is no less than the journey-work of the stars,
And the pismire[1] is equally perfect, and a grain of sand, and the egg
    of the wren,   661
And the tree-toad is a chef-d'œuvre for the highest,
And the running blackberry would adorn the parlors of heaven,
And the narrowest hinge in my hand puts to scorn all machinery,
And the cow crunching with depress'd head surpasses any statue,
And a mouse is miracle enough to stagger sextillions of infidels,
And I could come every afternoon of my life to look at the farmer's
    girl boiling her iron tea-kettle and baking shortcake.

I find I incorporate gneiss,[2] coal, long-threaded moss, fruits, grains,
    esculent[3] roots,
And am stucco'd with quadrupeds and birds all over,
And have distanced what is behind me for good reasons,   670
And call anything close again, when I desire it.

◆

I understand the large hearts of heroes,
The courage of present times and all times;
How the skipper saw the crowded and rudderless wreck of the steam-
    ship, and Death chasing it up and down the storm;
How he knuckled tight, and gave not back one inch, and was faithful
    of days and faithful of nights,
And chalk'd in large letters, on a board, *Be of good cheer, we will not
    desert you:*
How he follow'd with them, and tack'd with them—and would not give
    it up;
How he saved the drifting company at last:

1   an ant.
2   granite-like rock.
3   edible.

How the lank loose-gown'd women look'd when boated from the side
of their prepared graves;
How the silent old-faced infants, and the lifted sick, and the sharp-
lipp'd unshaved men:
All this I swallow—it tastes good—I like it well—it becomes mine;   830
I am the man—I suffer'd—I was there.

The disdain and calmness of olden martyrs;
The mother, condemn'd for a witch, burnt with dry wood, her children
gazing on;
The hounded slave that flags in the race, leans by the fence, blowing,
cover'd with sweat;
The twinges that sting like needles his legs and neck—the murderous
buckshot and the bullets;
All these I feel, or am.

I am the hounded slave, I wince at the bite of the dogs,
Hell and despair are upon me, crack and again crack the marksmen;
I clutch the rails of the fence, my gore dribs, thinn'd with the ooze of
my skin;
I fall on the weeds and stones;   840
The riders spur their unwilling horses, haul close,
Taunt my dizzy ears, and beat me violently over the head with whip-
stocks.

Agonies are one of my changes of garments;
I do not ask the wounded person how he feels—I myself become the
wounded person;
My hurts turn livid upon me as I lean on a cane and observe.

A Farm Picture

Through the ample open door of the peaceful country barn,
A sun-lit pasture field, with cattle and horses feeding;
And haze, and vista, and the far horizon, fading away.

Beat! Beat! Drums!

1

Beat! beat! drums!—Blow! bugles! blow!
Through the windows—through doors—burst like a ruthless force,
Into the solemn church, and scatter the congregation;
Into the school where the scholar is studying;
Leave not the bridegroom quiet—no happiness must he have now with
his bride;

Nor the peaceful farmer any peace, plowing his field or gathering his
    grain;
So fierce you whirr and pound, you drums—so shrill you bugles blow.

2

Beat! beat! drums!—Blow! bugles! blow!
Over the traffic of cities—over the rumble of wheels in the streets:
Are beds prepared for sleepers at night in the houses? No sleepers
    must sleep in those beds;   10
No bargainers' bargains by day—no brokers or speculators—Would
    they continue?
Would the talkers be talking? would the singer attempt to sing?
Would the lawyer rise in the court to state his case before the judge?
Then rattle quicker, heavier drums—you bugles wilder blow.

3

Beat! beat! drums!—Blow! bugles! blow!
Make no parley—stop for no expostulation;
Mind not the timid—mind not the weeper or prayer;
Mind not the old man beseeching the young man;
Let not the child's voice be heard, nor the mother's entreaties;
Make even the trestles to shake the dead, where they lie awaiting the
    hearses,   20
So strong you thump, O terrible drums—so loud you bugles blow.

Cavalry
Crossing a Ford

A line in long array, where they wind betwixt green islands;
They take a serpentine course—their arms flash in the sun—Hark to the
    musical clank;
Behold the silvery river—in it the splashing horses, loitering, stop to
    drink;
Behold the brown-faced men—each group, each person, a picture—the
    negligent rest on the saddles;
Some emerge on the opposite bank—others are just entering the ford—
    while,
Scarlet, and blue, and snowy white,
The guidon[1] flags flutter gaily in the wind.

An Army Corps
on the March

With its cloud of skirmishers in advance,
With now the sound of a single shot snapping like a whip, and now an
    irregular volley,

1   A guidon is a guide-flag carried by a cavalry troop.

The swarming ranks press on and on, the dense brigades press on;
Glittering dimly, toiling under the sun—the dust-cover'd men,
In columns rise and fall to the undulations of the ground,
With artillery interspers'd—the wheels rumble, the horses sweat,
As the army corps advances.

from Marches
Now the War
Is Over

Rhymes and rhymers pass away—poems distill'd from foreign poems
    pass away,
The swarms of reflectors and the polite pass, and leave ashes;
Admirers, importers, obedient persons, make but the soil of literature;
America justifies itself, give it time—no disguise can deceive it, or con-
    ceal from it—it is impassive enough,
Only toward the likes of itself will it advance to meet them,   222
If its poets appear, it will in due time advance to meet them—there is
    no fear of mistake,
(The proof of a poet shall be sternly deferr'd, till his country absorbs
    him as affectionately as he has absorb'd it.)

♦

I swear I begin to see the meaning of these things!
It is not the earth, it is not America, who is so great,
It is I who am great, or to be great—it is you up there, or any one;
It is to walk rapidly through civilizations, governments, theories,
Through poems, pageants, shows, to form great individuals.

♦

I will confront these shows of the day and night!
I will know if I am to be less than they!
I will see if I am not as majestic as they!
I will see if I am not as subtle and real as they!
I will see if I am to be less generous than they!   310
I will see if I have no meaning, while the houses and ships have
    meaning!
I will see if the fishes and birds are to be enough for themselves, and I
    am not to be enough for myself.

The Runner

On a flat road runs the well-train'd runner;
He is lean and sinewy, with muscular legs;
He is thinly clothed—he leans forward as he runs,
With lightly closed fists, and arms partially rais'd.

The World
Below the Brine

The world below the brine;
Forests at the bottom of the sea—the branches and leaves,
Sea-lettuce, vast lichens, strange flowers and seeds—the thick tangle, the openings, and the pink turf,
Different colors, pale gray and green, purple, white, and gold—the play of light through the water,
Dumb swimmers there among the rocks—coral, gluten,[1] grass, rushes— and the aliment of the swimmers,
Sluggish existences grazing there, suspended, or slowly crawling close to the bottom,
The sperm-whale at the surface, blowing air and spray, or disporting with his flukes,[2]
The leaden-eyed shark, the walrus, the turtle, the hairy sea-leopard, and the sting-ray;
Passions there—wars, pursuits, tribes—sight in those ocean-depths— breathing that thick-breathing air, as so many do;
The change thence to the sight here, and to the subtle air breathed by beings like us, who walk this sphere;
The change onward from ours, to that of beings who walk other spheres.

1 a sticky secretion.
2 the lobes of a whale's tail.

On the Beach,
at Night

1
On the beach, at night,
Stands a child, with her father,
Watching the east, the autumn sky.

Up through the darkness,
While ravening clouds, the burial clouds, in black masses spreading,
Lower, sullen and fast, athwart and down the sky,
Amid a transparent clear belt of ether yet left in the east,
Ascends, large and calm, the lord-star Jupiter;
And nigh at hand, only a very little above,
Swim the delicate brothers, the Pleiades.[1]   10

2
From the beach, the child, holding the hand of her father,
Those burial-clouds that lower, victorious, soon to devour all,
Watching, silently weeps.

1 a constellation of seven stars.

Weep not, child,
Weep not, my darling,
With these kisses let me remove your tears;
The ravening clouds shall not long be victorious,
They shall not long possess the sky—shall devour the stars only in
     apparition:
Jupiter shall emerge—be patient—watch again another night—the
     Pleiades shall emerge,
They are immortal—all those stars, both silvery and golden, shall shine
     out again,   20
The great stars and the little ones shall shine out again—they endure;
The vast immortal suns, and the long-enduring pensive moons, shall
     again shine.

3

Then, dearest child, mournest thou only for Jupiter?
Considerest thou alone the burial of the stars?

Something there is,
(With my lips soothing thee, adding, I whisper,
I give thee the first suggestion, the problem and indirection,)
Something there is more immortal even than the stars,
(Many the burials, many the days and nights, passing away,)
Something that shall endure longer even than lustrous Jupiter,   30
Longer than sun, or any revolving satellite,
Or the radiant brothers, the Pleiades.

MATTHEW ARNOLD [1822–1888]

Dover Beach

The sea is calm tonight,
The tide is full, the moon lies fair
Upon the straits;—on the French coast the light
Gleams and is gone; the cliffs of England stand,
Glimmering and vast out in the tranquil bay.
Come to the window, sweet is the night-air!

Only, from the long line of spray
Where the sea meets the moon-blanched land,
Listen! you hear the grating roar
Of pebbles which the waves draw back, and fling,   10
At their return, up the high strand,
Begin, and cease, and then again begin,
With tremulous cadence slow, and bring
The eternal note of sadness in.

Sophocles long ago
Heard it on the Aegean, and it brought
Into his mind the turbid ebb and flow
Of human misery; we
Find also in the sound a thought,
Hearing it by this distant northern sea.   20

The Sea of Faith
Was once, too, at the full, and round earth's shore
Lay like the folds of a bright girdle furled.
But now I only hear
Its melancholy, long, withdrawing roar,
Retreating, to the breath
Of the night-wind, down the vast edges drear
And naked shingles of the world.

Ah, love, let us be true
To one another! for the world, which seems   30
To lie before us like a land of dreams,
So various, so beautiful, so new,
Hath really neither joy, nor love, nor light,
Nor certitude, nor peace, nor help for pain;
And we are here as on a darkling plain
Swept with confused alarms of struggle and flight,
Where ignorant armies clash by night.

EMILY DICKINSON [1830–1884]

Success Is
Counted Sweetest

Success is counted sweetest
By those who ne'er succeed.
To comprehend a nectar
Requires sorest need.

Not one of all the purple Host
Who took the Flag today
Can tell the definition
So clear of Victory

As he defeated—dying—
On whose forbidden ear
The distant strains of triumph
Burst agonized and clear!

I Like a
Look of Agony

I like a look of Agony,
Because I know it's true—
Men do not sham Convulsion,
Nor simulate, a Throe—

The Eyes glaze once—and that is Death—
Impossible to feign
The Beads upon the Forehead
By homely Anguish strung.

The Soul Selects
Her Own Society

The Soul selects her own Society—
Then—shuts the Door—
To her divine Majority—
Present no more—

Unmoved—she notes the Chariots—pausing—
At her low Gate—
Unmoved—an Emperor be kneeling
Upon her Mat—

I've known her—from an ample nation—
Choose One—
Then—close the Valves of her attention—
Like Stone—

After Great Pain,
a Formal Feeling Comes

After great pain, a formal feeling comes—
The Nerves sit ceremonious, like Tombs—
The stiff Heart questions was it He, that bore,
And Yesterday, or Centuries before?

The Feet, mechanical, go round—
Of Ground, or Air, or Ought—
A Wooden way
Regardless grown,
A Quartz contentment, like a stone—

This is the Hour of Lead—
Remembered, if outlived,
As Freezing persons, recollect the Snow—
First—Chill—then Stupor—then the letting go—

There's Been a Death, in the Opposite House

There's been a Death, in the Opposite House,
As lately as Today—
I know it, by the numb look
Such Houses have—alway—

The Neighbors rustle in and out—
The Doctor—drives away—
A Window opens like a Pod—
Abrupt—mechanically—

Somebody flings a Mattrass out—
The Children hurry by—
They wonder if it died—on that—
I used to—when a Boy—

The Minister—goes stiffly in—
As if the House were His—
And He owned all the Mourners—now—
And little Boys—besides—

And then the Milliner—and the Man
Of the Appalling Trade—
To take the measure of the House—
There'll be that Dark Parade—

Of Tassels—and of Coaches—soon—
It's easy as a Sign—
The Intuition of the News—
In just a Country Town—

They Shut Me Up in Prose

They shut me up in Prose—
As when a little Girl
They put me in the Closet—
Because they liked me "still"—

Still! Could themself have peeped—
And seen my Brain—go round—

They might as wise have lodged a Bird
For Treason—in the Pound—

Himself has but to will
And easy as a Star
Look down upon Captivity—
And laugh—No more have I—

The Way I Read
a Letter's—This

The Way I read a Letter's—this—
'Tis first—I lock the Door—
And push it with my fingers—next—
For transport it be sure—

And then I go the furthest off
To counteract a knock—
Then draw my little Letter forth
And slowly pick the lock—

Then—glancing narrow, at the Wall—
And narrow at the floor
For firm Conviction of a Mouse
Not exorcised before—

Peruse how infinite I am
To no one that You—know—
And sigh for lack of Heaven—but not
The Heaven God bestow—

The Name—
of It—Is "Autumn"

The name—of it—is "Autumn"—
The hue—of it—is Blood—
An Artery—upon the Hill—
A Vein—along the Road—

Great Globules—in the Alleys—
And Oh, the Shower of Stain—
When Winds—upset the Basin—
And spill the Scarlet Rain—

It sprinkles Bonnets—far below—
It gathers ruddy Pools—
Then—eddies like a Rose—away—
Upon Vermilion Wheels—

Ah, Teneriffe!¹

Ah, Teneriffe!
Retreating Mountain!
Purples of Ages—pause for *you*—

Sunset—reviews her Sapphire Regiment—
Day—drops you her Red Adieu!

Still—Clad in your Mail of ices—
Thigh of Granite—and thew—of Steel—
Heedless—alike—of pomp—or parting

Ah, Teneriffe!
I'm kneeling—still—

1   Teneriffe: one of the Canary Islands,
a chain of mountainous islands in the
Atlantic, off the west coast of Africa.

A Drunkard Cannot Meet a Cork

A Drunkard cannot meet a Cork
Without a Revery—
And so encountering a Fly
This January Day
Jamaicas of Remembrance stir
That send me reeling in—
The moderate drinker of Delight
Does not deserve the spring—
Of juleps, part are in the Jug
And more are in the joy—
Your connoisseur in Liquors
Consults the Bumble Bee—

LEWIS CARROLL   [1832–1898]

The White Knight's Song¹

"I'll tell thee everything I can:
    There's little to relate.
I saw an aged aged man,
    A-sitting on a gate.
'Who are you, aged man?' I said,
    'And how is it you live?'

1   a parody of Wordsworth's "Resolution and Independence."

And his answer trickled through my head
    Like water through a sieve.

"He said, 'I look for butterflies,
    That sleep among the wheat;   10
I make them into mutton pies,
    And sell them in the street.
I sell them unto men,' he said,
    'Who sail on stormy seas;
And that's the way I get my bread—
    A trifle, if you please!'

"But I was thinking of a plan
    To dye one's whiskers green,
And always use so large a fan
    That they could not be seen.   20
So, having no reply to give
    To what the old man said,
I cried, 'Come, tell me how you live!'
    And thumped him on the head.

"His accents mild took up the tale:
    He said, 'I go my ways,
And when I find a mountain rill,
    I set it in a blaze;
And there they make a stuff they call
    Rowland's Macassar oil—[2]   30
Yet twopence halfpenny is all
    They give my for my toil.'

"But I was thinking of a way
    To feed oneself on batter
And so go on from day to day
    Getting a little fatter.
I shook him well from side to side,
    Until his face was blue:
'Come, tell me how you live,' I cried,
    'And what it is you do?'   40

"He said, 'I hunt for haddocks' eyes
    Among the heather bright,
I work them into waistcoat buttons
    In the silent night.
And these I do not sell for gold
    Or coin of silvery shine,
But for a copper halfpenny,
    And that will purchase nine.

2   hair oil.

" 'I sometimes dig for buttered rolls,
    Or set limed twigs for crabs: 50
I sometimes search the grassy knolls
    For wheels of hansom cabs;
And that's the way' (he gave a wink)
    'By which I get my wealth—
And very gladly will I drink
    Your honor's noble health.'

"I heard him then, for I had just
    Completed my design
To keep the Menai Bridge[3] from rust
    By boiling it in wine.   60
I thanked him much for telling me
    The way he got his wealth,
But chiefly for his wish that he
    Might drink my noble health.

"And now, if e'er by chance I put
    My fingers into glue,
Or madly squeeze a right-hand foot
    Into a left-hand shoe,
Or if I drop upon my toe
    A very heavy weight,   70
I weep, for it reminds me so
Of that old man I used to know—
Whose look was mild, whose speech was slow,
Whose hair was whiter than the snow,
Whose face was very like a crow,
    With eyes, like cinders, all aglow,
Who seemed distracted with his woe,
Who rocked his body to and fro,
And muttered mumblingly and low,
As if his mouth were full of dough,   80
Who snorted like a buffalo—
That summer evening long ago,
    A-sitting on a gate."

Jabberwocky

'Twas brillig, and the slithy toves
    Did gyre and gimble in the wabe:
All mimsy were the borogoves,
    And the mome raths outgrabe.

3   The Menai Strait separates Wales from the Isle of Anglesey and is crossed by two famous bridges, one by Telford and one by Robert Stephenson.

"Beware the Jabberwock, my son!
    The jaws that bite, the claws that catch!
Beware the Jubjub bird, and shun
    The frumious Bandersnatch!"

He took his vorpal sword in hand:
    Long time the manxome foe he sought—
So rested he by the Tumtum tree
    And stood awhile in thought.

And, as in uffish thought he stood,
    The Jabberwock, with eyes of flame,
Came whiffling through the tulgey wood,
    And burbled as it came!

One, two! One, two! and through and through
    The vorpal blade went snicker snack!
He left it dead and with his head
    He went galumphing back.

"And hast thou slain the Jabberwock?
    Come to my arms, my beamish boy!
O frabjous day! Callooh! Callay!"
    He chortled in his joy.

'Twas brillig, and the slithy toves
    Did gyre and gimble in the wabe:
All mimsy were the borogoves,
    And the mome raths outgrabe.[1]

1   "You seem very clever at explaining words, Sir," said Alice. "Would you
kindly tell me the meaning of the poem called '*Jabberwocky?*' "
    "Let's hear it," said Humpty Dumpty. "I can explain all the poems that ever
were invented—and a good many that haven't been invented just yet."
    This sounded very hopeful, so Alice repeated the first verse:—

> " *'Twas brillig, and the slithy toves*
>   *Did gyre and gimble in the wabe:*
> *All mimsy were the borogoves,*
>   *And the mome raths outgrabe.*"

    "That's enough to begin with," Humpty Dumpty interrupted: "there are
plenty of hard words there. '*Brillig*' means four o'clock in the afternoon—the
time when you begin *broiling* things for dinner."
    "That'll do very well," said Alice: "and '*slithy*'?"
    "Well, '*slithy*' means 'lithe and slimy.' 'Lithe' is the same as 'active.' You
see it's like a portmanteau—there are two meanings packed up into one word."
    "I see it now," Alice remarked thoughtfully: "and what are '*toves*'?"
    "Well, '*toves*' are something like badgers—they're something like lizards—and
they're something like corkscrews."
    "They must be very curious-looking creatures."
    "They are that," said Humpty Dumpty: "also they make their nest under
sun-dials—also they live on cheese."
    "And what's to '*gyre*' and to '*gimble*'?"
    "To '*gyre*' is to go round and round like a gyroscope. To '*gimble*' is to make
holes like a gimblet."
    "And '*the wabe*' is the grass-plot round a sun-dial, I suppose?" said Alice,
surprised at her own ingenuity.
    "Of course it is. It's called '*wabe*,' you know, because it goes a long way
before it, and a long way behind it—"

Drummer Hodge

They throw in Drummer Hodge, to rest
　　Uncoffined—just as found:
His landmark is a kopje-crest
　　That breaks the veldt around;[1]
And foreign constellations west
　　Each night above his mound.

Young Hodge the Drummer never knew—
　　Fresh from his Wessex home—
The meaning of the broad Karoo,
　　The Bush,[2] the dusty loam,
And why uprose to nightly view
　　Strange stars amid the gloam.

Yet portion of that unknown plain
　　Will Hodge for ever be;
His homely Northern breast and brain
　　Grow to some Southern tree,
And strange-eyed constellations reign
　　His stars eternally.

The Darkling Thrush

I leant upon a coppice gate
　　When Frost was specter-gray,
And Winter's dregs made desolate
　　The weakening eye of day.
The tangled bine-stems scored the sky
　　Like strings of broken lyres,

"And a long way beyond it on each side," Alice added.

"Exactly so. Well then, 'mimsy' is 'flimsy and miserable' (there's another portmanteau for you). And a 'borogove' is a thin shabby-looking bird with its feathers sticking out all round—something like a live mop."

"And then 'mome raths'?" said Alice. "I'm afraid I'm giving you a great deal of trouble."

"Well, a 'rath' is a sort of green pig; but 'mome' I'm not certain about. I think it's short for 'from home'—meaning that they'd lost their way, you know."

"And what does 'outgrabe' mean?"

"Well, 'outgribing' is something between bellowing and whistling, with a kind of sneeze in the middle: however, you'll hear it done, maybe—down in the wood yonder—and, when you've once heard it, you'll be quite content. Who's been repeating all that hard stuff to you?"

1　A kopje is a hillock in South African dialect; veldt is grassland.
2　Karoo is a region of dry flatland in South Africa; bush is uncleared land.

And all mankind that haunted nigh
    Had sought their household fires.

The land's sharp features seemed to be
    The Century's corpse outleant,   10
His crypt the cloudy canopy,
    The wind his death-lament.
The ancient pulse of germ and birth
    Was shrunken hard and dry,
And every spirit upon earth
    Seemed fervorless as I.

At once a voice arose among
    The bleak twigs overhead
In a full-hearted evensong
    Of joy illimited;   20
An aged thrush, frail, gaunt, and small,
    In blast-beruffled plume,
Had chosen thus to fling his soul
    Upon the growing gloom.

So little cause for carolings
    Of such ecstatic sound
Was written on terrestrial things
    Afar or nigh around,
That I could think there trembled through
    His happy good-night air   30
Some blessed Hope, whereof he knew
    And I was unaware.

The Man He Killed

    "Had he and I but met
      By some old ancient inn,
We should have sat us down to wet
      Right many a nipperkin![1]

    "But ranged, as infantry,
      And staring face to face,
I shot at him as he at me,
      And killed him in his place.

    "I shot him dead because—
      Because he was my foe,
Just so: my foe of course he was;
      That's clear enough; although

1   a short beer.

"He thought he'd 'list, perhaps,
        Off-hand like—just as I—
Was out of work—had sold his traps—[2]
        No other reason why.

"Yes; quaint and curious war is!
        You shoot a fellow down
You'd treat if met where any bar is,
        Or help to half-a-crown."[3]

2   equipment.
3   two shillings and sixpence; about thirty cents.

When I Set Out for Lyonnesse[1]

When I set out for Lyonnesse,
        A hundred miles away,
        The rime was on the spray,
And starlight lit my lonesomeness
When I set out for Lyonnesse
        A hundred miles away.

What would bechance at Lyonnesse
        While I should sojourn there
        No prophet durst declare,
Nor did the wisest wizard guess
What would bechance at Lyonnesse
        While I should sojourn there.

When I came back from Lyonnesse
        With magic in my eyes,
        All marked with mute surmise
My radiance rare and fathomless,
When I came back from Lyonnesse
        With magic in my eyes.

"Ah, Are You Digging on My Grave?"

"Ah, are you digging on my grave
        My loved one?—planting rue?"
—"No: yesterday he went to wed
One of the brightest wealth has bred.
'It cannot hurt her now,' he said,
        'That I should not be true.'"

1   legendary country off the south coast of Cornwall, England—scene of
Arthurian romance. It is said to have disappeared suddenly beneath the sea.

"Then who is digging on my grave?
        My nearest dearest kin?"
—"Ah, no: they sit and think, 'What use!
What good will planting flowers produce?   10
No tendance of her mound can loose
        Her spirit from Death's gin.' "

"But some one digs upon my grave?
        My enemy?—prodding sly?"
—"Nay: when she heard you had passed the Gate
That shuts on all flesh soon or late,
She thought you no more worth her hate,
        And cares not where you lie."

"Then, who is digging on my grave?
        Say—since I have not guessed!"   20
—"O it is I, my mistress dear,
Your little dog, who still lives near,
And much I hope my movements here
        Have not disturbed your rest?"

"Ah, yes!   *You* dig upon my grave . . .
        Why flashed it not on me
That one true heart was left behind!
What feeling do we ever find
To equal among human kind
        A dog's fidelity!"   30

"Mistress, I dug upon your grave
        To bury a bone, in case
I should be hungry near this spot
When passing on my daily trot.
I am sorry, but I quite forgot
        It was your resting-place."

Afterwards

When the Present has latched its postern behind my tremulous stay,
    And the May month flaps its glad green leaves like wings,
Delicate-filmed as new-spun silk, will the neighbors say,
    "He was a man who used to notice such things"?

If it be in the dusk when, like an eyelid's soundless blink,
    The dewfall-hawk comes crossing the shades to alight
Upon the wind-warped upland thorn, a gazer may think,
    "To him this must have been a familiar sight."

If I pass during some nocturnal blackness, mothy and warm,
    When the hedgehog travels furtively over the lawn,
One may say, "He strove that such innocent creatures should come to
        no harm,
    But he could do little for them; and now he is gone."

If, when hearing that I have been stilled at last, they stand at the
    door,
  Watching the full-starred heavens that winter sees,
Will this thought rise on those who will meet my face no more,
    "He was one who had an eye for such mysteries"?

And will any say when my bell of quittance is heard in the gloom,
    And a crossing breeze cuts a pause in its outrollings,
Till they rise again, as they were a new bell's boom,
    "He hears it not now, but used to notice such things"?

GERARD MANLEY HOPKINS [1844–1889]

The Starlight Night

Look at the stars! look, look up at the skies!
  O look at all the fire-folk sitting in the air!
  The bright boroughs, the circle-citadels there!
Down in dim woods the diamond delves! the elves'-eyes!
The grey lawns cold where gold, where quickgold lies!
  Wind-beat whitebeam! airy abeles[1] set on a flare!
  Flake-doves sent floating forth at a farmyard scare!—
Ah well! it is all a purchase, all is a prize.

Buy then! bid then!—What?—Prayer, patience, alms, vows.
Look, look: a May-mess, like on orchard boughs!
  Look! March-bloom, like on mealed-with-yellow shallows![2]
These are indeed the barn; withindoors house
The shocks. This piece-bright paling shuts the spouse
  Christ home, Christ and his mother and all his hallows.[3]

1   white poplars.
2   willows.
3   saints.

The Windhover[1]

TO CHRIST OUR LORD

I caught this morning morning's minion,[2] king-
    dom of daylight's dauphin,[3] dapple-dawn-drawn Falcon, in his
    riding
Of the rolling level underneath him steady air, and striding
High there, how he rung[4] upon the rein of a wimpling[5] wing

1   European falcon.
2   darling.
3   heir to the throne.
4   In falconry "to ring" is to rise in the air spirally; "to ring a horse" is to
guide it in a circle on a long rein.
5   rippling; turning.

In his ecstasy! then off, off forth on swing,
As a skate's heel sweeps smooth on a bow-bend: the hurl and
    gliding
Rebuffed the big wind. My heart in hiding
Stirred for a bird,—the achieve of, the mastery of the thing!

Brute beauty and valor and act, oh, air, pride, plume, here
Buckle![6] AND the fire that breaks from thee then, a billion
Times told lovelier, more dangerous, O my chevalier![7]

No wonder of it: sheer plod makes plough down sillion[8]
Shine, and blue-bleak embers, ah my dear,
    Fall, gall themselves, and gash gold-vermilion.

6 gather together (and dive).
7 knight.
8 the ridge between plowed furrows.

Pied Beauty

Glory be to God for dappled things—
    For skies of couple-color as a brinded[1] cow;
        For rose-moles all in stipple[2] upon trout that swim;
Fresh-firecoal chestnut-falls;[3] finches' wings;
    Landscape plotted and pieced—fold, fallow, and plow;
        And all trades, their gear and tackle and trim.
All things counter,[4] original, spare,[5] strange;
    Whatever is fickle, freckled (who knows how?)
        With swift, slow; sweet, sour; adazzle, dim;
He fathers-forth whose beauty is past change:
        Praise Him.

Binsey Poplars

My aspens dear, whose airy cages quelled,
    Quelled or quenched in leaves the leaping sun,
All felled, felled, are all felled;
        Of a fresh and following folded rank
                Not spared, not one
                That dandled a sandalled
            Shadow that swam or sank
On meadow and river and wind-wandering weed-winding bank.

1 archaic form of "brindled."
2 painted in small touches of color.
3 chestnuts without their husks.
4 opposite, contrary.
5 rare.

234

O if we but knew what we do
When we delve or hew—
Hack and rack the growing green!
Since country is so tender
To touch, her being so slender,
That, like this sleek and seeing ball
But a prick will make no eye at all,
Where we, even where we mean
To mend her we end her,
When we hew or delve:
After-comers cannot guess the beauty been.
Ten or twelve, only ten or twelve
Strokes of havoc unselve
The sweet especial scene,
Rural scene, a rural scene,
Sweet especial rural scene.

Felix Randal

Felix Randal the farrier, O is he dead then? my duty all ended,
Who have watched his mould of man, big-boned and hardy-handsome
Pining, pining, till time when reason rambled in it and some
Fatal four disorders, fleshed there, all contended?

Sickness broke him. Impatient, he cursed at first, but mended
Being anointed and all; though a heavenlier heart began some
Months earlier, since I had our sweet reprieve and ransom
Tendered to him. Ah well, God rest him all road ever he offended!

This seeing the sick endears them to us, us too it endears.
My tongue had taught thee comfort, touch had quenched thy tears,
Thy tears that touched my heart, child, Felix, poor Felix Randal;

How far from then forethought of, all thy more boisterous years,
When thou at the random grim forge, powerful amidst peers,
Didst fettle for the great grey drayhorse his bright and battering
sandal!

Spring and Fall:
To a Young Child

Márgarét, are you gríeving
Over Goldengrove unleaving?
Leáves, líke the things of man, you
With your fresh thoughts care for, can you?
Ah! ás the heart grows older

It will come to such sights colder
By and by, nor spare a sigh
Though worlds of wanwood leafmeal lie;
And yet you will weep and know why.
Now no matter, child, the name:
Sórrow's springs áre the same.
Nor mouth had, no nor mind, expressed
What heart heard of, ghost guessed:
It ís the blight man was born for,
It is Margaret you mourn for.

No Worst,
There Is None

No worst, there is none. Pitched past pitch of grief,
More pangs will, schooled at forepangs, wilder wring.
Comforter, where, where is your comforting?
Mary, mother of us, where is your relief?
My cries heave, herds-long; huddle in a main, a chief
Woe, world-sorrow; on an age-old anvil wince and sing—
Then lull, then leave off. Fury had shrieked "No lingering! Let me be
      fell: force I must be brief."

   O the mind, mind has mountains; cliffs of fall
Frightful, sheer, no-man fathomed. Hold them cheap
May who ne'er hung there. Nor does long our small
Durance deal with that steep or deep. Here! creep,
Wretch, under a comfort serves in a whirlwind: all
Life death does end and each day dies with sleep.

My Own Heart
Let Me More
Have Pity On

My own heart let me more have pity on; let
Me live to my sad self hereafter kind,
Charitable; not live this tormented mind
With this tormented mind tormenting yet.

I cast for comfort I can no more get
By groping round my comfortless, than blind
Eyes in their dark can day or thirst can find
Thirst's all-in-all in all a world of wet.

Soul, self; come, poor Jackself, I do advise
You, jaded, let be; call off thoughts awhile
Elsewhere; leave comfort root-room; let joy size

At God knows when to God knows what; whose smile
's not wrung, see you; unforeseen times rather—as skies
Betweenpie mountains—lights a lovely mile.

JOHN DAVIDSON   [1857–1909]

Thirty Bob
a Week[1]

I couldn't touch a stop[2] and turn a screw,
   And set the blooming world a-work for me,
Like such as cut their teeth—I hope, like you—
   On the handle of a skeleton gold key;
I cut mine on a leek, which I eat it every week:
   I'm a clerk at thirty bob as you can see.

But I don't allow it's luck and all a toss;
   There's no such thing as being starred and crossed;
It's just the power of some to be a boss,
   And the bally power of others to be bossed:
I face the music, sir; you bet I ain't a cur;
   Strike me lucky if I don't believe I'm lost!

For like a mole I journey in the dark,
   A-travelling along the underground
From my Pillar'd Halls and broad Suburbean Park,
   To come the daily dull official round;
And home again at night with my pipe all alight,
   A-scheming how to count ten bob a pound.

And it's often very cold and very wet,
   And my missis stitches towels for a hunks;[3]
And the Pillar'd Halls is half of it to let—
   Three rooms about the size of travelling trunks.
And we cough, my wife and I, to dislocate a sigh,
   When the noisy little kids are in their bunks.

But you never hear her do a growl or whine,
   For she's made of flint and roses, very odd;
And I've got to cut my meaning rather fine,
   Or I'd blubber, for I'm made of greens and sod:

10

20

1   bob (slang): one shilling. The plural is the same: bob. Thirty shillings
would be about $3.75 today.
2   valve used as a shut off.
3   bad-tempered old miser.

So p'r'aps we are in Hell for all that I can tell,
    And lost and damn'd and served up hot to God.   30

I ain't blaspheming, Mr. Silver-tongue;
    I'm saying things a bit beyond your art:
Of all the rummy starts you ever sprung,
    Thirty bob a week's the rummiest start!
With your science and your books and your the'ries about spooks
    Did you ever hear of looking in your heart?

I didn't mean your pocket, Mr., no:
    I mean that having children and a wife,
With thirty bob on which to come and go,
    Isn't dancing to the tabor and the fife: 40
When it doesn't make you drink, by Heaven! it makes you think,
    And notice curious items about life.

I step into my heart and there I meet
    A god-almighty devil singing small,
Who would like to shout and whistle in the street,
    And squelch the passers flat against the wall;
If the whole world was a cake he had the power to take,
    He would take it, ask for more, and eat it all.

And I meet a sort of simpleton beside,
    The kind that life is always giving beans;   50
With thirty bob a week to keep a bride
    He fell in love and married in his teens:
At thirty bob he stuck; but he knows it isn't luck:
    He knows the seas are deeper than tureens.

And the god-almighty devil and the fool
    That meet me in the High Street on the strike,
When I walk about my heart a-gathering wool,
    Are my good and evil angels if you like.
And both of them together in every kind of weather
    Ride me like a double-seated bike.   60

That's rough a bit and needs its meaning curled.
    But I have a high old hot un in my mind—
A most engrugious notion of the world,
    That leaves your lightning 'rithmetic behind
I give it at a glance when I say "There ain't no chance,
    Nor nothing of the lucky-lottery kind."

And it's this way that I make it out to be:
    No fathers, mothers, countries, climates—none;
Not Adam was responsible for me,
    Nor society, nor systems, nary one: 70

A little sleeping seed, I woke—I did, indeed—
   A million years before the blooming sun.

I woke because I thought the time had come;
   Beyond my will there was no other cause;
And everywhere I found myself at home,
   Because I chose to be the thing I was;
And in whatever shape of mollusc or of ape
   I always went according to the laws.

I was the love that chose my mother out;
   I joined two lives and from the union burst;   80
My weakness and my strength without a doubt
   Are mine alone for ever from the first:
It's just the very same with a difference in the name
   As "Thy will be done." You say it if you durst!

They say it daily up and down the land
   As easy as you take a drink, it's true;
But the difficultest go to understand,
   And the difficultest job a man can do,
Is to come it brave and meek with thirty bob a week,
   And feel that that's the proper thing for you.   90

It's a naked child against a hungry wolf;
   It's playing bowls upon a spluttering wreck;
It's walking on a string across a gulf
   With millstones fore-and-aft about your neck;
But the thing is daily done by many and many a one;
   And we fall, face forward, fighting, on the deck.

A. E. HOUSMAN   [1859–1936]

On Forelands
High in Heaven

On forelands high in heaven,
   'Tis many a year gone by,
Amidst the fall of even
   Would stand my friends and I.
Before our foolish faces
   Lay lands we did not see;
Our eyes were in the places
   Where we should never be.

Oh, the pearl seas are yonder,
   The amber-sanded shore;   10

Shires where the girls are fonder,
  Towns where the pots hold more.
And here fret we and moulder
  By grange and rick and shed
And every moon are older,
  And soon we shall be dead.

Heigho, 'twas true and pity;
  But there we lads must stay.
Troy was a steepled city,
  But Troy was far away.   20
And round we turned lamenting
  To homes we longed to leave,
And silent hills indenting
  The orange band of eve.

I see the air benighted
  And all the dusking dales,
And lamps in England lighted,
  And evening wrecked in Wales;
And starry darkness paces
  The road from sea to sea,   30
And blots the foolish faces
  Of my poor friends and me.

RUDYARD KIPLING   [1865–1936]

Danny Deever

"What are the bugles blowin' for?" said Files-on-Parade.
"To turn you out, to turn you out," the Color-Sergeant said.
"What makes you look so white, so white?" said Files-on-Parade.
"I'm dreadin' what I've got to watch," the Color-Sergeant said.
    For they're hangin' Danny Deever, you can hear the Dead March
        play,
      The Regiment's in 'ollow square—they're hangin' him today;
      They've taken of his buttons off an' cut his stripes away,
      An' they're hangin' Danny Deever in the mornin'.

"What makes the rear-rank breathe so 'ard?" said Files-on-Parade.
"It's bitter cold, it's bitter cold," the Color-Sergeant said.   10
"What makes that front-rank man fall down?" said Files-on-Parade.
"A touch o' sun, a touch o' sun," the Color-Sergeant said.
      They are hangin' Danny Deever, they are marchin' of 'im round,
      They 'ave 'alted Danny Deever by 'is coffin on the ground;

And' 'e'll swing in 'arf a minute for a sneakin' shootin' hound—
O they're hangin' Danny Deever in the mornin'!

" 'Is cot was right-'and cot to mine," said Files-on-Parade.
" 'E's sleepin' out an' far tonight," the Color-Sergeant said.
"I've drunk 'is beer a score o' times," said Files-on-Parade.
" 'E's drinkin' bitter beer alone," the Color-Sergeant said.   20
    They are hangin' Danny Deever, you must mark 'im to 'is place,
    For 'e shot a comrade sleepin'—you must look 'im in the face;
    Nine 'undred of 'is county an' the Regiment's disgrace,
    While they're hangin' Danny Deever in the mornin'.

"What's that so black agin the sun?" said Files-on-Parade.
"It's Danny fightin' 'ard for life," the Color-Sergeant said.
"What's that that whimpers over'ead?" said Files-on-Parade.
"It's Danny's soul that's passin' now," the Color-Sergeant said.
    For they're done with Danny Deever, you can 'ear the quickstep
      play,
    The Regiment's in column, an' they're marchin' us away;   30
    Ho! the young recruits are shakin', an' they'll want their beer
      today,
    After hangin' Danny Deever in the mornin'!

ARTHUR SYMONS [1865–1945]

White Heliotrope

The feverish room and that white bed,
The tumbled skirts upon a chair,
The novel flung half-open where
Hat, hair-pins, puffs, and paints, are spread;

The mirror that has sucked your face
Into its secret deep of deeps,
And there mysteriously keeps
Forgotten memories of grace;

And you, half dressed and half awake,
Your slant eyes strangely watching me,
And I, who watch you drowsily,
With eyes that, having slept not, ache;

This (need one dread? nay, dare one hope?)
Will rise, a ghost of memory, if
Ever again my handkerchief
Is scented with White Heliotrope.

WILLIAM BUTLER YEATS [1865–1939]

The Lake Isle
of Innisfree

I will arise and go now, and go to Innisfree,
And a small cabin build there, of clay and wattles made;
Nine bean rows will I have there, a hive for the honey bee,
And live alone in the bee-loud glade.

And I shall have some peace there, for peace comes dropping slow,
Dropping from the veils of the morning to where the cricket sings;
There midnight's all a glimmer, and noon a purple glow,
And evening full of the linnet's wings.

I will arise and go now, for always night and day
I hear lake water lapping with low sounds by the shore;
While I stand on the roadway, or on the pavements grey,
I hear it in the deep heart's core.

Paudeen[1]

Indignant at the fumbling wits, the obscure spite
Of our old Paudeen in his shop, I stumbled blind
Among the stones and thorn-trees, under morning light;
Until a curlew cried and in the luminous wind
A curlew answered; and suddenly thereupon I thought
That on the lonely height where all are in God's eye,
There cannot be, confusion of our sound forgot,
A single soul that lacks a sweet crystalline cry.

1   the Irish name for Paddy.

Easter 1916[1]

I have met them at close of day
Coming with vivid faces
From counter or desk among grey
Eighteenth-century houses.
I have passed with a nod of the head
Or polite meaningless words,
Or have lingered awhile and said

1   On Easter Monday, 1916, Irish rebels against the English government
occupied several buildings in Dublin, including the Post Office. Troops were
brought to Dublin and after bitter fighting the rebels surrendered. The leaders of
the rebellion were tried by court martial; fifteen were executed and others were
sentenced to penal servitude. Among those executed were Padraic Pearse,
Thomas MacDonagh, and James Connolly, whom Yeats names. Constance
Markievicz, for "using a revolver with great skill," was given a life sentence.

Polite meaningless words,
And thought before I had done
Of a mocking tale or a gibe
To please a companion
Around the fire at the club,
Being certain that they and I
But lived where motley is worn:
All changed, changed utterly:
A terrible beauty is born.

That woman's[2] days were spent
In ignorant good-will,
Her nights in argument
Until her voice grew shrill.
What voice more sweet than hers
When, young and beautiful,
She rode to harriers?
This man[3] had kept a school
And rode our wingéd horse;
This other[4] his helper and friend
Was coming into his force;
He might have won fame in the end,
So sensitive his nature seemed,
So daring and sweet his thought.
This other man[5] I had dreamed
A drunken, vainglorious lout.
He had done most bitter wrong
To some who are near my heart,
Yet I number him in the song;
He, too, has resigned his part
In the casual comedy;
He, too, has been changed in his turn,
Transformed utterly:
A terrible beauty is born.

Hearts with one purpose alone
Through summer and winter seem
Enchanted to a stone
To trouble the living stream.
The horse that comes from the road,
The rider, the birds that range
From cloud to tumbling cloud,
Minute by minute they change;
A shadow of cloud on the stream

10

20

30

40

2   Constance Markievicz. She came of an Anglo-Irish family, the Gore-Booths of
Sligo where Yeats spent much of his boyhood.
3   Padraic Pearse, who was a strong supporter of the Irish language movement.
4   the poet Thomas MacDonagh.
5   John MacBride, husband of Maud Gonne. Yeats had been in love with her
and had written about it in his poems.

Changes minute by minute; 50
A horse-hoof slides on the brim,
And a horse plashes within it;
The long-legged moor-hens dive,
And hens to moor-cocks call;
Minute by minute they live:
The stone's in the midst of all.

Too long a sacrifice
Can make a stone of the heart.
O when may it suffice? 60
That is Heaven's part, our part
To murmur name upon name,
As a mother names her child
When sleep at last has come
On limbs that had run wild.
What is it but nightfall?
No, no, not night but death;
Was it needless death after all?
For England may keep faith[6]
For all that is done and said.
We know their dream; enough 70
To know they dreamed and are dead;
And what if excess of love
Bewildered them till they died?
I write it out in a verse—
MacDonagh and MacBride
And Connolly[7] and Pearse
Now and in time to be,
Wherever green is worn,
Are changed, changed utterly:
A terrible beauty is born. 80

September 25, 1916

The Second Coming

Turning and turning in the widening gyre[1]
The falcon cannot hear the falconer;
Things fall apart; the centre cannot hold;

6   Yeats means: England may grant Ireland Home Rule. In 1914 the Liberal
party in England proposed a bill in Parliament granting Home Rule to Ireland.
In spite of Tory opposition and the opposition of Unionists in Northern Ireland
who were preparing to resist Home Rule with armed force, the bill passed and
was in the statute book, waiting to be put into effect. Then Britain went to war
with Germany, and Home Rule was deferred for the duration.
7   James Connolly, one of the executed rebels. A Marxist labor organizer,
his ideas are still influential in Irish politics.

1   a circling, spiraling motion.

Mere anarchy is loosed upon the world,
The blood-dimmed tide is loosed, and everywhere
The ceremony of innocence is drowned;
The best lack all conviction, while the worst
Are full of passionate intensity.

Surely some revelation is at hand;
Surely the Second Coming is at hand.
The Second Coming! Hardly are those words out
When a vast image out of *Spiritus Mundi*[2]
Troubles my sight: somewhere in sands of the desert
A shape with lion body and the head of a man,
A gaze blank and pitiless as the sun,
Is moving its slow thighs, while all about it
Reel shadows of the indignant desert birds.
The darkness drops again; but now I know
That twenty centuries of stony sleep
Were vexed to nightmare by a rocking cradle,
And what rough beast, its hour come round at last,
Slouches towards Bethlehem to be born?

2   "What spiritualists call the subliminal mind, what Jung
considers the racial unconscious, and what Henry More called
Anima Mundi."—Richard Ellmann, *The Identity of Yeats*

Sailing
to Byzantium[1]

1

That is no country for old men. The young
In one another's arms, birds in the trees
—Those dying generations—at their song,
The salmon-falls, the mackerel-crowded seas,
Fish, flesh, or fowl, commend all summer long
Whatever is begotten, born, and dies.
Caught in that sensual music all neglect
Monuments of unageing intellect.

2

An aged man is but a paltry thing,
A tattered coat upon a stick, unless   10
Soul clap its hands and sing, and louder sing
For every tatter in its mortal dress,
Nor is there singing school but studying
Monuments of its own magnificence;

1   ancient Greek city, renamed Constantinople by the Roman emperor
Constantine I, which became the capital of the Eastern Roman or Byzantine
Empire after the fall of Rome in 476 A.D. The city is famous for its mosaics
and other works of art.

And therefore I have sailed the seas and come
To the holy city of Byzantium.

3

O sages standing in God's holy fire
As in the gold mosaic of a wall,
Come from the holy fire, perne in a gyre,[2]
And be the singing-masters of my soul.   20
Consume my heart away; sick with desire
And fastened to a dying animal
It knows not what it is; and gather me
Into the artifice of eternity.

4

Once out of nature I shall never take
My bodily form from any natural thing,
But such a form as Grecian goldsmiths make
Of hammered gold and gold enameling
To keep a drowsy Emperor awake;
Or set upon a golden bough to sing   30
To lords and ladies of Byzantium
Of what is past, or passing, or to come.

Byzantium

The unpurged images of day recede;
The Emperor's drunken soldiery are abed;
Night resonance recedes, night-walkers' song
After great cathedral gong;
A starlit or a moonlit dome disdains
All that man is,
All mere complexities,
The fury and the mire of human veins.

Before me floats an image, man or shade,
Shade more than man, more image than a shade;   10
For Hades' bobbin bound in mummy-cloth
May unwind the winding path;
A mouth that has no moisture and no breath
Breathless mouths may summon;
I hail the superhuman;
I call it death-in-life and life-in-death.

2 "To perne" is a verb invented by Yeats. He had been told that the noun
"pern" was an Irish name for a spool on which thread is wound; hence, to turn,
spin; "gyre" (pronounced with a hard g) is a pattern formed by a circling or
spiraling motion.

Miracle, bird or golden handiwork,
More miracle than bird or handiwork,
Planted on the star-lit golden bough,
Can like the cocks of Hades crow,   20
Or, by the moon embittered, scorn aloud
In glory of changeless metal
Common bird or petal
And all complexities of mire or blood.

At midnight on the Emperor's pavement flit
Flames that no fagot feeds, nor steel has lit,
Nor storm disturbs, flames begotten of flame,
Where blood-begotten spirits come
And all complexities of fury leave,
Dying into a dance,   30
An agony of trance,
An agony of flame that cannot singe a sleeve.

Astraddle on the dolphin's mire and blood,
Spirit after spirit! The smithies break the flood,
The golden smithies of the Emperor!
Marbles of the dancing floor
Break bitter furies of complexity,
Those images that yet
Fresh images beget,
That dolphin-torn, that gong-tormented sea.   40

Meru

Civilization is hooped together, brought
Under a rule, under the semblance of peace
By manifold illusion; but man's life is thought,
And he, despite his terror, cannot cease
Ravening through century after century,
Ravening, raging, and uprooting that he may come
Into the desolation of reality:
Egypt and Greece, good-bye, and good-bye, Rome!

Hermits upon Mount Meru or Everest,
Caverned in night under the drifted snow,
Or where that snow and winter's dreadful blast
Beat down upon their naked bodies, know
That day brings round the night, that before dawn
His glory and his monuments are gone.

Lapis Lazuli[1]

FOR HARRY CLIFTON[2]

I have heard that hysterical women say
They are sick of the palette and fiddle-bow,
Of poets that are always gay,
For everybody knows or else should know
That if nothing drastic is done
Aeroplane and Zeppelin will come out,
Pitch like King Billy bomb-balls[3] in
Until the town lie beaten flat.

All perform their tragic play,
There struts Hamlet, there is Lear,   10
That's Ophelia, that Cordelia;
Yet they, should the last scene be there,
The great stage curtain about to drop,
If worthy their prominent part in the play,
Do not break up their lines to weep.
They know that Hamlet and Lear are gay;
Gaiety transfiguring all that dread.
All men have aimed at, found and lost;
Black out; Heaven blazing into the head:
Tragedy wrought to its uttermost.   20
Though Hamlet rambles and Lear rages,
And all the drop-scenes drop at once
Upon a hundred thousand stages,
It cannot grow by an inch or an ounce.

On their own feet they came, or on shipboard,
Camel-back, horse-back, ass-back, mule-back,
Old civilizations put to the sword.
Then they and their wisdom went to rack:
No handiwork of Callimachus,[4]
Who handled marble as if it were bronze,   30
Made draperies that seemed to rise
When sea-wind swept the corner, stands;
His long lamp-chimney shaped like the stem
Of a slender palm, stood but a day;
All things fall and are built again,
And those that build them again are gay.

1   a deep-blue stone used chiefly for ornament.
2   friend of Yeats, who had given him a lapis lazuli medallion, on which were carved the figures of an old man and a servant.
3   William III, King of England from 1689 to 1702. He made war with cannon balls that exploded on impact. "King Billy" also refers to Kaiser Wilhelm II, whose zeppelins and airplanes harried the English in World War I.
4   Greek sculptor of the fifth century B.C.

Two Chinamen, behind them a third,
Are carved in lapis lazuli,
Over them flies a long-legged bird,
A symbol of longevity;   40
The third, doubtless a serving-man,
Carries a musical instrument.

Every discoloration of the stone,
Every accidental crack or dent,
Seems a water-course or an avalanche,
Or lofty slope where it still snows
Though doubtless plum or cherry-branch
Sweetens the little half-way house
Those Chinamen climb towards, and I
Delight to imagine them seated there;   50
There, on the mountain and the sky,
On all the tragic scene they stare.
One asks for mournful melodies;
Accomplished fingers begin to play.
Their eyes mid many wrinkles, their eyes,
Their ancient, glittering eyes, are gay.

A Crazed Girl

That crazed girl improvising her music,
Her poetry, dancing upon the shore,
Her soul in division from itself
Climbing, falling she knew not where,
Hiding amid the cargo of a steamship,
Her knee-cap broken, that girl I declare
A beautiful lofty thing, or a thing
Heroically lost, heroically found.

No matter what disaster occurred
She stood in desperate music wound,
Wound, wound, and she made in her triumph
Where the bales and the baskets lay
No common intelligible sound
But sang, "O sea-starved, hungry sea."

Long-Legged Fly

That civilization may not sink,
Its great battle lost,
Quiet the dog, tether the pony
To a distant post;

Our master Caesar is in the tent
Where the maps are spread,
His eyes fixed upon nothing,
A hand under his head.
Like a long-legged fly upon the stream
His mind moves upon silence.   10

That the topless towers be burnt
And men recall that face,
Move most gently if move you must
In this lonely place.
She thinks, part woman, three parts a child,
That nobody looks; her feet
Practise a tinker shuffle
Picked up on a street.
Like a long-legged fly upon the stream
Her mind moves upon silence.   20

That girls at puberty may find
The first Adam in their thought,
Shut the door of the Pope's chapel,
Keep those children out.
There on that scaffolding reclines
Michael Angelo.
With no more sound than the mice make
His hand moves to and fro.
Like a long-legged fly upon the stream
His mind moves upon silence.   30

Politics

> *In our time the destiny of man presents its meaning*
> *in political terms*—THOMAS MANN[1]

How can I, that girl standing there,
My attention fix
On Roman or on Russian
Or on Spanish politics?
Yet here's a travelled man that knows
What he talks about,
And there's a politician
That has read and thought,
And maybe what they say is true
Of war and war's alarms,
But O that I were young again
And held her in my arms!

1   German   novelist   (1875–1955).

ROBERT FROST [1875–1963]

Mending Wall

Something there is that doesn't love a wall,
That sends the frozen-ground-swell under it
And spills the upper boulders in the sun,
And makes gaps even two can pass abreast.
The work of hunters is another thing:
I have come after them and made repair
Where they have left not one stone on a stone,
But they would have the rabbit out of hiding,
To please the yelping dogs. The gaps I mean,
No one has seen them made or heard them made,   10
But at spring mending-time we find them there.
I let my neighbor know beyond the hill;
And on a day we meet to walk the line
And set the wall between us once again.
We keep the wall between us as we go.
To each the boulders that have fallen to each.
And some are loaves and some so nearly balls
We have to use a spell to make them balance:
"Stay where you are until our backs are turned!"
We wear our fingers rough with handling them.   20
Oh, just another kind of outdoor game,
One on a side. It comes to little more:
There where it is we do not need the wall:
He is all pine and I am apple orchard.
My apple trees will never get across
And eat the cones under his pines, I tell him.
He only says, "Good fences make good neighbors."
Spring is the mischief in me, and I wonder
If I could put a notion in his head:
"*Why* do they make good neighbors? Isn't it   30
Where there are cows? But here there are no cows.
Before I built a wall I'd ask to know
What I was walling in or walling out,
And to whom I was like to give offense.
Something there is that doesn't love a wall,
That wants it down." I could say "Elves" to him,
But it's not elves exactly, and I'd rather
He said it for himself. I see him there,
Bringing a stone grasped firmly by the top
In each hand, like an old-stone savage armed.   40
He moves in darkness as it seems to me,
Not of woods only and the shade of trees.
He will not go behind his father's saying,
And he likes having thought of it so well
He says again, "Good fences make good neighbors."

The Code

There were three in the meadow by the brook
Gathering up windrows, piling cocks of hay,
With an eye always lifted toward the west
Where an irregular sun-bordered cloud
Darkly advanced with a perpetual dagger
Flickering across its bosom. Suddenly
One helper, thrusting pitchfork in the ground,
Marched himself off the field and home. One stayed.
The town-bred farmer failed to understand.

"What is there wrong?"   10

                              "Something you just now said."

"What did I say?"

                              "About our taking pains."

"To cock the hay?—because it's going to shower?
I said that more than half an hour ago.
I said it to myself as much as you."

"You didn't know. But James is one big fool.
He thought you meant to find fault with his work.
That's what the average farmer would have meant.
James would take time, of course, to chew it over   20
Before he acted: he's just got round to act."

"He *is* a fool if that's the way he takes me."

"Don't let it bother you. You've found out something.
The hand that knows his business won't be told
To do work better or faster—those two things.
I'm as particular as anyone:
Most likely I'd have served you just the same.
But I know you don't understand our ways.
You were just talking what was in your mind,
What was in all our minds, and you weren't hinting.   30
Tell you a story of what happened once:
I was up here in Salem, at a man's
Named Sanders, with a gang of four or five
Doing the haying. No one liked the boss.
He was one of the kind sports call a spider,
All wiry arms and legs that spread out wavy
From a humped body nigh as big's a biscuit.
But work! that man could work, especially
If by so doing he could get more work

Out of his hired help. I'm not denying   40
He was hard on himself. I couldn't find
That he kept any hours—not for himself.
Daylight and lantern-light were one to him:
I've heard him pounding in the barn all night.
But what he liked was someone to encourage.
Them that he couldn't lead he'd get behind
And drive, the way you can, you know, in mowing—
Keep at their heels and threaten to mow their legs off.
I'd seen about enough of his bulling tricks
(We call that bulling). I'd been watching him.   50
So when he paired off with me in the hayfield
To load the load, thinks I, Look out for trouble.
I built the load and topped it off; old Sanders
Combed it down with a rake and says, 'O.K.'
Everything went well till we reached the barn
With a big jag to empty in a bay.
You understand that meant the easy job
For the man up on top, of throwing *down*
The hay and rolling it off wholesale,
Where on a mow it would have been slow lifting.   60
You wouldn't think a fellow'd need much urging
Under those circumstances, would you now?
But the old fool seizes his fork in both hands,
And looking up bewhiskered out of the pit,
Shouts like an army captain, 'Let her come!'
Thinks I, D'ye mean it? 'What was that you said?'
I asked out loud, so's there'd be no mistake,
'Did you say, "Let her come"?' 'Yes, let her come.'
He said it over, but he said it softer.
Never you say a thing like that to a man,   70
Not if he values what he is. God, I'd as soon
Murdered him as left out his middle name.
I'd built the load and knew right where to find it.
Two or three forkfuls I picked lightly round for
Like meditating, and then I just dug in
And dumped the rackful on him in ten lots.
I looked over the side once in the dust
And caught sight of him treading-water-like,
Keeping his head above. 'Damn ye,' I says,
'That gets ye!' He squeaked like a squeezed rat.   80
That was the last I saw or heard of him.
I cleaned the rack and drove out to cool off.
As I sat mopping hayseed from my neck,
And sort of waiting to be asked about it,
One of the boys sings out, 'Where's the old man?'
'I left him in the barn under the hay.
If ye want him, ye can go and dig him out.'
They realized from the way I swabbed my neck

More than was needed, something must be up.
They headed for the barn; I stayed where I was. 90
They told me afterward. First they forked hay,
A lot of it, out into the barn floor.
Nothing! They listened for him. Not a rustle.
I guess they thought I'd spiked him in the temple
Before I buried him, or I couldn't have managed.
They excavated more. 'Go keep his wife
Out of the barn.' Someone looked in a window,
And curse me if he wasn't in the kitchen
Slumped way down in a chair, with both his feet
Against the stove, the hottest day that summer. 100
He looked so clean disgusted from behind
There was no one that dared to stir him up,
Or let him know that he was being looked at.
Apparently I hadn't buried him
(I may have knocked him down); but my just trying
To bury him had hurt his dignity.
He had gone to the house so's not to meet me.
He kept away from us all afternoon.
We tended to his hay. We saw him out
After a while picking peas in his garden: 110
He couldn't keep away from doing something."

"Weren't you relieved to find he wasn't dead?"

"No! and yet I don't know—it's hard to say.
I went about to kill him fair enough."

"You took an awkward way. Did he discharge you?"

"Discharge me? No! He knew I did just right."

Stopping by Woods
on a Snowy Evening

Whose woods these are I think I know.
His house is in the village though;
He will not see me stopping here
To watch his woods fill up with snow.

My little horse must think it queer
To stop without a farmhouse near
Between the woods and frozen lake
The darkest evening of the year.

He gives his harness bells a shake
To ask if there is some mistake.

The only other sound's the sweep
Of easy wind and downy flake.

The woods are lovely, dark and deep,
But I have promises to keep,
And miles to go before I sleep,
And miles to go before I sleep.

Design

I found a dimpled spider, fat and white,
On a white heal-all,[1] holding up a moth
Like a white piece of rigid satin cloth—
Assorted characters of death and blight
Mixed ready to begin the morning right,
Like the ingredients of a witch's broth—
A snow-drop spider, a flower like froth,
And dead wings carried like a paper kite.

What had that flower to do with being white,
The wayside blue and innocent heal-all?
What brought the kindred spider to that height,
Then steered the white moth thither in the night?
What but design of darkness to appall?—
If design govern in a thing so small.

EDWARD THOMAS   [1878–1917]

The Gallows

There was a weasel lived in the sun
With all his family,
Till a keeper shot him with his gun
And hung him up on a tree,
Where he swings in the wind and rain,
In the sun and in the snow,
Without pleasure, without pain,
On the dead oak tree bough.

There was a crow who was no sleeper,
But a thief and a murderer   10
Till a very late hour; and this keeper
Made him one of the things that were,
To hang and flap in rain and wind

1   a blue flower.

In the sun and in the snow.
There are no more sins to be sinned
On the dead oak tree bough.

There was a magpie, too,
Had a long tongue and a long tail;
He could both talk and do—
But what did that avail? 20
He, too, flaps in the wind and rain
Alongside weasel and crow,
Without pleasure, without pain,
On the dead oak tree bough.

And many other beasts
And birds, skin, bone, and feather,
Have been taken from their feasts
And hung up there together.
To swing and have endless leisure
In the sun and in the snow, 30
Without pain, without pleasure,
On the dead oak tree bough.

Aspens

All day and night, save winter, every weather,
Above the inn, the smithy, and the shop,
The aspens at the cross-roads talk together
Of rain, until their last leaves fall from the top.

Out of the blacksmith's cavern comes the ringing
Of hammer, shoe, and anvil; out of the inn
The clink, the hum, the roar, the random singing—
The sounds that for these fifty years have been.

The whisper of the aspens is not drowned,
And over lightless pane and footless road,
Empty as sky, with every other sound
Not ceasing, calls their ghosts from their abode,

A silent smithy, a silent inn, nor fails
In the bare moonlight or the thick-furred gloom,
In tempest or the night of nightingales,
To turn the cross-roads to a ghostly room.

And it would be the same were no house near.
Over all sorts of weather, men, and times,
Aspens must shake their leaves and men may hear
But need not listen, more than to my rhymes.

Whatever wind blows, while they and I have leaves
We cannot other than an aspen be
That ceaselessly, unreasonably grieves,
Or so men think who like a different tree.

WALLACE STEVENS [1879–1955]

Hibiscus on the Sleeping Shores

I say now, Fernando, that on that day
The mind roamed as a moth roams,
Among the blooms beyond the open sand;

And that whatever noise the motion of the waves
Made on the sea-weeds and the covered stones
Disturbed not even the most idle ear.

Then it was that that monstered moth
Which had lain folded against the blue
And the colored purple of the lazy sea,

And which had drowsed along the bony shores,
Shut to the blather that the water made,
Rose up besprent and sought the flaming red

Dabbled with yellow pollen—red as red
As the flag above the old café—
And roamed there all the stupid afternoon.

Disillusionment of Ten O'Clock

The houses are haunted
By white night-gowns.
None are green,
Or purple with green rings,
Or green with yellow rings,
Or yellow with blue rings.
None of them are strange,
With socks of lace
And beaded ceintures.
People are not going
To dream of baboons and periwinkles.

Only, here and there, an old sailor,
Drunk and asleep in his boots,
Catches tigers
In red weather.

Bantams
in Pine-Woods

Chieftain Iffucan of Azcan in caftan
Of tan with henna hackles, halt!

Damned universal cock, as if the sun
Was blackamoor to bear your blazing tail.

Fat! Fat! Fat! Fat! I am the personal.
Your world is you. I am my world.

You ten-foot poet among inchlings. Fat!
Begone! An inchling bristles in these pines,

Bristles, and points their Appalachian tangs,
And fears not portly Azcan nor his hoos.

Peter Quince[1]
at the Clavier

1

Just as my fingers on these keys
Make music, so the selfsame sounds
On my spirit make a music, too.

Music is feeling, then, not sound;
And thus it is that what I feel,
Here in this room, desiring you,

Thinking of your blue-shadowed silk,
Is music. It is like the strain
Waked in the elders by Susanna.[2]

Of a green evening, clear and warm,   10
She bathed in her still garden, while
The red-eyed elders watching, felt

1   the carpenter who directed the play before the Duke of Athens in
Shakespeare's *Midsummer Night's Dream*.
2   In the apocryphal Old Testament story, Susanna, the faithful wife, was spied
on by two elders while her husband was away. When she rejected their
advances, they accused her of adultery, but she was saved from death by the
prophet Daniel.

The basses of their beings throb
In witching chords, and their thin blood
Pulse pizzicati of Hosanna.[3]

2

In the green water, clear and warm,
Susanna lay.
She searched
The touch of springs,
And found   20
Concealed imaginings.
She sighed,
For so much melody.

Upon the bank, she stood
In the cool
Of spent emotions.
She felt, among the leaves,
The dew
Of old devotions.

She walked upon the grass,   30
Still quavering.
The winds were like her maids,
On timid feet,
Fetching her woven scarves,
Yet wavering.

A breath upon her hand
Muted the night.
She turned—
A cymbal crashed,
And roaring horns.   40

3

Soon, with a noise like tambourines,
Came her attendant Byzantines.

They wondered why Susanna cried
Against the elders by her side;

And as they whispered, the refrain
Was like a willow swept by rain.

Anon, their lamps' uplifted flame
Revealed Susanna and her shame.

And then, the simpering Byzantines
Fled, with a noise like tambourines.   50

3   "Pizzicati" are plucking of strings instead of bowing; a Hosanna is a song
of praise to God.

4

Beauty is momentary in the mind—
The fitful tracing of a portal;
But in the flesh it is immortal.

The body dies; the body's beauty lives.
So evenings die, in their green going,
A wave, interminably flowing.
So gardens die, their meek breath scenting
The cowl of winter, done repenting.
So maidens die, to the auroral
Celebration of a maiden's choral.   60
Susanna's music touched the bawdy strings
Of those white elders; but, escaping,
Left only Death's ironic scraping.
Now, in its immortality, it plays
On the clear viol of her memory,
And makes a constant sacrament of praise.

Study of Two Pears

1

Opusculum pædagogum.[1]
The pears are not viols,
Nudes or bottles.
They resemble nothing else.

2

They are yellow forms
Composed of curves
Bulging toward the base.
They are touched red.

3

They are not flat surfaces
Having curved outlines.
They are round
Tapering toward the top.

4

In the way they are modeled
There are bits of blue.
A hard dry leaf hangs
From the stem.

1   "a little pedagogical work."

5

The yellow glistens.
It glistens with various yellows,
Citrons, oranges and greens
Flowering over the skin.

6

The shadows of the pears
Are blobs on the green cloth.
The pears are not seen
As the observer wills.

Mrs. Alfred Uruguay

So what said the others and the sun went down
And, in the brown blues of evening, the lady said,
In the donkey's ear, "I fear that elegance
Must struggle like the rest." She climbed until
The moonlight in her lap, mewing her velvet,
And her dress were one and she said, "I have said no
To everything, in order to get at myself.
I have wiped away moonlight like mud. Your innocent ear
And I, if I rode naked, are what remain."

The moonlight crumbled to degenerate forms,   10
While she approached the real, upon her mountain,
With lofty darkness. The donkey was there to ride,
To hold by the ear, even though it wished for a bell,
Wished faithfully for a falsifying bell.
Neither the moonlight could change it. And for her,
To be, regardless of velvet, could never be more
Than to be, she could never differently be,
Her no and no made yes impossible.

Who was it passed her there on a horse all will,
What figure of capable imagination?   20
Whose horse clattered on the road on which she rose,
As it descended, blind to her velvet and
The moonlight? Was it a rider intent on the sun,
A youth, a lover with phosphorescent hair,
Dressed poorly, arrogant of his streaming forces,
Lost in an integration of the martyrs' bones,
Rushing from what was real; and capable?

The villages slept as the capable man went down,
Time swished on the village clocks and dreams were alive,
The enormous gongs gave edges to their sounds,   30

As the rider, no chevalere and poorly dressed,
Impatient of the bells and midnight forms,
Rode over the picket rocks, rode down the road,
And, capable, created in his mind,
Eventual victor, out of the martyrs' bones,
The ultimate elegance: the imagined land.

The Plain Sense
of Things

After the leaves have fallen, we return
To a plain sense of things. It is as if
We had come to an end of the imagination,
Inanimate in an inert savoir.

It is difficult even to choose the adjective
For this blank cold, this sadness without cause.
The great structure has become a minor house.
No turban walks across the lessened floors.

The greenhouse never so badly needed paint.
The chimney is fifty years old and slants to one side.
A fantastic effort has failed, a repetition
In a repetitiousness of men and flies.

Yet the absence of the imagination had
Itself to be imagined. The great pond,
The plain sense of it, without reflections, leaves,
Mud, water like dirty glass, expressing silence

Of a sort, silence of a rat come out to see,
The great pond and its waste of the lilies, all this
Had to be imagined as an inevitable knowledge,
Required, as a necessity requires.

Song of
Fixed Accord

Rou-cou spoke the dove,
Like the sooth lord of sorrow,
Of sooth love and sorrow,
And a hail-bow, hail-bow,
To this morrow.

She lay upon the roof,
A little wet of wing and woe,
And she rou-ed there,

Softly she piped among the suns
And their ordinary glare,

The sun of five, the sun of six,
Their ordinariness,
And the ordinariness of seven,
Which she accepted,
Like a fixed heaven,

Not subject to change . . .
Day's invisible beginner,
The lord of love and of sooth sorrow,
Lay on the roof
And made much within her.

WILLIAM CARLOS WILLIAMS [1883–1963]

Danse Russe

If I when my wife is sleeping
and the baby and Kathleen
are sleeping
and the sun is a flame-white disc
in silken mists
above shining trees,—
if I in my north room
dance naked, grotesquely
before my mirror
waving my shirt round my head
and singing softly to myself:
"I am lonely, lonely.
I was born to be lonely,
I am best so!"
If I admire my arms, my face
my shoulders, flanks, buttocks
against the yellow drawn shades,—

Who shall say I am not
the happy genius of my household?

January Morning

SUITE:

1

I have discovered that most of
the beauties of travel are due to
the strange hours we keep to see them:

the domes of the Church of
the Paulist Fathers in Weehawken
against a smoky dawn—the heart stirred—
are beautiful as Saint Peters
approached after years of anticipation.

2

Though the operation was postponed
I saw the tall probationers   10
in their tan uniforms
                    hurrying to breakfast!

3

—and from basement entries
neatly coiffed, middle aged gentlemen
with orderly moustaches and
well-brushed coats

4

—and the sun, dipping into the avenues
streaking the tops of
the irregular red houselets,
                              and   20
the gay shadows dropping and dropping.

5

—and a young horse with a green bed-quilt
on his withers shaking his head:
bared teeth and nozzle high in the air!

6

—and a semicircle of dirt-colored men
about a fire bursting from an old
ash can,

7

            —and the worn,
blue car rails (like the sky!)
gleaming among the cobbles!   30

8

—and the rickety ferry-boat "Arden"![1]
What an object to be called "Arden"
among the great piers,—on the
ever new river!
                "Put me a Touchstone[2]
at the wheel, white gulls, and we'll

1   named after the Forest of Arden in Shakespeare's *As You Like It*.
2   the clown in *As You Like It*.

follow the ghost of the *Half Moon*[3]
to the North West Passage—and through!
(at Albany!) for all that!"

9

Exquisite brown waves—long   40
circlets of silver moving over you!
enough with crumbling ice crusts among you!
The sky has come down to you,
lighter than tiny bubbles, face to
face with you!
        His spirit is
a white gull with delicate pink feet
and a snowy breast for you to
hold to your lips delicately!

10

The young doctor is dancing with happiness   50
in the sparkling wind, alone
at the prow of the ferry! He notices
the curdy barnacles and broken ice crusts
left at the slip's base by the low tide
and thinks of summer and green
shell-crusted ledges among
        the emerald eel-grass!

11

Who knows the Palisades[4] as I do
knows the river breaks east from them
above the city—but they continue south   60
—under the sky—to bear a crest of
little peering houses that brighten
with dawn behind the moody
water-loving giants of Manhattan.

12

Long yellow rushes bending
above the white snow patches;
purple and gold ribbon
of the distant wood:
        what an angle
you make with each other as   70
you lie there in contemplation.

3   the name of Henry Hudson's ship on his third voyage of discovery. Looking
for a new route to China, in 1609 Hudson sailed from Holland to New York
and ascended the river now called Hudson to the vicinity of the present Albany.
On the fourth voyage, 1610, looking for a northwest passage, he reached what
is now called Hudson's Bay.
4   cliffs on the New Jersey side of the Hudson River.

13

Work hard all your young days
and they'll find you too, some morning
staring up under
your chiffonier at its warped
bass-wood bottom and your soul—
out!
—among the little sparrows
behind the shutter.

14

—and the flapping flags are at   80
half mast for the dead admiral.

15

All this—
       was for you, old woman.
I wanted to write a poem
that you would understand.
For what good is it to me
if you can't understand it?
           But you got to try hard—
But—
    Well, you know how   90
the young girls run giggling
on Park Avenue after dark
when they ought to be home in bed?
Well,
that's the way it is with me somehow.

To Elsie

The pure products of America
go crazy—
mountain folk from Kentucky

or the ribbed north end of
Jersey
with its isolate lakes and

valleys, its deaf-mutes, thieves
old names
and promiscuity between

devil-may-care men who have taken   10
to railroading
out of sheer lust of adventure—

and young slatterns, bathed
in filth
from Monday to Saturday

to be tricked out that night
with gauds
from imaginations which have no

peasant traditions to give them
character   20
but flutter and flaunt

sheer rags—succumbing without
emotion
save numbed terror

under some hedge of choke-cherry
or viburnum—
which they cannot express—

Unless it be that marriage
perhaps
with a dash of Indian blood   30

will throw up a girl so desolate
so hemmed round
with disease or murder

that she'll be rescued by an
agent—
reared by the state and

sent out at fifteen to work in
some hard pressed
house in the suburbs—

some doctor's family, some Elsie—   40
voluptuous water
expressing with broken

brain the truth about us—
her great
ungainly hips and flopping breasts

addressed to cheap
jewelry
and rich young men with fine eyes

as if the earth under our feet
were   50
an excrement of some sky

and we degraded prisoners
destined
to hunger until we eat filth

while the imagination strains
after deer
going by fields of goldenrod in

the stifling heat of September
Somehow
it seems to destroy us 60

It is only in isolate flecks that
something
is given off

No one
to witness
and adjust, no one to drive the car

Poem

As the cat
climbed over
the top of

the jamcloset
first the right
forefoot

carefully
then the hind
stepped down

into the pit of
the empty
flowerpot

This Is
Just To Say

I have eaten
the plums
that were in
the icebox

and which
you were probably
saving
for breakfast

Forgive me
they were delicious
so sweet
and so cold

Iris

a burst of iris so that
come down for
breakfast

we searched through the
rooms for
that

sweetest odor and at
first could not
find its

source then a blue as
of the sea
struck

startling us from among
those trumpeting
petals

The Artist

Mr. T.
        bareheaded
                in a soiled undershirt
his hair standing out
        on all sides
                stood on his toes
heels together
        arms gracefully
                for the moment
curled above his head.
        Then he whirled about
                bounded
into the air
        and with an *entrechat*[1]
                perfectly achieved
completed the figure.
        My mother
                taken by surprise
where she sat
        in her invalid's chair
                was left speechless.

1   a leap made by a ballet dancer during which he crosses his legs, sometimes
with a beating motion.

Bravo! she cried at last
   and clapped her hands.
      The man's wife
came from the kitchen:
   What goes on here? she said.
      But the show was over.

The Sparrow

TO MY FATHER

This sparrow
   who comes to sit at my window
      is a poetic truth
more than a natural one.
   His voice,
      his movements,
his habits—
   how he loves to
      flutter his wings
in the dust—   10
   all attest it;
      granted he does it
to rid himself of lice
   but the relief he feels
      makes him
cry out lustily—
   which is a trait
      more related to music
than otherwise.
   Wherever he finds himself   20
      in early spring,
on back streets
   or beside palaces,
      he carries on
unaffectedly
   his amours.
      It begins in the egg,
his sex genders it:
   What is more pretentiously
      useless   30
or about which
   we more pride ourselves?
      It leads as often as not
to our undoing.
   The cockerel, the crow
      with their challenging voices

cannot surpass
            the insistence
                        of his cheep!
Once
            at El Paso
                        toward evening,
I saw—and heard!—
            ten thousand sparrows
                        who had come in from
the desert
            to roost. They filled the trees
                        of a small park. Men fled
(with ears ringing!)
            from their droppings,
                        leaving the premises
to the alligators
            who inhabit
                        the fountain. His image
is familiar
            as that of the aristocratic
                        Unicorn, a pity
there are not more oats eaten
            now-a-days
                        to make living easier
for him.
            At that,
                        his small size,
keen eyes,
            serviceable beak
                        and general truculence
assure his survival—
            to say nothing
                        of his innumerable
brood.
            Even the Japanese
                        know him
and have painted him
            sympathetically,
                        with profound insight
into his minor
            characteristics.
                        Nothing even remotely
subtle
            about his lovemaking.
                        He crouches
before the female,
            drags his wings,
                        waltzing,

throws back his head
           and simply—
                  yells! The din
is terrific.
           The way he swipes his bill
                  across a plank   90
to clean it,
           is decisive.
                  So with everything
he does. His coppery
           eyebrows
                  give him the air
of being always
           a winner—and yet
                  I saw once,
the female of his species   100
           clinging determinedly
                  to the edge of
a waterpipe,
           catch him
                  by his crown-feathers
to hold him
           silent,
                  subdued,
hanging above the city streets
           until   110
                  she was through with him.
What was the use
           of that?
                  She hung there
herself,
           puzzled at her success.
                  I laughed heartily.
Practical to the end,
           it is the poem
                  of his existence   120
that triumphed
           finally;
                  a wisp of feathers
flattened to the pavement,
           wings spread symmetrically
                  as if in flight,
the head gone,
           the black escutcheon
                  undecipherable,
an effigy of a sparrow,   130
           a dried wafer only,
                  left to say

and it says it
        without offense,
               beautifully;
This was I,
      a sparrow.
             I did my best;
farewell.

D. H. LAWRENCE [1885–1930]

The Song of a Man Who Has Come Through

Not I, not I, but the wind that blows through me!
A fine wind is blowing the new direction of Time.
If only I let it bear me, carry me, if only it carry me!
If only I am sensitive, subtle, oh, delicate, a winged gift!
If only, most lovely of all, I yield myself and am borrowed
By the fine, fine wind that takes its course through the chaos of the
    world
Like a fine, an exquisite chisel, a wedge-blade inserted;
If only I am keen and hard like the sheer tip of a wedge
Driven by invisible blows,
The rock will split, we shall come at the wonder, we shall find the
    Hesperides.[1]

Oh, for the wonder that bubbles into my soul,
I would be a good fountain, a good well-head,
Would blur no whisper, spoil no expression.

What is the knocking?
What is the knocking at the door in the night?
It is somebody wants to do us harm.

No, no, it is the three strange angels.
Admit them, admit them.

Humming-bird

I can imagine, in some otherworld
Primeval-dumb, far back

1   in Greek mythology, a garden producing golden apples.

In that most awful stillness, that only gasped and hummed,
Humming-birds raced down the avenues.

Before anything had a soul,
While life was a heave of Matter, half inanimate,
This little bit chipped off in brilliance
And went whizzing through the slow, vast, succulent stems.

I believe there were no flowers then,
In the world where the humming-bird flashed ahead of creation.
I believe he pierced the slow vegetable veins with his long beak.

Probably he was big
As mosses, and little lizards, they say, were once big.
Probably he was a jabbing, terrifying monster.

We look at him through the wrong end of the long telescope of Time,
Luckily for us.

Kangaroo

In the northern hemisphere
Life seems to leap at the air, or skim under the wind
Like stags on rocky ground, or pawing horses, or springy scut-tailed
        rabbits.

Or else rush horizontal to charge at the sky's horizon,
Like bulls or bisons or wild pigs.

Or slip like water slippery towards its ends,
As foxes, stoats, and wolves, and prairie dogs.

Only mice, and moles, and rats, and badgers, and beavers, and per-
        haps bears
Seem belly-plumbed to the earth's mid-navel.
Or frogs that when they leap come flop, and flop to the center of the
        earth.   10

But the yellow antipodal Kangaroo, when she sits up,
Who can unseat her, like a liquid drop that is heavy, and just touches
        earth.

The downward drip
The down-urge.
So much denser than cold-blooded frogs.

Delicate mother Kangaroo
Sitting up there rabbit-wise, but huge, plumb-weighted,
And lifting her beautiful slender face, oh! so much more gently and
        finely lined than a rabbit's, or than a hare's,
Lifting her face to nibble at a round white peppermint drop which she
        loves, sensitive mother Kangaroo.

Her sensitive, long, pure-bred face.
Her full antipodal eyes, so dark,
So big and quiet and remote, having watched so many empty dawns
    in silent Australia.

Her little loose hands, and drooping Victorian shoulders.
And then her great weight below the waist, her vast pale belly
With a thin young yellow little paw hanging out, and straggle of a
    long thin ear, like ribbon,
Like a funny trimming to the middle of her belly, thin little dangle of
    an immature paw, and one thin ear.

Her belly, her big haunches
And, in addition, the great muscular python-stretch of her tail.

There, she shan't have any more peppermint drops.
So she wistfully, sensitively sniffs the air, and then turns, goes off in
    slow sad leaps   30

On the long flat skis of her legs,
Steered and propelled by that steel-strong snake of a tail.

Stops again, half turns, inquisitive to look back.
While something stirs quickly in her belly, and a lean little face comes
    out, as from a window,
Peaked and a bit dismayed,
Only to disappear again quickly away from the sight of the world, to
    snuggle down in the warmth,
Leaving the trail of a different paw hanging out.

Still she watches with eternal, cocked wistfulness!
How full her eyes are, like the full, fathomless, shining eyes of an
    Australian black-boy
Who has been lost so many centuries on the margins of existence!   40

She watches with insatiable wistfulness.
Untold centuries of watching for something to come,
For a new signal from life, in that silent lost land of the South.

Where nothing bites but insects and snakes and the sun, small life.
Where no bull roared, no cow ever lowed, no stag cried, no leopard
    screeched, no lion coughed, no dog barked,
But all was silent save for parrots occasionally, in the haunted blue
    bush.

Wistfully watching, with wonderful liquid eyes.
And all her weight, all her blood, dripping sack-wise down towards
    the earth's center,
And the live little-one taking in its paw at the door of her belly.

Leap then, and come down on the line that draws to the earth's deep,
    heavy center.   50

To Women, As Far As I'm Concerned

The feelings I don't have I don't have.
The feelings I don't have, I won't say I have.
The feelings you say you have, you don't have.
The feelings you would like us both to have, we neither of us have.
The feelings people ought to have, they never have.
If people say they've got feelings, you may be pretty sure they haven't
    got them.
So if you want either of us to feel anything at all
You'd better abandon all idea of feelings altogether.

Energetic Women

Why are women so energetic?
prancing their knees under their tiny skirts
like war-horses; or war-ponies at least!

Why are they so centrifugal?
Why are they so bursting, flinging themselves about?
Why, as they grow older, do they suffer from blood-pressure?

Why are they never happy to be still?
Why did they cut off their long hair
which they could comb by the hour in luxurious quiet?

I suppose when the men all started being Willy wet-legs
women felt it was no longer any use being a linger-longer-Lucy.

Volcanic Venus

What has happened in the world?
the women like little volcanoes
all more or less in eruption.

It is very unnerving, moving in a world of smouldering volcanoes.
It is rather agitating, sleeping with a little Vesuvius.

And exhausting, penetrating the lava-crater of a tiny Ixtaccihuatl
and never knowing when you'll provoke an earthquake.

It's No Good!

It's no good, the women are in eruption,
and those that have been good so far
now begin to steam ominously,
and if they're over forty-five, hurl great stones into the air

which are very like to hit you on the head as you sit
on the very slopes of the matrimonial mountain
where you've sat peacefully all these years.

Vengeance is mine, saith the Lord,
but the women are my favorite vessels of wrath.

Bavarian Gentians

Not every man has gentians in his house
in Soft September, at slow, sad Michaelmas.[1]
Bavarian gentians, big and dark, only dark
darkening the day-time, torch-like with the smoking blueness of
      Pluto's[2] gloom,
ribbed and torch-like, with their blaze of darkness spread blue
down flattening into points, flattened under the sweep of white day
torch-flower of the blue-smoking darkness, Pluto's dark-blue daze,
black lamps from the halls of Dis, burning dark blue,
giving off darkness, blue darkness, as Demeter's pale lamps give off
      light,
lead me then, lead the way.

Reach me a gentian, give me a torch!
let me guide myself with the blue, forked torch of this flower
down the darker and darker stairs, where blue is darkened on blueness
even where Persephone goes, just now, from the frosted September
to the sightless realm where darkness is awake upon the dark
and Persephone herself is but a voice
or a darkness invisible enfolded in the deeper dark
of the arms Plutonic, and pierced with the passion of dense gloom,
among the splendor of torches of darkness, shedding darkness on the
      lost bride and her groom.

EZRA POUND [1885–   ]

The Study
in Aesthetics

The very small children in patched clothing,
Being smitten with an unusual wisdom,
Stopped in their play as she passed them
And cried up from their cobbles:

1   feast of the archangel Michael, September 29.
2   Pluto (Dis) was god of the underworld. He came upon Persephone—
daughter of Zeus and Demeter, the corn goddess—as she was gathering flowers
and carried her off. Demeter searched for her daughter in vain; in her grief she
caused a famine, and men would have died had Zeus not persuaded Pluto to let
Persephone return to earth for a part of the year.

Guarda! Ahi, guarda! ch'è be'a![1]

But three years after this
I heard the young Dante, whose last name I do not know—
For there are, in Sirmione,[2] twenty-eight young Dantes and thirty-four
        Catulli;[3]
And there had been a great catch of sardines,
And his elders
Were packing them in the great wooden boxes
For the market in Brescia,[4] and he
Leapt about, snatching at the bright fish
And getting in both of their ways;
And in vain they commanded him to *sta fermo!*[5]
And when they would not let him arrange
The fish in the boxes
He stroked those which were already arranged,
Murmuring for his own satisfaction
This identical phrase:

Ch'è be'a.

And at this I was mildly abashed.

1   "Look, oh look, how beautiful!"
2   a peninsula on Lake Garda in northern Italy.
3   Latin plural of Catullus, Roman lyric poet.
4   town in northern Italy.
5   be still.

from Hugh Selwyn Mauberley
(LIFE AND CONTACTS)

"Vocat Aestus in Umbram," Nemesianus, Ec. IV[1]

I

E. P. ODE POUR L'ELECTION
DE SON SEPULCHRE[1]

For three years, out of key with his time,
He strove to resuscitate the dead art
Of poetry; to maintain "the sublime"
In the old sense. Wrong from the start—

No, hardly, but seeing he had been born
In a half savage country, out of date;
Bent resolutely on wringing lilies from the acorn;
Capaneus;[2] trout for factitious bait;

1   *"Vocat Aestus . . .":* "the heat calls us into the shade." "*E. P. Ode . . .":*
"Ezra Pound: ode for the election of his sepulcher," adapted from Pierre
Ronsard's "Ode de l'élection de son sépulchre" (1550).
2   one of the seven heroes who marched against Thebes. He defied Zeus and
was struck down by a thunderbolt as he was climbing the Theban walls.

"Ἴδμεν γάρ τοι πάνθ' ὅσ' ἐνὶ Τροίη³
Caught in the unstopped ear;
Giving the rocks small lee-way
The chopped seas held him, therefore, that year.

His true Penelope was Flaubert,
He fished by obstinate isles;
Observed the elegance of Circe's⁴ hair
Rather than the mottoes on sun-dials.

Unaffected by "the march of events,"
He passed from men's memory in *l'an trentiesme
De son eage;*⁵ the case presents
No adjunct to the Muses' diadem.

II

The age demanded an image
Of its accelerated grimace,
Something for the modern stage,
Not, at any rate, an Attic grace;

Not, not certainly, the obscure reveries
Of the inward gaze;
Better mendacities
Than the classics in paraphrase!

The "age demanded" chiefly a mould in plaster,
Made with no loss of time,
A prose kinema,⁶ not, not assuredly, alabaster
Or the "sculpture" of rhyme.

III

The tea-rose tea-gown, etc.
Supplants the mousseline of Cos,
The pianola "replaces"
Sappho's barbitos.⁷

Christ follows Dionysus,⁸
Phallic and ambrosial
Made way for macerations;⁹
Caliban casts out Ariel.¹⁰

3 "For we know all the things that in Troy [the Greeks and Trojans endured by the will of the gods]," *Odyssey*, XII. 189.
4 Penelope was Odysseus' faithful wife, and a symbol of devotion; Flaubert was a nineteenth-century French novelist who aimed at perfection of form and precision of words; Circe is the goddess who bewitched the followers of Odysseus.
5 "the thirtieth year of his age"; paraphrased from François Villon's *Grand Testament*.
6 movement.
7 Sappho was a Greek poetess of Lesbos, and the barbitos was her lyre; Cos is a Greek island famous for its silks.
8 the wine god.
9 macerate: to soften, waste away.
10 Caliban the bestial, and Ariel the ethereal man in Shakespeare's *The Tempest*.

All things are a flowing,
Sage Heracleitus[11] says;
But a tawdry cheapness
Shall outlast our days.

Even the Christian beauty
Defects—after Samothrace;
We see τὸ καλὸν[12]
Decreed in the market place.

Faun's flesh is not to us,
Nor the saint's vision.   50
We have the press for wafer;
Franchise for circumcision.

All men, in law, are equals.
Free of Pisistratus,[13]
We choose a knave or an eunuch
To rule over us.

O bright Apollo,
τὶν' ἀνδρα, τὶν ἤρωα, τινα θεὸν,[14]
What god, man, or hero
Shall I place a tin wreath upon!   60

                        IV
These fought in any case,
and some believing,
                        pro domo,[15] in any case . . .
Some quick to arm,
some for adventure,
some from fear of weakness,
some from fear of censure,
some for love of slaughter, in imagination,
learning later . . .
some in fear, learning love of slaughter;   70

Died some, pro patria,
                        non "dulce" non "et decor"[16]. . . .
walked eye-deep in hell
believing in old men's lies, then unbelieving
came home, home to a lie,
home to many deceits,

11   pre-Socratic philosopher who emphasized the doctrine that all is in flux.
12   "the beautiful"; Samothrace is the Greek island where the statue of the
Winged Victory was found.
13   Athenian tyrant.
14   "what man, what hero, what god [shall we praise]?"—Pindar, "Second
Olympian Ode."
15   "for home."
16   referring to Horace's line *Dulce et decorum est pro patria mori*, "It is
sweet and proper to die for one's country."

home to old lies and new infamy;
usury age-old and age-thick
and liars in public places.

Daring as never before, wastage as never before.   80
Young blood and high blood,
fair cheeks, and fine bodies;

fortitude as never before

frankness as never before,
disillusions as never told in the old days,
hysterias, trench confessions,
laughter out of dead bellies.

V

There died a myriad,
And of the best, among them,
For an old bitch gone in the teeth,   90
For a botched civilization,

Charm, smiling at the good mouth,
Quick eyes gone under earth's lid,

For two gross of broken statues,
For a few thousand battered books.

YEUX GLAUQUES[17]

Gladstone was still respected,
When John Ruskin produced
"King's Treasuries";[18] Swinburne
And Rossetti still abused.

Fœtid Buchanan lifted up his voice   100
When that faun's head of hers[19]
Became a pastime for
Painters and adulterers.

The Burne-Jones cartons
Have preserved her eyes;
Still, at the Tate, they teach
Cophetua[20] to rhapsodize;

Thin like brook-water,
With a vacant gaze.

17   sea-green eyes. Pound's French translation of the title of a poem by Théophile
Gautier, *Caerulei Oculi*.
18   Ruskin's "Of Kings' Treasuries," the opening lecture in *Sesame and Lilies*.
19   Buchanan attacked Rossetti and Swinburne in an article titled "The Fleshly
School of Poetry"; "faun's head of hers" refers to Elizabeth Siddal, a painter's
model whom Rossetti married. Two years later she killed herself.
20   "Cophetua and the Beggar Maid" is a painting by Burne-Jones now at the
Tate Gallery.

The English Rubaiyat was still-born   110
In those days.

The thin, clear gaze, the same
Still darts out faun-like from the half-ruin'd face,
Questing and passive. . . .
"Ah, poor Jenny's[21] case" . . .

Bewildered that a world
Shows no surprise
At her last maquero's[22]
Adulteries.

"SIENA MI FE';
DISFECEMI MAREMMA"[23]

Among the pickled fœtuses and bottled bones,   120
Engaged in perfecting the catalogue,
I found the last scion of the
Senatorial families of Strasbourg, Monsieur Verog.[24]

For two hours he talked of Gallifet;
Of Dowson; of the Rhymers' Club;[25]
Told me how Johnson (Lionel) died
By falling from a high stool in a pub . . .

But showed no trace of alcohol   ·
At the autopsy, privately performed—
Tissue preserved—the pure mind   130
Arose toward Newman[26] as the whiskey warmed.

Dowson found harlots cheaper than hotels;
Headlam for uplift; Image impartially imbued
With raptures for Bacchus, Terpsichore and the Church.
So spoke the author of "The Dorian Mood,"[27]

M. Verog, out of step with the decade,
Detached from his contemporaries,
Neglected by the young,
Because of these reveries.

21   the prostitute in a poem by Rossetti. Also, in Shakespeare's *Merry Wives of
Windsor*, Mistress Quickly says, "Vengeance of Jinny's case. Fie on her! Never
name her, child, if she be a whore."
22   pimp's.
23   "Siena made me; Maremma undid me." Dante, *Purgatorio*, V. 135. Dante's
line is spoken by Pia de' Tolomei of Siena, whose husband, in order to marry
another woman, murdered her at his castle in the Tuscan Maremma.
24   Dr. Victor Gustave Plarr was born in Strasbourg but lived in England,
where he was a friend of Dowson and Lionel Johnson, and was librarian to the
Royal College of Surgeons.
25   a literary club, whose members included Ernest Dowson, Lionel Johnson,
and W. B. Yeats. Galliffet was a French general.
26   Cardinal John Henry Newman, English theologian and writer.
27   The Reverend Steward Headlam was an associate of the Rhymers' Club and
gave parties where churchmen and theater people mixed. Professor Selwyn
Image was a friend of Lionel Johnson and Plarr; Plarr wrote a book of verse
called *In the Dorian Mood*.

BRENNBAUM[28]

The sky-like limpid eyes,   140
The circular infant's face,
The stiffness from spats to collar
Never relaxing into grace;

The heavy memories of Horeb, Sinai and the forty years,
Showed only when the daylight fell
Level across the face
Of Brennbaum "The Impeccable."

MR. NIXON[29]

In the cream gilded cabin of his steam yacht
Mr. Nixon advised me kindly, to advance with fewer
Dangers of delay. "Consider   150
        "Carefully the reviewer.

"I was as poor as you are;
"When I began I got, of course,
"Advance on royalties, fifty at first," said Mr. Nixon,
"Follow me, and take a column,
"Even if you have to work free.

"Butter reviewers. From fifty to three hundred
"I rose in eighteen months;
"The hardest nut I had to crack
"Was Dr. Dundas.   160

"I never mentioned a man but with the view
"Of selling my own works.
"The tip's a good one, as for literature
"It gives no man a sinecure.

"And no one knows, at sight, a masterpiece.
"And give up verse, my boy,
"There's nothing in it."

        .   .   .   .   .

Likewise a friend of Bloughram's[30] once advised me:
Don't kick against the pricks,
Accept opinion. The "Nineties" tried your game   170
And died, there's nothing in it.

                X
Beneath the sagging roof
The stylist[31] has taken shelter,

28   the English writer and caricaturist, Max Beerbohm.
29   Arnold Bennett, to whom Pound refers in his letters as an author who
frankly declared that his real interest in literature was financial.
30   Blougram is a bishop in a poem by Robert Browning.
31   Ford Madox Ford, novelist.

Unpaid, uncelebrated,
At last from the world's welter

Nature receives him;
With a placid and uneducated mistress
He exercises his talents
And the soil meets his distress.

The haven from sophistications and contentions   180
Leaks through its thatch;
He offers succulent cooking;
The door has a creaking latch.

XI

"Conservatrix of Milésien"[32]
Habits of mind and feeling,
Possibly. But in Ealing
With the most bank-clerkly of Englishmen?

No, "Milésian" is an exaggeration.
No instinct has survived in her
Older than those her grandmother   190
Told her would fit her station.

XII

"Daphne[33] with her thighs in bark
Stretches toward me her leafy hands,"—
Subjectively. In the stuffed-satin drawing-room
I await The Lady Valentine's commands,

Knowing my coat has never been
Of precisely the fashion
To stimulate, in her,
A durable passion;

Doubtful, somewhat, of the value   200
Of well-gowned approbation
Of literary effort,
But never of The Lady Valentine's vocation:

Poetry, her border of ideas,
The edge, uncertain, but a means of blending
With other strata
Where the lower and higher have ending;

A hook to catch the Lady Jane's attention,
A modulation toward the theatre,

32   Pound's adaptation of a phrase from a story by Rémy de Goncourt:
Femmes, conservatrices des traditions milésiennes, "Women, conservators of
Milesian traditions." The *Milesian Tales* were a collection of short stories of love
and adventure, by Aristides of Miletus (second century B.C.).
33   Daphne was loved by Apollo, from whom she escaped by being transformed
into a laurel tree. The two lines quoted are a translation from a poem by
Théophile Gautier, *Le Château du Souvenir.*

Also, in the case of revolution,   210
A possible friend and comforter.

.   .   .   .   .

Conduct, on the other hand, the soul
"Which the highest cultures have nourished"
To Fleet St.[34] where
Dr. Johnson flourished;

Beside this thoroughfare
The sale of half-hose has
Long since superseded the cultivation
Of Pierian roses.[35]

ENVOI (1919)

Go, dumb-born book,[36]   220
Tell her that sang me once that song of Lawes:
Hadst thou but song
As thou hast subjects known,
Then were there cause in thee that should condone
Even my faults that heavy upon me lie,
And build her glories their longevity.

Tell her that sheds
Such treasure in the air,
Recking naught else but that her graces give
Life to the moment,   230
I would bid them live
As roses might, in magic amber laid,
Red overwrought with orange and all made
One substance and one color
Braving time.

Tell her that goes
With song upon her lips
But sings not out the song, nor knows
The maker of it, some other mouth,
May be as fair as hers,   240
Might, in new ages, gain her worshippers,
When our two dusts with Waller's shall be laid,
Siftings on siftings in oblivion,
Till change hath broken down
All things save Beauty alone.

34   a street in London of printers and publishers, now taken over by
haberdashers.
35   One of Sappho's poems addresses a woman of no culture who will "have
no share in the roses from Pieria." Pieria was a part of ancient Macedonia
where the Muses were worshipped.
36   based on Edmund Waller's "Go, Lovely Rose," which was set to music by
Henry Lawes, a seventeenth-century composer.

from Canto LXXXI

What thou lovest well remains,
                                the rest is dross
What thou lov'st well shall not be reft from thee
What thou lov'st well is thy true heritage
Whose world, or mine or theirs
                        or is it of none?
First came the seen, then thus the palpable
        Elysium, though it were in the halls of hell,
What thou lovest well is thy true heritage
What thou lov'st well shall not be reft from thee   10

The ant's a centaur in his dragon world.
Pull down thy vanity, it is not man
Made courage, or made order, or made grace,
        Pull down thy vanity, I say pull down.
Learn of the green world what can be thy place
In scaled invention or true artistry,
Pull down thy vanity,
                        Paquin[1] pull down!
The green casque has outdone your elegance.

"Master thyself, then others shall thee beare"   20
        Pull down thy vanity
Thou art a beaten dog beneath the hail,
A swollen magpie in a fitful sun,
Half black half white
Nor knowst'ou wing from tail
Pull down thy vanity
        How mean thy hates
Fostered in falsity,
        Pull down thy vanity,
Rathe to destroy, niggard in charity,   30
Pull down thy vanity,
        I say pull down.

But to have done instead of not doing
        this is not vanity
To have, with decency, knocked
That a Blunt[2] should open
        To have gathered from the air a live tradition
or from a fine old eye the unconquered flame
This is not vanity.
        Here error is all in the not done,   40
all in the diffidence that faltered.

1 Parisian dress designer.
2 English scholar, poet, and traveler (1840–1922).

ROBINSON JEFFERS [1887–1962]

New Mexican Mountain

I watch the Indians dancing to help the young corn at Taos pueblo.
  The old men squat in a ring
And make the song, the young women with fat bare arms, and a few
  shame-faced young men, shuffle the dance.

The lean-muscled young men are naked to the narrow loins, their
  breasts and backs daubed with white clay,
Two eagle-feathers plume the black heads. They dance with reluc-
  tance, they are growing civilized; the old men persuade them.

Only the drum is confident, it thinks the world has not changed; the
  beating heart, the simplest of rhythms,
It thinks the world has not changed at all; it is only a dreamer, a brain-
  less heart, the drum has no eyes.

These tourists have eyes, the hundred watching the dance, white
  Americans, hungrily too, with reverence, not laughter;
Pilgrims from civilization, anxiously seeking beauty, religion, poetry;
  pilgrims from the vacuum.

People from cities, anxious to be human again. Poor show how they
  suck you empty! The Indians are emptied,
And certainly there was never religion enough, nor beauty nor poetry
  here . . . to fill Americans.

Only the drum is confident, it thinks the world has not changed. Apparently only myself and the strong
Tribal drum, and the rockhead of Taos mountain, remember that
  civilization is a transient sickness.

Love the Wild Swan

"I hate my verses, every line, every word.
Oh pale and brittle pencils ever to try
One grass-blade's curve, or the throat of one bird
That clings to twig, ruffled against white sky.
Oh cracked and twilight mirrors ever to catch
One color, one glinting flash, of the splendor of things.
Unlucky hunter, Oh bullets of wax,
The lion beauty, the wild-swan wings, the storm of the wings."
—This wild swan of a world is no hunter's game.
Better bullets than yours would miss the white breast,

Better mirrors than yours would crack in the flame.
Does it matter whether you hate your . . . self? At least
Love your eyes that can see, your mind that can
Hear the music, the thunder of the wings. Love the wild swan.

T. S. ELIOT [1888–1965]

The Love Song
of J. Alfred Prufrock

S'io credesse che mia riposta fosse
A persona che mai tornasse al mondo,
Questa fiamma staria senza piu scosse.
Ma perciocche giammai di questo fondo
Non torno vivo alcun, s'i'odo il vero,
Senza tema d'infamia ti rispondo.[1]

Let us go then, you and I,
When the evening is spread out against the sky
Like a patient etherized upon a table;
Let us go, through certain half-deserted streets,
The muttering retreats
Of restless nights in one-night cheap hotels
And sawdust restaurants with oyster-shells:
Streets that follow like a tedious argument
Of insidious intent
To lead you to an overwhelming question . . .   10
Oh, do not ask, "What is it?"
Let us go and make our visit.

In the room the women come and go
Talking of Michelangelo.

The yellow fog that rubs its back upon the window-panes,
The yellow smoke that rubs its muzzle on the window-panes
Licked its tongue into the corners of the evening,
Lingered upon the pools that stand in drains,
Let fall upon its back the soot that falls from chimneys,
Slipped by the terrace, made a sudden leap,   20
And seeing that it was a soft October night,
Curled once about the house, and fell asleep.

1 "If I believed that my answer would be to one who would ever return to
the world, this flame would shake no more; but since no one ever returns
alive from this depth, if what I hear is true, I answer you without fear of
infamy." This is Guido da Montefeltro's answer to Dante when asked why he
is being punished in hell (Dante's *Inferno*, XXVII, 61–66).

And indeed there will be time
For the yellow smoke that slides along the street,
Rubbing its back upon the window-panes;
There will be time, there will be time
To prepare a face to meet the faces that you meet;
There will be time to murder and create,
And time for all the works and days[2] of hands
That lift and drop a question on your plate;   30
Time for you and time for me,
And time yet for a hundred indecisions,
And for a hundred visions and revisions,
Before the taking of a toast and tea.

In the room the women come and go
Talking of Michelangelo.

And indeed there will be time
To wonder, "Do I dare?" and, "Do I dare?"
Time to turn back and descend the stair,
With a bald spot in the middle of my hair—   40
[They will say: "How his hair is growing thin!"]
My morning coat, my collar mounting firmly to the chin,
My necktie rich and modest, but asserted by a simple pin—
[They will say: "But how his arms and legs are thin!"]
Do I dare
Disturb the universe?
In a minute there is time
For decisions and revisions which a minute will reverse.

For I have known them all already, known them all:—
Have known the evenings, mornings, afternoons,   50
I have measured out my life with coffee spoons;
I know the voices dying with a dying fall
Beneath the music from a farther room.
    So how should I presume?

And I have known the eyes already, known them all—
The eyes that fix you in a formulated phrase,
And when I am formulated, sprawling on a pin,
When I am pinned and wriggling on the wall,
Then how should I begin
To spit out all the butt-ends of my days and ways?   60
    And how should I presume?

And I have known the arms already, known them all—
Arms that are braceleted and white and bare
[But in the lamplight, downed with light brown hair!]

2   an allusion to Hesiod's *Works and Days*, a poem praising hard work in the
fields.

Is it perfume from a dress
That makes me so digress?
Arms that lie along a table, or wrap about a shawl.
 And should I then presume?
 And how should I begin?

   .   .   .   .   .

Shall I say, I have gone at dusk through narrow streets   70
And watched the smoke that rises from the pipes
Of lonely men in shirt-sleeves, leaning out of windows? . . .

I should have been a pair of ragged claws
Scuttling across the floors of silent seas.

    .   .   .   .   .

And the afternoon, the evening, sleeps so peacefully!
Smoothed by long fingers,
Asleep . . . tired . . . or it malingers,
Stretched on the floor, here beside you and me.
Should I, after tea and cakes and ices,
Have the strength to force the moment to its crisis?   80
But though I have wept and fasted, wept and prayed,
Though I have seen my head [grown slightly bald] brought in upon a
   platter,[3]
I am no prophet—and here's no great matter;
I have seen the moment of my greatness flicker,
And I have seen the eternal Footman hold my coat, and snicker,
And in short, I was afraid.

And would it have been worth it, after all,
After the cups, the marmalade, the tea,
Among the porcelain, among some talk of you and me,
Would it have been worth while,   90
To have bitten off the matter with a smile,
To have squeezed the universe into a ball
To roll it toward some overwhelming question,
To say: "I am Lazarus, come from the dead,[4]
Come back to tell you all, I shall tell you all"—
If one, settling a pillow by her head,
 Should say: "That is not what I meant at all.
 That is not it, at all."

And would it have been worth it, after all,
Would it have been worth while   100
After the sunsets and the dooryards and the sprinkled streets,

3 like the head of John the Baptist. At the request of Salome he was executed,
and his head was brought in to Herod on a platter (Matt., xiv. 1–11).
4 the brother of Mary and Martha, who was raised from death by Christ
(John, xi. 1–44).

After the novels, after the teacups, after the skirts that trail along the
        floor—
And this, and so much more?—
It is impossible to say just what I mean!
But as if a magic lantern threw the nerves in patterns on a screen:
Would it have been worth while,
If one, settling a pillow or throwing off a shawl,
And turning toward the window, should say:
    "That is not it at all,
    That is not what I meant, at all."   110

                .   .   .   .   .

No! I am not Prince Hamlet, nor was meant to be;
Am an attendant lord, one that will do
To swell a progress, start a scene or two,
Advise the prince; no doubt, an easy tool,
Deferential, glad to be of use,
Politic, cautious, and meticulous;
Full of high sentence, but a bit obtuse;
At times, indeed, almost ridiculous—
Almost, at times, the Fool.

I grow old . . . I grow old . . .   120
I shall wear the bottoms of my trousers rolled.[5]

Shall I part my hair behind? Do I dare to eat a peach?
I shall wear white flannel trousers, and walk upon the beach.
I have heard the mermaids singing, each to each.

I do not think that they will sing to me.

I have seen them riding seaward on the waves
Combing the white hair of the waves blown back
When the wind blows the water white and black.

We have lingered in the chambers of the sea
By sea-girls wreathed with seaweed red and brown   130
Till human voices wake us, and we drown.

Preludes

1

The winter evening settles down
With smell of steaks in passageways.
Six o'clock.
The burnt-out ends of smoky days.

5   trousers with cuffs, a new fashion then.

And now a gusty shower wraps
The grimy scraps
Of withered leaves about your feet
And newspapers from vacant lots;
The showers beat
On broken blinds and chimney-pots,   10
And at the corner of the street
A lonely cab-horse steams and stamps.
And then the lighting of the lamps.

                    2
The morning comes to consciousness
Of faint stale smells of beer
From the sawdust-trampled street
With all its muddy feet that press
To early coffee-stands.
With the other masquerades
That time resumes,   20
One thinks of all the hands
That are raising dingy shades
In a thousand furnished rooms.

                    3
You tossed a blanket from the bed,
You lay upon your back, and waited;
You dozed, and watched the night revealing
The thousand sordid images
Of which your soul was constituted;
They flickered against the ceiling.
And when all the world came back   30
And the light crept up between the shutters
And you heard the sparrows in the gutters,
You had such a vision of the street
As the street hardly understands;
Sitting along the bed's edge, where
You curled the papers from your hair,
Or clasped the yellow soles of feet
In the palms of both soiled hands.

                    4
His soul stretched tight across the skies
That fade behind a city block,   40
Or trampled by insistent feet
At four and five and six o'clock;
And short square fingers stuffing pipes,
And evening newspapers, and eyes
Assured of certain certainties,
The conscience of a blackened street
Impatient to assume the world.

I am moved by fancies that are curled
Around these images, and cling:
The notion of some infinitely gentle   50
Infinitely suffering thing.

Wipe your hand across your mouth, and laugh;
The worlds revolve like ancient women
Gathering fuel in vacant lots.

Gerontion[1]

*Thou hast nor youth nor age
But as it were an after dinner sleep
Dreaming of both.*[2]

Here I am, an old man in a dry month,
Being read to by a boy, waiting for rain.[3]
I was neither at the hot gates[4]
Nor fought in the warm rain
Nor knee deep in the salt marsh,[5] heaving a cutlass,
Bitten by flies, fought.
My house is a decayed house,
And the jew squats on the window sill, the owner,
Spawned in some estaminet[6] of Antwerp,
Blistered in Brussels, patched and peeled in London.   10
The goat coughs at night in the field overhead;
Rocks, moss, stonecrop, iron, merds.
The woman keeps the kitchen, makes tea,
Sneezes at evening, poking the peevish gutter.
                                        I an old man,
A dull head among windy spaces.

Signs are taken for wonders. "We would see a sign!"[7]
The word within a word, unable to speak a word,
Swaddled with darkness. In the juvescence of the year
Came Christ the tiger   20
In depraved May, dogwood and chestnut, flowering judas,[8]

1   Greek: little old man.
2   Shakespeare, *Measure for Measure*, Act III, Scene 1.
3   from a life of Edward Fitzgerald: "in a dry month, old and blind, being
read to by a country boy, longing for rain."
4   hot gates: translation of the Greek place name Thermopylae.
5   Sigismondo Malatesta, fifteenth-century Italian mercenary soldier, writes of
fighting in the marshes. See also Ezra Pound's *Cantos*.
6   café.
7   Matt. xvi and John vi: Jesus has been asked for a sign that he is the son
of God. In Matthew he replies that no sign shall be given; in John he says that
he is the sign.
8   This description is taken from *The Education of Henry Adams*. Adams
compares the rank growth and depravity of the spring in Washington with the
strict moral tone of New England.

To be eaten, to be divided, to be drunk
Among whispers; by Mr. Silvero
With caressing hands, at Limoges
Who walked all night in the next room;

By Hakagawa, bowing among the Titians;
By Madame de Tornquist, in the dark room
Shifting the candles; Fräulein von Kulp
Who turned in the hall, one hand on the door.⁹ Vacant shuttles
Weave the wind. I have no ghosts,   30
An old man in a draughty house
Under a windy knob.

After such knowledge, what forgiveness? Think now
History has many cunning passages, contrived corridors¹⁰
And issues, deceives with whispering ambitions,
Guides us by vanities. Think now
She gives when our attention is distracted
And what she gives, gives with such supple confusions
That the giving famishes the craving. Gives too late
What's not believed in, or if still believed,   40
In memory only, reconsidered passion. Gives too soon
Into weak hands, what's thought can be dispensed with
Till the refusal propagates a fear. Think
Neither fear nor courage saves us. Unnatural vices
Are fathered by our heroism. Virtues
Are forced upon us by our impudent crimes.
These tears are shaken from the wrath-bearing tree.

The tiger springs in the new year. Us he devours. Think at last
We have not reached conclusion, when I
Stiffen in a rented house. Think at last   50
I have not made this show purposelessly
And it is not by any concitation
Of the backward devils.
I would meet you upon this honestly.
I that was near your heart was removed therefrom
To lose beauty in terror, terror in inquisition.
I have lost my passion: why should I need to keep it
Since what is kept must be adulterated?
I have lost my sight, smell, hearing, taste and touch:
How should I use them for your closer contact?   60

These with a thousand small deliberations
Protract the profit of their chilled delirium,

9   Mr. Silvero, Hakagawa, Madame de Tornquist, and Fräulein von Kulp seem
to be imaginary characters.
10   In 1919, shortly before this poem was written, the leaders of the
victorious Allied powers meeting at Versailles had "contrived" a corridor from
Poland to the sea This same corridor would be one of the matters of dispute
that brought on the Second World War.

Excite the membrane, when the sense has cooled,
With pungent sauces, multiply variety
In a wilderness of mirrors. What will the spider do,
Suspend its operations, will the weevil
Delay? De Bailhache, Fresca, Mrs. Cammel,[11] whirled
Beyond the circuit of the shuddering Bear
In fractured atoms. Gull against the wind, in the windy straits
Of Belle Isle, or running on the Horn.   70
White feathers in the snow, the Gulf claims,
And an old man driven by the Trades
To a sleepy corner.

                              Tenants of the house,
Thoughts of a dry brain in a dry season.

11   Again, these are apparently imaginary characters.

The Hollow Men

Mistah Kurtz—he dead.
A penny for the Old Guy[1]

1

We are the hollow men
We are the stuffed men
Leaning together
Headpiece filled with straw. Alas!
Our dried voices, when
We whisper together
Are quiet and meaningless
As wind in dry grass
Or rats' feet over broken glass
In our dry cellar   10

Shape without form, shade without color,
Paralyzed force, gesture without motion;

Those who have crossed
With direct eyes, to death's other Kingdom
Remember us—if at all—not as lost
Violent souls, but only
As the hollow men
The stuffed men.

2

Eyes I dare not meet in dreams
In death's dream kingdom   20

1   The first epigraph is the cabin boy announcing Kurtz's death in Joseph
Conrad's story, *Heart of Darkness*. The second is the cry of children collecting
on Guy Fawkes Day, celebrating the discovery of a plot to blow up the House
of Parliament.

These do not appear:
There, the eyes are
Sunlight on a broken column
There, is a tree swinging
And voices are
In the wind's singing
More distant and more solemn
Than a fading star.

Let me be no nearer
In death's dream kingdom   30
Let me also wear
Such deliberate disguises
Rat's coat, crowskin, crossed staves
In a field
Behaving as the wind behaves
No nearer—

Not that final meeting
In the twilight kingdom

                    3
This is the dead land
This is cactus land   40
Here the stone images
Are raised, here they receive
The supplication of a dead man's hand
Under the twinkle of a fading star.

Is it like this
In death's other kingdom
Waking alone
At the hour when we are
Trembling with tenderness
Lips that would kiss   50
Form prayers to broken stone.

                    4
The eyes are not here
There are no eyes here
In this valley of dying stars
In this hollow valley
This broken jaw of our lost kingdoms

In this last of meeting places
We grope together
And avoid speech
Gathered on this beach of the tumid river[2]   60

2   the river Acheron in the underworld.

296

Sightless, unless
The eyes reappear
As the perpetual star
Multifoliate rose[3]
Of death's twilight kingdom
The hope only
Of empty men.

5

Here we go round the prickly pear
Prickly pear prickly pear
Here we go round the prickly pear   70
At five o'clock in the morning.

Between the idea
And the reality
Between the motion
And the act
Falls the Shadow
                    For Thine is the Kingdom

Between the conception
And the creation
Between the emotion   80
And the response
Falls the Shadow
                              Life is very long

Between the desire
And the spasm
Between the potency
And the existence
Between the essence
And the descent
Falls the Shadow   90
                    For Thine is the Kingdom

For Thine is
Life is
For Thine is the

This is the way the world ends
This is the way the world ends
This is the way the world ends
Not with a bang but a whimper.

3   an emblem of Christ and the Virgin.

Macavity:
the Mystery Cat

Macavity's a Mystery Cat: he's called the Hidden Paw—
For he's the master criminal who can defy the Law.
He's the bafflement of Scotland Yard, the Flying Squad's despair:
For when they reach the scene of crime—*Macavity's not there!*

Macavity, Macavity, there's no one like Macavity,
He's broken every human law, he breaks the law of gravity.
His powers of levitation would make a fakir stare,
And when you reach the scene of crime—*Macavity's not there!*
You may seek him in the basement, you may look up in the air—
But I tell you once and once again, *Macavity's not there!*   10

Macavity's a ginger cat, he's very tall and thin;
You would know him if you saw him, for his eyes are sunken in.
His brow is deeply lined with thought, his head is highly domed;
His coat is dusty from neglect, his whiskers are uncombed.
He sways his head from side to side, with movements like a snake;
And when you think he's half asleep, he's always wide awake.

Macavity, Macavity, there's no one like Macavity,
For he's a fiend in feline shape, a monster of depravity.
You may meet him in a by-street, you may see him in the square—
But when a crime's discovered, then *Macavity's not there!*   20

He's outwardly respectable. (They say he cheats at cards.)
And his footprints are not found in any file of Scotland Yard's.
And when the larder's looted, or the jewel-case is rifled,
Or when the milk is missing, or another Peke's been stifled,
Or the greenhouse glass is broken, and the trellis past repair—
Ay, there's the wonder of the thing! *Macavity's not there!*

And when the Foreign Office find a Treaty's gone astray,
Or the Admiralty lose some plans and drawings by the way,
There may be a scrap of paper in the hall or on the stair—
But it's useless to investigate—*Macavity's not there!*   30
And when the loss has been disclosed, the Secret Service say:
"It *must* have been Macavity!"—but he's a mile away.
You'll be sure to find him resting, or a-licking of his thumbs,
Or engaged in doing complicated long division sums.

Macavity, Macavity, there's no one like Macavity,
There never was a Cat of such deceitfulness and suavity.
He always has an alibi, and one or two to spare:
At whatever time the deed took place—MACAVITY WASN'T THERE!

And they say that all the Cats whose wicked deeds are widely known
(I might mention Mungojerrie, I might mention Griddlebone)   40
Are nothing more than agents for the Cat who all the time
Just controls their operations: the Napoleon of Crime!

JOHN CROWE RANSOM [1888–   ]

Bells for John Whiteside's Daughter

There was such speed in her little body,
And such lightness in her footfall,
It is no wonder her brown study
Astonishes us all.

Her wars were bruited in our high window.
We looked among orchard trees and beyond
Where she took arms against her shadow,
Or harried unto the pond

The lazy geese, like a snow cloud
Dripping their snow on the green grass,
Tricking and stopping, sleepy and proud,
Who cried in goose, Alas,

For the tireless heart within the little
Lady with rod that made them rise
From their noon apple-dreams and scuttle
Goose-fashion under the skies!

But now go the bells and we are ready,
In one house we are sternly stopped
To say we are vexed at her brown study,
Lying so primly propped.

Dog

Cock-a-doodle-doo the brass-lined rooster goes,
Brekekekex intones the fat Greek frog,
These fantasies do not worry me as does
The bow-wow-wow of dog.

I had a doggie who used to sit and beg,
A pretty little creature with tears in his eyes

And anomalous hand extended on a leg.
Housebroken was my Huendchen, and so wise.

Booms a big dog's voice like a fireman's bell.
But Fido sits at dusk on Madame's lap   10
And bored beyond his tongue's poor skill to tell
Rehearses his pink paradigm, To yap.

However. Up the lane the tender bull
Proceeds unto his kine; he yearns for them,
Whose eyes adore him and are beautiful,
Love speeds him, and no treason or mayhem.

But having come to the gateway in the fence,
Listen! again the hateful barking dog,
Like a numerous army rattling the battlements
With shout, though it is but his monologue,   20
With lion's courage and sting-bee's virulence
Though he is but one dog.

Shrill is the fury of the royal bull,
His knees quiver, and the honeysuckle vine
Expires with anguish as his voice, dreadful,
Cries, "What do you want of my bonded lady kine?"

Now the air trembles to the sorrowing Moo
Of twenty blameless ladies of the mead
Who fear their lord's precarious set-to.
It is the sunset and the heavens bleed.   30

The hooves of the brave bull slither the claybank
And cut the green tendrils of the vine; the horn
Slices the young birch into splinter and shank
But lunging leaves the bitch's boy untorn.

Across the late sky comes master, Hodge by name,
Upright, two-legged, tall-browed, and self-assured,
In his hand a cudgel, in his blue eye a flame:
"Have I beat my dog so sore and he is not cured?"

Old Hodge stays not his hand, but whips to kennel
The renegade. God's peace betide the souls   40
Of the pure in heart! But from the box in the fennel
Blaze two red eyes as hot as cooking-coals.

The Bonnie Broukit° Bairn°

dirty / child

Mars is braw° in crammasy,°   *gaily dressed / crimson*
Venus in a green silk goun,
The auld mune shak's her gowden° feathers,   *golden*
Their starry talk's a wheen° o' blethers,°   *a good deal / nonsense*
Nane for thee a thochtie° sparin',   *a little thought*
Earth, thou bonnie broukit bairn!
—But greet,° an' in your tears ye'll drown   *cry*
The haill° clanjamfrie!°   *whole / worthless bunch*

Crowdieknowe

Oh to be at Crowdieknowe
When the last trumpet blaws,
An' see the deid° come loupin' owre   *dead*
The auld grey wa's.°   *walls*

Muckle° men wi' tousled beards.   *large*
I grat° as a bairn°   *wept / child*
'll scramble frae the croodit° clay   *thickened*
Wi' feck° o' swearin'.   *plenty*

An' glower° at God an' a' his gang   *stare*
O' angels i' the lift°   *sky*
—Thae trashy bleezin° French-like folk   *drunk*
Wha gar'd° them shift!   *forced*

Fain° the weemun-folk'll seek   *gladly*
To mak' them haud° their row   *hold*
—Fegs,° God's no blate° gin he stirs up   *Truly / not shy*
The men o' Crowdieknowe!

from The Kind of Poetry I Want

The poetry of one the Russians call "a broad nature"
And the Japanese call "flower heart,"
And we, in Scottish Gaeldom, "*ionraic.*"[1]
The poetry of one who practices his art
Not like a man who works that he may live
But as one who is bent on doing nothing but work

1   Gaelic.

Confident that he who lives does not work,
That one must die to life in order to be
Utterly a creator—refusing to sanction 130
The irresponsible lyricism in which sense impressions
Are employed to substitute ecstasy for information,
Knowing that feeling, warm heart-felt feeling,
Is always banal and futile.
Only the irrations and icy ecstasies
Of the artist's corrupted nervous system
Are artistic—the very gift of style, of form and expression,
Is nothing else than this cool and fastidious attitude
Towards humanity. The artist is happiest
With an idea which can become 140
All emotion, and an emotion all idea.

      .   .   .   .

   And, constantly, I seek 190
A poetry of facts. Even as
The profound kinship of all living substance
Is made clear by the chemical route.
Without some chemistry one is bound to remain
Forever a dumbfounded savage
In the face of vital reactions.
The beautiful relations
Shown only by biochemistry
Replace a stupefied sense of wonder
With something more wonderful 200
Because natural and understandable.
Nature is more wonderful
When it is at least partly understood.
Such an understanding dawns
On the lay reader when he becomes
Acquainted with the biochemistry of the glands
In their relation to diseases such as goiter
And in their effects on growth, sex, and reproduction.
He will begin to comprehend a little
The subtlety and beauty of the action 210
Of enzymes, viruses, and bacteriophages,
Those substances which are on the borderland
Between the living and the non-living.
He will understand why the biochemist
Can speculate on the possibility
Of the synthesis of life without feeling
That thereby he is shallow or blasphemous.
He will understand that, on the contrary,
He finds all the more
Because he seeks for the endless 220
—"Even our deepest emotions
May be conditioned by traces
Of a derivative of phenanthrene!"

Crystals Like Blood

I remember how, long ago, I found
Crystals like blood in a broken stone.

I picked up a broken chunk of bed-rock
And turned it this way and that,
It was heavier than one would have expected
From its size. One face was caked
With brown limestone. But the rest
Was a hard greenish-gray quartz-like stone
Faintly dappled with darker shadows,
And in this quartz ran veins and beads
Of bright magenta.

And I remember how later on I saw
How mercury is extracted from cinnebar
—The double ring of iron piledrivers
Like the multiple legs of a fantastically symmetrical spider
Rising and falling with monotonous precision,
Marching round in an endless circle
And pounding up and down with a tireless, thunderous force,
While, beyond, another conveyor drew the crumbled ore
From the bottom and raised it to an opening high
In the side of a gigantic gray-white kiln.

So I remember how mercury is got
When I contrast my living memory of you
And your dear body rotting here in the clay
—And feel once again released in me
The bright torrents of felicity, naturalness, and faith
My treadmill memory draws from you yet.

WILFRED OWEN [1893–1918]

Insensibility

1

Happy are men who yet before they are killed
Can let their veins run cold.
Whom no compassion fleers[1]
Or makes their feet
Sore on the alleys cobbled with their brothers.
The front line withers,
But they are troops who fade, not flowers
For poets' tearful fooling:

1 scoffs at.

Men, gaps for filling:
Losses who might have fought   10
Longer; but no one bothers.

2
And some cease feeling
Even themselves or for themselves.
Dullness best solves
The tease and doubt of shelling,
And Chance's strange arithmetic
Comes simpler than the reckoning of their shilling.
They keep no check on armies' decimation.

3
Happy are these who lose imagination:
They have enough to carry with ammunition.   20
Their spirit drags no pack,
Their old wounds, save with cold, can not more ache.
Having seen all things red,
Their eyes are rid
Of the hurt of the color of blood for ever.
And terror's first constriction over,
Their hearts remain small-drawn.
Their senses in some scorching cautery of battle
Now long since ironed,
Can laugh among the dying, unconcerned.   30

4
Happy the soldier home, with not a notion
How somewhere, every dawn, some men attack,
And many sighs are drained.
Happy the lad whose mind was never trained:
His days are worth forgetting more than not.
He sings along the march
Which we march taciturn, because of dusk,
The long, forlorn, relentless trend
From larger day to huger night.

5
We wise, who with a thought besmirch   40
Blood over all our soul,
How should we see our task
But through his blunt and lashless eyes?
Alive, he is not vital overmuch;
Dying, not mortal overmuch;
Nor sad, nor proud,
Nor curious at all.
He cannot tell
Old men's placidity from his.

6

But cursed are dullards whom no cannon stuns, 50
That they should be as stones;
Wretched are they, and mean
With paucity that never was simplicity.
By choice they made themselves immune
To pity and whatever moans in man
Before the last sea and the hapless stars;
Whatever mourns when many leave these shores;
Whatever shares
The eternal reciprocity of tears.

The Send-Off

Down the close, darkening lanes they sang their way
To the siding-shed,
And lined the train with faces grimly gay.

Their breasts were stuck all white with wreath and spray
As men's are, dead.

Dull porters watched them, and a casual tramp
Stood staring hard,
Sorry to miss them from the upland camp.
Then, unmoved, signals nodded, and a lamp
Winked to the guard.

So secretly, like wrongs hushed-up, they went.
They were not ours:
We never heard to which front these were sent.

Nor there if they yet mock what women meant
Who gave them flowers.

Shall they return to beatings of great bells
In wild train-loads?
A few, a few, too few for drums and yells,
May creep back, silent, to still village wells
Up half-known roads.

Exposure

Our brains ache, in the merciless iced east winds that knive us . . .
Wearied we keep awake because the night is silent . . .
Low, drooping flares confuse our memory of the salient . . .
Worried by silence, sentries whisper, curious, nervous,
                    But nothing happens.

Watching, we hear the mad gusts tugging on the wire,
Like twitching agonies of men among its brambles.
Northward, incessantly, the flickering gunnery rumbles,
Far off, like a dull rumor of some other war.
   What are we doing here?   10

The poignant misery of dawn begins to grow . . .
We only know war lasts, rain soaks, and clouds sag stormy.
Dawn massing in the east her melancholy army
Attacks once more in ranks on shivering ranks of gray,
   But nothing happens.

Sudden successive flights of bullets streak the silence.
Less deadly than the air that shudders black with snow,
With sidelong flowing flakes that flock, pause, and renew;
We watch them wandering up and down the wind's nonchalance,
   But nothing happens.   20

Pale flakes with fingering stealth come feeling for our faces—
We cringe in holes, back on forgotten dreams, and stare, snow-dazed,
Deep into grassier ditches. So we drowse, sun-dozed,
Littered with blossoms trickling where the blackbird fusses.
   Is it that we are dying?

Slowly our ghosts drag home: glimpsing the sunk fires, glozed
With crusted dark-red jewels; crickets jingle there;
For hours the innocent mice rejoice: the house is theirs;
Shutters and doors, all closed: on us the doors are closed,—
   We turn back to our dying.   30

Since we believe not otherwise can kind fires burn;
Nor ever suns smile true on child, or field, or fruit.
For God's invincible spring our love is made afraid;
Therefore, not loath, we lie out here; therefore were born,
   For love of God seems dying.

To-night, His frost will fasten on this mud and us,
Shriveling many hands, puckering foreheads crisp.
The burying-party, picks and shovels in their shaking grasp,
Pause over half-known faces. All their eyes are ice,
   But nothing happens.   40

Disabled

He sat in a wheeled chair, waiting for dark,
And shivered in his ghastly suit of gray,
Legless, sewn short at elbow. Through the park
Voices of boys rang saddening like a hymn,

Voices of play and pleasures after day,
Till gathering sleep had mothered them from him.

About this time Town used to swing so gay
When glow-lamps budded in the light blue trees,
And girls glanced lovelier as the air grew dim,—
In the old times, before he threw away his knees.   10
Now he will never feel again how slim
Girls' waists are, or how warm their subtle hands;
All of them touch him like some queer disease.

There was an artist silly for his face,
For it was younger than his youth, last year.
Now, he is old; his back will never brace;
He's lost his color very far from here,
Poured it down shell-holes till the veins ran dry,
And half his lifetime lapsed in the hot race,
And leap of purple spurted from his thigh.   20

One time he liked a blood-smear down his leg,
After the matches, carried shoulder-high.
It was after football, when he'd drunk a peg,
He thought he'd better join.—He wonders why.
Someone had said he'd look a god in kilts,
That's why; and may be, too, to please his Meg;
Aye, that was it, to please the giddy jilts
He asked to join. He didn't have to beg;

Smiling they wrote his lie; aged nineteen years.
Germans he scarcely thought of; all their guilt,   30
And Austria's, did not move him. And no fears
Of Fear came yet. He thought of jeweled hilts
For daggers in plaid socks; of smart salutes;
And care of arms; and leave; and pay arrears;
Esprit de corps, and hints for young recruits.
And soon he was drafted out with drums and cheers.

Some cheered him home, but not as crowds cheer Goal.
Only a solemn man who brought him fruits
Thanked him; and then inquired about his soul.

Now, he will spend a few sick years in Institutes,   40
And do what things the rules consider wise,
And take whatever pity they may dole.
Tonight he noticed how the women's eyes
Passed from him to the strong men that were whole.
How cold and late it is! Why don't they come
And put him into bed? Why don't they come?

Portrait

Buffalo Bill's
defunct
      who used to
      ride a watersmooth-silver
              stallion
and break onetwothreefourfive pigeonsjustlikethat
                        Jesus
he was a handsome man
              and what i want to know is
how do you like your blueeyed boy
Mister Death

Poem,
or Beauty
Hurts Mr. Vinal

take it from me kiddo
believe me
my country, 'tis of

you, land of the Cluett
Shirt Boston Garter and Spearmint
Girl With The Wrigley Eyes (of you
land of the Arrow Ide
and Earl &
Wilson
Collars) of you i
sing:land of Abraham Lincoln and Lydia E. Pinkham,
land above all of Just Add Hot Water And Serve—
from every B. V. D.

let freedom ring

amen. i do however protest, anent the un
-spontaneous and otherwise scented merde which
greets one (Everywhere Why) as divine poesy per
that and this radically defunct periodical. i would

suggest that certain ideas gestures
rhymes, like Gillette Razor Blades
having been used and reused
to the mystical moment of dullness emphatically are
Not To Be Resharpened. (Case in point

10

20

if we are to believe these gently O sweetly
melancholy trillers amid the thrillers
these crepuscular violinists among my and your
skyscrapers—Helen & Cleopatra were Just Too Lovely,
The Snail's On The Thorn enter Morn and God's
In His andsoforth

do you get me?) according   30
to such supposedly indigenous
throstles Art is O World O Life
a formula: example, Turn Your Shirttails Into
Drawers and If It Isn't An Eastman It Isn't A
Kodak therefore my friends let
us now sing each and all fortissimo A-
mer
i

ca, I
love,   40
You. And there're a
hun-dred-mil-lion-oth-ers, like
all of you successfully if
delicately gelded (or spaded)
gentlemen (and ladies)—pretty

littleliverpill-
hearted-Nujolneeding-There's-A-Reason
americans (who tensetendoned and with
upward vacant eyes, painfully
perpetually crouched, quivering, upon the   50
sternly allotted sandpile
—how silently
emit a tiny violetflavored nuisance: Odor?

ono.
comes out like a ribbon lies flat on the brush

my sweet
old etcetera

my sweet old etcetera
aunt lucy during the recent

war could and what
is more did tell you just
what everybody was fighting

for,
my sister

isabel created hundreds
(and
hundreds)of socks not to
mention shirts fleaproof earwarmers

etcetera wristers etcetera, my
mother hoped that

i would die etcetera
bravely of course my father used
to become hoarse talking about how it was
a privilege and if only he
could meanwhile my

self etcetera lay quietly
in the deep mud et

cetera
(dreaming,
et
    cetera, of
Your smile
eyes knees and of your Etcetera)

somewhere i have never travelled, gladly beyond

somewhere i have never travelled,gladly beyond
any experience,your eyes have their silence:
in your most frail gesture are things which enclose me,
or which i cannot touch because they are too near

your slightest look easily will unclose me
though i have closed myself as fingers,
you open always petal by petal myself as Spring opens
(touching skilfully,mysteriously)her first rose

or if your wish be to close me,i and
my life will shut very beautifully,suddenly,
as when the heart of this flower imagines
the snow carefully everywhere descending;

nothing which we are to perceive in this world equals
the power of your intense fragility:whose texture
compels me with the color of its countries,
rendering death and forever with each breathing

(i do not know what it is about you that closes
and opens;only something in me understands
the voice of your eyes is deeper than all roses)
nobody,not even the rain,has such small hands

a he as o

a he as o
ld as who stag
geri
ng up some streetfu

l of peopl
e lurche
s viv
idly

from ti(& d
esperate
ly)m
e to ti

me shru
gg
ing as if to say b
ut for chreyesake how ca

n
i s
ell drunk if i
be pencils

old age sticks

old age sticks
up Keep
Off
signs)&

youth yanks them
down(old
age
cries No

Tres)&(pas)
youth laughs
(sing
old age

scolds Forbid
den Stop
Must
n't Don't

&) youth goes
right on
gr
owing old

ALLEN TATE [1899–   ]

The Swimmers

SCENE: *Montgomery County, Kentucky, July 1911*

Kentucky water, clear springs: a boy fleeing
   To water under the dry Kentucky sun,
   His four little friends in tandem with him, seeing

Long shadows of grapevine wriggle and run
   Over the green swirl; mullein under the ear
   Soft as Nausicaä's[1] palm; sullen fun

Savage as childhood's thin harmonious tear:
   O fountain, bosom source undying-dead
   Replenish me the spring of love and fear

And give me back the eye that looked and fled   10
   When a thrush idling in the tulip tree
   Unwound the cold dream of the copperhead.

—Along the creek the road was winding; we
   Felt the quicksilver sky. I see again
   The shrill companions of that odyssey:

Bill Eaton, Charlie Watson, "Nigger" Layne
   The doctor's son, Harry Duèsler who played
   The flute; and Tate, with water on the brain.

Dog-days: the dusty leaves where rain delayed
   Hung low on poison-oak and scuppernong,   20
   And we were following the active shade

Of water, that bells and bickers all night long.
   "No more'n a mile," Layne said. All five stood still.
   Listening, I heard what seemed at first a song;

1   In the *Odyssey* of Homer, Nausicaä is the daughter of Alcinous,
king of the Phoeacians.

Peering, I heard the hooves come down the hill.
    The posse passed, twelve horse; the leader's face
    Was worn as limestone on an ancient sill.

Then, as sleepwalkers shift from a hard place
    In bed, and rising to keep a formal pledge
    Descend a ladder into empty space,   30

We scuttled down the bank below a ledge
    And marched stiff-legged in our common fright
    Along a hog-track by the riffle's edge:

Into a world where sound shaded the sight
    Dropped the dull hooves again; the horsemen came
    Again, all but the leader: it was night

Momently and I feared: eleven same
    Jesus-Christers unmembered and unmade,
    Whose Corpse had died again in dirty shame.

The bank then levelling in a speckled glade,   40
    We stopped to breathe above the swimming-hole;
    I gazed at its reticulated shade

Recoiling in blue fear, and felt it roll
    Over my ears and eyes and lift my hair
    Like seaweed tossing on a sunk atoll.

I rose again. Borne on the copper air
    A distant voice green as a funeral wreath
    Against a grave: "That dead nigger there."

The melancholy sheriff slouched beneath
    A giant sycamore; shaking his head   50
    He plucked a sassafras twig and picked his teeth:

"We come too late." He spoke to the tired dead
    Whose ragged shirt soaked up the viscous flow
    Of blood in which It lay discomfited.

A butting horse-fly gave one ear a blow
    And glanced off, as the sheriff kicked the rope
    Loose from the neck and hooked it with his toe

Away from the blood.—I looked back down the slope:
    The friends were gone that I had hoped to greet.—
    A single horseman came at a slow lope   60

And pulled up at the hanged man's horny feet;
    The sheriff noosed the feet, the other end
    The stranger tied to his pommel in a neat

Slip-knot. I saw the Negro's body bend
    And straighten, as a fish-line cast transverse
    Yields to the current that it must subtend.

The sheriff's Goddamn was a murmured curse
   Not for the dead but for the blinding dust
   That boxed the cortège in a cloudy hearse

And dragged it towards our town. I knew I must   70
   Not stay till twilight in that silent road;
   Sliding my bare feet into the warm crust,

I hopped the stonecrop like a panting toad
   Mouth open, following the heaving cloud
   That floated to the court-house square its load

Of limber corpse that took the sun for shroud.
   There were three figures in the dying sun
   Whose light were company where three was crowd.

My breath crackled the dead air like a shotgun
   As, sheriff and the stranger disappearing,   80
   The faceless head lay still. I could not run

Or walk, but stood. Alone in the public clearing
   This private thing was owned by all the town,
   Though never claimed by us within my hearing.

HART CRANE   [1899–1932]

For the Marriage
of Faustus and Helen[1]

> "And so we may arrive by Talmud skill
> And profane Greek to raise the building up
> Of Helen's house against the Ismaelite,
> King of Thogarma, and his habergeons
> Brimstony, blue and fiery; and the force
> Of King Abaddon, and the beast of Cittim;
> Which Rabbi David Kimchi, Onkelos,
> And Aben Ezra do interpret Rome."
>
> THE ALCHEMIST[2]

1

The mind has shown itself at times
Too much the baked and labeled dough
Divided by accepted multitudes.

1   Faust: a legendary necromancer who sold his soul to the Devil in exchange
for supernatural powers. Christopher Marlowe and Goethe, among others, wrote
works of which Faust is the protagonist. In Marlowe's play, *Doctor Faustus*,
some of the most famous lines in English poetry describe the appearance of
Helen of Troy to Faust:
    Was this the face that launched a thousand ships
    And burnt the topless towers of Ilium?
    Sweet Helen, make me immortal with a kiss.
In Greek mythology Helen was the wife of the Greek king Menelaus; she was
abducted by Paris, prince of Troy, and so the Greeks went to war with Troy.
2 = a play by Ben Jonson. Alchemy was the art of turning base metals into gold.

Across the stacked partitions of the day—
Across the memoranda, baseball scores,
The stenographic smiles and stock quotations
Smutty wings flash out equivocations.

The mind is brushed by sparrow wings;
Numbers, rebuffed by asphalt, crowd
The margins of the day, accent the curbs,   10
Convoying divers dawns on every corner
To druggist, barber and tobacconist,
Until the graduate opacities of evening
Take them away as suddenly to somewhere
Virginal perhaps, less fragmentary, cool.

> There is the world dimensional for
> those untwisted by the love of things
> irreconcilable . . .

And yet, suppose some evening I forgot
The fare and transfer, yet got by that way   20
Without recall,—lost yet poised in traffic.
Then I might find your eyes across an aisle,
Still flickering with those prefigurations—
Prodigal, yet uncontested now,
Half-riant before the jerky window frame.

There is some way, I think, to touch
Those hands of yours that count the nights
Stippled with pink and green advertisements.
And now, before its arteries turn dark
I would have you meet this bartered blood.   30
Imminent in his dream, none better knows
The white wafer cheek of love, or offers words
Lightly as moonlight on the eaves meets snow.

Reflective conversion of all things
At your deep blush, when ecstasies thread
The limbs and belly, when rainbows spread
Impinging on the throat and sides . . .
Inevitable, the body of the world
Weeps in inventive dust for the hiatus
That winks above it, bluet in your breasts.   40

The earth may glide diaphanous to death;
But if I lift my arms it is to bend
To you who turned away once, Helen, knowing
The press of troubled hands, too alternate
With steel and soil to hold you endlessly.
I meet you, therefore, in that eventual flame

You found in final chains, no captive then—
Beyond their million brittle, bloodshot eyes;
White, through white cities passed on to assume
That world which comes to each of us alone.   50

Accept a lone eye riveted to your plane,
Bent axle of devotion along companion ways
That beat, continuous, to hourless days—
One inconspicuous, glowing orb of praise.

                    2
Brazen hypnotics glitter here;
Glee shifts from foot to foot,
Magnetic to their tremolo.
This crashing opéra bouffe,[3]
Blest excursion! this ricochet
From roof to roof—   60
Know, Olympians, we are breathless
While nigger cupids scour the stars!

A thousand light shrugs balance us
Through snarling hails of melody.
White shadows slip across the floor
Splayed like cards from a loose hand;
Rhythmic ellipses lead into canters
Until somewhere a rooster banters.

Greet naïvely—yet intrepidly
New soothings, new amazements   70
That cornets introduce at every turn—
And you may fall downstairs with me
With perfect grace and equanimity.
Or, plaintively scud past shores
Where, by strange harmonic laws
All relatives, serene and cool,
Sit rocked in patent armchairs.

O, I have known metallic paradises
Where cuckoos clucked to finches
Above the deft catastrophes of drums.   80
While titters hailed the groans of death
Beneath gyrating awnings I have seen
The incunabula[4] of the divine grotesque.
This music has a reassuring way.

The siren of the springs of guilty song—
Let us take her on the incandescent wax

3   light comic opera.
4   books printed before 1501.

Striated with nuances, nervosities
That we are heir to: she is still so young,
We cannot frown upon her as she smiles,
Dipping here in this cultivated storm   90
Among slim skaters of the gardened skies.

                      3
Capped arbiter of beauty in this street
That narrows darkly into motor dawn,—
You, here beside me, delicate ambassador
Of intricate slain numbers that arise
In whispers, naked of steel;
                              religious gunman!
Who faithfully, yourself, will fall too soon,
And in other ways than as the wind settles
On the sixteen thrifty bridges of the city: 100
Let us unbind our throats of fear and pity.

                              We even,
Who drove speediest destruction
In corymbulous[5] formations of mechanics,—
Who hurried the hill breezes, spouting malice
Plangent over meadows, and looked down
On rifts of torn and empty houses
Like old women with teeth unjubilant
That waited faintly, briefly and in vain:

We know, eternal gunman, our flesh remembers   110
The tensile boughs, the nimble blue plateaus,
The mounted, yielding cities of the air!

That saddled sky that shook down vertical
Repeated play of fire—no hypogeum[6]
Of wave or rock was good against one hour.
We did not ask for that, but have survived,
And will persist to speak again before
All stubble streets that have not curved
To memory, or known the ominous lifted arm
That lowers down the arc of Helen's brow   120
To saturate with blessing and dismay.

A goose, tobacco and cologne—
Three-winged and gold-shod prophecies of heaven,
The lavish heart shall always have to leaven
And spread with bells and voices, and atone
The abating shadows of our conscript dust.

5   A corymb is the floral configuration in which a flat-surfaced cluster is formed
from flower stalks all arising from the same stem, the lower stalks being longer
than the upper.
6   cellar, catacomb.

Anchises'[7] navel, dripping of the sea,—
The hands Erasmus[8] dipped in gleaming tides,
Gathered the voltage of blown blood and vine;
Delve upward for the new and scattered wine,   130
O brother-thief of time, that we recall.
Laugh out the meager penance of their days
Who dare not share with us the breath released,
The substance drilled and spent beyond repair
For golden, or the shadow of gold hair.

Distinctly praise the years, whose volatile
Blamed bleeding hands extend and thresh the height
The imagination spans beyond despair,
Outpacing bargain, vocable and prayer.

7   in Greek mythology, a nobleman, the father of Aeneas. For
revealing the name of Aeneas' mother (the goddess Aphrodite),
Anchises was struck blind by lightning.
8   Erasmus (1466–1536) was a Dutch theologian who
prepared the way for the Reformation by his commentaries on
Church abuses. Later he opposed Luther.

from The Bridge

TO BROOKLYN BRIDGE

How many dawns, chill from his rippling rest
The seagull's wings shall dip and pivot him,
Shedding white rings of tumult, building high
Over the chained bay waters Liberty[1]—

Then, with inviolate curve, forsake our eyes
As apparitional as sails that cross
Some page of figures to be filed away;
—Till elevators drop us from our day . . .

I think of cinemas, panoramic sleights
With multitudes bent toward some flashing scene   10
Never disclosed, but hastened to again,
Foretold to other eyes on the same screen;

And Thee, across the harbor, silver-paced
As though the sun took step of thee, yet left
Some motion ever unspent in thy stride,—
Implicitly thy freedom staying thee!

Out of some subway scuttle, cell or loft
A bedlamite speeds to thy parapets,
Tilting there momently, shrill shirt ballooning,
A jest falls from the speechless caravan.   20

1   Statue of Liberty in New York harbor.

Down Wall, from girder into street noon leaks,
A rip-tooth of the sky's acetylene;
All afternoon the cloud-flown derricks turn . . .
Thy cables breathe the North Atlantic still.

And obscure as that heaven of the Jews,
Thy guerdon . . . Accolade thou dost bestow
Of anonymity time cannot raise:
Vibrant reprieve and pardon thou dost show.

O harp and altar, of the fury fused,
(How could mere toil align thy choiring strings!)   30
Terrific threshold of the prophet's pledge,
Prayer of pariah, and the lover's cry,—

Again the traffic lights that skim thy swift
Unfractioned idiom, immaculate sigh of stars,
Beading thy path—condense eternity:
And we have seen night lifted in thine arms.

Under thy shadow by the piers I waited;
Only in darkness is thy shadow clear.
The City's fiery parcels all undone,
Already snow submerges an iron year . . .   40

O Sleepless as the river under thee,
Vaulting the sea, the prairies' dreaming sod,
Unto us lowliest sometime sweep, descend
And of the curveship lend a myth to God.

NATIONAL WINTER GARDEN

Outspoken buttocks in pink beads
Invite the necessary cloudy clinch
Of bandy eyes. . . . No extra mufflings here:
The world's one flagrant, sweating cinch.

And while legs waken salads in the brain
You pick your blonde out neatly through the smoke.
Always you wait for someone else though, always—
(Then rush the nearest exit through the smoke).

Always and last, before the final ring
When all the fireworks blare, begins
A tom-tom scrimmage with a somewhere violin,
Some cheapest echo of them all—begins.

And shall we call her whiter than the snow?
Sprayed first with ruby, then with emerald sheen—
Least tearful and least glad (who knows her smile?)
A caught slide shows her sandstone gray between.

Her eyes exist in swivelings of her teats,
Pearls whip her hips, a drench of whirling strands.
Her silly snake rings begin to mount, surmount
Each other—turquoise fakes on tinseled hands.

We wait that writhing pool, her pearls collapsed,
—All but her belly buried in the floor;
And the lewd trounce of a final muted beat!
We flee her spasm through a fleshless door. . . .

Yet, to the empty trapeze of your flesh,
O Magdalene,[1] each comes back to die alone.
Then you, the burlesque of our lust—and faith,
Lug us back lifeward—bone by infant bone.

LANGSTON HUGHES   [1902–1967]

Children's Rhymes

When I was a chile we used to play,
"One—two—buckle my shoe!"
and things like that. But now, Lord,
listen at them little varmits!

> *By what sends*
> *the white kids*
> *I ain't sent:*
> *I know I can't*
> *be President.*

There is two thousand children
in this block, I do believe!

> *What don't bug*
> *them white kids*
> *sure bugs me:*
> *We knows everybody*
> *ain't free!*

Some of these young ones is cert'ly bad—
One batted a hard ball right through my window
and my gold fish et the glass.

> *What's written down*
> *for white folks*
> *ain't for us a-tall:*
> *"Liberty and Justice—*
> *Huh—For All."*

1   Mary Magdalene.

Oop-pop-a-da!
    Skee! Daddle-de-do!
    Be-bop!
Salt'peanuts!
    De-dop!

Night Funeral
in Harlem

Night funeral
in Harlem:

*Where did they get
Them two fine cars?*

Insurance man, he did not pay—
His insurance lapsed the other day—
Yet they got a satin box
For his head to lay.

Night funeral
in Harlem: 10

*Who was it sent
That wreath of flowers?*

Them flowers came
from that poor boy's friends—
They'll want flowers, too,
When they meet their ends.

Night funeral
in Harlem:

*Who preached that
Black boy to his grave?*   20

Old preacher-man
Preached that boy away—
Charged Five Dollars
His girl friend had to pay.

Night funeral
in Harlem:

When it was all over
And the lid shut on his head
and the organ had done played
and the last prayers been said   30
and six pallbearers
Carried him out for dead

And off down Lenox Avenue
That long black hearse sped,
 The street light
 At his corner
 Shined just like a tear—
That boy that they was mournin'
Was so dear, so dear
To them folks that brought the flowers,   40
To that girl who paid the preacher-man—
It was all their tears that made
 That poor boy's
 Funeral grand.

 Night funeral
 in Harlem.

Harlem

What happens to a dream deferred?

 Does it dry up
 like a raisin in the sun?
 Or fester like a sore—
 And then run?
 Does it stink like rotten meat?
 Or crust and sugar over—
 like a syrupy sweet?

 Maybe it just sags
 like a heavy load.

 Or does it explode?

Same in Blues

I said to my baby,
Baby, take it slow.
I can't, she said, I can't!
I got to go!

 *There's a certain
 amount of traveling
 in a dream deferred.*

Lulu said to Leonard,
I want a diamond ring.
Leonard said to Lulu,   10
You won't get a goddam thing!

A certain
amount of nothing
in a dream deferred.

Daddy, daddy, daddy,
All I want is you.
You can have me, baby—
but my lovin' days is through.

A certain
amount of impotence   20
in a dream deferred.

Three parties
On my party line—
But that third party,
Lord, ain't mine!

There's liable
to be confusion
in a dream deferred.

From river to river
Uptown and down,   30
There's liable to be confusion
when a dream gets kicked around.

CARL RAKOSI [1903–   ]

Americana IX

Your correspondent must be kidding when he says
that OK came to us from Obediah Kelly, a freight agent
who used to sign his initials on bills of lading.

Why, there are a dozen explanations more intriguing,
such as, an invention of the early telegraphers;

or, variant of okeh, a Choctaw word meaning "IT IS SO"
(which may account
                    for Mrs. Nicholas Murray Butler's[1] *horror*
at finding it in English drawing rooms by 1935
and, worse still, in The Oxford Dictionary);   10

or, a corruption of the harvest word, hoacky,
the last load brought in from the fields;

or, the identification letters for the outer keel
which used to be laid first by the early shipbuilders.

1   wife of the president of Columbia University.

At one time it was even used as an incantation
against fleas,
     which may explain why some people thought
it had its origin in a sign: THE PEOPLE IS OLL KORRECT

painted by Thomas Daniels, a local handyman,
on a farm wagon drawn by twenty-four horses   20
carrying thirty-six young women dressed in white
to a Whig rally in a grove in Champaign County, Ohio.

Another possibility is that OK stood
for Old Kinderhook, the birthplace of Martin Van Buren,[2]
known to his supporters as The Sage of Kinderhook
and to his enemies as The Kinderhook Fox

but after five hundred of his loyal rowdies
using OK as a rallying cry were thrown out
        of a Whig meeting,
the *Daily Express* suggested that the word was Arabic   30
which read backwards meant Kicked Out.

The possibility I like best, however, is that OK stood
for Aux Quais where the French sailors
used to date American girls during the Revolutionary War.

At any rate, OK is the first word
       learned by immigrants
and makes them instant
     democrats.

Americana XV
Simplicity

o rare circle,
you are not in favor now.
Not much is written about you.
Perhaps not much is known about you.
But when I hear this,

"I am just a widow woman.
What do I know?"

and when I see the father of many children
hurrying to the polls in Saigon
to pick the candidate whose symbol is the plow

and when I hear an eighteen year old tell the judge
"So here is Tom Rodd.
     I wanted to go to Selma
and Montgomery but I didn't.

2 eighth president of the United States, 1837–1841.

I wanted to go to Washington and confront the President
                              but I didn't.
But this war is too much for me to say I didn't.
So I'm prepared to go to jail.
                              I have no beef against this court.
I want my friends to know that I'm an optimist.
I drink beer and I play the banjo."

O rare simplicity,
                 when I hear this,
I know I am in your honest presence.

Young Couples
Strolling By

When we get a good day here
                              the bee is at meridian
and little girls in worn-out slippers
charm the adversary
                 in the stranger's eye.

Incognito then enters
                 the coupling influence of the sun
licking an ice cream cone
and Swedes become Italians
                              and Italians become lizards
and Diogenes[1] goes sailing.

W. H. AUDEN [1907–   ]

On This Island

Look, stranger, on this island now
The leaping light for your delight discovers,
Stand stable here
And silent be,
That through the channels of the ear
May wander like a river
The swaying sound of the sea.

Here at a small field's ending pause
When the chalk wall falls to the foam and its tall ledges

1   Greek philosopher, fourth century B.C., originator of the sect of Cynics.
Said to have lived in a tub.

Oppose the pluck
And knock of the tide,
And the shingle scrambles after the suck-
-ing surf,
And a gull lodges
A moment on its sheer side.

Far off like floating seeds the ships
Diverge on urgent voluntary errands,
And this full view
Indeed may enter
And move in memory as now these clouds do,
That pass the harbor mirror
And all the summer through the water saunter.

Musée
des Beaux Arts[1]

About suffering they were never wrong,
The Old Masters: how well they understood
Its human position; how it takes place
While someone else is eating or opening a window or just walking
      dully along;
How, when the aged are reverently, passionately waiting
For the miraculous birth, there always must be
Children who did not specially want it to happen, skating
On a pond at the edge of the wood:
They never forgot
That even the dreadful martyrdom must run its course
Anyhow in a corner, some untidy spot
Where the dogs go on with their doggy life and the torturer's horse
Scratches its innocent behind on a tree.

In Brueghel's *Icarus*,[2] for instance: how everything turns away
Quite leisurely from the disaster; the ploughman may
Have heard the splash, the forsaken cry,
But for him it was not an important failure; the sun shone
As it had to on the white legs disappearing into the green
Water; and the expensive delicate ship that must have seen
Something amazing, a boy falling out of the sky,
Had somewhere to get to and sailed calmly on.

1   Museum of Fine Arts.
2   "The Fall of Icarus," a sixteenth-century painting by Pieter Brueghel.
Daedalus constructed wings of wax. His son, Icarus, flew too near the sun, the
wax melted, and he fell into the sea and drowned.

The Fall
of Rome

FOR CYRIL CONNOLLY

The piers are pummeled by the waves;
In a lonely field the rain
Lashes an abandoned train;
Outlaws fill the mountain caves.

Fantastic grow the evening gowns;
Agents of the Fisc[1] pursue
Absconding tax-defaulters through
The sewers of provincial towns.

Private rites of magic send
The temple prostitutes to sleep;
All the literati keep
An imaginary friend.

Cerebrotonic Catos[2] may
Extol the Ancient Disciplines,
But the muscle-bound Marines
Mutiny for food and pay.

Caesar's double-bed is warm
As an unimportant clerk
Writes I DO NOT LIKE MY WORK
On a pink official form.

Unendowed with wealth or pity,
Little birds with scarlet legs,
Sitting on their speckled eggs,
Eye each flu-infected city.

Altogether elsewhere, vast
Herds of reindeer move across
Miles and miles of golden moss,
Silently and very fast.

Since

On a mid-December day,
frying sausages
for myself, I abruptly
felt under fingers

1　British revenue department.
2　"cerebrotonic," intellectually invigorating; Cato the Elder was a Roman
statesman, Cato the Younger, a Stoic philosopher.

thirty years younger the rim
of a steering wheel,
on my cheek the parching wind
of an August noon,
as passenger beside me
You as then you were.   10

Slap across a veg-growing
alluvial plain
we raced in clouds of white dust,
and geese fled screaming
as we missed them by inches,
making a bee-line
for mountains gradually
enlarging eastward,
joyfully certain nightfall
would occasion joy.   20

It did. In a flagged kitchen
we were served broiled trout
and a rank cheese: for a while
we talked by the fire,
then, carrying candles, climbed
steep stairs. Love was made
then and there: so halcyoned,[1]
soon we fell asleep
to the sound of a river
swabbling through a gorge.   30

Since then, other enchantments
have blazed and faded,
enemies changed their address,
and War made ugly
an unaccountable number
of unknown neighbors,
precious as us to themselves:
but round your image
there is no fog, and the Earth
can still astonish.   40

Of what, then, should I complain,
pottering about
a neat suburban kitchen?
Solitude? Rubbish!
It's social enough with real

1   halcyon (adjective): calm, undisturbed, tranquil; (verb—obs.): to
tranquillize.

faces and landscapes
for whose friendly countenance
I at least can learn
to live with obesity
and a little fame.

. 50

THEODORE ROETHKE   [1908–1963]

Night Journey

Now as the train bears west,
Its rhythm rocks the earth,
And from my Pullman berth
I stare into the night
While others take their rest.
Bridges of iron lace,
A suddenness of trees,
A lap of mountain mist
All cross my line of sight,
Then a bleak wasted place,
And a lake below my knees.
Full on my neck I feel
The straining at a curve;
My muscles move with steel,
I wake in every nerve.
I watch a beacon swing
From dark to blazing bright;
We thunder through ravines
And gullies washed with light.
Beyond the mountain pass
Mist deepens on the pane;
We rush into a rain
That rattles double glass.
Wheels shake the roadbed stone,
The pistons jerk and shove,
I stay up half the night
To see the land I love.

My Papa's Waltz

The whiskey on your breath
Could make a small boy dizzy;
But I hung on like death:
Such waltzing was not easy.

We romped until the pans
Slid from the kitchen shelf;
My mother's countenance
Could not unfrown itself.

The hand that held my wrist
Was battered on one knuckle;
At every step you missed
My right ear scraped a buckle.

You beat time on my head
With a palm caked hard by dirt,
Then waltzed me off to bed
Still clinging to your shirt.

Dolor

I have known the inexorable sadness of pencils,
Neat in their boxes, dolor of pad and paper-weight,
All the misery of manilla folders and mucilage,
Desolation in immaculate public places,
Lonely reception room, lavatory, switchboard,
The unalterable pathos of basin and pitcher,
Ritual of multigraph, paper-clip, comma,
Endless duplication of lives and objects.
And I have seen dust from the walls of institutions,
Finer than flour, alive, more dangerous than silica,
Sift, almost invisible, through long afternoons of tedium,
Dropping a fine film on nails and delicate eyebrows,
Glazing the pale hair, the duplicate grey standard faces.

Elegy for Jane
My Student, Thrown by a Horse

I remember the neckcurls, limp and damp as tendrils;
And her quick look, a sidelong pickerel smile;
And how, once startled into talk, the light syllables leaped for her,
And she balanced in the delight of her thought,
A wren, happy, tail into the wind,
Her song trembling the twigs and small branches.
The shade sang with her;
The leaves, their whispers turned to kissing;
And the mold sang in the bleached valleys under the rose.

Oh, when she was sad, she cast herself down into such a pure depth,
Even a father could not find her:
Scraping her cheek against straw;
Stirring the clearest water.

My sparrow, you are not here,
Waiting like a fern, making a spiny shadow.
The sides of wet stones cannot console me,
Nor the moss, wound with the last light.

If only I could nudge you from this sleep,
My maimed darling, my skittery pigeon.
Over this damp grave I speak the words of my love:
I, with no rights in this matter,
Neither father nor lover.

The Waking

I wake to sleep, and take my waking slow.
I feel my fate in what I cannot fear.
I learn by going where I have to go.

We think by feeling. What is there to know?
I hear my being dance from ear to ear.
I wake to sleep, and take my waking slow.

Of those so close beside me, which are you?
God bless the Ground! I shall walk softly there,
And learn by going where I have to go.

Light takes the Tree; but who can tell us how?
The lowly worm climbs up a winding stair;
I wake to sleep, and take my waking slow.

Great Nature has another thing to do
To you and me; so take the lively air,
And, lovely, learn by going where to go.

This shaking keeps me steady. I should know.
What falls away is always. And is near.
I wake to sleep, and take my waking slow.
I learn by going where I have to go.

The Rose

1

There are those to whom place is unimportant,
But this place, where sea and fresh water meet,
Is important—
Where the hawks sway out into the wind,
Without a single wingbeat,
And the eagles sail low over the fir trees,
And the gulls cry against the crows
In the curved harbors,

And the tide rises up against the grass
Nibbled by sheep and rabbits.   10

A time for watching the tide,
For the heron's hieratic fishing,
For the sleepy cries of the towhee,
The morning birds gone, the twittering finches,
But still the flash of the kingfisher, the wingbeat of the scoter,
The sun a ball of fire coming down over the water,
The last geese crossing against the reflected afterlight,
The moon retreating into a vague cloud-shape
To the cries of the owl, the eerie whooper.
The old log subsides with the lessening waves,   20
And there is silence.

I sway outside myself
Into the darkening currents,
Into the small spillage of driftwood,
The waters swirling past the tiny headlands.
Was it here I wore a crown of birds for a moment
While on a far point of the rocks
The light heightened,
And below, in a mist out of nowhere,
The first rain gathered?   30

                    2
As when a ship sails with a light wind—
The waves less than the ripples made by rising fish,
The lacelike wrinkles of the wake widening, thinning out,
Sliding away from the traveler's eye,
The prow pitching easily up and down,
The whole ship rolling slightly sideways,
The stern high, dipping like a child's boat in a pond—
Our motion continues.

But this rose, this rose in the sea-wind,
Stays,   40
Stays in its true place,
Flowering out of the dark,
Widening at high noon, face upward,
A single wild rose, struggling out of the white embrace of the morning-
      glory,
Out of the briary hedge, the tangle of matted underbrush,
Beyond the clover, the ragged hay,
Beyond the sea pine, the oak, the wind-tipped madrona,
Moving with the waves, the undulating driftwood,
Where the slow creek winds down to the black sand of the shore
With its thick grassy scum and crabs scuttling back into their glisten-
      ing craters.   50

And I think of roses, roses,
White and red, in the wide six-hundred-foot greenhouses,
And my father standing astride the cement benches,
Lifting me high over the four-foot stems, the Mrs. Russells, and his
    own elaborate hybrids,
And how those flowerheads seemed to flow toward me, to beckon me,
    only a child, out of myself.

What need for heaven, then,
With that man, and those roses?

3
What do they tell us, sound and silence?
I think of American sounds in this silence:
On the banks of the Tombstone, the wind-harps having their say,   60
The thrush singing alone, that easy bird,
The killdeer whistling away from me,
The mimetic chortling of the catbird
Down in the corner of the garden, among the raggedy lilacs,
The bobolink skirring from a broken fencepost,
The bluebird, lover of holes in old wood, lilting its light song,
And that thin cry, like a needle piercing the ear, the insistent cicada,
And the ticking of snow around oil drums in the Dakotas,
The thin whine of telephone wires in the wind of a Michigan winter,
The shriek of nails as old shingles are ripped from the top of a roof,
The bulldozer backing away, the hiss of the sandblaster,   71
And the deep chorus of horns coming up from the streets in early
    morning.
I return to the twittering of swallows above water,
And that sound, that single sound,
When the mind remembers all,
And gently the light enters the sleeping soul,
A sound so thin it could not woo a bird,

Beautiful my desire, and the place of my desire.

I think of the rock singing, and light making its own silence,
At the edge of a ripening meadow, in early summer,   80
The moon lolling in the close elm, a shimmer of silver,
Or that lonely time before the breaking of morning
When the slow freight winds along the edge of the ravaged hillside,
And the wind tries the shape of a tree,
While the moon lingers,
And a drop of rain water hangs at the tip of a leaf
Shifting in the wakening sunlight
Like the eye of a new-caught fish.

4
I live with the rocks, their weeds,
Their filmy fringes of green, their harsh   90

Edges, their holes
Cut by the sea-slime, far from the crash
Of the long swell,
The oily, tar-laden walls
Of the toppling waves,
Where the salmon ease their way into the kelp beds,
And the sea rearranges itself among the small islands.

Near this rose, in this grove of sun-parched, wind-warped madronas,
Among the half-dead trees, I came upon the true ease of myself,
As if another man appeared out of the depths of my being,   100
And I stood outside myself,
Beyond becoming and perishing,
A something wholly other,
As if I swayed out on the wildest wave alive,
And yet was still.
And I rejoiced in being what I was:
In the lilac change, the white reptilian calm,
In the bird beyond the bough, the single one
With all the air to greet him as he flies,
The dolphin rising from the darkening waves;   110

And in this rose, this rose in the sea-wind,
Rooted in stone, keeping the whole of light,
Gathering to itself sound and silence—
Mine and the sea-wind's.

DYLAN THOMAS [1914–1953]

The Force That
Through the Green Fuse
Drives the Flower

The force that through the green fuse drives the flower
Drives my green age; that blasts the roots of trees
Is my destroyer.
And I am dumb to tell the crooked rose
My youth is bent by the same wintry fever.

The force that drives the water through the rocks
Drives my red blood; that dries the mouthing streams
Turns mine to wax.
And I am dumb to mouth unto my veins
How at the mountain spring the same mouth sucks.

The hand that whirls the water in the pool
Stirs the quicksand; that ropes the blowing wind

Hauls my shroud sail.
And I am dumb to tell the hanging man
How of my clay is made the hangman's lime.

The lips of time leech to the fountain head;
Love drips and gathers, but the fallen blood
Shall calm her sores.
And I am dumb to tell a weather's wind
How time has ticked a heaven round the stars.

And I am dumb to tell the lover's tomb
How at my sheet goes the same crooked worm.

Fern Hill

Now as I was young and easy under the apple boughs
About the lilting house and happy as the grass was green,
    The night above the dingle starry,
      Time let me hail and climb
    Golden in the heydays of his eyes,
And honored among wagons I was prince of the apple towns
And once below a time I lordly had the trees and leaves
      Trail with daisies and barley
    Down the rivers of the windfall light.

And as I was green and carefree, famous among the barns   10
About the happy yard and singing as the farm was home,
    In the sun that is young once only,
      Time let me play and be
    Golden in the mercy of his means,
And green and golden I was huntsman and herdsman, the calves
Sang to my horn, the foxes on the hills barked clear and cold,
      And the sabbath rang slowly
    In the pebbles of the holy streams.

All the sun long it was running, it was lovely, the hay
Fields high as the house, the tunes from the chimneys, it was air   20
    And playing, lovely and watery
      And fire green as grass.
    And nightly under the simple stars
As I rode to sleep the owls were bearing the farm away,
All the moon long I heard, blessed among stables, the nightjars
      Flying with the ricks, and the horses
      Flashing into the dark.

And then to awake, and the farm, like a wanderer white
With the dew, come back, the cock on his shoulder: it was all
    Shining, it was Adam and maiden,   30
      The sky gathered again

And the sun grew round that very day.
So it must have been after the birth of the simple light
In the first, spinning place, the spellbound horses walking warm
    Out of the whinnying green stable
      On to the fields of praise.

And honored among foxes and pheasants by the gay house
Under the new made clouds and happy as the heart was long,
    In the sun born over and over,
      I ran my heedless ways,   40
    My wishes raced through the house high hay
And nothing I cared, at my sky blue trades, that time allows
In all his tuneful turning so few and such morning songs
    Before the children green and golden
      Follow him out of grace,

Nothing I cared, in the lamb white days, that time would take me
Up to the swallow thronged loft by the shadow of my hand,
    In the moon that is always rising,
      Nor that riding to sleep
    I should hear him fly with the high fields   50
And wake to the farm forever fled from the childless land.
Oh as I was young and easy in the mercy of his means,
      Time held me green and dying
    Though I sang in my chains like the sea.

Do Not
Go Gentle into
That Good Night

Do not go gentle into that good night,
Old age should burn and rave at close of day;
Rage, rage against the dying of the light.

Though wise men at their end know dark is right,
Because their words have forked no lightning they
Do not go gentle into that good night.

Good men, the last wave by, crying how bright
Their frail deeds might have danced in a green bay,
Rage, rage against the dying of the light.

Wild men who caught and sang the sun in flight,
And learn, too late, they grieved it on its way,
Do not go gentle into that good night.

Grave men, near death, who see with blinding sight
Blind eyes could blaze like meteors and be gay,
Rage, rage against the dying of the light.

And you, my father, there on the sad height,
Curse, bless, me now with your fierce tears, I pray.
Do not go gentle into that good night.
Rage, rage against the dying of the light.

DUDLEY RANDALL [1914–   ]

Blackberry Sweet

Black girl black girl
lips as curved as cherries
full as grape bunches
sweet as blackberries

Black girl black girl
when you walk you are
magic as a rising bird
or a falling star

Black girl black girl
what's your spell to make
the heart in my breast
jump   stop   shake

HENRY REED [1914–   ]

Naming of Parts

Today we have naming of parts. Yesterday,
We had daily cleaning. And tomorrow morning,
We shall have what to do after firing. But today,
Today we have naming of parts. Japonica
Glistens like coral in all of the neighboring gardens,
      And today we have naming of parts.

This is the lower sling swivel. And this
Is the upper sling swivel, whose use you will see,
When you are given your slings. And this is the piling swivel,
Which in your case you have not got. The branches   10
Hold in the gardens their silent, eloquent gestures,
      Which in our case we have not got.

This is the safety-catch, which is always released
With an easy flick of the thumb. And please do not let me
See anyone using his finger. You can do it quite easy
If you have any strength in your thumb. The blossoms
Are fragile and motionless, never letting anyone see
      Any of them using their finger.

And this you can see is the bolt. The purpose of this
Is to open the breech, as you see. We can slide it   20
Rapidly backwards and forwards: we call this
Easing the spring. And rapidly backwards and forwards
The early bees are assaulting and fumbling the flowers:
    They call it easing the Spring.

They call it easing the Spring: it is perfectly easy
If you have any strength in your thumb: like the bolt,
And the breech, and the cocking-piece, and the point of balance,
Which in our case we have not got; and the almond-blossom
Silent in all of the gardens and the bees going backwards and forwards,
    For today we have naming of parts.   30

DAVID IGNATOW [1914–   ]

Get the Gasworks

Get the gasworks into a poem,
and you've got the smoke and smokestacks,
the mottled red and yellow tenements,
and grimy kids who curse with the pungency
of the odor of gas. You've got America, boy.

Sketch in the river and barges,
all dirty and slimy.
How do the seagulls stay so white?
And always cawing like little mad geniuses?
You've got the kind of living
that makes the kind of thinking we do:
gaswork smokestack whistle tooting wisecracks.
They don't come because we like it that way,
but because we find it outside our window each morning,
in soot on the furniture,
and trucks carrying coal for gas,
the kid hot after the ball under the wheel.
He gets it over the belly, all right.
He dies there.

So the kids keep tossing the ball around
after the funeral.
So the cops keep chasing them,
so the mamas keep hollering,
and papa flings his newspaper outward,
in disgust with discipline.

from Between
the Porch
and the Altar

IV. *At the Altar*

I sit at a gold table with my girl
Whose eyelids burn with brandy. What a whirl
Of Easter eggs is colored by the lights,
As the Norwegian dancer's crystalled tights
Flash with her naked leg's high-booted skate,
Like Northern Lights upon my watching plate.
The twinkling steel above me is a star;
I am a fallen Christmas tree. Our car   100
Races through seven red-lights—then the road
Is unpatrolled and empty, and a load
Of ply-wood with a tail-light makes us slow.
I turn and whisper in her ear. You know
I want to leave my mother and my wife,
You wouldn't have me tied to them for life . . .
Time runs, the windshield runs with stars. The past
Is cities from a train, until at last
Its escalating and black-windowed blocks
Recoil against a Gothic church. The clocks   110
Are tolling. I am dying. The shocked stones
Are falling like a ton of bricks and bones
That snap and splinter and descend in glass
Before a priest who mumbles through his Mass
And sprinkles holy water; and the Day
Breaks with its lightning on the man of clay,
Dies amara valde.[1] Here the Lord
Is Lucifer in harness: hand on sword,
He watches me for Mother, and will turn
The bier and baby-carriage where I burn.   120

1   "a very bitter day."

Mr. Edwards[1]
and the Spider

I saw the spiders marching through the air,
   Swimming from tree to tree that mildewed day
      In latter August when the hay
         Came creaking to the barn. But where

1   Jonathan Edwards, eighteenth-century Calvinist theologian, born in East
Windsor, Connecticut.

The wind is westerly,
Where gnarled November makes the spiders fly
Into the apparitions of the sky,
They purpose nothing but their ease and die
Urgently beating east to sunrise and the sea;

What are we in the hands of the great God?   10
It was in vain you set up thorn and briar
    In battle array against the fire
    And treason crackling in your blood;
        For the wild thorns grow tame
And will do nothing to oppose the flame;
Your lacerations tell the losing game
You play against a sickness past your cure.
How will the hands be strong? How will the heart endure?

A very little thing, a little worm,
Or hourglass-blazoned spider, it is said,   20
    Can kill a tiger. Will the dead
    Hold up his mirror and affirm
        To the four winds the smell
And flash of his authority? It's well
If God who holds you to the pit of hell,
Much as one holds a spider, will destroy,
Baffle and dissipate your soul. As a small boy

On Windsor Marsh, I saw the spider die
When thrown into the bowels of fierce fire:
    There's no long struggle, no desire   30
    To get up on its feet and fly—
        It stretches out its feet
And dies. This is the sinner's last retreat;
Yes, and no strength exerted on the heat
Then sinews the abolished will, when sick
And full of burning, it will whistle on a brick.

But who can plumb the sinking of that soul?
Josiah Hawley,[2] picture yourself cast
    Into a brick-kiln where the blast
    Fans your quick vitals to a coal—   40
        If measured by a glass,
How long would it seem burning! Let there pass
A minute, ten, ten trillion; but the blaze
Is infinite, eternal: this is death,
To die and know it. This is the Black Widow, death.

2   Edwards' cousin, who opposed his revivalist preachings.

Memories
of West Street
and Lepke

Only teaching on Tuesdays, book-worming
in pajamas fresh from the washer each morning,
I hog a whole house on Boston's
"hardly passionate Marlborough Street,"[1]
where even the man
scavenging filth in the back alley trash cans,
has two children, a beach wagon, a helpmate,
and is a "young Republican."
I have a nine months' daughter,
young enough to be my granddaughter.   10
Like the sun she rises in her flame-flamingo infants' wear.

These are the tranquillized *Fifties*,
and I am forty. Ought I to regret my seedtime?
I was a fire-breathing Catholic C.O.,[2]
and made my manic statement,
telling off the state and president, and then
sat waiting sentence in the bull pen
beside a Negro boy with curlicues
of marijuana in his hair.

Given a year,   20
I walked on the roof of the West Street Jail,[3] a short
enclosure like my school soccer court,
and saw the Hudson River once a day
through sooty clothesline entanglements
and bleaching khaki tenements.
Strolling, I yammered metaphysics with Abramowitz,[4]
a jaundice-yellow ("it's really tan")
and fly-weight pacifist,
so vegetarian,
he wore rope shoes and preferred fallen fruit.   30
He tried to convert Bioff and Brown,
the Hollywood pimps, to his diet.
Hairy, muscular, suburban,
wearing chocolate double-breasted suits,
they blew their tops and beat him black and blue.

1   Henry James said an example of extreme understatement would be that
Marlborough Street was hardly passionate.
2   conscientious objector.
3   jail in New York from which prisoners were sent elsewhere. Lowell says
that "all sorts of people were there, including German bundists and Jehovah's
Witnesses."
4   Robert Lowell recounts that "Abramowitz didn't eat meat—or fruit, unless
fallen from the tree; his clothes were made of fallen vegetables. Bioff and
Brown attacked him."

I was so out of things, I'd never heard
of the Jehovah's Witnesses.
"Are you a C.O.?" I asked a fellow jailbird.
"No," he answered, "I'm a J.W."
He taught me the "hospital tuck,"   40
and pointed out the T shirted back
of *Murder Incorporated's* Czar Lepke,[5]
there piling towels on a rack,
or dawdling off to his little segregated cell full
of things forbidden the common man:
a portable radio, a dresser, two toy American
flags tied together with a ribbon of Easter palm.
Flabby, bald, lobotomized,
he drifted in a sheepish calm,
where no agonizing reappraisal   50
jarred his concentration on the electric chair—
hanging like an oasis in his air
of lost connections. . . .

5   Lou (Lepke) Buchalter, one of the leaders of
New York's labor and industrial rackets, and a
member of the ruling board of Murder, Inc. He went
to the electric chair in 1944. Lowell says, "He was
a mild soul—looked like an art critic I knew but
less dangerous. Lepke was evil as a negative
reality."

For the Union Dead

"Relinquunt Omnia Servare Rem Publicam."[1]

The old South Boston Aquarium stands
in a Sahara of snow now. Its broken windows are boarded.
The bronze weathervane cod has lost half its scales.
The airy tanks are dry.

Once my nose crawled like a snail on the glass;
my hand tingled
to burst the bubbles
drifting from the noses of the cowed, compliant fish.

My hand draws back. I often sigh still
for the dark downward and vegetating kingdom   10
of the fish and reptile. One morning last March,
I pressed against the new barbed and galvanized

fence on the Boston Common. Behind their cage,
yellow dinosaur steamshovels were grunting
as they cropped up tons of mush and grass
to gouge their underworld garage.

Parking spaces luxuriate like civic
sandpiles in the heart of Boston.

1   "They gave up everything to serve the State."

A girdle of orange, Puritan-pumpkin colored girders
braces the tingling Statehouse,   20

shaking over the excavations, as it faces Colonel Shaw[2]
and his bell-cheeked Negro infantry
on St. Gaudens'[3] shaking Civil War relief,
propped by a plank splint against the garage's earthquake.

Two months after marching through Boston,
half the regiment was dead;
at the dedication,
William James[4] could almost hear the bronze Negroes breathe.

Their monument sticks like a fishbone
in the city's throat.   30
Its Colonel is as lean
as a compass-needle.

He has an angry wrenlike vigilance,
a greyhound's gentle tautness;
he seems to wince at pleasure,
and suffocate for privacy.

He is out of bounds now. He rejoices in man's lovely,
peculiar power to choose life and die—
when he leads his black soldiers to death,
he cannot bend his back.   40

On a thousand small town New England greens,
the old white churches hold their air
of sparse, sincere rebellion; frayed flags
quilt the graveyards of the Grand Army of the Republic.

The stone statues of the abstract Union Soldier
grow slimmer and younger each year—
wasp-waisted, they doze over muskets
and muse through their sideburns . . .

Shaw's father wanted no monument
except the ditch,   50
where his son's body was thrown
and lost with his "niggers."

The ditch is nearer.
There are no statues for the last war here;
on Boyleston Street, a commercial photograph
shows Hiroshima boiling

2   Robert Gould Shaw, born in Boston in 1837 and killed at Fort Wagner,
South Carolina in 1863. Shaw enlisted as a private in the Union Army in 1861,
was promoted to captain, and in 1863 became colonel of the 54th Massachusetts,
the first regiment of Negro troops from a free state mustered into the U.S.
service. A statue by Saint-Gaudens of Shaw stands on Boston Common.
3   Augustus Saint-Gaudens, American sculptor, 1848–1907.
4   American psychologist and philosopher, 1842–1910.

over a Mosler Safe, the "Rock of Ages"
that survived the blast. Space is nearer.
When I crouch to my television set,
the drained faces of Negro school-children rise like balloons.   60

Colonel Shaw
is riding on his bubble,
he waits
for the blessèd break.

The Aquarium is gone. Everywhere,
giant finned cars nose forward like fish;
a savage servility
slides by on grease.

ROBERT DUNCAN [1919–   ]

Two Presentations

1

[*After my mother's death in December 1960, there were two returns
of her presence in February and March of 1961. The first came in a
dream.*]

"*We send you word of the Mother.*"
Was it my mother? our mother?
In the dream it was a blessing or a key
she brought, a message.
Was it H.D.'s[1] frail script?

It was she, I thought, but the sign
was of another. It was a help
(for my mind is in great trouble)
to receive the letter.

But I was cold, lying in the narrow bed,   10
naked. When did I lie there so?
        The first light of morning
came in over me, a cold thin wave
where nerves shrank back from the bruise.

Who gave me the note? Only I
accuse myself of lying here in the cold,
shaking in the drafts of light,
hugging to the scant cover.
For I have lost heart,
my mind is divided.   20

1   Hilda Doolittle, American poet, 1886–1961.

[AFTERTHOUGHTS: November 1961. Working on the H.D. Book,
I had begun to fear her death as a forfeit or foundation of the work.

My first mother in whom I took my first nature, the formal imperative
of my physical body and signature, died when I was born. I was
motherless then, "in the cold," for six months before my second
mother found and adopted me. But the "When did I lie there so?"
seems to refer to some cold back of this period of loss, as, in turn,
"the Mother" is back of my mothers.

When I was born, what gave birth to me fell back dead or died in
the labor towards my success. Was she alive or dead when I drew my
first "breath" and utterd, threw out, my first cry? In taking heart,
another heart was lost. What blessing, what key then?]

2

[In the change from my birth name, Edward Howard Duncan, to my
name by adoption, Robert Edward Symmes, the hidden or lost name
is Howard.

The second presentation came while I was riding the Union-Howard
busline from the Marina to North Beach.[2] I had begun a poem
addresst to my mother, when the hysterical talk of a school-girl broke
in, dictating fragments of a message that seemd meant for me and at
the same time to direct the poem.]

You are gone and I send
as I used to
    with the salutation *Dear Mother*
the beginning of a letter
    as if it could reach you.

Yet *Dear Mother* could catch at my heart to say
    —and did when I was a child, as you
are now a child among shades—
    as if the words betrayd
a painful nearness and separation.   30

"It's this poem I wrote and I calld it *My Soul!*"
Was she talking to me? Her voice carries
above the din of high-school girls chattering,
crowding the bus with shrill bird voices.

"It's this poem I wrote, see!"

She waits, and when I look up from where I am writing . . .
Did she see me writing here? How did I hear
    her voice if not directed in the crowd to me?
Laughing, the fat little Hindu girl
turns her eyes from my glance, triumphant.   40

2   places in San Francisco.

"I write so many, see, all the time.
 And this one I lost. That's why I say
 I lost *My Soul*."

Does she say anything that comes into her head
to hold my attention?
"Well, you didnt go over and pull me out,"
she shouts to some girl I can't see.

"I had such a cramp in my leg
 and I almost drownd.
 I thought I was all alone."   50

Like *that* then. Her voice, too,
came thru to me,
swimming in the flood of voices as if alone,
catching my attention
—a sheaf of poems hysterical girls
might carry about, carry-on about,
their souls or names . . .
loves? "You'll never love anyone," you said, Mother,
so long ago.

                        ❋

                    Caught in the swirl of waters,   60
bobbing heads of the young girls, pubescent,
        descending from the bus,
pass on or out, into the street beyond
        —one dark Hindu face among them passes
        out of my ken.

Are you out there alone then like that?
Or did your own mother come, close in,
to meet you. As your sister, looking forward or back
from her eighty years, said,
"Mother will be there when I die,   70
waiting for me." Her throat
catching at the evocation.

        But, of that other Great Mother
or metre, of the matter . . .

My letter always went alone
        to where
I never knew you reading.

KEITH DOUGLAS [1920–1944]

Vergissmeinicht[1]

Three weeks gone and the combatants gone,
returning over the nightmare ground
we found the place again, and found
the soldier sprawling in the sun.

The frowning barrel of his gun
overshadowing. As we came on
that day, he hit my tank with one
like the entry of a demon.

Look. Here in the gunpit spoil
the dishonored picture of his girl
who has put: *Steffi. Vergissmeinicht*
in a copybook gothic script.

We see him almost with content
abased, and seeming to have paid
and mocked at by his own equipment
that's hard and good when he's decayed.

But she would weep to see today
how on his skin the swart flies move;
the dust upon the paper eye
and the burst stomach like a cave.

For here the lover and killer are mingled
who had one body and one heart.
And death who had the soldier singled
has done the lover mortal hurt.

1   "forget me not."

RICHARD WILBUR [1921–   ]

The Beautiful
Changes

One wading a Fall meadow finds on all sides
The Queen Anne's Lace lying like lilies
On water; it glides
So from the walker, it turns
Dry grass to a lake, as the slightest shade of you
Valleys my mind in fabulous blue Lucernes.[1]

1   Lucerne, a lake in Switzerland.

The beautiful changes as a forest is changed
By a chameleon's tuning his skin to it;
As a mantis, arranged
On a green leaf, grows
Into it, makes the leaf leafier, and proves
Any greenness is deeper than anyone knows.

Your hands hold roses always in a way that says
They are not only yours; the beautiful changes
In such kind ways,
Wishing ever to sunder
Things and things' selves for a second finding, to lose
For a moment all that it touches back to wonder.

Love Calls Us to the Things of This World

The eyes open to a cry of pulleys,
And spirited from sleep, the astounded soul
Hangs for a moment bodiless and simple
As false dawn.
        Outside the open window
The morning air is all awash with angels.

Some are in bed-sheets, some are in blouses,
Some are in smocks: but truly there they are.
Now they are rising together in calm swells
Of halcyon feeling, filling whatever they wear   10
With the deep joy of their impersonal breathing;

Now they are flying in place, conveying
The terrible speed of their omnipresence, moving
And staying like white water; and now of a sudden
They swoon down into so rapt a quiet
That nobody seems to be there.
        The soul shrinks

From all that it is about to remember,
From the punctual rape of every blessèd day,
And cries,   20
        "Oh, let there be nothing on earth but laundry,
Nothing but rosy hands in the rising steam
And clear dances done in the sight of heaven."

Yet, as the sun acknowledges
With a warm look the world's hunks and colors,
The soul descends once more in bitter love
To accept the waking body, saying now
In a changed voice as the man yawns and rises,

"Bring them down from their ruddy gallows;
Let there be clean linen for the backs of thieves;   30
Let lovers go fresh and sweet to be undone,
And the heaviest nuns walk in a pure floating
Of dark habits,
                    keeping their difficult balance."

Piazza di Spagna, Early Morning[1]

            I can't forget
    How she stood at the top of that long marble stair
    Amazed, and then with a sleepy pirouette
Went dancing slowly down to the fountain-quieted square;

        Nothing upon her face
But some impersonal loneliness,—not then a girl,
        But as it were a reverie of the place,
            A called-for falling glide and whirl;

        As when a leaf, petal, or thin chip
Is drawn to the falls of a pool and, circling a moment above it,
            Rides on over the lip—
    Perfectly beautiful, perfectly ignorant of it.

PHILIP LARKIN [1922–   ]

Within the Dream You Said

Within the dream you said:
Let us kiss then,
In this room, in this bed,
But when all's done
We must not meet again.

Hearing this last word,
There was no lambing-night,
No gale-driven bird
Nor frost-encircled root
As cold as my heart.

1 a square in Rome with a flight of stairs and a fountain at the bottom.

Night-Music

At one the wind rose,
And with it the noise
Of the black poplars.

Long since had the living
By a thin twine
Been led into their dreams
Where lanterns shine
Under a still veil
Of falling streams;
Long since had the dead
Become untroubled
In the light soil.
There were no mouths
To drink of the wind,
Nor any eyes
To sharpen on the stars'
Wide heaven-holding,
Only the sound
Long sibilant-muscled trees
Were lifting up, the black poplars.

And in their blazing solitude
The stars sang in their sockets through the night:
"Blow bright, blow bright
The coal of this unquickened world."

Mr Bleaney

"This was Mr Bleaney's room. He stayed
The whole time he was at the Bodies,[1] till
They moved him." Flowered curtains, thin and frayed,
Fall to within five inches of the sill,

Whose window shows a strip of building land,
Tussocky, littered. "Mr Bleaney took
My bit of garden properly in hand."
Bed, upright chair, sixty-watt bulb, no hook

Behind the door, no room for books or bags—
"I'll take it." So it happens that I lie
Where Mr Bleaney lay, and stub my fags
On the same saucer-souvenir, and try

Stuffing my ears with cotton-wool, to drown
The jabbering set he egged her on to buy.
I know his habits—what time he came down,
His preference for sauce to gravy, why

1   automobile factory (slang).

350

He kept on plugging at the four aways[2]—
Likewise their yearly frame: the Frinton folk
Who put him up for summer holidays,
And Christmas at his sister's house in Stoke.

But if he stood and watched the frigid wind
Tousling the clouds, lay on the fusty bed
Telling himself that this was home, and grinned,
And shivered, without shaking off the dread

That how we live measures our own nature,
And at his age having no more to show
Than one hired box should make him pretty sure
He warranted no better, I don't know.

Wild Oats

About twenty years ago
Two girls came in where I worked—
A bosomy English rose
And her friend in specs I could talk to.
Faces in those days sparked
The whole shooting-match off, and I doubt
If ever one had like hers:
But it was the friend I took out,

And in seven years after that
Wrote over four hundred letters,
Gave a ten-guinea ring
I got back in the end, and met
At numerous cathedral cities
Unknown to the clergy. I believe
I met beautiful twice. She was trying
Both times (so I thought) not to laugh.

Parting, after about five
Rehearsals, was an agreement
That I was too selfish, withdrawn,
And easily bored to love.
Well, useful to get that learnt.
In my wallet are still two snaps
Of bosomy rose with fur gloves on.
Unlucky charms, perhaps.

2   The "four aways" section of British football-pool forms requires competitors
to gamble on a prediction of four Association Football teams winning matches
"away" from their home grounds—more difficult, supposedly, than predicting
"home" wins, but attracting some gamblers because they need make fewer
predictions. Mr. Bleaney might argue that persistence in this limited field would
be more likely to bring prizes.—Alan Brownjohn

JAMES DICKEY   [1923–   ]

Listening
to Foxhounds

When in that gold
Of fires, quietly sitting
With the men whose brothers are hounds,

You hear the first tone
Of a dog on scent, you look from face
To face, to see whose will light up.

When that light comes
Inside the dark light of the fire,
You know which chosen man has heard

A thing like his own dead   10
Speak out in a marvelous, helpless voice
That he has been straining to hear.

Miles away in the dark,
His enchanted dog can sense
How his features glow like a savior's,

And begins to hunt
In a frenzy of desperate pride.
Among us, no one's eyes give off a light

For the red fox
Playing in and out of his scent,   20
Leaping stones, doubling back over water.

Who runs with the fox
Must sit here like his own image,
Giving nothing of himself

To the sensitive flames,
With no human joy rising up,
Coming out of his face to be seen.

And it is hard,
When the fox leaps into his burrow,
To keep that singing down,   30

To sit with the fire
Drawn into one's secret features,
And all eyes turning around

From the dark wood
Until they come, amazed, upon
A face that does not shine

Back from itself,
That holds its own light and takes more,
Like the face of the dead, sitting still,

Giving no sign, 40
Making no outcry, no matter
Who may be straining to hear.

Cherrylog Road

Off Highway 106
At Cherrylog Road I entered
The '34 Ford without wheels,
Smothered in kudzu,
With a seat pulled out to run
Corn whiskey down from the hills,

And then from the other side
Crept into an Essex
With a rumble seat of red leather
And then out again, aboard 10
A blue Chevrolet, releasing
The rust from its other color,

Reared up on three building blocks.
None had the same body heat;
I changed with them inward, toward
The weedy heart of the junkyard,
For I knew that Doris Holbrook
Would escape from her father at noon

And would come from the farm
To seek parts owned by the sun 20
Among the abandoned chassis,
Sitting in each in turn
As I did, leaning forward
As in a wild stock-car race

In the parking lot of the dead.
Time after time, I climbed in
And out the other side, like
An envoy or movie star
Met at the station by crickets.
A radiator cap raised its head, 30

Become a real toad or a kingsnake
As I neared the hub of the yard,
Passing through many states,

Many lives, to reach
Some grandmother's long Pierce-Arrow
Sending platters of blindness forth

From its nickel hubcaps
And spilling its tender upholstery
On sleepy roaches,
The glass panel in between   40
Lady and colored driver
Not all the way broken out,

The back-seat phone
Still on its hook.
I got in as though to exclaim,
"Let us go to the orphan asylum,
John; I have some old toys
For children who say their prayers."

I popped with sweat as I thought
I heard Doris Holbrook scrape   50
Like a mouse in the southern-state sun
That was eating the paint in blisters
From a hundred car tops and hoods.
She was tapping like code,

Loosening the screws,
Carrying off headlights,
Sparkplugs, bumpers,
Cracked mirrors and gear-knobs,
Getting ready, already,
To go back with something to show   60

Other than her lips' new trembling
I would hold to me soon, soon,
Where I sat in the ripped back seat
Talking over the interphone,
Praying for Doris Holbrook
To come from her father's farm

And to get back there
With no trace of me on her face
To be seen by her red-haired father
Who would change, in the squalling barn,   70
Her back's pale skin with a strop,
Then lay for me

In a bootlegger's roasting car
With a string-triggered 12-gauge shotgun
To blast the breath from the air.

Not cut by the jagged windshields,
Through the acres of wrecks she came
With a wrench in her hand,

Through dust where the blacksnake dies
Of boredom, and the beetle knows   80
The compost has no more life.
Someone outside would have seen
The oldest car's door inexplicably
Close from within:

I held her and held her and held her,
Convoyed at terrific speed
By the stalled, dreaming traffic around us,
So the blacksnake, stiff
With inaction, curved back
Into life, and hunted the mouse   90

With deadly overexcitement,
The beetles reclaimed their field
As we clung, glued together,
With the hooks of the seat springs
Working through to catch us red-handed
Amidst the gray breathless batting

That burst from the seat at our backs.
We left by separate doors
Into the changed, other bodies
Of cars, she down Cherrylog Road   100
And I to my motorcycle
Parked like the soul of the junkyard

Restored, a bicycle fleshed
With power, and tore off
Up Highway 106, continually
Drunk on the wind in my mouth,
Wringing the handlebar for speed,
Wild to be wreckage forever.

DENISE LEVERTOV [1923–   ]

February Evening
in New York

As the stores close, a winter light
    opens air to iris blue,
    glint of frost through the smoke,
    grains of mica, salt of the sidewalk.

As the buildings close, released autonomous
   feet pattern the streets
   in hurry and stroll; balloon heads
   drift and dive above them; the bodies
   aren't really there.
As the lights brighten, as the sky darkens,
   a woman with crooked heels says to another woman
   while they step along at a fair pace,
   "You know, I'm telling you, what I love best
   is life. I love life! Even if I ever get
   to be old and wheezy—or limp! You know?
   Limping along?—I'd still . . ." Out of hearing.
To the multiple disordered tones
   of gears changing, a dance
   to the compass points, out, four-way river.
   Prospect of sky
   wedged into avenues, left at the ends of streets,
   west sky, east sky: more life tonight! A range
   of open time at winter's outskirts.

In Mind

There's in my mind a woman
of innocence, unadorned but

fair-featured, and smelling of
apples or grass. She wears

a utopian smock or shift, her hair
is light brown and smooth, and she

is kind and very clean without
ostentation—
         but she has
no imagination.
           And there's a
turbulent moon-ridden girl

or old woman, or both,
dressed in opals and rags, feathers

and torn taffeta,
who knows strange songs—

but she is not kind.

Advent 1966

Because in Vietnam the vision of a Burning Babe[1]
is multiplied, multiplied,
               the flesh on fire
not Christ's, as Southwell saw it, prefiguring
the Passion upon the Eve of Christmas,

but wholly human and repeated, repeated,
infant after infant, their names forgotten,
their sex unknown in the ashes,
set alight, flaming but not vanishing,
not vanishing as his vision but lingering,

cinders upon the earth or living on
moaning and stinking in hospitals three abed;

because of this my strong sight,
my clear caressive sight, my poet's sight I was given
that it might stir me to song,
is blurred.
        There is a cataract filming over
my inner eyes. Or else a monstrous insect
has entered my head, and looks out
from my sockets with multiple vision,

seeing not the unique Holy Infant
burning sublimely, an imagination of redemption,
furnace in which souls are wrought into new life,
but, as off a beltline, more, more senseless figures aflame.

And this insect (who is not there—
it is my own eyes do my seeing, the insect
is not there, what I see is there)
will not permit me to look elsewhere,

or if I look, to see except dulled and unfocused
the delicate, firm, whole flesh of the still unburned.

10

20

30

LOUIS SIMPSON [1923–   ]

Frogs

The storm broke, and it rained,
And water rose in the pool,
And frogs hopped into the gutter,

With their skins of yellow and green,
And just their eyes shining above the surface
Of the warm solution of slime.

1 See "The Burning Babe" by Robert Southwell (1561–1595).

At night, when fireflies trace
Light-lines between the trees and flowers
Exhaling perfume,

The frogs speak to each other
In rhythm. The sound is monstrous,
But their voices are filled with satisfaction.

In the city I pine for the country;
In the country I long for conversation—
Our happy croaking.

The Inner Part

When they had won the war[1]
And for the first time in history
Americans were the most important people—

When the leading citizens no longer lived in their shirt sleeves,
And their wives did not scratch in public;
Just when they'd stopped saying "Gosh!"—

When their daughters seemed as sensitive
As the tip of a fly rod,
And their sons were as smooth as a V-8 engine—

Priests, examining the entrails of birds,
Found the heart misplaced, and seeds
As black as death, emitting a strange odor.

Simplicity

Climbing the staircase
step by step, feeling my way . . .
I seem to have some trouble with my vision.
The stairs are littered with paper,
eggshells, and other garbage.
Then she comes to the door.
Without eye-shadow or lipstick,
with her hair tied in a bun,
in a white dress, she seems ethereal.

"Peter," she says, "how nice!   10
I thought that you were Albert,
but he hardly ever comes."

1 World War II.

She says, "I hope you like my dress.
It's simple. I made it myself.
Nowadays everyone's wearing simple things.
The thing is to be sincere,
and then, when you're tired of something,
you just throw it away."

I'll spare you the description
of all her simple objects: 20
the bed pushed in one corner;
the naked bulb that hangs
on a wire down from the ceiling
that is stamped out of metal
in squares, each square containing
a pattern of leaves and flowers;
the window with no blinds, admitting
daylight, and the wall
where a stream of yellow ice hangs down
in waves.   30

                    She is saying
"I have sat in this room
all day. There is a time
when you just stare at the wall
all day, and nothing moves.
I can't go on like this any longer,
counting the cracks in the wall,
doting on my buttons."

I seem to be disconnected
from the voice that is speaking   40
and the sound of the voice that answers.
Things seem to be moving into a vacuum.
I put my head in my hands
and try to concentrate.
But the light shines through my hands,

and then (how shall I put it
exactly?) it's as though she begins
giving off vibrations,
waves of resentment, an aura
of hate you could cut with a knife. . . .   50
Squirming, looking over her shoulder. . . .
Her whole body seems
to shrink, and she speaks in hisses:

"They want to remove my personality.
They're giving me psychotherapy
and *ikebana*, the art of flower-arrangement.

Some day, I suppose, I'll be cured,
and then I'll go and live in the suburbs,
doting on dogs and small children."

I go down the stairs, feeling my way   60
step by step. When I come out,
the light on the snow is blinding.
My shoes crunch on ice and my head
goes floating along, and a voice
from a high, barred window cries
"Write me a poem!"

JOHN A. WILLIAMS [1925–   ]

Safari West

The South Atlantic clouds rode low
in the sky; blue-fringed with rain that
would come later.
Popo Channel ran strong beneath its mud-green
undulating surface and the boatmen pointed
and told me
there were barracudas there. They swam in
from the ocean side, just to take a look,
hoping, perhaps
that slavery had returned and rebellious   10
and sick and dying blacks were being dumped
into the waters again.
Badagry, the town roofed over with rusted
tin and walled concrete hard mud, peddles a
view of its baracoon.
For a Nigerian pound; for two you can heft
old irons worn thin and trod the cells.
Ah, God!
Chains for the rebellious, the old, the strong;
chains for the weak, the children, all westbound,   20
all black.
And I raised each crude instrument to places
where gone, gone brothers had worn them,
the ankles,
wrists, necks, and mouths, and did not wipe
my lips, hoping some terribly dormant
all-powerful
germ of saliva would dart quickly within
and shock awake memory, fury, wisdom
and retribution.   30
It did. And Nigerians drowsed in the heat

or floated through it, their voices truly
musical,
and wondered at this black man clothed in
the cloth of the West, his eyes swinging
angrily
out over Popo Island and beyond, West,
West to the Middle Passage, eyes swinging
with wet anger.
There is an old one-pounder in the village;   40
it stands where a missionary, prelude to
Western armies
once had a church. When the ships rounded
Popo and stood swollen in the channel,
the missionary,
forgetful of his role, fired the cannon to
warn his flock that the slavers had come.
    Again.
As the vessels rode high in the channel
with light cargoes of cloth, trinkets and other   50
Western waste and
lowered their sails in the humid wind,
the blacks ran and traitors ran with them
deep into the bush.
They could not run fast or far enough or fear
quite enough. The Badagry baracoon stand
today,
somewhat maintained, I think, in the manner
in which Dachau is maintained in something of
greater degree.   60

ALLEN GINSBERG [1926–   ]

from Howl

FOR CARL SOLOMON

I

I saw the best minds of my generation destroyed by madness, starving
        hysterical naked,
dragging themselves through the negro streets at dawn looking for an
        angry fix,
angelheaded hipsters burning for the ancient heavenly connection to
        the starry dynamo in the machinery of night,
who poverty and tatters and hollow-eyed and high sat up smoking in
        the supernatural darkness of cold-water flats floating across the
        tops of cities contemplating jazz,

who bared their brains to Heaven under the El and saw Mohammedan
angels staggering on tenement roofs illuminated,
who passed through universities with radiant cool eyes hallucinating
Arkansas and Blake-light tragedy among the scholars of war,
who were expelled from the academies for crazy & publishing obscene
odes on the windows of the skull,
who cowered in unshaven rooms in underwear, burning their money
in wastebaskets and listening to the Terror through the wall,
who got busted in their pubic beards returning through Laredo with
a belt of marijuana for New York,
who ate fire in paint hotels or drank turpentine in Paradise Alley,
death, or purgatoried their torsos night after night   10
with dreams, with drugs, with waking nightmares, alcohol and cock
and endless balls,
incomparable blind streets of shuddering cloud and lightning in the
mind leaping toward poles of Canada & Paterson, illuminating
all the motionless world of Time between,
Peyote solidities of halls, backyard green tree cemetery dawns, wine
drunkenness over the rooftops, storefront boroughs of teahead
joyride neon blinking traffic light, sun and moon and tree
vibrations in the roaring winter dusks of Brooklyn, ashcan
rantings and kind king light of mind,
who chained themselves to subways for the endless ride from Battery
to holy Bronx on benzedrine until the noise of wheels and
children brought them down shuddering mouth-wracked and
battered bleak of brain all drained of brilliance in the drear
light of Zoo,
who sank all night in submarine light of Bickford's floated out and sat
through the stale beer afternoon in desolate Fugazzi's, listening
to the crack of doom on the hydrogen jukebox,
who talked continuously seventy hours from park to pad to bar to
Bellevue to museum to the Brooklyn Bridge,
a lost battalion of platonic conversationalists jumping down the stoops
off fire escapes off windowsills off Empire State out of the
moon,
yacketayakking screaming vomiting whispering facts and memories
and anecdotes and eyeball kicks and shocks of hospitals and
jails and wars,
whole intellects disgorged in total recall for seven days and nights
with brilliant eyes, meat for the Synagogue cast on the pavement,
who vanished into nowhere Zen New Jersey leaving a trail of ambiguous picture postcards of Atlantic City Hall,   20
suffering Eastern sweats and Tangerian bone-grindings and migraines
of China under junk-withdrawal in Newark's bleak furnished
room,
who wandered around and around at midnight in the railroad yard
wondering where to go, and went, leaving no broken hearts,

who lit cigarettes in boxcars boxcars boxcars racketing through snow
  toward lonesome farms in grandfather night,
who studied Plotinus Poe St. John of the Cross telepathy and bop
  kaballa[1] because the cosmos instinctively vibrated at their feet
  in Kansas,
who loned it through the streets of Idaho seeking visionary indian
  angels who were visionary indian angels,
who thought they were only mad when Baltimore gleamed in supernatural ecstasy,
who jumped in limousines with the Chinaman of Oklahoma on the
  impulse of winter midnight streetlight smalltown rain,
who lounged hungry and lonesome through Houston seeking jazz or
  sex or soup, and followed the brilliant Spaniard to converse
  about America and Eternity, a hopeless task, and so took ship
  to Africa,
who disappeared into the volcanoes of Mexico leaving behind nothing
  but the shadow of dungarees and the lava and ash of poetry
  scattered in fireplace Chicago,
who reappeared on the West Coast investigating the F.B.I. in beards
  and shorts with big pacifist eyes sexy in their dark skin passing
  out incomprehensible leaflets . . .   30

1   mystical interpretations of the Scriptures by certain Jewish rabbis.

ROBERT CREELEY [1926–   ]

After Lorca[1]

FOR M. MARTI

The church is a business, and the rich
are the business men.
                        When they pull on the bells, the
poor come piling in and when a poor man dies, he has a wooden
cross, and they rush through the ceremony.

But when a rich man dies, they
drag out the Sacrament
and a golden Cross, and go *doucement, doucement*[2]
to the cemetery.

And the poor love it
and think its crazy.

1   Federico García Lorca, modern Spanish poet and playwright, supported the
Loyalists in the Spanish civil war and was killed by persons unknown.
2   slowly, slowly.

I Know
a Man

As I sd to my
friend, because I am
always talking,—John, I

sd, which was not his
name, the darkness sur-
rounds us, what

can we do against
it, or else, shall we &
why not, buy a goddamn big car,

drive, he sd, for
christ's sake, look
out where yr going.

Kore

As I was walking
   I came upon
chance walking
   the same road upon.

As I sat down
   by chance to move
later
   if and as I might,

light the wood was,
   light and green,
and what I saw
   before I had not seen.

It was a lady
   accompanied
by goat men
   leading her.

Her hair held earth.
   Her eyes were dark.
A double flute
   made her move.

"O love,
   where are you
leading
   me now?"

ROBERT BLY [1926–   ]

Waking from Sleep

Inside the veins there are navies setting forth,
Tiny explosions at the water lines,
And seagulls weaving in the wind of the salty blood.

It is the morning. The country has slept the whole winter.
Window seats were covered with fur skins, the yard was full
Of stiff dogs, and hands that clumsily held heavy books.

Now we wake, and rise from bed, and eat breakfast!—
Shouts rise from the harbor of the blood,
Mist, and masts rising, the knock of wooden tackle in the sunlight.

Now we sing, and do tiny dances on the kitchen floor.
Our whole body is like a harbor at dawn;
We know that our master has left us for the day.

Poem Against the British

1

The wind through the box-elder trees
Is like rides at dusk on a white horse,
Wars for your country, and fighting the British.

2

I wonder if Washington listened to the trees.
All morning I have been sitting in grass,
Higher than my eyes, beneath trees,
And listening upward, to the wind in leaves.
Suddenly I realize there is one thing more:
There is also the wind through the high grass.

3

There are palaces, boats, silence among white buildings,
Iced drinks on marble tops, among cool rooms;
It is good also to be poor, and listen to the wind.

Summer, 1960, Minnesota

1

After a drifting day, visiting the bridge near Louisberg,
With its hot muddy water flowing
Under the excited swallows,

Now, at noon
We plunge through the hot beanfields,
And the sturdy alfalfa fields, the farm groves
Like heavy green smoke close to the ground.

2

Inside me there is a confusion of swallows,
Birds flying through the smoke,
And horses galloping excitedly on fields of short grass.

3

Yet, we are falling,
Falling into the open mouths of darkness,
Into the Congo as if into a river,
Or as wheat into open mills.

Love Poem

When we are in love, we love the grass,
And the barns, and the lightpoles,
And the small mainstreets abandoned all night.

JAMES WRIGHT [1927–   ]

Lying in a Hammock
at William Duffy's Farm
in Pine Island, Minnesota

Over my head, I see the bronze butterfly,
Asleep on the black trunk,
Blowing like a leaf in green shadow.
Down the ravine behind the empty house,
The cowbells follow one another
Into the distances of the afternoon.
To my right,
In a field of sunlight between two pines,
The droppings of last year's horses
Blaze up into golden stones.
I lean back, as the evening darkens and comes on.
A chicken hawk floats over, looking for home.
I have wasted my life.

Autumn Begins
in Martins Ferry, Ohio

In the Shreve High football stadium,
I think of Polacks nursing long beers in Tiltonsville,
And gray faces of Negroes in the blast furnace at Benwood,
And the ruptured night watchman of Wheeling Steel,
Dreaming of heroes.

All the proud fathers are ashamed to go home.
Their women cluck like starved pullets,
Dying for love.

Therefore,
Their sons grow suicidally beautiful
At the beginning of October,
And gallop terribly against each other's bodies.

I Try to Waken
and Greet the World
Once Again

In a pine tree,
A few yards away from my window sill,
A brilliant blue jay is springing up and down, up and down,
On a branch.
I laugh, as I see him abandon himself
To entire delight, for he knows as well as I do
That the branch will not break.

DONALD HALL [1928–   ]

An Airstrip
in Essex, 1960

It is a lost road into the air.
It is a desert
among sugar beets.
The tiny wings
of the Spitfires of nineteen-forty-one
flake in the mud of the Channel.

Near the road a brick pillbox
totters under a load of grass,
where Home Guards waited
in the white fogs of the invasion winter.

Goodnight, old ruined war.

In Poland the wind rides on a jagged wall.
Smoke rises from the stones; no, it is mist.

Gold

Pale gold of the walls, gold
of the centers of daisies, yellow roses
pressing from a clear bowl. All day
we lay on the bed, my hand
stroking the deep
gold of your thighs and your back.
We slept and woke
entering the golden room together,
lay down in it breathing
quickly, then
slowly again,
caressing and dozing, your hand sleepily
touching my hair now.

We made in those days
tiny identical rooms inside our bodies
which the men who uncover our graves
will find in a thousand years,
shining and whole.

THOM GUNN [1929–   ]

My Sad Captains

One by one they appear in
the darkness: a few friends, and
a few with historical
names. How late they start to shine!
but before they fade they stand
perfectly embodied, all

the past lapping them like a
cloak of chaos. They were men
who, I thought, lived only to
renew the wasteful force they
spent with each hot convulsion.
They remind me, distant now.

True, they are not at rest yet,
but now that they are indeed
apart, winnowed from failures,
they withdraw to an orbit
and turn with disinterested
hard energy, like the stars.

TED HUGHES [1930–   ]

Crow's First Lesson

God tried to teach Crow how to talk.
"Love," said God. "Say, Love."
Crow gaped, and the white shark crashed into the sea
And went rolling downwards, discovering its own depth.

"No, no," said God, "Say Love. Now try it. LOVE."
Crow gaped, and a bluefly, a tsetse, a mosquito
Zoomed out and down
To their sundry flesh-pots.

"A final try," said God. "Now, LOVE."
Crow convulsed, gaped, retched and
Man's bodiless prodigious head
Bulbed out onto the earth, with swivelling eyes,
Jabbering protest—

And Crow retched again, before God could stop him.
And woman's vulva dropped over man's neck and tightened.
The two struggled together on the grass.
God struggled to part them, cursed, wept—

Crow flew guiltily off.

In Laughter

Cars collide and erupt luggage and babies
In laughter
The steamer upends and goes under saluting like a stuntman
In laughter
The nosediving aircraft concludes with a boom
In laughter
People's arms and legs fly off and fly on again
In laughter
The haggard mask on the bed rediscovers its pang
In laughter, in laughter   10
The meteorite crashes
With extraordinarily ill-luck on the pram

The ears and eyes are bundled up
Are folded up in the hair,
Wrapped in the carpet, the wallpaper, tied with the lampflex[1]
Only the teeth work on
And the heart, dancing on in its open cave
Helpless on the strings of laughter

While the tears are nickel-plated and come through doors with a bang

And the wails stun with fear   20
And the bones
Jump from the torment flesh has to stay for

Stagger some distance and fall in full view

Still laughter scampers around on centipede boots
Still it runs all over on caterpillar tread
And rolls back onto the mattress, legs in the air
But it's only human

And finally it's had enough—enough!
And slowly sits up, exhausted,
And slowly starts to fasten buttons,   30
With long pauses,

Like somebody the police have come for.

1   lamp cord.

Crow's Last Stand

Burning
        burning
                burning
                        there was finally something
The sun could not burn, that it had rendered
Everything down to—a final obstacle
Against which it raged and charred

And rages and chars

Limpid among the glaring furnace clinkers[1]
The pulsing blue tongues and the red and the yellow
The green lickings of the conflagration

Limpid and black—

Crow's eye-pupil, in the tower of its scorched fort.

1   in burning coal, hard masses formed from the impurities.

Truth Kills Everybody

So Crow found Proteus[1]—steaming in the sun.
Stinking with sea-bottom growths
Like the plug of the earth's sump-outlet.
There he lay—belching quakily.

Crow pounced and buried his talons—

And it was the famous bulging Achilles[2]—but he held him
The oesophagus of a staring shark—but he held it
A wreath of lashing mambas—but he held it

It was a naked powerline, 2000 volts—
He stood aside, watching his body go blue
As he held it and held it

It was a screeching woman and he had her by the throat—
He held it

A gone steering wheel bouncing towards a cliff edge—
He held it

A trunk of jewels dragging into a black depth—he held it

The ankle of a rising, fiery angel—he held it

Christ's hot pounding heart—he held it

The earth, shrunk to the size of a hand grenade

And he held it he held it and held it and

BANG!

He was blasted to nothing.

GREGORY CORSO [1930–   ]

Marriage

Should I get married? Should I be good?
Astound the girl next door with my velvet suit and faustus hood?
Don't take her to movies but to cemeteries
tell all about werewolf bathtubs and forked clarinets
then desire her and kiss her and all the preliminaries
and she going just so far and I understanding why
not getting angry saying You must feel! It's beautiful to feel!
Instead take her in my arms lean against an old crooked tombstone
and woo her the entire night the constellations in the sky—

1 in Greek mythology, an old man of the sea who could assume many shapes.
2 Greek warrior, hero of the *Iliad*. Also, a bulbous fish.

When she introduces me to her parents   10
back straightened, hair finally combed, strangled by a tie,
should I sit knees together on their 3rd degree sofa
and not ask Where's the bathroom?
How else to feel other than I am,
often thinking Flash Gordon soap—
O how terrible it must be for a young man
seated before a family and the family thinking
We never saw him before! He wants our Mary Lou!
After tea and homemade cookies they ask What do you do for a living?
Should I tell them? Would they like me then?   20
Say All right get married, we're losing a daughter
but we're gaining a son—
And should I then ask Where's the bathroom?

O God, and the wedding! All her family and her friends
and only a handful of mine all scroungy and bearded
just wait to get at the drinks and food—
And the priest! he looking at me as if I masturbated
asking me Do you take this woman for your lawful wedded wife?
And I trembling what to say say Pie Glue!
I kiss the bride all those corny men slapping me on the back   30
She's all yours, boy! Ha-ha-ha!
And in their eyes you could see some obscene honeymoon going on—
Then all that absurd rice and clanky cans and shoes
Niagara Falls! Hordes of us! Husbands! Wives! Flowers! Chocolates!
All streaming into cozy hotels
All going to do the same thing tonight
The indifferent clerk he knowing what was going to happen
The lobby zombies they knowing what
The whistling elevator man he knowing
The winking bellboy knowing   40
Everybody knowing! I'd be almost inclined not to do anything!
Stay up all night! Stare that hotel clerk in the eye!
Screaming: I deny honeymoon! I deny honeymoon!
running rampant into those almost climactic suites
yelling Radio belly! Cat shovel!
O I'd live in Niagara forever! in a dark cave beneath the Falls
I'd sit there the Mad Honeymooner
devising ways to break marriages, a scourge of bigamy
a saint of divorce—

But I should get married I should be good   50
How nice it'd be to come home to her
and sit by the fireplace and she in the kitchen
aproned young and lovely wanting my baby
and so happy about me she burns the roast beef
and comes crying to me and I get up from my big papa chair
saying Christmas teeth! Radiant brains! Apple deaf!

God what a husband I'd make! Yes, I should get married!
So much to do! like sneaking into Mr Jones' house late at night
and cover his golf clubs with 1920 Norwegian books
Like hanging a picture of Rimbaud on the lawnmower   60
like pasting Tannu Tuva postage stamps all over the picket fence
like when Mrs Kindhead comes to collect for the Community Chest
grab her and tell her There are unfavorable omens in the sky!
And when the mayor comes to get my vote tell him
When are you going to stop people killing whales!
And when the milkman comes leave him a note in the bottle
Penguin dust, bring me penguin dust, I want penguin dust—

Yet if I should get married and it's Connecticut and snow
and she gives birth to a child and I am sleepless, worn,   69
up for nights, head bowed against a quiet window, the past behind me,
finding myself in the most common of situations a trembling man
knowledged with responsibility not twig-smear nor Roman coin soup—
O what would that be like!
Surely I'd give it for a nipple a rubber Tacitus
For a rattle a bag of broken Bach records
Tack Della Francesca all over its crib
Sew the Greek alphabet on its bib
And build for its playpen a roofless Parthenon

No, I doubt I'd be that kind of father
not rural not snow no quiet window   80
but hot smelly tight New York City
seven flights up, roaches and rats in the walls
a fat Reichian wife screeching over potatoes Get a job!
And five nose running brats in love with Batman
And the neighbors all toothless and dry haired
like those hag masses of the 18th century
all wanting to come in and watch TV
The landlord wants his rent
Grocery store Blue Cross Gas & Electric Knights of Columbus
Impossible to lie back and dream Telephone snow, ghost parking—
No! I should not get married I should never get married!   91
But—imagine If I were married to a beautiful sophisticated woman
tall and pale wearing an elegant black dress and long black gloves
holding a cigarette holder in one hand and a highball in the other
and we lived high up in a penthouse with a huge window
from which we could see all of New York and ever farther on clearer
          days
No, can't imagine myself married to that pleasant prison dream—

O but what about love? I forget love
not that I am incapable of love
it's just that I see love as odd as wearing shoes—   100
I never wanted to marry a girl who was like my mother

And Ingrid Bergman was always impossible
And there's maybe a girl now but she's already married
And I don't like men and—
but there's got to be somebody!
Because what if I'm 60 years old and not married,
all alone in a furnished room with pee stains on my underwear
and everybody else is married! All the universe married but me!

Ah, yet well I know that were a woman possible as I am possible
then marriage would be possible—   110
Like SHE in her lonely alien gaud waiting her Egyptian lover
so I wait—bereft of 2,000 years and the bath of life.

GARY SNYDER [1930–   ]

Milton by Firelight

Piute Creek, August 1955

"O hell, what do mine eyes
            with grief behold?"[1]
Working with an old
Singlejack miner, who can sense
The vein and cleavage
In the very guts of rock, can
Blast granite, build
Switchbacks that last for years
Under the beat of snow, thaw, mule-hooves.
What use, Milton, a silly story   10
Of our lost general parents,
            eaters of fruit?

The Indian, the chainsaw boy,
And a string of six mules
Came riding down to camp
Hungry for tomatoes and green apples.
Sleeping in saddle-blankets
Under a bright night-sky
Han River slantwise by morning.
Jays squall   20
Coffee boils

In ten thousand years the Sierras
Will be dry and dead, home of the scorpion.
Ice-scratched slabs and bent trees.
No paradise, no fall,

1   Satan's exclamation upon first seeing Adam and Eve in Eden (Milton,
Paradise Lost, Book IV).

Only the weathering land
The wheeling sky,
Man, with his Satan
Scouring the chaos of the mind.
Oh Hell!   30

Fire down
Too dark to read, miles from a road
The bell-mare clangs in the meadow
That packed dirt for a fill-in
Scrambling through loose rocks
On an old trail
All of a summer's day.

Hay for
the Horses

He had driven half the night
From far down San Joaquin
Through Mariposa, up the
Dangerous mountain roads,
And pulled in at eight a.m.
With his big truckload of hay
                    behind the barn.
With winch and ropes and hooks
We stacked the bales up clean
To splintery redwood rafters
High in the dark, flecks of alfalfa
Whirling through shingle-cracks of light,
Itch of haydust in the
                    sweaty shirt and shoes.
At lunchtime under black oak
Out in the hot corral,
—The old mare nosing lunchpails,
Grasshoppers crackling in the weeds—
"I'm sixty-eight" he said,
"I first bucked hay when I was seventeen.
I thought, that day I started,
I sure would hate to do this all my life.
And dammit, that's just what
I've gone and done."

Nansen[1]

I found you on a rainy morning
After a typhoon
In a bamboo grove at Daitoku-ji.[2]
Tiny wet rag with a
Huge voice, you crawled under the fence
To my hand. Left to die.
I carried you home in my raincoat.
"Nansen, cheese!" you'd shout an answer
And come running.
But you never got big,
Bandy-legged bright little dwarf—
Sometimes not eating, often coughing
Mewing bitterly at inner twinge.

Now, thin and older, you won't eat
But milk and cheese. Sitting on a pole
In the sun. Hardy with resigned
Discontent.
You just weren't made right. I saved you,
And your three-year life has been full
Of mild, steady pain.

1   In Zen Buddhism there is a story of a Zen
master named Nansen who heard two monks
quarreling over a cat. He asked them to say a
word of Zen, or he'd kill the cat. They
couldn't, and he killed it.
2   in Japan.

December[1]

Three a.m.—a far bell
        coming closer:
fling up useless futon[2] on the shelf;
outside, ice-water in the hand & wash the face.
        Ko the bird-head, silent, skinny,
        swiftly cruise the room with
        salt plum tea.

Bell from the hondo[3] chanting sutras.[4] Gi:[5]
deep bell, small bell, wooden drum.

1   This poem describes the day of a monk or layman in a Zen Buddhist
monastery.
2   cushion.
3   main hall, usually a separate building, in a Japanese monastery, used
principally for lectures and meals.
4   part of the Canon containing the dialogue or discourses of the Buddha.
5   temple.

sanzen[6] at four   10
    kneel on icy polisht boards in line;

Shukuza rice and pickles
barrel and bucket
dim watt bulb.
    till daybreak nap upright.
                        sweep
        garden and hall.
        frost outside
                        wind through walls

At eight the lecture bell. high chair.   20
Ke helps the robe—red, gold,
        black lacquer in the shadow
        sun and cold

Saiza[7] a quarter to ten
soup and rice dab on the bench
feed the hungry ghosts
        back in the hall by noon.
two o clock sanzen
three o clock bellywarmer
        boild up soup-rice mush.   30
dinging and scuffing. out back smoke,
                        and talk.

At dusk, at five,
black robes draw into the hall.
        stiff joints, sore knees bend
        the jiki[8] pads by with his incense lit,
                        bells,
        wood block crack
& stick slips round the room
on soft straw sandals.   40

seven, sanzen
tea, and a leaf-shaped candy.
kinhin[9] at eight with folded hands—
        single-file racing in flying robes leaning
                    to wake—

6   interview between Zen master (roshi) and the monk or layman undergoing
Zen training.
7   break.
8   person who presides over sessions of meditation.
9   pacing and meditating.

377

nine o clock one more sanzen
ten, hot noodles,
three bowls each.

Sit until midnight. chant.
    make three bows and pull the futon down.   50
    roll in the bed—
    black.

A far bell coming closer

Looking
At Pictures
To Be Put Away

Who was this girl
In her white night gown
Clutching a pair of jeans

On a foggy redwood deck.
She looks up at me tender,
Calm, surprised,

What will we remember
Bodies thick with food and lovers
After twenty years.

SYLVIA PLATH [1932–1963]

Morning Song

Love set you going like a fat gold watch.
The midwife slapped your footsoles, and your bald cry
Took its place among the elements.

Our voices echo, magnifying your arrival. New statue.
In a drafty museum, your nakedness
Shadows our safety. We stand round blankly as walls.

I'm no more your mother
Than the cloud that distils a mirror to reflect its own slow
Effacement at the wind's hand.

All night your moth-breath
Flickers among the flat pink roses. I wake to listen:
A far sea moves in my ear.

One cry, and I stumble from bed, cow-heavy and floral
In my Victorian nightgown.
Your mouth opens clean as a cat's. The window square

Whitens and swallows its dull stars. And now you try
Your handful of notes;
The clear vowels rise like balloons.

Daddy

You do not do, you do not do
Any more, black shoe
In which I have lived like a foot
For thirty years, poor and white,
Barely daring to breathe or Achoo.

Daddy, I have had to kill you.
You died before I had time—
Marble-heavy, a bag full of God,
Ghastly statue with one grey toe
Big as a Frisco seal   10

And a head in the freakish Atlantic
Where it pours bean green over blue
In the waters off beautiful Nauset.
I used to pray to recover you.
Ach, du.[1]

In the German tongue, in the Polish town
Scraped flat by the roller
Of wars, wars, wars.
But the name of the town is common.
My Polack friend   20

Says there are a dozen or two.
So I never could tell where you
Put your foot, your root,
I never could talk to you.
The tongue stuck in my jaw.

It stuck in a barb wire snare.
Ich,[2] ich, ich, ich,
I could hardly speak.
I thought every German was you.
And the language obscene   30

An engine, an engine
Chuffing me off like a Jew.

1   German: you.
2   German: I.

A Jew to Dachau, Auschwitz, Belsen.
I began to talk like a Jew.
I think I may well be a Jew.

The snows of the Tyrol, the clear beer of Vienna
Are not very pure or true.
With my gypsy ancestress and my weird luck
And my Taroc[3] pack and my Taroc pack
I may be a bit of a Jew.   40

I have always been scared of *you*,
With your Luftwaffe, your gobbledygoo.
And your neat moustache
And your Aryan eye, bright blue.
Panzer-man, panzer-man, O You—

Not God but a swastika[4]
So black no sky could squeak through.
Every woman adores a Fascist,
The boot in the face, the brute
Brute heart of a brute like you.   50

You stand at the blackboard, daddy,
In the picture I have of you,
A cleft in your chin instead of your foot
But no less a devil for that, no not
Any less the black man who

Bit my pretty red heart in two.
I was ten when they buried you.
At twenty I tried to die
And get back, back, back to you.
I thought even the bones would do.   60

But they pulled me out of the sack,
And they stuck me together with glue.
And then I knew what to do.
I made a model of you,
A man in black with a Meinkampf[5] look

And a love of the rack and the screw.
And I said I do, I do.
So daddy, I'm finally through.
The black telephone's off at the root,
The voices just can't worm through.   70

If I've killed one man, I've killed two——
The vampire who said he was you
And drank my blood for a year,

3   cards used in fortune telling.
4   emblem of the German Nazis.
5   Hitler, leader of the Nazis, wrote an autobiography titled *Mein Kampf*
(*My Struggle*).

Seven years, if you want to know.
Daddy, you can lie back now.

There's a stake in your fat black heart
And the villagers never liked you.
They are dancing and stamping on you.
They always *knew* it was you.
Daddy, daddy, you bastard, I'm through.   80

The Bee Meeting

Who are these people at the bridge to meet me? They are the
              villagers——
The rector, the midwife, the sexton, the agent for bees.
In my sleeveless summery dress I have no protection,
And they are all gloved and covered, why did nobody tell me?
They are smiling and taking out veils tacked to ancient hats.

I am nude as a chicken neck, does nobody love me?
Yes, here is the secretary of bees with her white shop smock,
Buttoning the cuffs at my wrists and the slit from my neck to my
              knees.
Now I am milkweed silk, the bees will not notice.
They will not smell my fear, my fear, my fear.   10

Which is the rector now, is it that man in black?
Which is the midwife, is that her blue coat?
Everybody is nodding a square black head, they are knights in visors,
Breastplates of cheesecloth knotted under the armpits.
Their smiles and their voices are changing. I am led through a bean-
              field.

Strips of tinfoil winking like people,
Feather dusters fanning their hands in a sea of bean flowers,
Creamy bean flowers with black eyes and leaves like bored hearts.
Is it blood clots the tendrils are dragging up that string?
No, no, it is scarlet flowers that will one day be edible.   20

Now they are giving me a fashionable white straw Italian hat
And a black veil that moulds to my face, they are making me one of
              them.
They are leading me to the shorn grove, the circle of hives.
Is it the hawthorn that smells so sick?
The barren body of hawthorn, etherizing its children.

Is it some operation that is taking place?
It is the surgeon my neighbours are waiting for,
This apparition in a green helmet,

Shining gloves and white suit.
Is it the butcher, the grocer, the postman, someone I know?   30

I cannot run, I am rooted, and the gorse hurts me
With its yellow purses, its spiky armoury.
I could not run without having to run forever.
The white hive is snug as a virgin,
Sealing off her brood cells, her honey, and quietly humming.

Smoke rolls and scarves in the grove.
The mind of the hive thinks this is the end of everything.
Here they come, the outriders, on their hysterical elastics.
If I stand very still, they will think I am cow parsley,
A gullible head untouched by their animosity,   40

Not even nodding, a personage in a hedgerow.
The villagers open the chambers, they are hunting the queen.
Is she hiding, is she eating honey? She is very clever.
She is old, old, old, she must live another year, and she knows it.
While in their fingerjoint cells the new virgins

Dream of a duel they will win inevitably,
A curtain of wax dividing them from the bride flight,
The upflight of the murderess into a heaven that loves her.
The villagers are moving the virgins, there will be no killing.
The old queen does not show herself, is she so ungrateful?   50

I am exhausted, I am exhausted——
Pillar of white in a blackout of knives.
I am the magician's girl who does not flinch.
The villagers are untying their disguises, they are shaking hands.
Whose is that long white box in the grove, what have they accomplished, why am I cold?

LEROI JONES [1934–   ]

Preface to
a Twenty Volume
Suicide Note

(FOR KELLIE JONES, BORN 16 MAY 1959)

Lately, I've become accustomed to the way
The ground opens up and envelopes me
Each time I go out to walk the dog.
Or the broad edged silly music the wind
Makes when I run for a bus . . .

Things have come to that.

And now, each night I count the stars,
And each night I get the same number.
And when they will not come to be counted,
I count the holes they leave.

Nobody sings anymore.

And then last night, I tiptoed up
To my daughter's room and heard her
Talking to someone, and when I opened
The door, there was no one there . . .
Only she on her knees, peeking into

Her own clasped hands.

JACK ANDERSON [1935–   ]

The Invention
of New Jersey

Place a custard stand in a garden
or in place of a custard stand
   place a tumbled-down custard stand
in place of a tumbled-down custard stand
   place miniature golf in a garden
   and an advertisement for miniature golf
     shaped for no apparent reason
     like an old Dutch windmill
in place of a swamp
   place a swamp   10

       or a pizzeria called the Tower of Pizza
        sporting a scale model
         of the Tower of Pisa
       or a water tower resembling
        a roll-on deodorant
       or a Dixie Cup factory
        with a giant metal Dixie Cup on the roof

In place of wolverines, rabbits, or melons
   place a vulcanizing plant
in place of a deer   20
   place an iron deer
   at a lawn furniture store
   selling iron deer

Negro jockeys
Bavarian gnomes
and imitation grottoes
with electric Infants of Prague[1]
in place of phosphorescence
of marshy ground at night
place smears of rubbish fires   30
in place of brown water with minnows
place brown water
gigantic landlords
in the doorways of apartment houses
which look like auto showrooms
auto showrooms which look like diners
diners which look like motels
motels which look like plastic chair covers
plastic chair covers which look like
plastic table covers which look like plastic bags   40

the mad scientist of Secaucus
invents a plastic cover
to cover the lawn
with millions of perforations
for the grass to poke through

In place of the straight lines of grasses
place the straight lines of gantries
in place of lights in the window
place lighted refineries
in place of a river   50
place the road like a slim pair of pants
set to dry beside a neon frankfurter
in place of New Jersey
place a plastic New Jersey

on weekends a guy has nothing to do
except drive around in a convertible
counting the shoe stores
and thinking of screwing
his date beside him
a faintly bilious look   60
perpetually on her face

1   replica of a statue in Prague, made in 1628, representing the Christ Child.
An object of popular devotion.

LUCILLE CLIFTON [1936–   ]

The 1st

What I remember about that day
is boxes stacked across the walk
and couch springs curling through the air
and drawers and tables balanced on the curb
and us, hollering,
leaping up and around
happy to have a playground;

nothing about the emptied rooms
nothing about the emptied family

Still

still
it was nice
when the scissors man come round
running his wheel
rolling his wheel
and the sparks shooting
out in the dark
across the lot
and over to the white folks section

still
it was nice
in the light of Maizie's store
to watch the wheel
and catch the wheel—
fire spinning in the air
and our edges
and our points
sharpening good as anybodys'

Good Times

My Daddy has paid the rent
and the insurance man is gone
and the lights is back on
and my uncle Brud has hit
for one dollar straight
and they is good times
good times
good times

My Mama has made bread
and Grampaw has come
and everybody is drunk
and dancing in the kitchen
and singing in the kitchen
oh these is good times
good times
good times

oh children think about the
good times

Willie B (2)

Why I would bring a wagon into battle
is
a wagon is a help to a soldier
with his bricks
and when he want to rest
also
today is Mama's birthday
and I'm gone get her that tv
out of old Steinhart's store

Admonitions

boys
i don't promise you nothing
but this
what you pawn
i will redeem
what you steal
i will conceal
my private silence to
your public guilt
is all i got

girls
first time a white man
opens his fly
like a good thing
we'll just laugh
laugh real loud my
black women

children
when they ask you
why is your mama so funny
say
she is a poet
she don't have no sense

DIANE WAKOSKI [1937–   ]

The Ice Eagle

It was with resolution that she gave up the
powerful teardrops in her eyes—
that crystal, the Venus[1]-soft lizard-eyed creature called woman, gazes
through, her philosopher's stone,
the sweet glass
that drops from the sky.
Ancients,
in sacrifice,
cut off tears
with knives.   10

*   *   *

The 50 lb. eagle carved out of ice
sitting in the silver punch bowl
turned her attention to physical details.
                    Why am I saying
                    "her"?
                    It is I,
                    undoubtedly I,
                    the life a dream work.
Undoubtedly the life has been confused with the movies,
I, Gloria Swanson,[2] walking discontented   20
for all parties become that to me. I cannot
walk through the rituals
without my golden mask,
alas, 3 dozen of them hang on my wall,
the thick lips reminding me of what has been eaten
and has not nourished.
Physical details: the lawn that sloped down to the sea cliffs,
the swallows building their nests in rafters,
the stone house punctured with courts and patios,
Bougainvillea winding up its sides,   30
raw old Spanish wood composing chests and high still chairs

1   goddess of love.
2   movie actress famous in the 1930's.

387

moved and touched into water-like smoothness,
the gravel driveway balancing the cutaway heels
of beautiful women,
the men swimming through the night in dinner jackets like papercups
floating on the ocean;
yes, her eyes—
>   again why do I say
>   "her,"
>   I must insist it is I.   40
my eyes are informed of silk and the obsidian minds of the rich.
Here is a thick glossy black smooth idea—sex and nothing else.
The rich are born bored
and look for purposes, causes, projects
to keep them busy.
The women make up wild malachite eyes, green with beautiful
sleep and restless knowledge of new plays,
new dancers,
new books,
new jazz. They   50
can ring their Egyptian eyes with kohl
and be aesthetes
and in veils walk down the rock path to the sea;
riding black tigers of Sartre and Camus and Ionesco,[3]
yards of chiffon trailing their heels and they despair
the men,
they, I, we
>   all women when it gets past social class
despair the men who have only the moon in their milky fluid fingers.
Yes, they wait,   60
the sun god we wait,
to find him naked in a blaze of fire.
We are stuck with vulgar substitutes—
the fashionable avant-garde dancer,
the sensational beat poet,
the jazz trumpeter,
the negro novelist,
and Amen-ra,[4] Amen-ra, our father, they are all glorious sun-brilliant
artists, but
homosexuals   70
fucking each other, riding on their own black panthers
wading into the iron waters.
Again the women must rest their bodies against each other and moan.
It is not the mysteries that draw the men,
but the fear of that great mystery

3   Jean Paul Sartre (born 1905): French playwright, novelist, and philosopher
of Existentialism. Albert Camus (1913–1960): French playwright, novelist, and
essayist. Eugene Ionesco (born 1912): French dramatist of Rumanian descent.
4   the Egyptian sun god. It was believed that he was born each day in the
east, traveled across the sky in his boat and died each evening in the west.
Isis took advantage of his waning powers toward evening and persuaded him
to reveal his secrets to her. Thus she acquired sovereign power.

the veiled woman, Isis,[5]
mother, whom they fear to be greater than all else.

And I am sick unto death. Sick,
I say, sick. We live in a world where men have forgotten their offices
only taking the woman   80
        like good debaters
        assigned to the positive side
        on whom rests the burden of
        proof
only taking her on the surface—
she, I, we, can peel off layer after layer where you
have taken her and yet find the bottom deep and tight and untouched
and longing for the greater measure.

She, no it was I, walked with the moon in Pisces,
and felt the trout slipping down into the ocean.   90
The carved ice eagle of that party
was melting
into the gin and strawberries.
In its beak
someone had placed an American flag.
I found it hard to believe myself in this slippery unreal
man-made country. Look, look, look
I want to say; the eagle is a powerful bird.
In your fear, all you can do is carve him out of ice.
And that leaves only one alternative   100
in this temperate climate.
The ice eagle can do nothing
but melt.

5   Egyptian goddess, enchantress, wife-sister of King Osiris.
Her powers and her love for Osiris were so great that by
mourning him she brought him back to life.

JIM HARRISON [1937–   ]

Ghazals[1]

     23

I imagined her dead, killed by some local maniac who
crept upon the house with snowmobile at low throttle.

Alcohol that lets me play out hates and loves and fights;
in each bottle is a woman, the betrayer and the slain.

1   "The ghazal is an antique form dating from the thirteenth century and
practiced by hundreds of poets since in languages as varied as Urdu, Arabic,
Pashto, Turkish, Persian, German, French, Spanish. Even Goethe and Schlegel
wrote ghazals. . . . I have not adhered to the strictness of metrics and structure
of the ancient practitioners, with the exception of using a minimum of five
couplets. The couplets are not related by reason of logic and their only continuity
is made by a metaphorical jump. Ghazals are essentially lyrics and I have
worked with whatever aspect of our life now that seemed to want to enter my
field of vision."—Jim Harrison

I insist on a one-to-one relationship with nature.
If Thursday I'm a frog it will have to be my business.

You are well. You grow taller. Friends think I've bought you
stilts but it is I shrinking, up past my knees in marl.

She said take out the garbage. I trot through a field with the
sack in my teeth. At the dump I pause to snarl at a rat.

48

Dog, the lightning frightened us, dark house and both of us
silvered by it. Now we'll have three months of wind and cold.

Safe. From miracles and clouds, cut off from you and your
earthly city, parades of rats, froth, and skull tympanums.

The breathing in the thicket behind the beech tree was a deer
that hadn't heard me, a doe. I had hoped for a pretty girl.

Flickers gathering, swallows already gone. I'm going South
to the Yucatan or Costa Rica and foment foment and fish.

In the sudan grass waving, roots white cords, utterly hidden
and only the hounds could find me assuming someone would look.

This sun shines coldly. I aim my shotgun at a ship at sea
and say nothing. The dog barks at the ship and countless waves.

62

She climbed the ladder looking over the wall at the party
given for poets by the Prince of China. Fun was had by all.

A certain gracelessness entered his walk and gestures. A tumor
the size of a chick-pea grew into a pink balloon in his brain.

I won't die in Paris or Jerusalem as planned but by electrocution
when I climb up the windmill to unscrew the shorted yardlights.

Samadhi. When I slept in the woods I awoke before dawn
and drank brandy and listened to birds until the moon disappeared.

When she married she turned from a beautiful girl into a
useless sow with mud on her breasts and choruses of oinks.

O the bard is sure he loves the moon. And the inanimate moon
loves him back with silences, and moonbeams made of chalk.

LEBERT BETHUNE [1937–]

A Juju[1]
of My Own

To make a Juju of my own
For I was tired of strange ghosts
Whose cool bones
Lived on the green furnace of my blood
Was always my destiny
So she warned me—my grandmother,
And now and now
When I kindle again her small eyes with their quick
lights
Darting ancient love into my infancy
And when I break through to her easy voice
That voice like the pliant red clay she baked
She sings the only lullaby she sang me

"Me no care for Bakra[2] whip
Me no care fe fum-fum
Come Juju come"

So I am fashioning this thing
My own Juju
Out of her life and our desire
Out of an old black love
I am baking my destiny to a lullaby—

"Me no care fe Bakra whip
Me no care fe fum-fum
Come Juju come . . ."

1   an object venerated by West African
natives and used as a charm or protection.
2   Boss's.

MICHAEL BENEDIKT [1937–]

Clement Attlee[1]

1
Except for me, nobody remembers Clement Attlee.
The winds of change and cold snows, too, have flowed all over his
features and figure, and now all we can see is a Sherlock
Holmes cap and large pair of earmuffs.

1   English Labour Party leader (born 1883) who was Prime Minister from
1945 to 1951.

Occasionally, a bear comes by and finds a boot to bite.
Oh, wake up Clement Attlee, another inch of time and not only will
    no one admit to remembering you, but nobody will be able to
    be found who has really ever heard of you!
Clement, Clement!—Hi ho, first post-war English Labourite and some-
    what socialist Prime Minister—hi ho, hoo-hoo.

2

The other day, in the moviehouse (after all these years, *I* should say
    "cinema"?) a hundred people chuckled when a French general
    with large weights affixed to his eyelids said he had once been
    a member of the "underground resistance."
Upstairs, twelve students from nursery school are discussing the New
    Order.
At a party, I finally meet God. He is with a student. He grimaces a
    lot, the student.
Elsewhere, a graduate of Sarah Lawrence College is entering a
    mosque.
Apocalypse!

3

Outside the covers of the bed, place from which all creation is sent
    forth, I feel a shiny bald head, a bristly walrus moustache, and
    imagine that under the covers, I am wearing checquered
    knickers and carrying a walking stick. Cautiously, a frayed
    black monocle cord starts to make its way back across my
    cheek . . .

TONY HARRISON   [1937–   ]

Schwiegermutterlieder[1]

FOR ROSEMARIE

1

Mother and daughter German refugees
were not much wanted in nineteen
forty five. She had to skivvy[2] for rich Jews
in Manchester's posh "Palestine."

I never really could believe
her story of your being thrown out
by some, one *snowy* Christmas Eve,
for having real wax candles on your conifer,
their children shouting: *Kraut! Kraut!*[3]

1   mother-in-law song.
2   to work as a female house servant doing the dirty work.
3   cabbage, insulting name for a German.

until she brought the tea-chests out of store. 10

Then I saw the hotel towels, the stolen
London cafe spoons,
bits of half-eaten *Stollen*,[4]
casserole and cooking pans
packed hot from the oven.

Kleptomaniac,
dear *Schwiegermutter*,
did you have to pack
a ½ lb. Kosher butter?

I've seen her waltz 20
off with rare, bright plants she's pinched
from Kew,[5] but the good bed-linen
was her own, brought bunched
up in bundles from Berlin,
embroidered: *Mein Heim ist Mein Stolz.*[6]

After 13 years she fished
out her treasures; none any use.
She gave us a perished
red-rubber douche.

2
After the wedding she insisted on 30
a head-and-shoulders photograph that just
got her *real* violets on your breast
but not your belly in.

She sang and spun round in a raven
black, hook-buttoned waitress dress.
She was in some sort of heaven,
Viennese with happiness,
her arms round everybody's neck,
warbling from pre-war musicals,
and *Rŭ-, Rŭ-, Ruženka Maria*, your name in Czech, 40
with cracked ecstatic trills.—

But dying uncle Bertolt
made his '14–18 amputation tender
by stamping his tin foot, when he was told
you'd married an *Englander*.

3
Else Crossfield, Dietzsch,
née Schubert—*British* bitch!

4   a sweet bread containing fruits and nuts.
5   It isn't far from London.
6   "My home is my pride."

JOHN LENNON [1940–   ] AND PAUL McCARTNEY [1942–   ]

Eleanor Rigby

Ah, look at all the lonely people!
Ah, look at all the lonely people!

Eleanor Rigby
Picks up the rice in the church where a wedding has been,
Lives in a dream,
Waits at the window
Wearing the face that she keeps in a jar by the door.
Who is it for?

All the lonely people,
Where do they all come from?   10
All the lonely people,
Where do they all belong?

Father McKenzie,
Writing the words of a sermon that no one will hear,
No one comes near
Look at him working,
Darning his socks in the night when there's nobody there.
What does he care?

All the lonely people
Where do they all come from?   20
All the lonely people
Where do they all belong?

Eleanor Rigby
Died in the church and was buried along with her name.
Nobody came.
Father McKenzie,
Wiping the dirt from his hands as he walks from the grave,
No one was saved.

All the lonely people,
Where do they all come from?   30
All the lonely people,
Where do they all belong?

Ah, look at all the lonely people!
Ah, look at all the lonely people!

BOB DYLAN [1941–   ]

Desolation Row[1]

They're selling postcards of the hanging
They're painting the passports brown
The beauty parlor's filled with sailors
The circus is in town
Here comes the blind commissioner
They've got him in a trance
One hand's tied to the tight-rope walker
The other is in his pants
And the riot squad they're restless
They need somewhere to go   10
As lady and I look out tonight
From Desolation Row

Cinderella she seems so easy
It takes one to know one she smiles
Then puts her hands in her back pocket
Bette Davis style
Then in comes Romeo he's moaning
You belong to me I believe
Then someone says you're in the wrong place my friend
You'd better leave   20
And the only sound that's left
After the ambulances go
Is Cinderella sweeping up
On Desolation Row.

Now the moon is almost hidden
The stars are beginning to hide
The fortune telling lady
Has even taken all her things inside
All except for Cain and Abel
And the hunchback of Notre Dame   30
Everybody is making love
Or else expecting rain
And the good samaritan he's dressing
He's getting ready for the show
He's going to the carnival
Tonight on Desolation Row.

Einstein disguised as Robin Hood
With his memories in a trunk
Passed this way an hour ago
With his friend a jealous monk   40

He looked so immaculately frightful
As he bummed a cigarette
Then he went off sniffing drain pipes
And reciting the alphabet
Now you would not think to look at him
But he was famous long ago
For playing the electric violin
On Desolation Row.

Doctor filth he keeps his word
Inside of a leather cup   50
But all his sexless patients
They're trying to blow it up
Now his nurse some local loser
She's in charge of the cyanide hold
And she also keeps the cards that read
Have mercy on his soul
They all play on penny whistles
You can hear them blow
If you lean your head out far enough
From Desolation Row.   60

Across the street they've nailed the curtains
They're getting ready for the feast
The phantom of the opera
A perfect image of a priest
They're spoon feeding Casanova
To get him to feel more assured
Then they'll kill him with self confidence
After poisoning him with words
And the phantom shouting to skinny girls
Get outta here if you don't know   70
Casanova is just being punished
For going to Desolation Row.

Now at midnight all the agents
And the super human crew
Come out and round up everyone
That knows more than they do
Then they bring them to the factory
Where the heart attack machine
Is strapped across their shoulders
And then the kerosene   80
Is brought down from the castles
By insurance men who go
Check to see that nobody is escaping
To Desolation Row.

Praise be to Nero's Neptune
The Titanic sails at dawn
Everybody's shouting
Which side are you on?
And Ezra Pound and T. S. Eliot
Are fighting in the captain's tower   90
While calypso singers laugh at them
And fishermen hold flowers
Between the windows of the sea
Where lovely mermaids flow
And nobody has to think too much
About Desolation Row.

NIKKI GIOVANNI [1943–   ]

Knoxville, Tennessee

I always like summer
best
you can eat fresh corn
from daddy's garden
and okra
and greens
and cabbage
and lots of
barbecue
and buttermilk
and homemade ice-cream
at the church picnic
and listen to
gospel music
outside
at the church
homecoming
and go to the mountains with
your grandmother
and go barefooted
and be warm
all the time
not only when you go to bed
and sleep

GLOSSARY

ACATALECTIC. Not catalectic; not lacking a syllable in the last foot. Acatalectic verse has the full number of syllables required by the pattern of meter. See CATALEXIS, HYPERMETER.

ACCENT. The emphasis given to certain syllables in a line of verse. *Word accent* is the normally spoken pattern of stressed and unstressed syllables. *Rhetorical accent* is the emphasis given to a word because of its importance in a sentence. *Metrical accent* is the stress pattern set up by a regular verse meter. *Wrenched accent:* the meter forces a shift in the normal word accent, as in ballads. *Hovering accent:* it is difficult to decide which of two adjacent syllables should receive greater stress.

ACEPHALOUS. See HEADLESS LINE.

AESTHETICISM (AESTHETIC MOVEMENT). A literary movement in the nineteenth century whose motto was "art for art's sake." It arose in opposition to the utilitarian doctrine that everything, including art, must be "useful" and contribute to the material progress of society; in practice this ideology had led to cynical materialism and self-righteous middle class morality. Led by Walter Pater and Oscar Wilde, the Aesthetic Movement insisted that art was independent of any didactic end and of any theory of what was morally good or useful. Later, however, the movement deteriorated to interest merely in stylistic polish and unusual subject matter. The term *fin de siècle* ("end of the century"), which had once connoted "Progress," came to connote "decadence." If capitalized, "Decadence" often refers to the Aesthetic Movement itself.

AFFECTIVE FALLACY. In the New Criticism, the alleged error of judging a literary work according to the emotional effect it produces in the reader. "Affect" is the technical term in psychology meaning "feeling or emotion"; it is related to the word "affection."

ALBA. Provençal, a song by lovers when they part at dawn. In French, *aubade;* German, *Tagelied.*

ALEXANDRINE. In English, a line of iambic hexameter. The line conventionally has a *caesura,* or pause, in the middle, dividing it into two symmetrical halves called *hemistiches:*

A needless Alexandrine ends the song
That, like a wounded snake, // drags its slow length along.

Pope, An Essay on Criticism

The Alexandrine has been common in French poetry since the twelfth century, and is used in elevated verse such as the tragedies of Racine. In English, the Spenserian stanza (q.v.) ends with an Alexandrine.

ALLEGORY. An extended metaphor, with subordinate metaphors depending from the main. In allegorical narrative, the literal action evokes another, parallel action composed of ideas. In simple allegory, there is a one-to-one correspondence of literal and abstract meanings.

Many a green isle needs must be
In the deep wide sea of Misery,
Or the mariner, worn and wan,
Never thus could voyage on—
Day and night, and night and day,
Drifting on his weary way . . .

Shelley, "Lines Written Among the Euganean Hills"

Here happiness is a green island, misery is a sea, man is a mariner, and life is a voyage. But allegorical narrative may be a great deal more complicated, with several levels of meaning. In the first book of Spenser's *Faerie Queene*, the Redcross Knight passes through actual adventures. He fights with a real fire-breathing dragon, is seduced by a real woman, suffers actual pain and imprisonment. This is the literal narrative. But at the same time the poem is an allegory of man's spiritual pilgrimage. The Redcross Knight is seeking holiness. In this he is aided by Una (Truth) and misled by Duessa (False Religion) and Archimago (Illusion). Moreover, there is an historical allegory. Redcross is an Englishman; he falls prey to the Church of Rome (the giant Orgoglio); he is rescued by Prince Arthur (the Reformation), and finally weds Una (Anglicanism).

If the story, literally told, pleases as much as the original, and in the same way, to what purpose was the allegory employed? For the function of allegory is not to hide but to reveal, and it is properly used only for that which cannot be said, or so well said, in literal speech. The inner life, and specially the life of love, religion, and spiritual adventure, has therefore always been the field of true allegory; for here there are intangibles which only allegory can fix and reticences which only allegory can overcome.

C. S. Lewis, The Allegory of Love, 1936

ALLITERATION (INITIAL RHYME). Repetition of sounds usually at the beginning of words.

Hast thou *f*orgot me then, and do I *s*eem
Now in thine eye so *f*oul, once deemed so *f*air

Milton, Paradise Lost

Alliteration unifies these lines and emphasizes the alliterated words and their relationships of unity and contrast with each other. *Hidden alliteration* is the repetition of sounds within the words, as the "s" sound above in "Ha*s*t" and on*c*e."

Old English poetry was written in *alliterative meter* arranged in tight patterns. Each line was divided by a pause into two verses; the verse-pairs were linked by the alliteration of one or two stressed syllables in the first verse with the first stressed syllable of the second verse. Alliterative meter was characteristic of Middle English prosody also; the patterns, however, were less regular.

A faire felde ful of folke   fonde I there bytwene.

William Langland, Piers Plowman

ALLUSION. A reference, usually brief, to something outside the literary text itself. In the following example, "three-days personage" refers to Christ:

He does not become a three-days personage,
Imposing his separation,
Calling for pomp.

Stevens, "The Death of a Soldier"

Addison says of the use of allusions:

It is this talent of affecting the imagination that gives an embellishment to good sense, and makes one man's compositions more agreeable than another's. It sets off all writings in general, but it is the very life and highest perfection of poetry. Where it shines in an eminent degree, it has preserved several poems for many ages, that have nothing else to recommend them; and where all the other beauties are present, the work appears dry and insipid, if this single one be wanting. It has something in it like creation; it bestows a kind of existence, and draws up to the reader's view several objects which are not to be found in being. It makes additions to nature, and gives a greater variety to God's works. In a word, it is able to beautify and adorn the most illustrious scenes in the universe, or to fill the mind with more glorious shows and apparitions, than can be found in any part of it.

Addison, The Spectator, 1711-12

AMBIGUITY (MULTIPLE MEANING). The use of language so that more than one interpretation of a word or passage is relevant to the meaning. In the following passage from *Paradise Lost,* the army of devils is facing the army of angels. The devils have artillery concealed in their ranks and are preparing to use it. Satan, leader of the devils, is speaking:

"Vanguard, to right and left the front unfold;
That all may see who hate us, how we seek
Peace and composure, and with open breast
Stand ready to receive them, if they like
Our overture, and turn not back perverse;
But that I doubt; however, witness Heaven,
Heaven witness thou anon, while we discharge
Freely our part. Ye who appointed stand,

Do as you have in charge, and briefly touch
What we propound, and loud that all may hear."
  So scoffing in ambiguous words, he scarce
Had ended, when . . .

The words "discharge," "charge," and "touch" are puns, a form of
ambiguity. They contain hidden references to the use of artillery:
"discharge"—to shoot; "charge"—the load in a gun; "touch"—to set off
gunpowder. The lines

That all may see who hate us, how we seek
Peace and composure . . .

are ambiguous, for the devils seek peace by making war. "Turn not
back perverse" hints at what will happen to the angels when the artillery hits them, with a pun on "perverse," meaning both wrongheaded
and bowled over. "Propound" is ambiguous; the word sounds like the
double thunder of cannon.
  In these lines by Dylan Thomas, "grave" is ambiguous, meaning
both serious and having to do with death:

I shall not murder
The mankind of her going with a grave truth . . .
    "A Refusal to Mourn the Death, by Fire, of a Child in London"

AMPHIBRACH. A metrical foot of three syllables: one weak, one strong, and
one weak ($\smile - \smile$), as in the word "arrangement."

AMPHIMACER. A metrical foot of three syllables: one strong, one weak, and
one strong ($- \smile -$). Also called the cretic foot.

Hēar mў lōve, / hēar mў prāyer / . . .
                    Plautus, *Curculio* (trans. G. E. Duckworth)

ANACREONTIC VERSE. Verse written in the style of Anacreon, a Greek poet
of the sixth century B.C., who sang of wine, love, and other pleasures.
The regular Anacreontic meter is exemplified in Longfellow's *Hia-
watha:*

Ŏn thĕ shōres ŏf/ Gītchĕ Gūmee . . .

ANACRUSIS. The addition of one or more unstressed syllables before the first
word of a line whose meter normally begins with a stress, as in the
second line of the following:

When the stars threw down their spears,
And watered heaven with their tears,
Did he smile his work to see?
                    Blake, "The Tiger"

ANALOGY. A comparison of two like relationships, e.g., the relationship of
man to God is compared to the relationship of a child to his father.
For an analogy in verse, see CONCEIT, the lines quoted from Donne's
"A Valediction Forbidding Mourning." Loosely, "analogy" may mean
any similarity between things.

404

ANAPEST, ANAPESTIC. A metrical foot of three syllables, with two weak stresses and one strong thus: ᵕ ᵕ —. See also METER and RISING METER.

ANTISTROPHE. See ODE.

APOCAPATED RHYME. See RHYME.

APOLLO. The Greek god of poetry—also of medicine, archery, light, youth, prophecy, and music, especially the lyre. *Apollonian* connotes a sense of classical order, moderation, reason, and culture. See DIONYSUS.

APOSTROPHE. A figure of speech in which an absent person, or a personification, is addressed.

> Come, seeling night,
> Scarf up the tender eye of pitiful day.

Shakespeare, Macbeth

APPROXIMATE RHYME. See RHYME.

ARCADIA, ARCADY. A mountainous region of Greece which became, in the conventions of pastoral poetry, the symbol of a retreat from the complexities of the real word to a simple, happy, and uncorrupted world of singing shepherds. See PASTORAL.

ARCHAISM. A word, expression, or spelling that is obsolete.

ARGUMENT OF A POEM. The plot or sequence of ideas that is the poem's intellectual substructure.

ASSOCIATION. A process of thinking in which a given work or image recalls, suggests, or connotes certain other images or emotions.

ASSONANCE. Repetition of vowel sounds preceded and followed by different consonant sounds, as in "time" and "mind." Assonance may be described loosely as a resemblance of vowel sounds.

ATMOSPHERE. The emotional setting in which a fictive world exists—its mood, as perceived by the reader: calm, humorous, mysterious, sinister, oppressive, etc.

AUBADE. See ALBA.

AUGUSTAN AGE. In Roman literature, the period of the reign of Caesar Augustus (27 B.C.–14 A.D.), which included the classical authors Ovid, Horace, and Virgil. In English literature, the term is applied to the early eighteenth century, when the authors Pope, Swift, Addison, and Steele were writing. Cf. CLASSICAL and NEOCLASSICAL.

BALLAD. A narrative poem, originally intended to be sung. The story is told in compact dramatic scenes, with simple dialogue and concrete imagery, and often a refrain. A *folk*, or *popular ballad*, is an anonymous communal creation transmitted orally from one person to another, and therefore may exist in more than one version. See "Sir Patrick Spens," "Thomas the Rhymer," and "Edward, Edward," pp. 50-55. A *literary ballad* is a ballad written by a single author in deliberate imitation of the folk ballad. Coleridge's "Rime of the Ancient Mariner" and Keats's "La Belle Dame sans Merci" are well-known literary ballads (pp. 156, 194).

BALLAD STANZA. A quatrain that alternates tetrameter with trimeter lines, and usually rhymes *a b c b*.

"The very deep did rot: O Christ!
That ever this should be!
Yea, slimy things did crawl with legs
Upon the slimy sea.
Coleridge, "The Rime of the Ancient Mariner"

BALLADE. A fixed verse form having three identically rhymed 8- or 10-line stanzas and an envoy, whose refrain (R) is the same as that of each stanza. (Rhyme scheme is *a b a b b c b R* in the octaves and *b c b R* in the envoy; or it is *a b a b b c d c R* in the 10-line stanzas and *c c d c R* in the envoy.) A *double ballade* has six regular stanzas but often no envoy. Ballades are more common in French than in English, and in English are usually employed for light verse.

BARD. Originally, a Celtic minstrel-poet who entertained warriors by singing of their feats; later, any poet.

BATHOS (SINKING). A sudden and unintentional descent from the exalted in style and content to the ridiculous, often because the author is straining for sublimity.

The Eternal heard, and from the heavenly quire
    Chose out the cherub with the flaming sword,
And bad him swiftly drive the approaching fire
    From where our naval magazines were stored.
Dryden, "Annus Mirabilis"

        Hast thou then survived—
Mild offspring of infirm humanity,
Meek infant! among all forlornest things
The most forlorn—one life of that bright star,
The second glory of the Heavens?—Thou hast.
Wordsworth, "Address to My Infant Daughter"

Bathos may simply mean language that is flat, dismal, or ridiculous.

"Lord Byron" was an Englishman
    A poet I believe,
His first works in old England
    Was poorly received.
Perhaps it was "Lord Byron's" fault
    And perhaps it was not.
His life was full of misfortunes,
    Ah, strange was his lot.
Julia Moore (the Sweet Singer of Michigan), "Lord Byron's Life"

This last is bathos, but not sinking, for the Sweet Singer was sunk from the start. And whenever the subject comes up, someone will quote McGonagall. Everyone has his favorite passage from McGonagall—this is mine:

Oh! ill-fated Bridge of the Silv'ry Tay,
I must now conclude my lay
By telling the world fearlessly without the least dismay,
That your central girders would not have given way,
At least many sensible men do say,
Had they been supported on each side with buttresses,
At least many sensible men confesses,
For the stronger we our houses do build,
The less chance we have of being killed.

William McGonagall, "The Tay Bridge Disaster"

BEAST EPIC. A related series of tales (*beast fables*) about animals with human characteristics. The medieval beast epic was often an allegory aimed at social satire, in which Reynard the Fox could be interpreted as the Church, Noble the Lion as the king, and Ysengrim the Wolf as the aristocracy. Chauntecleer the Cock was a favorite character. The genre is as old as Aesop's fables of the sixth century B.C.

BEAT POETRY. A kind of verse first written in the United States in the late 1950's. Originally "beat" may have meant "worn out," "exhausted"; it has also been said to mean "beatific." The most famous of the Beats (Beat poets) is Allen Ginsberg, whose *Howl* epitomized attitudes and techniques of the movement. Beat poetry is usually written in free verse. The language is slangy. The poet writes about his personal habits, friends, experiences of sex, use of hallucinatory drugs. Frequently the beat writer expresses his dislike for middle class ("square") people.

BEAUTY

The sense of beauty is intuitive, and beauty itself is all that inspires pleasure without, and aloof from, and even contrarily to, interest.

Coleridge, *Biographia Literaria*

What the imagination seizes as Beauty must be truth—whether it existed before or not—for I have the same Idea of all our passions as of Love; they are all in their sublime, creative of essential Beauty.

Keats, Letter to Benjamin Bailey

BESTIARY. A medieval collection of descriptions of animals, real and fictitious, which allegorized Christian doctrines; e.g., the phoenix, a legendary bird that rises anew from the ashes of its pyre, represents the immortal soul, and the unicorn is a metaphor for Christ.

BLANK VERSE. Unrhymed iambic pentameter. After its introduction by Surrey in the sixteenth century, blank verse was widely used in the drama. Later it was used for nondramatic poetry. The tradition includes the drama of Marlowe and Shakespeare, Milton's *Paradise Lost,* Wordsworth's *The Prelude,* and some of Browning's dramatic monologues.

But, soft! What light through yonder window breaks?
It is the east, and Juliet is the sun.

Shakespeare, Romeo and Juliet

BOMBAST. Originally, cotton stuffing to make bulges in garments, according to Elizabethan fashion. Bombastic language is pretentious and inflated:

Pistol. I'll see her damned first; to Pluto's damned lake, by this hand, to the infernal deep, with Erebus and tortures vile also.

Shakespeare, Henry IV, Part 2

BROKEN RHYME. See RHYME.

BUCOLIC. 1. referring to shepherds. 2. a pastoral poem.

BURLESQUE. Any imitation of other literary works, or of people's actions and attitudes, which aims to amuse and to ridicule by distortion or by incongruity of style and subject. *High burlesque* uses a high style and a low subject. Examples of high burlesque are the *parody* (q.v.), which mocks a specific literary work by applying its style to a trivial subject, and the *mock epic,* or *mock heroic* style, which ridicules a trivial subject by treating it with the high style of the epic, as in Pope's "Rape of the Lock." *Low burlesque,* in contrast, uses a low style with a high subject, as in a *travesty,* which ridicules a specific literary work by treating its dignified subject in a grotesque low style that exaggerates the peculiarities of the original. See also SATIRE.

BYRONIC. Referring to romantic behavior patterned on the attitudes and opinions of Lord Byron. Symptoms include veiled guilt, proud scorn of society, and rhapsodizing about nature.

CACOPHONY. A combination of sounds that is harsh, discordant, or hard to articulate, usually because of clusters of consonants. Cacophony can be used to support meaning.

Blow, winds, and crack your cheeks! rage! blow!

Shakespeare, King Lear

Cf. DISSONANCE.

CADENCE. (Derived from Latin *cadens,* falling.) The rising and falling rhythmic flow of spoken language, resulting from the pattern of stressed and unstressed syllables. See FREE VERSE.

CAESURA. A pause within a line of verse, dictated by speech rhythm rather than meter. In scanning verse, the caesura may be indicated by vertical bars.

Know then thyself, // presume not God to scan;
The proper study of Mankind // is Man.

Pope, An Essay on Man

CANON (and APOCRYPHA). A canon is a list of an author's works accepted as authentic, e.g., there are thirty-six plays in the canon of Shakespeare. Works doubtfully ascribed to an author are apocrypha.

CANTO. A subdivision of an epic or narrative poem, corresponding to a chapter in a novel.

CANZONE. A Provençal or Italian lyric, sometimes set to music. There are a number of verse forms with different metrical patterns.

CAROL. Originally, a song for a circle dance, as around the Christmas crib in the Middle Ages; later, traditional Christmas songs or drinking songs.

CAROLINE. (Derived from Latin *Carolus*, Charles.) Of the period of King Charles I of England, 1625–1649. See CAVALIER POETS.

CARPE DIEM MOTIF. The Latin words mean "Seize the day." A poetic theme as ancient as Greek and Latin lyrics: make the most of the present.

CATALEXIS (TRUNCATION). A *catalectic* line omits the final unaccented syllables of the meter.

Tiger!/Tiger!/burning/bright [‿]
In the forests of the night

Blake, "The Tiger"

See ACATALECTIC.

CAVALIER POETS. Seventeenth-century poets who were sympathetic to King Charles I (1625–1649): Herrick, Carew, Suckling, Lovelace, and Waller. Much of their poetry is in the manner of a song: gallant, witty, devil-may-care.

CELTIC RENAISSANCE (IRISH LITERARY REVIVAL). The nationalistic Irish literary movement of the late nineteenth and early twentieth centuries, in which Irish intellectuals and writers asserted their cultural independence from Britain. The aim was for art rooted in the Celtic and Gaelic heritage, or in Irish life, as in the writings of Yeats and Synge.

CHANSON. French for "song." *Chanson courtois:* "courtly song." *Chanson de geste:* "song of noble deeds," a type of Old French (eleventh to fourteenth century) epic tale in verse, centered on a legendary or historical hero, such as Charlemagne. The most famous is the *Chanson de Roland,* or *Song of Roland. Chanson populaire:* "song of the people."

CHANT ROYAL. A French fixed verse form having five stanzas of eleven lines each, rhyming *a b a b c c d d e d R*—R being a refrain—and an envoy that rhymes *d d e d R.* Uncommon in English.

CHIASMUS. (Derived from Greek *chiazein,* "to mark crosswise.") A rhetorical figure with two syntactically parallel constructions, one of which has the word order reversed:

They fall successive, and successive rise.

CHORIAMB. A metrical unit consisting of a trochee (choree) and an iamb (— ‿ ‿ —). Frequent in Greek dramatic choruses and lyric poetry—rare in English.

Ah, thy|snow-coloured hands!|once they were chains,|mighty to

bind|me fast.

Swinburne, "Choriambics"

CLASSIC. A work generally recognized as being of enduring significance; a model or a standard of excellence.

CLASSICAL. Referring to Greek and Roman literature.

CLASSICISM. An aesthetic that stresses tradition, convention, form, decorum, balance, restraint, moderation, simplicity, dignity, austerity. These qualities have been thought to be attributes of ancient Greek and Roman culture, but reading Greek or Roman literature, or a little history, will dispel the illusion. See ROMANTICISM.

CLICHÉ. A stale, trite figure of speech. As Pope remarked:

Where'er you find "the cooling western breeze,"
In the next line, it "whispers through the trees";
If crystal streams "with pleasing murmurs creep,"
The reader's threatened (not in vain) with "sleep."

An Essay on Criticism

CLOSED COUPLET. An end-stopped, rhymed couplet that contains a complete thought.

Let such teach others who themselves excel,
And censure freely who have written well.

Pope, *An Essay on Criticism*

COMMONWEALTH (PURITAN INTERREGNUM). The parliamentary government that controlled England between the execution of Charles I in 1649 and the restoration of Charles II to the throne in 1660.

COMPLAINT. Usually a lyric poem in which the speaker laments the absence or unresponsiveness of his beloved. But poets may complain about anything; for example, Chaucer's "Complaint to his Purse."

COMPLETE RHYME. See RHYME.

CONCEIT. A far-fetched comparison between things seemingly unlike. The *Petrarchan conceit,* as written by the Italian poet Petrarch (1304–74), was a Platonic idealization—usually the poet's idealization of his mistress. He might compare her to precious stones, artifacts, beautiful birds and animals, flowers, plants, and mythical creatures. The conceits in this passage from Spenser's "Epithalamion," in which he celebrates his marriage to Elizabeth Boyle, are in the manner of Petrarch:

Tell me ye merchants daughters did ye see
So fayre a creature in your towne before,
So sweet, so lovely, and so mild as she,
Adornd with beautyes grace and vertues store,
Her goodly eyes lyke Saphyres shining bright,
Her forehead yvory white,
Her cheekes lyke apples which the sun hath rudded,
Her lips lyke cherryes charming men to byte,
Her breast like to a bowle of creame vncrudded,
Her paps lyke lyllies budded,
Her snowie necke lyke to a marble towre,

410

And all her body like a pallace fayre,
Ascending uppe with many a stately stayre,
To honors seat and chastities sweet bowre.
Why stand ye still ye virgins in amaze,
Upon her so to gaze,
Whiles ye forget your former lay to sing,
To which the woods did answer and your eccho ring.

Conceits such as these were satirized by Shakespeare:

My mistress' eyes are nothing like the sun;
Coral is far more red than her lips' red;
If snows be white, why then her breasts are dun;
If hairs be wires, black wires grow on her head.

Metaphysical conceits, used by John Donne and his followers, exploited all fields of knowledge for comparisons—theology, astronomy, mythology, history, commerce, geography, metallurgy, alchemy, mathematics, etc. In 1693 Dryden said that John Donne's poetry "affects the metaphysics," or resembles the abstruse terms and arguments of the scholastic philosophers. In his "Life of Cowley" (1777) Dr. Johnson finds in the metaphysical poets "a combination of dissimilar images, or discovery of occult resemblances in things apparently unlike. Of wit, thus defined, they have more than enough. The most heterogeneous ideas are yoked by violence together; nature and art are ransacked for illustrations, comparisons, and allusions; their learning instructs, and their subtilty surprises; but the reader commonly thinks his improvement dearly bought, and, though he sometimes admires, is seldom pleased."

In the nineteenth century the metaphysical poets were neglected. Then, the research of scholars and an essay by T. S. Eliot titled "The Metaphysical Poets" (1921), in which he reviewed H. J. C. Grierson's *Metaphysical Lyrics and Poems of the Seventeenth Century,* roused new interest in these poets. They have had a strong influence on modern poetry, in the kind of verse in which complex ideas and concrete images are important, as in the poems of Eliot himself.

One of the more famous metaphysical conceits is Donne's comparison of two lovers to the legs of a mathematical compass, in "A Valediction Forbidding Mourning":

If they be two, they are two so
    As stiff twin compasses are two;
Thy soul, the fixed foot, makes no show
    To move, but doth, if th' other do.

And though it in the center sit,
    Yet when the other far doth roam,
It leans and hearkens after it,
    And grows erect, as that comes home.

Such wilt thou be to me, who must
    Like th' other foot, obliquely run;

Thy firmness makes my circle just,
  And makes me end where I begun.

In the following lines, from Crashaw's "Saint Mary Magdalene,"
metaphysical ingenuity falls into absurdity. The tearful eyes of the
repentant Magdalene are described as

  two faithful fountains
Two walking baths, two weeping motions,
Portable and compendious oceans.

Here is a modern metaphysical conceit in Eliot's "The Love Song of
J. Alfred Prufrock":

Let us go then, you and I,
When the evening is spread out against the sky
Like a patient etherised upon a table.

CONCRETE. A term applied to language that is full of images (words evoking sense perceptions); to be distinguished from language that is
abstract.

Taking the hands of someone you love,
You see they are delicate cages.
                              Robert Bly, "Taking the Hands"

Down the ravine behind the empty house,
The cowbells follow one another
Into the distances of the afternoon.
        James Wright, "Lying in a Hammock on William Duffy's Farm in
                                        Pine Island, Minnesota"

CONCRETE POETRY. Writing in which visual elements contribute essentially
to the effect. A letter of the alphabet may be printed repeatedly,
like a pattern in a carpet. A few words may be printed in different
combinations. The outline of the poem may resemble an object—e.g.,
the seventeenth-century poems "The Altar" and "Easter Wings" by
George Herbert (q.v.) and the "pattern poem" by Reinhard Döhl,
1965, on page 413. Parentheses may be scattered over the page like
bird wings, or there may be splatters of dots. Some critics make a
distinction between the concrete poem and the *shaped poem:* besides
having a shape that represents something—e.g., an altar—the shaped
poem has literary elements: significant language, meter, rhyme, etc.;
concrete poetry, on the other hand, is "the thing itself," purely a
design, without literary attributes. When concrete poetry consists only
of visual elements, it is arguable that it is not poetry but a form of
visual art.

ping pong
    ping pong ping
    pong ping pong
        ping pong
                              Eugen Gomringer, 1952

Apfel Apfel Apfel Apfel
Apfel Apfel Apfel Apfel A
Apfel Apfel Apfel Apfel Apfe
Apfel Apfel Apfel Apfel Apf
Apfel Apfel Apfel Apfel Apfel
Apfel Apfel Apfel Apfel Apfe
Apfel Apfel Apfel Apfel Apfel A
Apfel Apfel Apfel Apfel Apfe
Apfel Apfel Apfel Apfel Apfel
Apfel Apfel Apfel Apfel Apf
Apfel Apfel Apfel WurmAp
Apfel Apfel Apfel Apfel
Apfel Apfel Apfel
Apfel Apfel A
Apfel A

Reinhard Döhl, "Pattern Poem with an Elusive Intruder," 1965

Paul de Vree, "April in Paris," 1966

CONNOTATION. The significance of a word beyond its factual, neutral *denotation;* the associations, attitudes, and emotional meanings the word carries to or evokes from the reader by means of implication or suggestion. In the example below, instead of "boat" and "horses," words with more specific and romantic connotations have been used:

> There is no *frigate* like a book
> To take us lands away,
> Nor any *coursers* like a page
> Of prancing poetry.
>
> Emily Dickinson

See DENOTATION.

CONSONANCE. Repetition of consonant sounds where the vowels before the consonants differ, as in "stru*ts*" and "fre*ts*." Consonance may be used as a form of approximate rhyme (see RHYME). Sometimes the word "consonance" is used loosely to describe a repetition of consonant sounds.

CONSONANTAL RHYME. See RHYME.

CONVENTION. Any generally accepted feature of style or subject matter derived from past usage or custom. Conventions in poetry include rhyme, all stanza forms, genres (such as the pastoral elegy, dramatic monologue, and literary ballad), and stock characters (the epic hero, the languishing lover, and his cruel and beautiful mistress).

COUPLET. A pair of successive lines of verse, especially when they rhyme and are of the same length; a two-line stanza. See CLOSED COUPLET and HEROIC COUPLET.

DACTYL, DACTYLIC. A metrical foot of three syllables, with one strong stress and two weak, thus: — ⌣ ⌣. See also METER and FALLING METER.

DECADENCE. See AESTHETICISM.

DECORUM. The principle that the style and diction of a literary work should be appropriate to the genre, subject, speaker, audience, and occasion. A high (or grand or elevated) style is required for serious subjects and noble themes and characters in the epic, tragedy, elegy, and ode. A low (or plain) style, closer to everyday speech, may be used for comedy, satire, and lyrics.

Aristotle recommended that tragic poets write what is appropriate and avoid incongruities. Horace, in the *Art of Poetry*, said that a speaker's words should be in accord with his station: a slave should speak like a slave, an Assyrian like an Assyrian, and so on. Moreover, comic and tragic themes should never be mingled. These ideas prevailed in the theory of poetry throughout the Renaissance and long after. Neoclassic writers such as Tasso and Mazzoni went further, laying down rules for the epic poem, the dramatic, and the lyric, distinguishing one genre sharply from another and stating what style was appropriate for each. They emphasized propriety, elegance, and correct taste, excluding whatever was vulgar or unconventional.

However, medieval poets had not paid much attention to classical theory, and some Renaissance poets, influenced by the Bible and Christian literature, broke with decorum. They wrote tragical comedies, comical tragedies, histories, romances, naive lyrics, vulgar eclogues. These poets appealed to nature, and decorum has often been assaulted by poets who write out of their "feelings" rather than by rules. In 1800, in the Preface to *Lyrical Ballads,* Wordsworth attacked the decorum of the preceding age, arguing that poetry could be written about "humble and rustic" life, in a "selection of language really used by men."

DENOTATION. The dictionary definition of a word, referring to objects or facts, from which emotion is excluded. See CONNOTATION.

DIBRACH. See PYRRHIC.

DICTION. Choice of words, the vocabulary used in a literary text. The appropriateness of a particular word is determined by its context.

DIDACTIC. With intent to teach, especially to instruct in moral virtues or assert a doctrine or thesis as true, as in *Paradise Lost* where Milton's intent is to "justify the ways of God to men." *Didactic* is a neutral and descriptive, rather than a derogatory, critical term, because didactic works can be imaginative. As well as illustrating truths outside the text, they may be interesting and delightful in themselves. Some didactic poems convey practical information. The Greek poet Hesiod's *Works and Days* includes a farmer's almanac, a description of the work to be done at different seasons, advice on navigation, etc.

DIMETER. A line of two metrical feet, as the fourth line of

Tell me, where is fancy bred,
Or in the heart, or in the head?
How begot, how nourished?
　　Reply, reply.

Shakespeare, The Merchant of Venice

DIONYSUS. The Greek god of vegetation, vineyards, and wine. *Dionysian* connotes intoxication, ecstasy, frenzy, madness, and the deep irrational source of inspiration for music and poetry. See APOLLO.

DIPODIC VERSE. "Dipody" is Greek for "a combination of two feet." In dipodic verse, two metrical feet must be considered as one unit for scansion. The metrical unit is less the individual foot than a pair of feet, related but slightly different, one foot usually having a stronger stress than the other.

Taffy was a/ Welshman,

Taffy was a/ thief.

DIRGE (THRENODY). A lyric poem or song commemorating a death and expressing grief. A *monody* is a dirge sung by one person. Cf. ELEGY.

DISSOCIATION OF SENSIBILITY. A term made famous by T. S. Eliot's use of it in his essay "The Metaphysical Poets" (1921). In the metaphysical poets, according to Eliot, there was an immediate correlation between abstract thought and concrete phenomena. However, in later poets, especially Milton, the poet's thinking process was separated from his sense perceptions and, as a result, verse became inflated and its images empty of tangible intellectual application. Metaphors, for example, were merely decorative, instead of embodying thought in images so that the reader could "feel" the thought. "Tennyson and Browning are poets," wrote Eliot, "and they think; but they do not feel their thought as immediately as the odor of a rose. A thought to Donne was an experience . . ."

DISSONANCE. A discord of sounds. It may be intentional or unintentional. Dissonance may be cacophony, harsh and unpleasing, or it may be an interesting variation of sounds. See CACOPHONY.

DISTICH. A couplet.

DISTRIBUTED STRESS. See HOVERING STRESS.

DITHYRAMB. In ancient Greece, an irregular and wildly passionate choral hymn or chant sung in honor of Dionysus at a sacrificial festival; forerunner of Greek tragedy. A highly emotional or wildly lyrical piece of writing may be termed *dithyrambic*.

DOGGEREL. Rhymed verse that is too clumsy to be taken seriously. It is characterized by close-recurring rhymes, monotonous meter, and trivial thoughts. But doggerel can be written intentionally to be comic and humorous, as in Samuel Butler's *Hudibras:*

More peevish, cross, and splenetic
Than dog distract or monkey sick.

DOUBLE RHYME. See RHYME.

DRAMATIC IRONY. See IRONY.

DRAMATIC MONOLOGUE. A poem consisting of words spoken by a fictional character to a silent audience. Sometimes the speaker reveals aspects of his personality of which he himself is unaware. See PERSONA. Also, Robert Browning, "My Last Duchess," p. 207, and T. S. Eliot, "The Love Song of J. Alfred Prufrock," p. 288.

DUPLE METERS. Meters with feet consisting of two syllables. Iambic ($\smile$ $-$) and trochaic ($-$ $\smile$) are duple meters. See TRIPLE METERS.

ECLOGUE. A pastoral poem, especially a pastoral dialogue. In modern usage, any verse dialogue where the setting is important.

ELEGIAC QUATRAIN. Four lines of iambic pentameter rhyming *a b a b.*

How perfect was the calm! it seemed no sleep;
No mood, which season takes away, or brings:
I could have fancied that the mighty Deep
Was even the gentlest of all gentle Things.

Wordsworth, "Elegiac Stanzas"

ELEGY. (Derived from the Greek, *E, E legein!* "To cry woe, woe!") As early as the time of Mimnermus (ca. 630 B.C.) it was the metrical form for love poetry, in couplets of a long dactylic hexameter and a shorter pentameter line. The elegiac meter was also used for martial verse, dirge and lamentation, and occasional poetry of a descriptive or topical sort. The pastoral elegy has an especially rich tradition.

In England in the sixteenth and early seventeenth century, the word "elegy" is used for Petrarchan love poems, laments, and essays. The elegies of Donne include witty poems on trivial topics; apparently serious defenses of outrageous propositions; dramatic situations, real or imaginary, in which elements of wit or paradox may be incidentally present (J. B. Leishman). Donne's "Anatomy of the World" (1611) applies the elegy to death—he said, "funeral elegy"—and Milton's "Lycidas" (1637) establishes the elegy as a genre, a lament for the dead.

In current usage the word "elegiac" may mean meditative. Or it may be applied to verse that expresses sorrow over the dead. See the following poems in the anthology: Milton, "Lycidas"; Dryden, "To the Memory of Mr. Oldham"; Gray, "Elegy"; Hardy, "Drummer Hodge"; Hopkins, "Felix Randal"; Ransom, "Bells for John Whiteside's Daughter"; Roethke, "Elegy for Jane."

ELEVATION. Use of a high style or subject; grand or lofty writing.

ELISION. The omission of part of a word (o'er, ne'er), or the dropping of an unaccented syllable to make a line conform to a metrical pattern.

And yet 'tis almost 'gainst my conscience.

> Shakespeare, *Hamlet*

ELIZABETHAN. The period of Queen Elizabeth I (1558–1603), which included Spenser, Sidney, Marlowe, and Shakespeare. The English Renaissance.

ELLIPSIS. Leaving out words that are needed to express a meaning completely.

EMOTIVE LANGUAGE. Language that expresses or evokes feelings and attitudes:

And my poor fool is hanged! No, no, no life!
Why should a dog, a horse, a rat, have life,
And thou no breath at all?

> Shakespeare, *King Lear*

Emotive language is contrasted to *referential language,* in which neutral statements are made about facts.

EMPATHY. (The equivalent word in German is *Einfuhlung,* meaning "feeling into.") A person's mental identification with an object of perception, imagining how it feels to be inside something that is outside himself. "If a Sparrow come before my Window, I take part in its existence and pick about the Gravel."—Keats

417

ENCOMIASTIC VERSE. A general term for poems which praise or glorify a person, object, or abstract idea, as Wordsworth's "Ode to Duty."

END RHYME. See RHYME.

END-STOPPED LINE. One in which the end of a syntactical unit (phrase, clause, or sentence) coincides with the end of the line.

> Good nature and good sense must ever join;
> To err is human, to forgive, divine.
>
> Pope, An Essay on Criticism

Cf. RUN-ON LINE.

ENJAMBMENT. See RUN-ON LINE.

ENVOY (ENVOI). French for "a sending on the way"; a concluding stanza, dedicating the poem (such as a ballade) to an important person (such as a prince).

> O conquerour of Brutes Albyoun,
> Which that by lyne and free eleccioun
> Been verray kyng, this song to yow I sende;
> And ye, that mowen alle oure harmes amende,
> Have mynde upon my supplicacioun!
>
> Chaucer, "The Complaynt of Chaucer to his Purse"

EPIC. A long narrative poem with an exalted style and a heroic theme. Some epics are modeled on Homer's *Iliad* and *Odyssey*.

> Homer has shown in what meter may best be written the deeds of kings and captains, and the sorrows of war.
>
> Horace, Art of Poetry

Homeric conventions include the poet's invocation to his muse for her aid; his asking her an epic question, the answer to which begins the narrative *in medias res*, or in the middle of things; the hero's noble deeds and adventures, such as a descent into the underworld and battles in which the gods (the "machinery") take part; and, throughout the poem, a ceremonial high style with epic similes, catalogues, and processions of characters. Virgil's *Aeneid* and Milton's *Paradise Lost* are in the Homeric tradition.

 The word "epic" may also be used to describe heroic narrative poems that do not follow the Homeric conventions—e.g., *Beowulf*, Dante's *Divine Comedy*, *La Chanson de Roland*, the *Ramayana*, and the *Mahabharata*. (For *mock epic*, see BURLESQUE.)

EPIC QUESTION. Asked by the writer of an epic to the Muse; the answer reveals what started the action.

> Who first seduced them to that foul revolt?
> The infernal Serpent; he it was, whose guile,
> Stirred up with envy and revenge, deceived
> The Mother of Mankind . . .
>
> Milton, Paradise Lost

EPIC SIMILE. In epics, an extended comparison in which one or both of the subjects compared are described in elaborate detail, and in which the secondary subject (the vehicle) may be developed beyond its specific likeness to the primary subject (the tenor).

> [Satan] stood and called
> His Legions, Angel Forms, who lay entranced
> Thick as Autumnal Leaves that strow the Brooks
> In Vallombrosa, where th' Etrurian shades
> High overarched imbower; or scattered sedge
> Afloat, when with fierce Winds Orion armed
> Hath vexed the Red-Sea Coast, whose waves o'erthrew
> Busiris and his Memphian Chivalry,
> While with perfidious hatred they pursued
> The Sojourners of Goshen, who beheld
> From the safe shore thir floating Carcasses
> And broken Chariot Wheels; so thick bestrown
> Abject and lost lay these, covering the Flood,
> Under amazement of thir hideous change.

Milton, Paradise Lost

EPIGRAM. A polished, terse, and often witty remark, either in prose or verse. In verse the form is usually a couplet or quatrain, but tone is what distinguishes the epigram, rather than form. In the Renaissance, epigrams were patterned on the satiric examples of Martial and other Roman writers, rather than on Greek epigrams, some of which are delicate lyrics. In England in the seventeenth and eighteenth century, when epigrams were fashionable, there was a variety of types: insults, compliments, and pithy sayings. Epigrams may be parts of a poem. Pope's *Essays* are a series of epigrammatic couplets, each of which is a separate, memorable saying:

> A little learning is a dangerous thing;
> Drink deep, or taste not the Pierian spring . . .

An Essay on Criticism

These epigrams by Blake and Landor show the range:

> A petty Sneaking Knave I knew—
> O Mr. Cromek, how do ye do?

> Stand close around, ye Stygian set,
>   With Dirce in one boat conveyed!
> Or Charon, seeing, may forget
>   That he is old and she a shade.

EPILOGUE. A concluding section, separated from the main body of the literary work.

EPISTLE. A verse epistle is a poem in the form of a letter addressed to a specific person, e.g., Pope's "Epistle to Dr. Arbuthnot."

EPITAPH. Writing that could be placed on a grave, though this may not be done or intended. The epitaph sums up a life; some epitaphs are panegyrics, others are ribald. There are epitaphs that satirize a living man or an institution. Milton's poem on Shakespeare is one kind of epitaph:

What needs my Shakespeare for his honored bones
The labor of an age in piled stones . . .

Ralegh's on Leicester is another:

Here lies the noble Warrior that never blunted sword;
Here lies the noble Courtier that never kept his word;
Here lies his Excellency that governed all the state;
Here lies the Lord of Leicester that all the world did hate.

EPITHALAMION. (Greek, "at the bridal chamber.") A lyric poem, either solemn or ribald, to be sung outside the bridal chamber on the wedding night.

EPITHET. A word or phrase that describes the characteristic quality of a person or thing, as "Ethelred the Unready" or Homer's "wine-faced sea" and "fleet-footed Achilles." A *transferred epithet* is an adjective, word, or phrase that is shifted from the noun it would most obviously modify and applied to an associated but unexpected noun. In Keats' "Ode to a Nightingale," the word "embalmed," which evokes the closeness of an overwhelming perfume of flowers, is applied to the night itself:

I cannot see what flowers are at my feet,
　Nor what soft incense hangs upon the boughs,
But, in embalmed darkness, guess each sweet
　Wherewith the seasonable month endows
The grass, the thicket, and the fruit-tree wild.

EPODE. See ODE.

EULOGY. A speech or composition in praise of a person or thing, especially a formal poem praising a dead person.

EUPHONY. A combination of sounds that is pleasant, musical, and fluent.

Full fathom five thy father lies;
　Of his bones are coral made;
Those are pearls that were his eyes.

Shakespeare, *The Tempest*

EXACT RHYME. See RHYME.

EXPLICATION. An explanation. Originally, a French classroom technique of line-by-line, word-by-word explanation. To explicate a poem is to make it clear by explaining its meaning.

EYE RHYME. See RHYME.

FABLE. A brief tale in prose or verse, intended to illustrate a moral. The characters are often talking animals, as in Aesop's fables. See the poems by Ted Hughes about Crow, pp. 369-371.

FABLIAU. (Plural: *fabliaux*.) Earthy, comic, medieval tales in verse or prose, which usually satirized the clergy and middle class morality, and were often obscene. Chaucer's "Miller's Tale" is a *fabliau*.

FALLING METER. Meter in which the movement falls away from the stressed syllable of each foot. The trochee $(- \smile)$ and the dactyl $(- \smile \smile)$ are falling meters.

FANCY (IMAGINATION). Fancy is the faculty of arranging ideas and images in pleasant combinations. The creations of fancy are casual, whimsical, and often amusing; they are less profound and exciting than those of *Imagination,* which seems to be discovering new images and ideas. Until the nineteenth century the words Fancy and Imagination were often used to mean the same thing, as in this passage from Edmund Burke's "On Taste," 1757:

Besides the ideas, with their annexed pains and pleasures, which are presented by the sense, the mind of man possesses a sort of creative power of its own; either in representing at pleasure the images of things in the order and manner in which they were received by the senses, or in combining those images in a new manner, and according to a different order. This power is called imagination; and to this belongs whatever is called wit, fancy, invention, and the like. But it must be observed, that this power of the imagination is incapable of producing anything absolutely new; it can only vary the disposition of those ideas which it has received from the senses.

However some writers had begun to distinguish between Fancy and Imagination. Imagination was originality:

Original Genius . . . above all . . . is distinguished by an inventive and plastic Imagination, by which it sketches out a creation of its own, discloses truths that were formerly unknown, and exhibits a succession of scenes and events which were never before contemplated or conceived.

William Duff, *An Essay on Original Genius,* 1767

In 1817 in *Biographia Literaria,* Coleridge differentiated between Fancy and Imagination in these words:

The imagination, then, I consider either as primary, or secondary. The primary imagination I hold to be the living power and prime agent of all human perception, and as a repetition in the finite mind of the eternal act of creation in the infinite I AM. The secondary imagination I consider as an echo of the former, coexisting with the conscious will, yet still as identical with the primary in the *kind* of its agency, and differing only in *degree* and in the *mode* of its operation. It dissolves, diffuses, dissipates, in order to recreate; or where this process is rendered impossible, yet still at all events it struggles to idealize and to unify. It is essentially *vital,* even as all objects (*as* objects) are essentially fixed and dead.

    Fancy, on the contrary, has no other counters to play with, but fixities and definites. The fancy is indeed no other than a mode of memory emancipated from the order of time and space; while it is blended with, and modified by that empirical phenomenon of the will, which we express by the word *choice*. But equally with the ordinary memory the fancy must receive all its materials ready made from the law of association.

See IMAGINATION.

FEMININE RHYME. See RHYME.

FIGURATIVE LANGUAGE. Language which means something more than or other than what it literally says. See TROPE, SIMILE, METAPHOR, METONOMY, SYNECDOCHE, PERSONIFICATION, SYMBOL, ALLEGORY, PARADOX, IRONY, HYPERBOLE, and UNDERSTATEMENT.

FIGURES OF SPEECH. Rhetorical devices which depart from the ordinary meaning of words by arranging the words to achieve special effects. In figurative language, on the other hand, the meaning of the words themselves is radically changed. See APOSTROPHE, CHIASMUS, INVOCATION, RHETORICAL QUESTION, and ZEUGMA.

FIN DE SIÈCLE. See AESTHETICISM.

FIXED FORM. Any of the standard, highly structured arrangements of meter and rhyme patterns that define a poem as a sonnet, or ballade, or villanelle, etc. Other forms are: ballad stanza, double ballade, chant royal, closed couplet, elegiac quatrain, heroic quatrain, ottava rima, rime royal (or Chaucerian stanza), rondeau, rondeau redouble, rondel, rondelet, roundel, sapphic, sestina, Spenserian stanza, terza rima, triolet, and virelay.

FLYTING. An impromptu folk contest in which two contenders heap abuse on each other. This is the model for flytings in verse, such as the dispute between Beowulf and Unferth in the Old English epic *Beowulf*, and "The Flyting of Dunbar and Kennedie."

Quod Kennedy to Dunbar
Dathane devillis sone, and dragon dispitous,
   Abironis birth, and bred with Beliall;
Wod werwolf, worme, and scorpion vennemous . . .

FOLK BALLAD. See BALLAD.

FOOT. A metric unit consisting of one stressed syllable ($-$) and one or more unstressed syllables ($\smile\ \smile$). For those feet most commonly used in English, see pp. 34-37.

FORMS. Conventional arrangements of meter and rhyme patterns. See FIXED FORM.

FOUND POETRY. A piece of writing that is read as poetry though it was not intended to be. Usually the poem is found in a passage of prose—it may be from a news item, advertisement, handbook, travel book, or catalogue—which is then divided into lines of verse. Most found poems, though not all, are satiric—the unexpected attention catching the writer off guard.

Rising and Sinking

> (from *The Beauties of Nature*, by Sir John Lubbock, F.R.S.)

The Welsh Mountains are older than the Vosges,
The Vosges than the Pyrenees,
The Pyrenees than the Alps,
And the Alps than the Andes.
Scandinavia is rising in the north,
And sinking at the south.
South America is rising on the west
And sinking in the east.
Slow subterranean movements
Are still in progress.

Shirley Kaufman

Order in the Streets

> (from instructions printed on a child's toy, Christmas 1968, as
> reported in the *New York Times*)

1. 2. 3.
Switch on.

Jeep rushes
to the scene
of riot.

Jeep goes
in all directions
by mystery action.

Jeep stops periodically
to turn hood over

machine gun appears
with realistic
shooting noise.

After putting down riot,
jeep goes
back to the headquarters.

Donald Justice

FOURTEENER. Elizabethan term for heptameter (q.v.).

FREE VERSE (VERS LIBRE). Poetry in which rhythm is based not on strict
meter, but on a highly organized pattern of the natural cadences of
the spoken language.

The Dream

Someone approaches to say his life is ruined
and to fall down at your feet
and pound his head upon the sidewalk.
Blood spreads in a puddle.
And you, in a weak voice, plead
with those nearby for help;

your life takes on his desperation.
He keeps pounding his head.
It is you who are fated;
and you fall down beside him.
It is then you are awakened,
the body gone, the blood washed from the ground,
the stores lit up with their goods.

David Ignatow

When this verse was first dictated to me, I consider'd a Monotonous
Cadence, like that used by Milton and Shakespeare & all writers of
English Blank Verse, derived from the modern bondage of Rhyming,
to be a necessary and indispensible part of Verse. But I soon found
that in the mouth of a true Orator such monotony was not only awkward, but as much a bondage as rhyme itself. I therefore have
produced a variety in every line, both of cadences and number of
syllables. Every word and every letter is studied and put into its fit
place; the terrific numbers are reserved for the terrific parts, the mild
& gentle for the mild & gentle parts, and the prosaic for inferior
parts; all are necessary for each other. Poetry Fetter'd Fetters the Human Race.

William Blake, Jerusalem

See the discussion of free verse, pp. 3-4.

FULL RHYME. See RHYME.

GENRE. A certain type of literature, distinguished rather by the subject and
the way the subject is usually treated than by the technical form.
Drama, for example, includes the genres of tragedy, comedy, and
melodrama. Poetry includes several major genres and many minor
ones: folk and literary ballad, beast epic, burlesque, carol, dirge,
dramatic monologue, eclogue, elegy, epic, epistle, epithalamion, hymn,
idyll, lampoon, lyric, mock epic, paean, parody, pastoral and pastoral
elegy, ode, prothalamion, and song.

GEORGIAN. Pertaining to the reign of any king named George, but *Georgian
poetry* refers to a kind of verse published in England after 1910, early
in the reign of George V. The Georgian poets were collected by Sir
Edward Marsh in five anthologies. They derived from the romantics,
but though they wrote a great deal about nature, there was little
pressure of thought. The best known of the Georgians were John
Masefield, W. H. Davies, Ralph Hodgson, Rupert Brooke, and a very
fine poet indeed—Walter de la Mare. For a while D. H. Lawrence
was counted among the Georgians. But Hardy and Yeats were omitted.
When Ezra Pound launched the Imagist movement, he ridiculed the
Georgians for their triteness of thought and technique.

GEORGIC. A poem about rural life, especially the labor of farming, as in
Virgil's *Georgics;* to be distinguished from the pastoral idyll of happy
shepherds.

GLOSS. An explanation or interpretation of a difficult word or passage in a
text, often by means of a footnote.

GNOMIC POETRY. Poetry that makes pithy, proverbial statements. A "gnome" is the statement of a truth, an aphorism.

Success is counted sweetest
By those who ne'er succeed.

Emily Dickinson

GOTHIC. Characterized by a medieval setting and an atmosphere that is mysterious, frightening, and often supernatural. Gothic influence is apparent in the poetry of the Graveyard School (q.v.) and in Romantic poetry such as Coleridge's "The Rime of the Ancient Mariner" and Byron's "Manfred."

GRAVEYARD SCHOOL. A group of mid-eighteenth century poets who wrote mysterious and melancholy poems on death. Unlike their neoclassical contemporaries, they are associated with the Gothic revival, which anticipated the melancholy aspects of the romantic period. Among the poets are Thomas Parnell, Robert Blair, Edward Young, and Thomas Gray, whose "Elegy Written in a Country Churchyard" is the most famous "Graveyard" poem.

HAIKU (HOKKU). A Japanese verse form of seventeen syllables divided into lines of five syllables, seven, and five. It is a very old form; the earliest extant examples date from the beginning of the thirteenth century. The haiku may be sad or gay, deep or frivolous, religious, humorous, or satirical. Haikus usually give an image that is a starting point for thought and emotion. The scene is only sketched; the reader infers the rest. In nearly all haiku there is a *kigo,* a word or expression that indicates the time of year.

Fallen petals rise
   back to the branch—I watch:
      oh . . . butterflies!

Moritake (1452–1540)

Old pond:
   frog jump-in
      water-sound.

Bashō (1644–1694)

Wild geese! I know
   that they did eat the barley;
      yet, when they go . . .

Yasui (1657–1743)
(trans. Harold G. Henderson)

HALF RHYME. See RHYME.

HARMONY. The principle by which parts are blended into a unified and pleasing whole.

HEAD RHYME. See RHYME and ALLITERATION.

HEADLESS LINE (ACEPHALOUS). A line with the first syllable missing, in the strict pattern of the meter. (Gr. *acephalous,* "headless").

Whān | thăt Ā|prĭll wĭth | hĭs shoūr|ĕs soōte.

Geoffrey Chaucer

HEMISTICH. See ALEXANDRINE.

HEPTAMETER (FOURTEENER, SEPTENARY). A line of fourteen syllables, usually seven iambic feet, commonly used in England in the sixteenth century, especially for narrative. The line divides into the ballad meter of four stresses followed by three.

The God now having laide aside his borrowed shape of Bull,
Had in his likenesse showed himself: And with his pretty trull
Tane landing in the Isle of Crete. When in that while her Sire
Not knowing where she was become, sent after to enquire.
                    Ovid, *Metamorphoses,* 1567 (trans. Arthur Golding)

HEROIC COUPLET. Two lines of rhymed iambic pentameter, end-stopped. Especially popular in the eighteenth century.

His fate was destined to a barren strand,
A petty fortress, and a dubious hand.
                    Johnson, "The Vanity of Human Wishes"

See END-STOPPED LINE and CLOSED COUPLET.

HEROIC QUATRAIN. Four lines of iambic pentameter, rhymed *a b a b*. Synonymous with *elegaic quatrain* (q.v.).

HEXAMETER. A line of six feet, as in the final line of

We look before and after,
    And pine for what is not:
Our sincerest laughter
    With some pain is fraught;
Our sweetest songs are those that tell of saddest thought.
                    Shelley, "To a Skylark"

See ALEXANDRINE.

HIDDEN ALLITERATION. See ALLITERATION.

HIGH BURLESQUE. See BURLESQUE.

HISTORICAL RHYME. See RHYME.

HORATIAN ODE. See ODE.

HOVERING STRESS (DISTRIBUTED STRESS). In metrics, an accent that could be placed equally well on either of two adjacent syllables, so that it seems to hover between them.

There is sweet music here that softer falls
Than petals from blown roses on the grass . . .
                    Tennyson, "The Lotus-Eaters"

HUDIBRASTIC VERSE. Octosyllabic couplets in iambic tetrameter, as in Samuel Butler's *Hudibras.*

See DOGGEREL.

HUMOURS. The theory of "humours" is referred to by writers from Chaucer to the seventeenth century. Though the theory may not be stated explicitly, character portraits are frequently based upon it. In Medieval and Renaissance psychology there were four humours, that is, four fluids of the human body, which released their vapors to the brain and thus influenced physical and psychological health. When the four humours were in balance, the person behaved normally, but if one humour became dominant, it stereotyped his personality. Too much blood made him sanguine: ruddy-faced, cheerful, and amorous. Too much phlegm made him phlegmatic: dull, unresponsive, and cowardly. Too much yellow bile made him choleric: irritable, obstinate, vengeful, and easily aroused to anger. Too much black bile made him melancholic: depressed, brooding, satiric, and gluttonous.

HYMN. From Greek *hymnos*, a song praising heroes or the gods. By extension, a literary hymn is a song of praise, such as Shelley's "Hymn to Intellectual Beauty."

HYPERBOLE. Overstatement or exaggeration for the sake of emphasis. Marvell's lines are hyperbolic:

My vegetable love should grow
Vaster than empires and more slow;
An hundred years should go to praise
Thine eyes, and on thy forehead gaze . . .

"To His Coy Mistress"

HYPERMETER. In metrics, the addition of one or more unstressed syllables at the beginning or end of a line.

To be, or not to be; that is the ques/tion:

IAMB(US), IAMBIC. A metrical foot of two syllables, with a weak stress followed by a strong, thus: ⌣ —. Iambic is the most common meter in English poetry. See also METER, BLANK VERSE, and RISING METER.

IDENTICAL RHYME. See RHYME.

IDYLL. A short picturesque poem idealizing rural life; the charming pastoral of singing shepherds, as distinguished from the mournful pastoral elegy.

Come live with me and be my Love,
And we will all the pleasures prove . . .
The shepherd swains shall dance and sing
For thy delight each May morning—

Marlowe, "The Passionate Shepherd to His Love"

See also ARCADIA.

IMAGE

An "image" is that which presents an intellectual and emotional complex in an instant of time.

Ezra Pound, "A Few Don'ts by an Imagiste"

In modern poetry, an image is a word or cluster of words that stimulate sense-perceptions. The words evoke the reader's sense of sight, hearing, smell, taste, or touch, and his imaginary experiences are, to a large extent, the meaning of the poem. In Pound's words, "A poem is an image or a succession of images."

> I am moved by fancies that are curled
> Around these images, and cling . . .
>
> T. S. Eliot, "Preludes"

> The hand that whirls the water in the pool
> Stirs the quicksand; that ropes the blowing wind
> Hauls my shroud sail.
> And I am dumb to tell the hanging man
> How of my clay is made the hangman's lime.
>
> Dylan Thomas, "The Force That Through
the Green Fuse Drives the Flower"

See IMAGISM, SYMBOLISM, SURREALISM.

IMAGERY. Images considered collectively, as the imagery of light in *Oedipus Rex*.

IMAGINATION

> The word is predominantly used in cases where, carried away by enthusiasm and passion, you think you see what you describe, and you place it before the eyes of your hearers.
>
> *On the Sublime,* traditionally ascribed to Longinus, first or second
century A.D.

> The poet's eye, in a fine frenzy rolling,
> Doth glance from heaven to earth, from earth to heaven;
> And, as imagination bodies forth
> The forms of things unknown, the poet's pen
> Turns them to shapes, and gives to airy nothing
> A local habitation and a name.
>
> Shakespeare, *A Midsummer-Night's Dream*

> The poet . . . brings the whole soul of man into activity. . . . He diffuses a tone and spirit of unity, that blends, and (as it were) *fuses,* each into each, by the synthetic and magical power, to which we have exclusively appropriated the name of imagination. This power . . . reveals itself in the balance or reconciliation of opposite or discordant qualities: of sameness, with difference; of the general, with the concrete; the idea, with the image; the individual, with the representative; the sense of novelty and freshness, with old and familiar objects; a more than usual state of emotion, with more than usual order; judgement ever awake and steady self-possession, with enthusiasm and feeling profound or vehement; and while it blends and harmonizes the natural and the artificial, still subordinates art to nature; the manner to the matter; and our admiration of the poet to our sympathy with the poetry.
>
> Coleridge, *Biographia Literaria*

See FANCY.

IMAGISM. A literary movement that started about 1910, including the critic T. E. Hulme and the poets Ezra Pound, T. S. Eliot, H. D. (Hilda Doolittle), John Gould Fletcher, F. S. Flint, and Richard Aldington. Amy Lowell contributed to the movement until she broke with Pound. Pound says, "The tenets of the Imagist faith were published in March 1913 as follows:

1. Direct treatment of the 'thing,' whether subjective or objective.
2. To use absolutely no word that does not contribute to the presentation.
3. As regarding rhythm: to compose in sequence of the musical phrase, not in sequence of the metronome."

Pound's two-line poem "In a Station of the Metro" is often quoted as an example of Imagist writing:

The apparition of these faces in the crowd;
Petals on a wet, black bough.

This poem, Pound says, originated in a ride on the metro, when he saw beautiful faces. They obsessed him, till they became

an equation . . . not in speech, but in little splotches of color. It was just that—a "pattern," or hardly a pattern, if by "pattern" you mean something with a "repeat" in it . . . My experience in Paris should have gone into paint . . . In a poem of this sort one is trying to record the precise instant when a thing outward and objective transforms itself, or darts into a thing inward and subjective.

"Vorticism"

The ideas of the imagists have had a powerful influence on writing in the twentieth century, both verse and prose.

See IMAGE, SURREALISM, and also the discussion of Imagism on pp. 26-27.

IMITATION

The poet being an imitator, like a painter or any other artist, must of necessity imitate one of three objects—things as they were or are, things as they are said or thought to be, or things as they ought to be.
Aristotle, *Poetics*

As Aristotle used it, *mimesis*, or "imitation," meant the artistic process of selecting and arranging material in order to show its true significance. Imitation was not, as S. H. Butcher explains, mere copying; it was creation:

"Imitation," in the sense in which Aristotle applies the word to poetry, is equivalent to "producing" or "creating according to a true idea," which forms part of the definition of art in general. The "true idea" for fine art is derived from the εἶδος, the general concept which the intellect spontaneously abstracts from the details of sense. There is an ideal form which is present in each individual phenomenon but imperfectly manifested. This form impresses itself as a sensuous appearance on the mind of the artist; he seeks to give it a more complete expression, to bring to light the ideal which is only half revealed in the world of reality. His distinctive work as an artist consists in stamping the given material with the impress of the form which is universal. . . . "Imitation," so understood, is a creative act.

S. H. Butcher, Aristotle's Theory of Poetry

After Aristotle, other critics have said that poetry originates in "imitation." However, for some of them the word seems to mean not bringing forth the ideal or universal form, but a clever representation of things as they are. Such is the effect of the following statement by Vico:

Children excel in imitation; we observe them generally amuse themselves by imitating what they are able to understand. This axiom shows that the world in its infancy was composed of poetic nations, for poetry is nothing but imitation. . . . all the arts of things necessary, useful, convenient, and even in large part those of human pleasure, were invented in the poetic centuries before the philosophers came . . . the arts are nothing but imitations of nature, poems in a certain way made of things.

Vico, The New Science

The word "imitation" may be used to mean learning from other men. "The Poet," says Ben Jonson, must be able to "convert the substance, or Riches, of another Poet to his owne use" (*Timber*, 1641). And poets write "imitations"—that is, poems modeled on other poems. Johnson's "Vanity of Human Wishes" is an imitation of Juvenal's "Tenth Satire."

IMPERFECT RHYME. See RHYME.

INCREMENTAL REPETITION. A term introduced by Francis B. Gummere in 1907 to describe a device of the ballad: repeating lines with changes in certain words to show a development of the story. See the questions and answers in "Edward, Edward," p. 53.

INITIAL RHYME. See RHYME and ALLITERATION.

INSPIRATION

A man cannot say, "I will compose poetry." The greatest poet even cannot say it; for the mind in creation is as a fading coal, which some invisible influence, like an inconstant wind, awakens to transitory brightness; this power arises from within, like the colour of a flower which fades and changes as it is developed, and the conscious portions of our natures are unprophetic either of its approach or its departure. Could this influence be durable in its original purity and force, it is impossible to predict the greatness of the results; but when composition begins, inspiration is already on the decline, and the most glorious poetry that has ever been communicated to the world is probably a feeble shadow of the original conceptions of the Poet.

Shelley, A Defense of Poetry

INTENSITY. Concentration of meaning.

> Language is a means of communication. To charge language with meaning to the utmost possible degree, we have . . . the three chief means:
>
> 1. throwing the object (fixed or moving) onto the visual imagination.
> 2. inducing emotional correlations by the sound and rhythm of the speech.
> 3. inducing both of the effects by stimulating the associations (intellectual or emotional) that have remained in the receiver's consciousness in relation to the actual words or word groups employed . . .
>
> Incompetence will show in the use of too many words.
>
> Pound, ABC of Reading

INTENTIONAL FALLACY. In the "new criticism," according to W. K. Wimsatt and M. C. Beardsley, the error of trying to judge a literary work according to the author's statement of his intention in writing it, or according to the known biographical and historical facts surrounding its production.

INTERNAL RHYME. See RHYME.

INTERREGNUM. See COMMONWEALTH.

INVENTION

> Invention is nothing other than the natural virtue of an imagination, conceiving the ideas and forms of all things that can be imagined, whether of heaven or of earth, living or inanimate, for the purpose of afterwards representing, describing, imitating: for just as the aim of the orator is to persuade, so that of the poet is to imitate, invent, and represent—things which are, or which may be—in a resemblance to truth.
>
> Ronsard, A Brief on the Art of French Poetry, 1565

INVERSION. 1. Reversal of the normal order of words, for emphasis or because the rhyme or meter demands it.

> Bird thou never wert.
>
> Shelley, "To a Skylark"

2. The use of a foot opposite from the one required by the meter. An inverted accent, foot, or stress substitutes a dactyl for an anapest or a trochee for an iamb (and vice versa).

INVOCATION. The poet's appeal to his muse for assistance at the beginning of an epic or other long work.

IRISH LITERARY REVIVAL. See CELTIC RENAISSANCE.

IRONY. A rhetorical device by which a writer implies a discrepancy or an additional meaning that is often contradictory to the literal meaning of his words. In *verbal irony*, the meaning is different from, and usually the opposite of, what is said, as in the words "pure" and "religious" in the anonymous sixteenth-century poem "Of Alphus":

No egg on Friday Alph will eat,
    But drunken will he be
On Friday still. Oh, what a pure
    Religious man is he!

In *dramatic irony,* there is a discrepancy between what a character says and what the author thinks: when Milton's Satan convinces Eve that she should eat the apple, we know that Milton is against it. Dramatic irony also may refer to the additional significance of a character's speech or action to the audience, when they know certain crucial information that he does not. In *irony of situation,* the outcome of a situation is inappropriate, or different from what was expected. In *romantic irony,* the author creates an illusion and then deliberately destroys it by a change of tone, personal comment, or contradicting statement.

ITALIAN SONNET. See SONNET.

JACOBEAN. (From the Latin *Jacobus,* James.) The period of King James I (1603–1625). At this time Chapman, Bacon, Drayton, Shakespeare, Jonson, Donne, Tourneur, Webster, Beaumont and Fletcher were writing, and the King James version of the Bible was made.

KENNING. A metaphorical compound word or phrase used in Old English and Old Norse poetry. The ocean is the "whale-road" or "the foaming fields"; a lord is "dispenser of rings." A kenning may describe complex emotion.

He bade a seaworthy
wave-cutter be fitted out for him; the warrior king
he would seek, he said, over swan's riding.
            Beowulf (trans. from the Anglo-Saxon by Michael Alexander)

LAKE POETS. Wordsworth, Coleridge, and Southey were called "the Lake Poets" because they lived in Cumberland, in the Lake District.

LAMENT. A literary work, often a poem, expressing intense grief.

I am the man that hath seen affliction by the rod of His wrath. . . .
How is the gold become dim! how is the most fine gold changed! the stones of the sanctuary are poured out in the top of every street.
The precious sons of Zion, comparable to fine gold, how are they esteemed as earthen pitchers, the work of the hands of the potter!
            The Lamentations of Jeremiah

LAMPOON. A satirical attack, in verse or prose, upon an individual person, such as Pope's attack on Colley Cibber in *The Dunciad.* Lampoons were common in seventeenth- and eighteenth-century England, until the introduction of libel laws.

LAY. A narrative poem of adventure. In Medieval France the *lai* was written in octosyllabic couplets—a form adopted by Walter Scott in *The Lay of the Last Minstrel* (1805).

LEONINE RHYME. See RHYME.

LIGHT VERSE. Verse written mainly to entertain or amuse. The category includes nonsense verse, limericks, nursery rhymes, witty epigrams, some lyrics, satire, parodies, occasional verse, and *vers de société*.

LIMERICK. An anapestic jingle, used for making jokes; very popular in English. President Woodrow Wilson is said to have been the author of the following limerick:

I sat next to the Duchess at tea;
It was just as I feared it would be:
   Her rumblings abdominal
   Were truly phenomenal,
And everyone thought it was me!

LINE. A row of words. In prose the lines run on; in poetry each line ends or breaks where the rhythm dictates. Prose-writers think in sentences, poets think in lines. A line of poetry may be called a verse. See END-STOPPED LINE, RUN-ON LINE.

LINKED RHYME. See RHYME.

LITERALISM. 1. Adherence to the letter, the exact words of the original: "a literal translation." 2. Understanding words only in their strict sense, in a matter-of-fact, unimaginative way.

LITERARY BALLAD. See BALLAD.

LOW BURLESQUE. See BURLESQUE.

LYRE. A musical instrument of ancient Greece, consisting of a sound box (originally a turtle shell), with two curving arms carrying a cross bar (yoke) from which strings were stretched to the body. It was used to accompany the voice in singing and recitation, and became a symbol for music and poetry.

... the lyre was invented by the Greek Mercury ... This lyre was given him by Apollo, god of civil light or of the nobility ... and with this lyre Orpheus, Amphion and other theological poets, who professed knowledge of laws, founded and established the humanity of Greece. ... the lyre was the union of the cords or forces of the fathers, of which the public force was composed which is called civil authority, which finally put an end to all private force and violence. Hence the law was defined with full propriety by the poets as *lyra regnorum*, "the lyre of kingdoms". ...

Vico, *The New Science*

LYRIC. In ancient Greece, a poem to be sung or recited accompanied by a lyre. Now, any poem expressing personal emotion rather than describing events. Sonnets, elegies, odes, hymns, etc. are lyric poems.

MACARONIC. Verse consisting of a mixture of languages, especially Latin and a modern language. It began as a burlesque of Medieval sermons in which the monks mixed Latin with the vernacular.

MADRIGAL. A short lyric poem to be sung in several (as many as eight) parts, often with elaborate counterpoint. The theme may be pastoral, satiric, or concerned with love. Writing madrigals was fashionable in England in the last quarter of the sixteenth century.

MASCULINE RHYME. See RHYME.

MEANING. The meaning of a poem is in the form, images, rhythm, and tone, as well as in those ideas which could equally well be expressed in prose. The meaning of a poem is the poem itself. *Four levels of meaning:* a medieval concept, useful for understanding Dante's *Divine Comedy* and other works; in the *Summa Theologica* Thomas Aquinas stated that works should be read for their allegorical, moral, and anagogic meanings as well as their primary, literal meaning:

So far as the things of the Old Law signify the things of the New Law, there is the allegorical sense; so far as the things done in Christ . . . are signs of what we ought to do, there is the moral sense. But so far as they signify what relates to eternal glory, there is the anagogical sense.

MEDIEVAL ROMANCE (METRICAL ROMANCE). A verse tale of adventure with a courtly background, on themes of loyalty, bravery, honor, and especially love. The romance originated in medieval France. At first, the word was applied to vernacular French, as opposed to Latin, literature; later it came to mean imaginative, as opposed to historical, writing. Critics have distinguished between the romance and the national epic. The romance is less heroic than the epic, more fanciful and sophisticated. The ideal of "courtly love" is essential; the hero undertakes "love service" for his lady and is ennobled by it. Romance cycles are: "The Matter of Britain"—tales of King Arthur and poems derived from Breton lays; "The Matter of Rome"—tales of Alexander, the Trojan war, Thebes, and the Orient; "The Matter of France"—Charlemagne. The best-known romances in English are *Sir Gawain and the Green Knight* and Sir Thomas Malory's *Morte d'Arthur*.

MEIOSIS. See UNDERSTATEMENT.

METAPHOR. An implied comparison, omitting explicit words of comparison such as "like," "as," "as if," and "than." A metaphor is more compressed than a simile, because it identifies two things with each other or substitutes one for the other: "My love is a rose." A *dead metaphor* is one that is no longer recognized as a comparison: "the arm of a chair." A *submerged metaphor* implies, rather than states, one of the two subjects: "my winged heart" implies that "my heart is a bird." In a *mixed metaphor,* the comparison is strikingly disparate: "to take arms against a sea of troubles." See the discussion of metaphor, pp. 1-2.

Tenor and *vehicle* are terms used by I. A. Richards to explain the process of metaphor. If we take the sentence "My love is a rose," the principal subject "my love" would be called the *tenor* (because it is what we are "holding on to" or talking about), and the secondary subject "rose" would be called the *vehicle* (because it carries the weight of the comparison).

METAPHYSICAL CONCEIT. See CONCEIT.

METAPHYSICAL POETS. Seventeenth-century poets whose style of writing had a colloquial tone, tightly knit syntax, irony, devices of wit such as puns and paradoxes, and the farfetched original comparisons called metaphysical conceits. The best-known metaphysical poets are John Donne, Andrew Marvell, John Cleveland, Abraham Cowley, George Herbert, Richard Crashaw, and Henry Vaughan. See CONCEIT, and the discussion of John Donne's "The Sun Rising," pp. 15-18.

METER. The regular recurrence of patterns of accented and unaccented syllables. The basic metrical unit is the foot, which can be iambic, trochaic, anapestic, dactylic, spondaic, or pyrrhic. The number of feet per line is indicated by the terms monometer, dimeter, trimeter, tetrameter, pentameter, hexameter, heptameter, or octameter. (For examples, see individual entries, e.g., IAMBIC, HEXAMETER, etc.) A line of poetry is called a verse, and it is described by naming the kind of feet and the number of them in the line, e.g., "iambic pentameter." *Scansion* is the practice of describing the metrical patterns of a poem. See ACCENT, BLANK VERSE, CADENCE, FOOT, FREE VERSE, QUANTITATIVE VERSE, RHYTHM, SCANSION, SPRUNG RHYTHM, VERSE, and the discussion of meter, pp. 34-38.

METONYMY. A figure of speech in which the thing or idea given to the reader represents some other thing or idea that is closely associated with it. The name of a writer often means "his works," as in the statement "I have read all of Shakespeare." "The crown" can mean "the monarch." Metonymy may be *synecdoche* (q.v.), using a part for the whole, as when "horse" is used to mean "cavalry."

METRICAL ACCENT. See ACCENT.

METRICAL ROMANCE. See MEDIEVAL ROMANCE.

MIMESIS. See IMITATION.

MIXED METAPHOR. See METAPHOR.

MOCK EPIC. See BURLESQUE.

MOCK HEROIC STYLE. See BURLESQUE.

MONODY. See DIRGE.

MONOLOGUE. See DRAMATIC MONOLOGUE.

MONOMETER. A line of one metrical foot.

> Thus I
> Passe by
> And die:
> As One,
> Unknown,
> And gon.

> Herrick, "Upon His Departure Hence"

MONOSYLLABIC FOOT. A foot of only one syllable:

Di̅ng, / do̅ng, / be̅ll;

Pu̅ssy̆s / i̅n thĕ / we̅ll.

MOTIF. A recurrent image, word, phrase, theme, character, or situation in a work of literature.

MULTIPLE MEANING. See AMBIGUITY.

MUSE. In Greek mythology, any of the nine daughters of Zeus and Mnemosyne, goddess of memory, who were the goddesses presiding over the arts. Clio was the muse of history, Calliope of epic poetry, Erato of love and lyric poetry, Euterpe of music, Melpomene of tragedy, Polyhymnia of songs to the gods, Terpsichore of the dance, Thalia of comedy, and Urania of astronomy. Later "the Muse" came to mean the goddess or power that inspired poets.

MUSICAL DEVICES. A general term for ways of using language that bring out its affinities to music, by the choice and arrangement of accents to form rhythm and meter, or by the choice and arrangement of sounds to form assonance, consonance, alliteration, rhymes, stanza patterns, and refrains.

NARRATIVE. A narrative poem is a poem that tells a story. Narrative poetry may be as simple as a nursery rhyme or as sophisticated as a poem by T. S. Eliot. The subject is vast, for anything that happens may be written in a poem. See ALLEGORY, BALLAD, EPIC, POETRY.

NATURALISM. 1. A kind of art that closely imitates nature. 2. Sometimes used to describe the work of a "nature" poet, such as Wordsworth, who describes country life and scenes. 3. A late nineteenth-century movement in literature, mainly the novel, sometimes described as the extreme form of realism. Its proponents sought to record actual life, documented in scientifically accurate detail, in order to prove that all human actions are determined by heredity and environment. This meant recording dispassionately, even photographically, a "slice of life." However, the slice was usually chosen from the lower class slums, so naturalism had a definite tendency to be sordid as well as deterministic. The major figure of the movement was Emile Zola, who called his technique "naturalism" to distinguish it from the "realism" of Balzac and Flaubert. There are naturalistic influences in the poems of Thomas Hardy, E. A. Robinson, and Edgar Lee Masters.

NATURE. "Nature" has been a controlling concept in Western thought since antiquity. In the Middle Ages nature was considered primarily as the entire universe created by God and sustained by Him. Beginning in the Renaissance and culminating in the eighteenth century, "nature" and "nature's laws" were increasingly separated from theological considerations and were emphasized as the universal and necessary foundation of religion, ethics, politics, law, and art. Nature was "One clear, unchanged, and universal light" (Pope, An Essay on Criticism).

Here are some basic definitions of "nature" as the word occurs in poetry:

1. The creative and regulative physical power which is conceived of as operating in the material world and as the immediate cause of all its phenomena.

Where Nature shall provide Green Grass,
And fat'ning Clover for their Fare.
Dryden, trans. of Virgil's Georgic III, 1697

2. The material world, or its collective objects and phenomena, especially those with which man is most directly in contact; frequently the features and products of the earth itself, as contrasted with those of civilization.

But all her shows did Nature yield,
To please and win this pilgrim wise.
He saw the partridge drum in the woods;
He heard the woodcock's evening hymn;
He found the tawny thrushes' broods;
And the shy hawk did wait for him;
Ralph Waldo Emerson, Woodnotes, I, 1840

3. *The* (or *a*) *state of nature:* (*a*) the moral state natural to man, as opposed to a state of grace; (*b*) the condition of man before the foundation of organized society; (*c*) an uncultivated or undomesticated condition.

Nor think, in NATURE'S STATE they blindly trod;
The state of Nature was the reign of God:
Self-love and Social at her birth began,
Union the bond of all things, and of Man.
Pride then was not; nor Arts, that Pride to aid;
Man walked with beast, joint tenant of the shade;
Pope, An Essay on Man

4. The inherent impulse, in men or animals, by which behavior is determined and controlled.

And smale foweles maken melodye,
That slepen al the nyght with open ye
So priketh hem nature in hir corages . . .
Chaucer, General Prologue to The Canterbury Tales

Yet do I fear thy nature;
It is too full o' the milk of human kindness
To catch the nearest way.
Shakespeare, Macbeth

NEAR RHYME. See RHYME.

NEGATIVE CAPABILITY

Several things dove-tailed in my mind, and at once it struck me what quality went to form a Man of achievement, especially in Literature, and which Shakespeare possessed so enormously—I mean *Negative Capability*, that is, when a man is capable of being in uncertainties, mysteries, doubts, without any irritable reaching after fact and reason

—Coleridge, for instance, would let go by a fine isolated verisimilitude caught from the Penetralium of mystery, from being incapable of remaining content with half-knowledge.

John Keats, Letter to George and Thomas Keats

NEOCLASSICAL. Referring to a revival of classicism during the Augustan Age in England. See AUGUSTAN AGE.

NEW CRITICISM. A term applied to the writings of the literary critics R. P. Blackmur, Cleanth Brooks, John Crowe Ransom, Allen Tate, Robert Penn Warren, and, with less certainty, to those of Kenneth Burke, T. S. Eliot, William Empson, I. A. Richards, and Yvor Winters. In general, New Critics regard a poem as an object for rigorously empirical, objective analysis (textual criticism). The poem is treated "primarily as poetry and not another thing," without reference to the author's life or intention (the intentional fallacy), to the history of the society in which the author lived, to the traditional genre of the work, or to the effect the work has upon either the reader's emotions (the affective fallacy) or later literary history.

NONSENSE VERSE. A kind of light verse with pleasant, orderly, even jingly sounds, absurd statements, and words that are not in the dictionary. The best-known writers of nonsense verse are Edward Lear and Lewis Carroll. See "By Way of Preface," p. 212, and "Jabberwocky," p. 227.

NUMBER POEM. Numbers arranged so as to make *concrete* or *sound poetry* (q.v.). The author of the numbers printed below says that they were written to be read aloud and that the numbers have no significance beyond their sound value. Each number is to be pronounced separately, e.g., 375 as "three seven five."

0 9

0 4 3 1

   1 3 1 3 1 8 5

     0 5

     0 5 5 5

     3 7 5

     0 9

Neil Mills, 1970

OBJECTIVE CORRELATIVE

The only way of expressing emotion in the form of art is by finding an "objective correlative"; in other words, a set of objects, a situation, a chain of events which shall be the formula of that *particular* emotion; such that when the external facts, which must terminate in sensory experience, are given, the emotion is immediately evoked.

T. S. Eliot, "Hamlet and His Problems"

OBJECTIVITY. See SUBJECTIVITY.

OBLIQUE RHYME. See RHYME.

OCCASIONAL POEM. A poem written to commemorate a specific event or occasion, e.g., Yeats's "Easter 1916."

OCTAMETER. A line of eight feet. Because of its awkward length, which often breaks into two tetrameters, the line is rare in English. It is used by Tennyson in *Frater Ave atque Vale:*

Row us out from Desenzano, to your Sirmione row!
So they rowed, and there we landed—"O venusta Sirmio!"

OCTAVE. The first eight lines of a Petrarchan sonnet. See SONNET.

OCTET. Synonym for *octave.*

OCTOSYLLABIC COUPLET. A stanza in which each of the two lines contains eight syllables.

ODE. In English, a serious and dignified lyric poem, usually fairly long, with an elaborate stanzaic structure for which there is no conventional fixed form (see Keats, "Ode to Psyche," "Ode to a Nightingale," and "Ode on a Grecian Urn," pp. 196-201). The Greek poet Pindar modeled his odes on the choric songs of the drama, in which the chorus chanted or sang the "strophe" while dancing to the left, the "antistrophe" while retracing the pattern to the right, and the metrically different "epode" while standing still. The Pindaric or *irregular* ode in English is an imitation of this, having the strophe and antistrophe in a stanzaic form different from that of the epode. The irregular ode was introduced into England by Cowley; it became popular after the Restoration (see Dryden, "A Song for St. Cecilia's Day," p. 115). The Pindaric ode is exalted and enthusiastic. The Horatian ode, modeled on the odes of the Latin poet Horace, is simpler—often one stanzaic pattern throughout—cool and sober (see Marvell, "An Horation Ode Upon Cromwell's Return from Ireland," p. 109).

OFF RHYME. See RHYME.

ONOMATOPOEIA. The use of words that imitate sounds: "bang," "buzz," "hiss," "scratch."

ORNAMENT. "Poetic ornament" is a critical term—no longer used—for an image, epithet, or figure of speech.

ORPHIC. Resembling the music of Orpheus, who is said to have charmed stones and wild beasts with his lyre. Entrancing, mystic, oracular.

OTTAVA RIMA. A stanza of eight lines of iambic pentameter rhymed *a b a b a b c c.* It was used by the Italian writers of comic epics, Pulci, Berni, and Ariosto. The stanza was introduced into England in the sixteenth century by Wyatt. Byron adopted it for his "Beppo," "The Vision of Judgment," and *Don Juan:*

Yes, Don Alfonso! husband now no more,
If ever you indeed deserved the name,

Is't worthy of your years?—you have three-score—
　　Fifty, or sixty, it is all the same—
Is't wise or fitting, causeless to explore
　　For facts against a virtuous woman's fame?
Ungrateful, perjured, barbarous Don Alfonso,
How dare you think your lady would go on so?

OVERSTATEMENT. See HYPERBOLE.

OXYMORON. A figurative use of language in which a paradox contains a
direct contradiction. Milton describes hell as "no light, but rather
darkness visible." See PARADOX.

PAEAN. A song or hymn of praise, joy, or triumph, originally sung by Greeks
in gratitude to Apollo.

PANEGYRIC. A formal speech or piece of writing praising someone. Cf.
ENCOMIASTIC VERSE, EULOGY.

PANTOUM. A Malayan verse form introduced into French and English. It
consists of any number of quatrains rhyming *a b a b*, the second and
fourth lines of each stanza used as the first and third of the next. In
the final stanza, the second and fourth lines are lines three and one
of the opening stanza, so that the poem ends with its first line.

PARABLE. A short, simple story intended to illustrate a moral lesson. Best
known are the parables of Jesus, such as "The Good Samaritan" and
"The Prodigal Son." If, instead of human beings, the characters in
the parable are abstract qualities, then it is an *allegory* (q.v.); if
they are animals, plants, or objects, then it is a *fable* (q.v.).

PARADOX. An apparent contradiction that is nevertheless in some sense true
and valid, as in the phrases "conspicuous by his absence" and "damn
by faint praise." An *oxymoron* (q.v.) combines direct contraries, as in
"living death."

PARAPHRASE. A restatement of the ideas of a text in words that are different
but as close as possible to the meaning of the original. See PROSE
PARAPHRASE.

PARARHYME. See RHYME.

PARNASSIANS. The *Parnassiens* were French poets, centering around Leconte
de Lisle, who began publishing in the 1860's. The characteristics of
their verse are "hardness," precision, clarity:

The best work is made
from hard, strong materials,
　　obstinately precise—
the line of the poem, onyx, steel.
　　　　　　　　　Théophile Gautier, *L'Art* (trans. Denise Levertov)

They wrote about history, science, nature, philosophy, and contemporary life, but some Parnassians were chiefly writers of lyrics. Re-
belling against the Romantic subjectivity and social concern of Hugo,
Vigny, and Lamartine, they wanted poetry to be impersonal, exclud-

ing both the personality of the author and any moral or social usefulness. In the latter, they anticipated the Aesthetic Movement, which adopted their motto, "art for art's sake." They revived the older French fixed verse forms, such as the ballade, rondeau, and villanelle. Baudelaire, Heredia, Sully-Prudhomme, François Coppée, Anatole France, and Mallarmé were associated with the movement at one time or another. In England in the 1870's, Austin Dobson, Edmund Gosse, and Andrew Lang imitated the Parnassians in form and style, though not in thought. The English poets were somewhat inhibited by Victorian conventions.

PARNASSUS. A mountain in central Greece, frequented by Apollo and the Muses. Parnassus is 8068 feet high.

PARODY. A form of *burlesque* (q.v.). Literary or critical parody is an imitation of another man's style or a particular work. Through distortion or exaggeration the parodist points out salient features of the original. Parody may be funny, or malicious, or flattering. Lewis Carroll's parody of Wordsworth's "Resolution and Independence" is funny, and also it is acute literary criticism, emphasizing Wordsworth's earnestness, the circumstantiality of the narrative, and the eccentricity of the character. See "Resolution and Independence," p. 150, and "The White Knight's Song," p. 225.

PARTIAL RHYME. See RHYME.

PASTORAL. A genre of poetry, based on classical models, that deals with rustic life, usually with shepherds. The Greek poet Theocritus (third century B.C.) wrote the first pastoral poetry, describing Sicilian shepherds, or "pastors." After he established the conventions, pastoral became a highly artificial genre based on literary imitation, especially of Theocritus and Virgil. The setting was often *Arcadia*, a perpetual summer of meadows, trees, and flowers where shepherds and shepherdesses, who did no work, had love affairs and composed and sang songs of three major kinds: the *eclogue*, or singing match between two shepherds; the *complaint*, in which a shepherd praises his mistress's beauty and laments her cruelty; and the *pastoral elegy*, in which the shepherd bewails the death of a fellow shepherd. The Renaissance developed the *pastoral romance*—long tales of love and adventure in a pastoral setting—and *pastoral drama*. Shakespeare's *As You Like It* is derived from these. The pastoral world is often presented as simple and uncorrupted, an escape from the complexities and frustration of urban life into peace and the satisfaction of desires. Pastoral may be called *bucolic* or *idyllic*. Christian literature incorporates some features of the pastoral: the minister is the "shepherd" of his "flock," etc.

PASTORAL ELEGY. An elegy that incorporates pastoral conventions, such as representing the poet and the person for whom he mourns as shepherds, invoking the muses and making references to classical myths, having all nature join in mourning for the dead shepherd, asking the nymphs where they were when death took their beloved and why they did not save him, questioning divine justice and lamenting the world's corrupt state, having a procession of mourners and a list of appropriate flowers to deck the hearse, and closing with a tone of peaceful assurance that death leads to a better life. Milton's "Lycidas" (q.v.) and Shelley's "Adonais" are the most famous examples of pastoral elegy in English.

PATHETIC FALLACY. The attribution of human characteristics to inanimate objects, in a way less complete and less formal than full personification:

The one red leaf, the last of its clan,
That dances as often as dance it can.

Coleridge, "Christabel"

The term "pathetic fallacy" is derived from *pathelikos* (Gr. sensitive). It does not mean that the fallacy is pathetic. John Ruskin introduced the term in 1856. He said that among the people who had the pathetic fallacy were those who felt strongly but reasoned weakly, and those who were inspired. The term has come to have a peforative sense, describing literature that credits nature with human emotions. However, the objection may not be to the point of view, but to its being expressed awkwardly, for many poets—Wordsworth and Hardy, for example—have written as though nature and the human mind were in sympathy, or were controlled by the same forces. Indeed, this is one of the oldest and most widely held of beliefs.

See NATURE.

PATHOS. The quality in a work of literature which evokes pity, sorrow, or tenderness from the reader. A pathetic situation is often one where the innocent and helpless suffer. Pathos should be distinguished from *bathos* (q.v.) and from *tragedy*.

PAUSE. A moment of hesitation in the rhythm of verse. A pause within a line is called a *caesura* (q.v.). A pause at the end of a line or stanza is called a *metrical pause*. A pause for intensified poetic effect is a *rhetorical pause*. A pause is often used to compensate for a missing syllable.

PEGASUS. In classical mythology, a winged horse that sprang from the blood of Medusa when she was slain by Perseus. With his hoof Pegasus caused the spring Hippocrene, the source of poetry, to well forth on Mount Helicon. Thus Pegasus is associated with the Muses and with poetry.

PENTAMETER. A line of five feet:

Rough winds / do shake / the dar/ling buds / of May

Shakespeare, *Sonnet 18*

PERFECT RHYME. See RHYME.

PERIPHRASIS. (From the Greek *periphrazein:* to speak around.) Circumlocution. Using a longer phrase or indirect, abstract way of stating ideas or naming things in place of a shorter and plainer expression. Periphrasis may be euphemistic—using mild words instead of strong:

"passing away" for "death"—or it may be descriptive, as in Old English *kenning* (q.v.). Periphrasis easily degenerates into verbosity and a habitual avoidance of plain speech:

Up springs the lark . . .
Amid the dawning clouds, and from their haunts
Calls up the *tuneful nations* . . .

James Thomson, "Spring," 1728

PERSONA. The fictitious narrator imagined by the poet to speak the words of a poem. The persona is a "voice" or "mask" which should not be confused with the author's private personality. In "The Love Song of J. Alfred Prufrock," the speaker is the persona, Prufrock, not T. S. Eliot. In these lines of Browning's dramatic monologue, "Soliloquy of the Spanish Cloister," the persona is not Robert Browning but a ridiculous monk:

Gr-r-r—there go, my heart's abhorrence!
  Water your damned flowerpots, do!
If hate killed men, Brother Lawrence,
  God's blood, would not mine kill you!

PERSONIFICATION. A figurative use of language in which human qualities or feelings are attributed to nonhuman organisms, inanimate objects, or abstract ideas:

the farm, like a wanderer white
With the dew, come back, the cock on his shoulder.

Dylan Thomas, "Fern Hill"

Personification may be the representation of an abstract quality or idea by a human figure. It is in this sense that Addison uses the word in the following passage:

. . . when the Author represents any Passion, Appetite, Virtue or Vice, under a visible Shape, and makes it a Person or an Actor in his Poem. Of this Nature are the Descriptions of Hunger and Envy in *Ovid*, of Fame in *Virgil*, and of Sin and Death in *Milton*. We find a whole Creation of the like shadowy Persons in *Spencer* [sic], who had an admirable Talent in Representations of this kind.

Addison, *The Spectator*, 1711–12

See ALLEGORY, PATHETIC FALLACY.

PETRARCHAN CONCEIT. See CONCEIT.

PETRARCHAN SONNET. See SONNET.

PINDARIC ODE. *See* ODE.

POET. One who writes poetry. The word is derived from the Greek *poiein*, "to make." The poet is traditionally regarded as a "maker" and the poem as *poiēma*, "something made."

POETIC LICENSE. The liberty taken by poets to depart from fact and to use the language in unconventional ways in order to achieve special effects.

POETICS. The branch of *rhetoric* (q.v.) that has to do with poetry.

POETRY. Many writers have tried to define poetry, describing the aim of poetry, the character of the poet, and how poems are written. Here are a few examples:

All good poets, epic as well as lyric, compose their beautiful poems not by art, but because they are inspired and possessed. . . . the lyric poets are not in their right mind when they are composing their beautiful strains . . . they are simply inspired to utter that to which the Muse impels them . . . God takes away the mind of poets and uses them as his ministers, as he also uses diviners and holy prophets, in order that we who hear them may know them to be speaking not of themselves who utter these priceless words in a state of unconsciousness, but that God himself is the speaker, and that through them He is conversing with us.

Plato, Ion, c. 390 B.C.

The aim of poets is either to be beneficial or to delight, or in their phrases to combine charm and high applicability to life . . . By at once delighting and teaching the reader, the poet who mixes the sweet with the useful has everybody's approval.

Horace (65-8 B.C.), Epistle to the Pisos (The Art of Poetry)

Roscommon paraphrases this: "A poet should instruct, or please, or both."

The end [of poetry] is the giving of instruction in pleasurable form, for poetry teaches, and does not simply amuse, as some used to think.

Scaliger, Poetics, 1561

The aim of the poet is to imitate, invent, and represent—things which are, or which may be—in a resemblance to truth.

Ronsard, A Brief on the Art of French Poetry, 1565

[The poet] commeth to you with words sent in delightful proportion, either accompanied with, or prepared for the well inchaunting skill of Music; and with a tale forsooth he commeth unto you: with a tale which holdeth children from play, and old men from the chimney corner. And pretending no more, doth intende the winning of the mind from wickednesse to vertue . . .

Sidney, An Apologie for Poetrie, 1595

He is called a *Poet,* not he which writeth in measure only; but that fayneth and formeth a fable, and writes things like the Truth. For, the Fable and Fiction is (as it were) the form and soul of any poetical work, or poem.

Ben Jonson, Timber: or, Discoveries, 1641

Poetry is the spontaneous overflow of powerful feelings: it takes its origin from emotion recollected in tranquillity; the emotion is contemplated till, by a species of reaction, the tranquillity gradually disappears, and an emotion, kindred to that which was before the subject of contemplation, is gradually produced, and does itself actually exist in the mind. In this mood successful composition generally begins, and in a mood similar to this it is carried on; but the emotion, of whatever kind, and in whatever degree, from various causes, is qualified by various pleasures, so that in describing any passions whatsoever, which are voluntarily described, the mind will, upon the whole, be in a state of enjoyment.

Wordsworth, Preface to *Lyrical Ballads*, 1800

As to the poetical Character itself (I mean that sort of which, if I am any thing, I am a Member; that sort distinguished from the Wordsworthian or egotistical sublime; which is a thing per se and stands alone) it is not itself—it has no self—it is everything and nothing—It has no character—it enjoys light and shade; it lives in gusto, be it foul or fair, high or low, rich or poor, mean or elevated—It has as much delight in conceiving an Iago as an Imogen. What shocks the virtuous philosopher, delights the chameleon Poet. It does no harm from its relish of the dark side of things any more than from its taste for the bright one; because they both end in speculation. A Poet is the most unpoetical of anything in existence; because he has no Identity—he is continually informing and filling some other Body—the Sun, the Moon, the Sea and Men and Women who are creatures of impulse are poetical and have about them an unchangeable attribute—the poet has none; no identity—he is certainly the most unpoetical of all God's Creatures.

Keats, Letter to Richard Woodhouse, 1818

A poem is the very image of life expressed in its eternal truth. . . . A Poet is a nightingale, who sits in darkness and sings to cheer its own solitude with sweet sounds. . . . Poetry is the record of the best and happiest moments of the happiest and best minds. . . . Poetry turns all things to loveliness; it exalts the beauty of that which is most beautiful, and it adds beauty to that which is most deformed. . . . Poets are the hierophants of an unapprehended inspiration; the mirrors of the gigantic shadows which futurity casts upon the present; the words which express what they understand not; the trumpets which sing to battle and feel not what they inspire; the influence which is moved not, but moves. Poets are the unacknowledged legislators of the world.

Shelley, *A Defence of Poetry*, 1821

I would define, in brief, the Poetry of words as *The Rhythmical Creation of Beauty*. Its sole arbiter is Taste. With the Intellect or with the Conscience, it has only collateral relations. Unless incidentally, it has no concern whatever either with Duty or with Truth.

Poe, "The Poetic Principle," 1848

Poetry is not magic. In so far as poetry, or any other of the arts, can be said to have an ulterior purpose, it is, by telling the truth, to disenchant and disintoxicate.

Auden, *The Dyer's Hand, and Other Essays*, 1962

With this idea of poetry, which is about as far removed from Plato's *Ion* as it is possible to get, I'll leave the question.

POPULAR BALLAD. See BALLAD.

POULTER'S MEASURE. Rhymed lines of twelve and fourteen syllables, alternating. Named from the poultryman's practice of giving twelve eggs for the first dozen, fourteen eggs for the second. The meter was used in the sixteenth century by Wyatt, Surrey, and other English poets.

PRE-RAPHAELITE. Referring to the mid-nineteenth-century movement in art and literature known as the Pre-Raphaelite Brotherhood. They turned to the art before Raphael for inspiration, aiming to represent nature in exact detail and to depict uplifting subjects. Of the poets, Dante Gabriel Rossetti was the most famous; his "The Blessed Damozel" has often been anthologized. In 1871, Rossetti was attacked by Robert Buchanan in an article titled "The Fleshly School of Poetry."

PROJECTIVE VERSE. A movement in contemporary American poetry influenced by the work of Ezra Pound and William Carlos Williams. Its practitioners include Charles Olson, Robert Creeley, Robert Duncan, and Denise Levertov. The theories of the school are stated by Charles Olson in an article, "Projective Verse," first published in 1950. Robert Creeley summarizes Olson's ideas as follows:

He outlines . . . the premise of "composition by field" (the value of which William Carlos Williams was to emphasize by reprinting it in part in his own *Autobiography*); and defines a basis for structure in the poem in term of its *'kinetics'* ("the poem itself must, at all points, be a high energy-construct and, at all points, an energy discharge . . ."), the *'principle'* of its writing (form is never more than an extension of content), and the *'process'* ("One PERCEPTION MUST IMMEDIATELY AND DIRECTLY LEAD TO A FURTHER PERCEPTION . . ."). He equally distinguishes between breathing and hearing, as these relate to the line: "And the line comes (I swear it) from the breath, from the breathing of the man who writes, at that moment that he writes . . ."

The New American Poetry, 1960

PROSE PARAPHASE. A restatement in prose of the content of a poem. The use of paraphrase is to help understanding, but the music and images are lost. In fact, the poetry is lost.

PROSODY. The systematic, technical study of versification, including meter, rhyme, sound effects, and stanza patterns. "Prosody" has nothing to do with prose. See "Meter, Rhyme, Stanza, and Sound," pp. 34-41.

PROTHALAMION. A poem or song heralding a marriage. Edmund Spenser coined the word and used it as the title of one of his poems.

PSEUDO-STATEMENT. In the writings of I. A. Richards (*Science and Poetry,* 1926), a pseudo-statement is a statement that is "true" though it is contradicted by fact.

A pseudo-statement is "true" if it suits and serves some attitude or links together attitudes which on other grounds are desirable . . . A pseudo-statement is a form of words which is justified entirely by its effect in releasing or organizing our impulses and attitudes (due regard being had for the better or worse organizations of these *inter se*); a statement, on the other hand, is justified by its truth, i.e. its correspondence, in a highly technical sense, with the fact to which it points.

The following are pseudo-statements:

Machines have made their god. They walk or fly.
The towers bend like Magi, mountains weep,
Needles go mad, and metal sheds a tear.

Louis Simpson, "Outward"

PUN. A play on words, use of a word in a context where two or more of its meanings are relevant.

O Nelly Gray! O, Nelly Gray!
  Is this your love so warm?
The love that loves a scarlet coat
  Should be more uniform!

Thomas Hood, "Faithless Nelly Gray"

PURE POETRY. In contrast to didactic poetry, the aim of which is to teach moral or other truth, pure poetry aims only to delight the reader by the beauty of its language, music, and imagery. As words have meanings, however, and reflect the opinions of the author, no poetry can be absolutely "pure."

PURITAN INTERREGNUM. See COMMONWEALTH.

PURPLE PASSAGE (or PURPLE PATCH). A passage so heightened in style that it stands out from its context. "Purple" because this was the color of royalty, associated with gorgeous, barbaric courts.

PYRRHIC. Also called *dibrach*. A metrical foot of two unstressed syllables, thus: ˘ ˘. Because the pyrrhic foot has no stress, it is rarely considered a legitimate foot in modern English scansion.

Nŏr shăll / dēath brāg / thŏu wăn/dĕr'st īn / hĭs shāde

Prosody is not an exact science. The line could just as well be scanned:

Nōr shăll / dēath brāg / thŏu wăn/dĕr'st ĭn / hĭs shāde

QUALITATIVE VERSE. Also called *accentual verse*. Verse in which the metrical system is based on the language's having stressed (or accented) and unstressed (or unaccented) syllables. English verse is qualitative. See QUANTITATIVE VERSE.

QUANTITATIVE VERSE. Verse in which the metrical system is based on the length of time it takes to pronounce the syllables of the language, as in classical Greek and Latin. A long syllable takes twice as much time to pronounce as a short syllable. One long syllable therefore is considered equal to two short ones; the principle of substitution in classical metrics is based on this relationship. A long syllable contains either a long vowel or diphthong, or a short vowel plus two or more consonants. Stress, or accent, is irrelevant in quantitative verse.

QUATRAIN. A four-line stanza.

REALISM. 1. Said to be possessed by a work that closely imitates the details and appearances of real life, especially of commonplace middle or lower class life; often contrasted to "romance," which invents imaginary worlds. 2. "Literary realism" was a nineteenth-century movement of realistic writers, led by Flaubert. At the extreme, literary realism showed the disillusion and determinism of *naturalism* (q.v.).

REFRAIN. A line or lines repeated at regular intervals in a poem, represented by capital "R" in the rhyme scheme. For example, *a a a R, b b b R, c c c R*. See REPETEND.

REPETEND. A recurring word or phrase. As distinguished from a refrain (q.v.), a repetend is an irregular, or partial rather than complete, repetition. See the following repetends in "The Love Song of J. Alfred Prufrock," p. 288: "Let us go," "there will be time," "I have known," "would it have been worth it."

RESTORATION PERIOD. Dating from the end of the Puritan Commonwealth, in 1660, when the monarchy (Charles II) was restored, until about 1700. John Milton and John Dryden were the major literary figures. Other poets were Marvell, Samuel Butler, and the Earl of Rochester; prose writers, Hobbes, Bunyan, Locke, Newton, Samuel Pepys, and Sir William Temple. The Puritan ban on theater productions was revoked, and playwrights such as Dryden, Etherege, Wycherley, and Congreve wrote comedies and heroic dramas.

RHAPSODY. An unusually intense and irregular poem or piece of prose, ecstatic and enthusiastic. The writer of rhapsodies is called a rhapsodist. However, men who merely recite rhapsodic poems are also called rhapsodists, as in this definition by Scaliger:

While the poet is the imitator of things, the rhapsodist is he who acts out the imitation, and according as the poet represents, the rhapsodist can reproduce.

Poetics

RHETORIC. In the broad sense, the art of persuasion. In the narrow sense, the study of techniques used in public speaking (oratory) and in writing: figures of speech, diction, structure, and rhythm. In the medieval curriculum, grammar, logic, and rhetoric constituted the *trivium* or four-year course of undergraduate study. Music, arithmetic, geometry, and astronomy made up the *quadrivium* or three-year course from the B.A. to M.A. degree. These were the seven liberal arts.

Critics have often tried to distinguish between rhetoric and *poetics,* the theory of making and judging poetry. Aristotle said that the aim of rhetoric was to persuade, the aim of poetry to imitate. In the following stanza, Davies says that it is meter that distinguishes poetry from rhetoric; if he had meant rhythm, rather than meter, I would agree:

For Rhetoric, clothing speech in rich array,
In looser numbers teacheth her to range

With twenty tropes, and turnings every way,
And various figures, and licentious change;
But poetry, with rule and order strange,
So curiously doth move each single pace,
As all is marred if she one foot misplace.

Orchestra

Attempts to distinguish between rhetoric and poetry are not conclusive, however, for rhetoric is a part of poetry.

RHETORICAL ACCENT. See ACCENT.

RHETORICAL FIGURES. See FIGURES OF SPEECH.

RHETORICAL QUESTION. A question asked for effect, to express a thought rather than to find out information.

O, Wind,
If Winter comes, can Spring be far behind?

Shelley, "Ode to the West Wind"

RHYME. The identity or similarity of sound patterns. Rhyme at the end of lines is called *end* or *terminal* rhyme. Rhyme occurring within a line is *internal* rhyme ("I conceive you may use any language you choose to indulge in . . ."). If the word before the caesura rhymes with the concluding words, the rhyme is *leonine* ("Oh! a private buffoon is a light-hearted loon . . ."). The most common rhyme in English is that of the final accented vowels and all following sounds (night-light, heaven-seven, fertility-puerility). This is called *complete, exact, full, perfect, true* rhyme, or *rime suffisante*. A rhyme that is not perfect and has only similarity rather than identity of sound patterns (once-France) can be called *approximate, half, imperfect, near, oblique, off, partial,* or *slant* rhyme. *Assonance, consonance,* and *pararhyme,* are forms of approximate rhyme. In *assonance,* the vowels in the words are identical, while the consonants coming directly before and after the vowels change (time-mind). In *consonance,* or *consonantal* rhyme, the vowels change but the consonant sounds after the vowels are identical—the consonant sounds preceding the vowels may be, but are not necessarily, identical (struts-frets, lives-loves, fleshed-flashed, tigress-progress). If the consonant sounds both before and after the changing vowels are identical (as in lives-loves), consonance may be called *pararhyme.* And *alliteration,* or *initial* or *head* rhyme (forgot-foul-fair), and *hidden alliteration* (hast-once) are sometimes considered variations of rhyme. In *masculine* rhyme, the final syllable is stressed (name-fame, support-retort, roundelay-month of May). In *feminine* rhyme, the stressed syllables are followed by unstressed ones (after–laughter); *double* rhyme rhymes two syllables (double-trouble), and *triple* rhyme—often found in comic verse—rhymes three syllables (intellectual-hen-pecked you all). *Eye* rhyme rhymes only the spellings (cough–bough–though–rough). If an eye rhyme was once pronounced as a true rhyme, it is called a *historical* rhyme. In *identical* rhyme, in contrast, the rhyming words have identical pronunciation but different spelling (to–too–two, their–there), or the same word is used twice with different meanings. This is also called *rime riche*. In *apocapated* rhyme, the final syllable of one of the rhyme words is discounted (mope–ropeless). In *broken* rhyme, one of the rhyming words is completed at the beginning of the next line. In *linked* rhyme, found in early Welsh verse, one of the rhyming words is formed by linking the final syllable of one line to the first sound of the next line:

Dame, at our *door*
Drowned, and among our shoals,
Remember us in the roads, the heaven-haven of the Re*ward*
> Gerard Manley Hopkins, "The Wreck of the Deutschland"

RHYME ROYAL. A seven-line stanza of iambic pentameter, having the rhyme scheme *a b a b b c c*. Rhyme royal took its name from James I of England's writing in this stanza, although he was not the first to use it. It is sometimes called the Chaucerian stanza.

Flee from the prees, and dwelle with sothfastness,
　Suffice unto thy good, though it be small;
For hord hath hate, and climbing tikelnesse,
　Prees hath envye, and well blent overall;
Savour no more than thee bihove shall;
　Reule well thyself, that other folk canst rede;
　And trouthe thee shall deliver, it is no drede.
> Geoffrey Chaucer, "Balade de Bon Conseyl"

RHYME SCHEME. The pattern formed by the terminal rhymes of all the lines in a stanza. The rhyming words are assigned letters in the order of their occurrence, and a letter is repeated to show that a later word rhymes with an earlier one. A quatrain, for instance, may have a rhyme scheme of *a b a b*, *a b c b*, or *a a b a*, etc.

RHYTHM. Repetition of stress. Regular rhythm in verse is *meter* (q.v.). Irregular rhythm is *free verse* (q.v.).

Rhythm is a form cut into time.
> Pound, *ABC of Reading*

Rhythm is the entire movement, the flow, the recurrence of stress and unstress that is related to the rhythms of the blood, the rhythms of nature. It involves certainly stress, time, pitch, the texture of the words, the total meaning of the poem.
> Theodore Roethke, "Some Remarks on Rhythm"

RIME. Alternate spelling for rhyme.

RISING METER. Meter in which the movement rises up to the stressed syllable of each foot. The iamb ($\smile$ $-$) and the anapest ($\smile$ $\smile$ $-$) are rising meters.

ROCKING RHYTHM. A rhythmic effect that occurs when the stressed syllables in a line of verse fall between two unstressed syllables, as with anapestic and dactylic meter.

Believe me / if all those / endearing / young charms . . .

ROMANTIC PERIOD. In British literature, the period of the late eighteenth and early nineteenth century when the poets Burns, Blake, Scott, Wordsworth, Coleridge, Byron, Shelley, and Keats were writing. Among prose writers there were Coleridge, Hazlitt, Lamb, De Quincey, Jane Austen, and Scott. The period is sometimes dated from the outbreak of the French Revolution (1789) to the death of Scott (1832).

ROMANTICISM. An aesthetic that stresses imagination, individualism, the visionary and mysterious, "the spontaneous overflow of powerful feelings." See CLASSICISM, NEOCLASSICAL, ROMANTIC PERIOD.

RONDEAU. A French fixed verse form of three stanzas characterized by the use of a refrain and only two rhymes in the pattern *a a b b a, a a b R, a a b b a R*. The refrain is the first half of the opening line. The lines usually contain eight syllables.

RONDEL (and ROUNDEL). Both words are derived from the Old French *rondel, rond,* meaning "round," and have been used interchangeably. In English *rondel* usually refers to a poem having three stanzas and two rhymes, the rhyme scheme being *A B b a, a b A B, a b b a A (B)* —the capital letters standing for repeated lines. If there are thirteen lines, a refrain is made of the two opening lines, which are repeated as the seventh and eighth lines. If there are fourteen lines, the two-line refrain appears three times.

The *roundel* consists of eleven lines in three stanzas, rhyming *a b a R, b a b, a b a R*—R standing for the refrain. The refrain is made by taking the first word or a phrase from the opening line; if it is a phrase, the refrain usually rhymes with the second line.

RUN-ON LINE (ENJAMBMENT). A line that completes its grammatical unity and meaning by going into the next line without a pause. Running-on is marked by an absence of punctuation between the lines. The term is also used for carrying-over from one couplet or stanza to the next.

A thing of beauty is a joy for ever:
Its loveliness increases; it will never
Pass into nothingness; but still will keep
A bower quiet for us, and a sleep
Full of sweet dreams, and health, and quiet breathing.

Keats, *Endymion*

See END-STOPPED LINE.

SAPPHIC. A quatrain written in a meter derived from that of the Greek lyric poet Sappho. Each of the first three lines has eleven syllables, of which the fourth and eleventh may be either long or short: $- \smile /$ $- \smile / - \smile \smile / - \smile / - \smile$. The last line has only five syllables: $- \smile \smile / - \smile$.

All the night sleep came not upon my eyelids,
Shed not dew, nor shock nor unclosed a feather,
Yet with lips shut close and with eyes of iron,
    Stood and beheld me.

Swinburne, "Sapphics"

SATIRE. Dr. Johnson's definition is probably the best: "a poem in which wickedness or folly is censured." Satire may be Horatian or Juvenalian, after the Roman poet Horace, who was amused at man's foibles and gently mocked them, and Juvenal, who attacked vice with severe ridicule. Donne's "Satire IV" is Horatian; Johnson's "Vanity of Human Wishes" is modeled on Juvenal. Frequently the satiric poet feels called upon to justify his art, as Pope does in "An Epistle to Dr. Arbuthnot." The satirist presents himself as a mild, honest man who is compelled by the evil around him to speak out. See BURLESQUE.

SCANSION. The process of analyzing the metrical patterns of a poem. To scan a poem, one goes through it line by line marking the accented and unaccented syllables, then grouping them into metrical feet. One identifies the kind of feet, the number of feet per line, and the stanza pattern, if there is one. The stanza pattern is described by noting the rhyme scheme, with each letter followed by a numerical exponent to indicate the number of feet in the line. A ballad stanza, for instance, which alternates tetrameter and trimeter lines, is notated a^4 b^3 c^4 b^3. When the formal pattern of the verse is established, it is necessary to see how the rhetorical accents counterpoint with it.

SECONDARY STRESS. An accent on a syllable weaker than the primary stress of a word, but stronger than its unstressed syllables, e.g., the stress on the first syllable of the word "èvocátion."

SENSIBILITY. In the eighteenth century, "sensibility" referred to a person's capacity to respond emotionally, even tearfully, to the joy or distress of others, and to respond to beauty. In the twentieth century, "sensibility" has acquired a meaning closer to "sensitivity," referring to a person's capacity for aesthetic understanding and enjoyment.

SENTENTIA. Aphorisms, pointed statements alleging a truth, such as Aristotle's remark that "Education is learning to take pleasure in the right things." *Sententious verse* aims at instructing rather than giving pleasure. At the worst it is ponderous and trite. Unfortunately, as Northrop Frye says:

The sententious approach to literature is still the popular one, accounting for the wide appeal of such poems as Kipling's *If* or Longfellow's *Psalm of Life.*

The Well-Tempered Critic, 1963

SENTIMENTALISM. In the eighteenth century, self-conscious indulgence in emotional tenderness, pity, and sympathy—"the sadly pleasing tear," "the luxury of grief," "dear, delicious pain."

SENTIMENTALITY. Emotion in excess of what the occasion requires.

SEPTENARY. Synonym for *heptameter* (q.v.).

SESTET (also spelled SEXTET). A six-line poem or stanza. The term often refers to the final six lines of a Petrarchan sonnet. See SONNET.

SESTINA. A French fixed verse form having six unrhymed six-line stanzas with the same terminal words, in different orders, followed by a tercet using three of them, or all six if two are used per line. In the following diagram, each letter represents the terminal word of a line, and each horizontal line of letters represents one stanza:

a b c d e f
f a e b d c
c f d a b e
e c b f a d
d e a c f b
b d f e c a
  e c a

SHAKESPEAREAN SONNET. See SONNET.

SHAPED POEM. See CONCRETE POETRY.

SIMILE. An expressed comparison, often using the words "like," "as," "as if," "than":

My luve is *like* a red, red rose.

SINKING. See BATHOS.

SKELTONIC VERSE. Verse in the headlong, quick-rhyming, slapdash manner of John Skelton (1460?–1529).

For though my ryme be ragged,
Tattered and iagged,
Rudely rayne beaten,
Rusty and mothe eaten;
If ye take well therwith,
It hath in it some pyth.

John Skelton, "Colyn Cloute"

SLANT RHYME. See RHYME.

SLASH. See VIRGULE.

SOLILOQUY. In drama (especially Elizabethan), an extended speech by a solitary character expressing his thoughts aloud to himself and the audience. Hamlet's famous speech beginning "To be or not to be" is a soliloquy.

SONNET. A fixed verse form, having fourteen lines (occasionally twelve or sixteen) of iambic pentameter (in English) with an elaborate rhyme scheme. The *Petrarchan*, or *Italian*, sonnet is divided into an *octave* (or octet) rhyming *a b b a a b b a*, and a *sestet* usually rhyming *c d e c d e* or *c d c d c d*. Between the octet and sestet there is a significant break in meaning, a movement from question to answer, complaint to resolution, cause to effect, etc. The *Miltonic* sonnet has the Petrarchan scheme, but no significant break in meaning between the octave and sestet. The *Shakespearean*, or *English*, sonnet has three quatrains and a final couplet which usually contains an epigrammatic statement of the theme. The rhyme scheme is *a b a b, c d c d, e f e f, g g*, or else *a b b a, c d d c, e f f e, g g*. The *Spenserian*, or *"link"* sonnet rhymes *a b a b, b c b c, c d c d, e e*, and often has no break in meaning between the octave and sestet. See SONNET SEQUENCE.

SONNET SEQUENCE. A series of sonnets by one author. It may have a single theme.

SOUND POETRY. Verse in which sound effects are far more important than imagery or statement. Some "sound poems" have little or no meaning in the ordinary sense of the word; therefore, as with concrete poems (qv.) in which there are only visual elements, it is arguable that this is not poetry but another form of expression. The following "exclamation poem," according to the author, was written to be shouted aloud. It requires "voice, gesture and soapbox."

zacoatl !   seascarnal !
            manpoise !
FERNBLEST LANGERS SNORN
      snoflects & nervequil
                                              Neil Mills, 1970

SPENSERIAN STANZA. A nine-line stanza rhymed *a b a b b c b c c*. All of the lines are iambic pentameter, except the final one, which is iambic hexameter, an Alexandrine.

> He there does now enjoy eternall rest
> And happie ease, which thou doest want and craue,
> And further from it daily wanderest:
> What if some litle paine the passage haue.
> That makes fraile flesh to feare the bitter waue?
> Is not short paine well borne, that brings long ease,
> And layes the soule to sleepe in quiet graue?
> Sleepe after toyle, port after stormie seas,
> Ease after warre, death after life does greatly please.
>   Spenser, *The Faerie Queene*

SPONDEE, SPONDAIC. A metrical foot of two syllables, both of which are stressed, thus: — —. Spondee cannot be the basic meter of a poem. Rather, it is introduced as a variant or substitute foot, especially for an iamb or trochee. Spondee neither rises nor falls. See also METER.

SPRUNG RHYTHM. A term coined by Gerard Manley Hopkins to describe a kind of rhythm between strict meter and free verse. The verse is measured according to the number of stressed syllables, which may stand alone or be followed by any number of unstressed syllables. The stressed syllables are always considered to begin the feet, so the most common feet in Hopkins' verse are the spondee, dactyl, and trochee. Hopkins pointed out that sprung rhythm is characteristic of common speech, written prose, most music, and nursery rhymes: "Little Jack Horner sat in a corner . . ."

STANZA. A group of lines considered as a unit, forming a division of a poem, and recurring in the same pattern or variations of the pattern. A stanza pattern is determined by the number of lines, the kind of feet and the number of feet per line, and the rhyme scheme. Many stanzaic forms are conventional and have their own names: see FIXED FORM. The common name for a two-line stanza is "couplet," for a three-line

stanza, "tercet," and for a four-line stanza, "quatrain." See also SCAN-
SION.

STOCK CHARACTER. A familiar, conventional character who appears often in
certain kinds of literary works. Stock characters include the epic hero,
the knight and his lady, the disconsolate lover and his cruel mistress,
the villain, the braggart soldier, the clever servant, the cruel step-
mother, the clown or fool, the proud tragic hero, the virtuous heroine,
the *femme fatale,* etc.

STOCK EPITHET. Frequently repeated lines or phrases, such as occurred in the
long, orally recited heroic poems. For example, Homer's "rosy-fingered
dawn."

STOCK RESPONSE. An unsophisticated reader's predictable emotional reaction
to certain stimuli, such as the word "mother" in a poem. Stock re-
sponses are like sentimentality in that they suspend judgment and
prevent a deeper understanding and enjoyment of poetry.

STOCK SITUATION. Stock situations are circumstances that appear frequently
in literature: mistaken identities, love triangles, separations of twins
by shipwreck, etc.

STREAM OF CONSCIOUSNESS. A term coined by William James (*Principles of
Psychology,* 1890) to refer to the continuous flow of inner experiences.
In literature it refers to a technique of presenting the perceptions,
thoughts, and feelings of characters in a narrative. The narrative
progresses through psychological association rather than linguistic
conventions such as sentences. The term is usually applied to prose
fiction—e.g., James Joyce's *Ulysses*—but it might also be applied to the
floating consciousness of T. S. Eliot's Prufrock and to parts of *The
Waste Land* and Pound's *Cantos.*

STRESS. Synonym for "accent," the emphasis given to certain syllables of
words. If a word (usually longer than three syllables) has more than
one accented syllable, the heavier accent is called the primary stress,
the lighter is the secondary stress, and the other syllables are unstressed.

STROPHE. See ODE.

STRUCTURE. The underlying logic or arrangement and movement in a literary
text; its skeleton or paraphrasable content. The term "structure"
usually refers to the organization of elements other than words. For
the latter the term "style" is used. See ARGUMENT and TEXTURE.

STYLE. The choice and arrangement of words, sentences, and larger units in
a literary text. The term is very broad and includes consideration of
the choices a writer must make about diction, figurative and rhetorical
devices, tone, and sound patterns of the language (alliteration, rhyme,
meter, etc.). Styles may be classified according to authors (Miltonic,
Shakespearean), or periods (classical, Renaissance, romantic), or
books (Biblical), or subjects (legal, journalistic). Styles may also be
classified as high (or grand), middle, and low (or plain).

SUBJECTIVITY. The quality in a literary work which reveals the author's personality, his own feelings and attitudes. Wordsworth's *The Prelude* is subjective because it records the growth of the poet's own mind. Shakespeare's plays, in contrast, are impersonal and objective, for they tell us virtually nothing about the poet's personality. The term may be used to refer to the characters in a work, rather than to the author who created them; Browning's dramatic monologues are subjective in that they reveal the personality of the character, or persona, in the poem. In literary criticism, subjectivity means emphasis on the critic's personal taste and response, "impressionistic" criticism.

SUBLIMITY (THE SUBLIME).

Sublimity is a certain distinction and excellence in expression, and . . . it is from no other source than this that the greatest poets and writers have derived their eminence and gained an immortality of renown. The effect of elevated language upon an audience is not persuasion but transport. At every time and in every way imposing speech, with the spell it throws over us, prevails over that which aims at persuasion and gratification. Our persuasions we can usually control, but the influences of the sublime bring power and irresistible might to bear, and reign supreme over every hearer. . . . Sublimity flashing forth at the right moment scatters everything before it like a thunderbolt. . . . For, as if instinctively, our soul is uplifted by the true sublime; it takes a proud flight, and is filled with joy and vaunting, as though it had itself produced what it has heard.

On the Sublime, traditionally ascribed to Longinus

SUBSTITUTION. See INVERSION.

SURREALISM. A literary and artistic movement vigorous in the 1920's and 1930's, and still productive. Surrealists want to go "beyond" realism (normal perception of the outer world) deep into the inner world of the unconscious mind. Their work often resembles the stark, strange imagery and nonsyntactical narrative of dreams. In general, surrealists are hostile to, or "go beyond," rationality, bourgeois morality, and artistic conventions. The French poet Guillaume Appollinaire invented the word surrealism; André Breton led the movement. Poets who use surrealist techniques include Aragon and Eluard in French, Lorca and Neruda in Spanish, and Dylan Thomas in English. Max Ernst and Salvador Dali are surrealist painters. A *surrealist image* is not so much "the thing perceived" as "anything as it might be perceived." In practice, most surrealist images are merely juxtapositions of objects that have no relationship in the normal world. However, the effective surrealist images are more than this; they seem to be formed by a logic of the subconscious, as things are in dreams.

When the sun is only a drop of sweat
the sound of a bell
the red pearl falling down a vertical needle

Michel Leiris, "Marécage du sommeil"

Surrealist techniques have always existed in verse. Breton remarks that the eighteenth-century poetry of Edward Young, in *Night*

456

Thoughts, was surrealist. The deliberate, intense application of these techniques in the twentieth century has created a kind of literature that seems, in spite of absurdities, original and stimulating. The following poem by the Chilean Pablo Neruda, here printed in its entirety in translation by Angel Flores, describes the art of a surrealist and uses surrealistic techniques:

Ars Poetica
Between shadow and space, between garrisons and maidens,
endowed with singular heart and doleful dreams,
precipitately pale, the forehead withered,
and with the mourning of an angry widower for each day of life,
alas, for each invisible drop of water which I drink sleepily
and for each sound which I receive, trembling,
I have the same absent thirst and the same cold fever,
an ear that is born, an indirect anguish,
as if thieves or ghosts were approaching,
and in a shell of fixed and deep extent,
like a humiliated waiter, like a bell slightly hoarse,
like an old mirror, like the smell of a lonely house
whose roomers enter by night dead drunk,
and there is a smell of clothing thrown about on the floor, and an
    absence of flowers
possibly in some other way even less melancholy,
but, in truth, suddenly, the wind that strikes my chest
the nights of infinite substance dropped into my bedroom,
the noise of a day that burns with sacrifice,
demand, sadly, whatever there is of prophetic in me,
and there is a knocking of objects which call without being answered,
and a ceaseless movement, and a confused name.

SYLLABIC VERSE (SYLLABICS). Verse in which the system of measurement is based on the number of syllables in the line, rather than on stress or quantity. In the first of the following stanzas, the syllable count by lines is 5, 5, 6, 11, 10, 7. The second stanza is made on the same pattern—with a variation, 9 syllables in the fifth line.

They had their men tie
hippopotami
    and bring out dapple dog-
    cats to course antelopes, dikdik, and ibex;
        or used small eagles. They looked on as theirs,
        impallas and onigers,

the wild ostrich herd
with hard feet and bird
    necks rearing back in the
    dust like a serpent preparing to strike, cranes,
        mongooses, storks, anoas, Nile geese;
        and there were gardens for these—

                                        Marianne Moore, "The Jerboa"

See Thomas Campion, "Rose-Cheeked Laura," p. 79.

> Nature is a temple, in which living pillars sometimes utter a babel of words; man traverses it through forests of symbols, that watch him with knowing eyes.
>
> Charles Baudelaire, *Correspondances* (trans. Francis Scarfe)

A symbol is an image that stands not only for itself but for something else as well, and perhaps many things. Part of the meaning of a symbol is emotional and subconscious, in the psychic reality of myth. A symbol is often a means of making concrete and perceptible a meaning that otherwise would remain inexpressible. It is a "loaded" word or image from which meanings ray out; the meanings are determined by the context in which the symbol appears. A symbol may be an object (a rose), a situation (a journey), a character (Coleridge's Ancient Mariner), or the setting of a work (the sea). See SYMBOLISM and the discussion of "The Magi" by W. B. Yeats, pp. 23-25.

SYMBOLISM (SYMBOLIST MOVEMENT). A literary movement originating in late nineteenth-century France. Baudelaire was a forerunner of symbolism; Verlaine, Rimbaud, and Mallarmé were the leading Symbolists. Rimbaud said, "The poet makes himself a seer by means of a long, immense and calculated disordering of all the senses." In his *Bateau Ivre,* 1871, he created new rhythms, exotic descriptions of land and sea, and vivid colors, and employed symbols that evoked the creation of the world. Mallarmé evolved a technique of combining verbal music and typographic patterns to suggest his ideas. To Mallarmé, poetry was a mystery; the poet should suggest, not state: "To name a thing is to suppress three quarters of the joy of the poem, which consists in guessing, little by little: suggestion makes the dream." Donald Davie has described symbolist technique as setting the images at a certain distance from one another and letting the meaning flower out of the spaces between. Mallarmé called this forming "constellations." These men also were important in the movement: Jean Moréas, René Ghil, Gustave Khan, Stuart Merrill, Emile Verhaeren, Maurice Maeterlinck, Villiers de l'Isle Adam, Jules Laforgue, and Arthur Symons, who introduced W. B. Yeats to the symbolists.

> All sounds, all colors, all forms, either because of their pre-ordained energies or because of long associations, evoke undefinable and yet precise emotions, or, as I prefer to think, call down among us certain disembodied powers, whose footsteps over our hearts we call emotions; and when sound, and color, and form are in a musical relation, a beautiful relation to one another, they become as it were one sound, one color, one form, and evoke an emotion that is made out of their distinct evocations and yet is one emotion.
>
> Yeats, "The Symbolism of Poetry"

Among British and American poets, T. S. Eliot and Dylan Thomas were influenced by the symbolists, and many other poets have used symbolist techniques.

SYNCOPE. Omission of a letter or syllable in a word, as in "o'er" for "over."

SYNECDOCHE. A figurative use of language in which a part of something is substituted for the whole, or the whole for a part. "Roof" is used to mean "house," "sail" to mean "ship," etc. Synecdoche is often regarded as a special type of *metonymy* (q.v.).

SYNESTHESIA. Description of one kind of sense perception in words that usually describe another.

> There are perfumes fresh and cool as the bodies of children, mellow as oboes, green as fields; and others that are perverse, rich, and triumphant.
>
> Charles Baudelaire, *Correspondances* (trans. by Francis Scarfe)

TENOR. See METAPHOR.

TENSION. A technical term in the vocabulary of New Criticism (q.v.). Allen Tate arrived at it by "lopping the prefixes off the logical terms *ex*tension and *in*tension" and combining their meanings, so that the term "tension" refers to the extent to which the abstract and concrete elements in a poem have a integral relationship or are unified with the idea embodied in images. An additional meaning of the term "tension" involves "conflict-structures," listed by Robert Penn Warren as "tension between the rhythm of the poem and the rhythm of speech . . . between the formality of the rhythm and the informality of language; between the particular and the general, the concrete and the abstract; between the elements of even the simplest metaphor; between the beautiful and the ugly; between ideas; between the elements involved in irony; between prosisms and poeticisms."

TERCET. A three-line stanza. If there is a single rhyme for all three lines, the tercet is a triplet. The term "tercet" may also refer to half the sestet in a Petrarchan sonnet, or to the *terza rima* stanza.

TERMINAL RHYME. See RHYME.

TERZA RIMA. An Italian fixed verse form of tercets with rhymes interlocking in the pattern *a b a, b c b, c d c, d e d*, etc. The form was used by Dante in *The Divine Comedy*. See Shelley, "Ode to the West Wind," p. 188, and Allen Tate, "The Swimmers," p. 312.

TETRAMETER. A line of four metrical feet:

> Hōw thĕ / Chīmnĕy/ -swēepĕr's / crȳ
> Every black'ning Church appalls;
> And the hapless Soldier's sigh
> Runs in blood down Palace walls.
>
> Blake, "London"

TETRASTICH. A four-line stanza; synonym for quatrain.

TEXTURE. The surface detail of a text, especially the phonetic patterns, the sensory quality of the images, and the additional richness of meaning suggested by the connotations of the words. Texture is contrasted with structure, which is the argument or paraphrasable content of the work. With reference to meter, John Crowe Ransom calls the basic meter the structure and the variations on it the texture.

THEMATIC DEVELOPMENT. The process by which a theme unfolds to the reader or undergoes changes in a work.

THEME. A central idea or major point of a literary work; its thesis, as stated in sentence form. Also, loosely used, "theme" can mean the subject of a work, such as time, love, death, beauty, and so on.

THRENODY. See DIRGE.

TONE. The attitude of the writer toward his subject and his audience, as it is implied in the text and inferred by the reader. The tone may be serious or light, formal or intimate, scornful or sympathetic, straightforward or given a double edge by irony.

TRADITION. A body of beliefs, laws, and customs handed down from generation to generation. In literature, the totality of conventions—of technique, form, subject matter, and point of view or attitude—characteristic of a group of writers in a period. Thus we may speak of the Puritan tradition, the Cavalier tradition, the metaphysical tradition of the seventeenth century, the neoclassical tradition of the eighteenth century, or the romantic tradition of the nineteenth century. The term may also be used to refer to a complex of conventions and themes common to writers of various periods, such as the classical tradition, the Neoplatonic tradition, and the pastoral tradition.

TRANSFERRED EPITHET. See EPITHET.

TRAVESTY. See BURLESQUE.

TRIMETER. A line of three metrical feet.

My silks / and fine / array,
My smiles / and lan/guish'd air
By Love / are driv'n / away; . . .

Blake, "Song"

TRIOLET. A French fixed form used by late nineteenth-century English poets. It has eight lines, but only two rhymes; the first two lines are repeated as the last two, and the fourth is the same as the first. The rhyme scheme is *a b a a a b a b*.

TRIPLE METERS. Meters whose feet consist of three syllables. Dactylic ($-\smile\smile$) and anapestic ($\smile\smile-$) are triple meters. See DUPLE METERS.

TRIPLE RHYME. See RHYME.

TRIPLET. A three-line stanza with a single rhyme.

TRISTICH. A three-line stanza; synonym for *tercet*.

TROCHEE, TROCHAIC. A metrical foot of two syllables, with a strong stress followed by a weak: $-\smile$. See also METER and FALLING METER.

TROPE. Literally, a "turn," or use of a word with a definite change or extension of its meaning, from literal to figurative. See FIGURATIVE LANGUAGE.

TROUBADOUR. One of a class of lyric poets who flourished in southern France (and eastern Spain and northern Italy) from the eleventh to the thirteenth centuries. They wrote in the Provençal dialect about courtly love and chivalry. Their interest in metrical technique led to the development of many of the intricate French fixed verse forms. Among the more famous of the troubadours were Bertrans de Born, Arnaut Daniel, and William, Count of Poitiers. See also TROUVÈRE.

TROUVÈRE. One of a class of court poets of northern France who flourished at the same time as the Provençal troubadours and were greatly influenced by them. Trouvères, one of whom was Chrétien de Troyes, wrote chivalric romances, love lyrics, and *chansons de geste*.

TRUE RHYME. See RHYME.

TRUNCATION. See CATALEXIS.

TUMIDITY. Pompous, turgid, bombastic language or literary style.

"UBI SUNT" MOTIF. A common theme in lyric poetry: lamenting the vanished past. The phrase is Latin for "where are," as in Villon's "Where are the snows of yesteryear?".

UNDERSTATEMENT (MEIOSIS). A figurative use of language in which less is said than is meant. Only a part of the meaning is stated, so that the reader, in order to complete the thought, must enter into the mind and feelings of the author. In doing so, the reader obtains a better understanding than he would from explicit statement. Shakespeare's Othello says: "Keep up your bright swords, for the dew will rust them." He is speaking of a quarrel in the street, between men armed with swords, as though it were a promenade. The effect is to draw the reader into the heroic calm of Othello's mind. He is a man of experience, particularly of battle, to whom a streetfight would be insignificant.

> But now go the bells, and we are ready;
> In one house we are sternly stopped
> To say we are vexed at her brown study,
> Lying so primly propped.
> John Crowe Ransom, "Bells for John Whiteside's Daughter"

In this stanza about the death of a little girl, the "brown study" is death, and being "vexed" is being grieved. The words seem insufficient; in order to complete the poet's meaning, the reader is compelled to imagine the scene and give of his own feelings.

UNITY. The coherent relationship of all the parts of a work to the whole, with nothing essential omitted and nothing irrelevant included. The *"three unities"* of the drama are those of action, time, and place. During the Renaissance, French and Italian critics who derived the "unities" from Aristotle's *Poetics* insisted that a play should be the imitation of a single action taking place within a single day in a single place. However, the only unity that Aristotle himself had insisted upon was unity of action.

VEHICLE. See METAPHOR.

VERS DE SOCIÉTÉ. French for "society verse," brief epigrammatic or lyrical light verse concerning polite society. It is usually witty and highly polished, using a conversational tone and one of the intricate French fixed verse forms, such as the rondeau or villanelle. It may be gently satiric or elegantly amorous, paying a witty compliment to a lady.

VERS LIBRE. See FREE VERSE.

VERSE. 1. Any individual line of a poem. 2. Strictly metrical language; verse as distinguished from prose. Verse is not necessarily poetry, however; it may be mere doggerel.

> A rhymer, and a *poet,* are two things.
>
> Ben Jonson, *Timber*

VERSE PARAGRAPH. A group of lines, frequently in blank verse, considered as a rhetorical unit similar to a prose paragraph, and indicated as such by the indentation of the first line.

VERSIFICATION. Synonym for *prosody* (q.v.).

VICTORIAN PERIOD. The period dated from either 1832 (the first Reform Bill) or 1837 (the accession of Queen Victoria to the throne) until the Queen's death in 1901. Much of the writing of this period reflected contemporary social, economic, and intellectual problems, such as the Industrial Revolution, pressures for political and economic reforms, and the impact of the Darwinian theory of evolution. Tennyson, Browning, and Arnold were the more prominent poets. Arnold, Carlyle, and Ruskin were influential essayists. Among the novelists were Dickens, Thackeray, George Eliot, Meredith, Trollope, Hardy, and Samuel Butler.

VILLANELLE. A French fixed verse form of six stanzas (five tercets and a quatrain), characterized by the use of only two rhymes and the repetition of lines as refrains. The opening line is repeated at the ends of the second and fourth stanzas, and the third line at the ends of the third and fifth. The two refrain lines conclude the poem. The rhyme scheme is *a b a, a b a, a b a, a b a, a b a, a b a a.* The form was originally used for pastoral subjects (the name derives from *villa,* a farm or country house), and later used for light verse. See Theodore Roethke, "The Waking," p. 331, and Dylan Thomas, "Do Not Go Gentle into That Good Night," p. 336.

VIRELAY. A name applied to two verse forms derived from old French poetry, neither of which is strictly fixed in form or common in English. The short one has only two rhymes and alternates the first and second lines as refrains. The other has an indefinite number of stanzas with one rhyme in long lines and the other rhyme in short lines. The short lines always provide the rhyme for the long lines of the next stanza, and the short lines of the last stanza rhyme with the long lines of the first.

VIRGULE (SLASH). The short slanting line used to divide a line into feet, or to mark the division between one line and another when quoting poetry in a prose paragraph.

Now / my charms / are all / o'erthrown.

VOICE. T. S. Eliot has described "The Three Voices of Poetry":

> The first voice is the voice of the poet talking to himself—or to nobody. The second is the voice of the poet addressing an audience, whether large or small. The third is the voice of the poet when he attempts to create a dramatic character speaking in verse; when he is saying, not what he would say in his own person, but only what he can say within the limits of one imaginary character addressing another imaginary character.

See PERSONA.

WEAK ENDING. At the end of a line of verse, a syllable which, though it is stressed metrically, would be unstressed in ordinary speech, and leads right on to the following line:

> Thy mother was a piece of virtue, and
> She said thou wast my daughter.
>
> Shakespeare, *The Tempest*

WIT. 1. Intelligence or wisdom (Renaissance usage). 2. Fancy or nimbleness of thinking (seventeenth-century usage, often applied in discussion of metaphysical poetry). 3. The ability to see similarities, as opposed to "judgment," which was considered the ability to see differences (late seventeenth-century usage). 4. In the eighteenth century, according to Pope,

> True wit is Nature to advantage dressed,
> What oft was thought, but ne'er so well expressed.

5. In the twentieth century, wit is associated with humor in original, clever remarks.

WORD ACCENT. See ACCENT.

WRENCHED ACCENT. See ACCENT.

ZEUGMA. A Greek word literally meaning "yoking," and applying to the use of a single word standing in the same grammatical relationship to two other words, but with significant differences in meaning:

> Or *stain* her honor, or her new brocade.
>
> Pope, *The Rape of the Lock*

a he as o, 311
Absalom and Achitophel (selection), 18
Adam Lay I-bowndyn, 48
Admonitions, 386
Advent 1966, 357
After Great Pain, a Formal Feeling Comes, 222
After Lorca, 363
Afterwards, 232
"Ah, Are You Digging on My Grave?" 231
Ah, Teneriffe! 225
Airstrip in Essex, 1960, An, 367
ALFRED, LORD TENNYSON, 203–207
All, All of a Piece, 117
Altar, The, 93
Americana IX, 323
Americana XIII, 30
Americana XV Simplicity, 324
Americana XVII A Reminder of William Carlos Williams, 29
ANDERSON, JACK, 383–384
April in Paris, 313
Army Corps on the March, An, 217
ARNOLD, MATTHEW, 220–221
Artillery, 95
Art Thou Poor, 80
Artist, The, 269
As You Came from the Holy Land of Walsingham, 70
Aspens, 256
At the Altar, 339
"At the round earth's imagin'd corners, blow," 87
AUDEN, W. H., 325–329
Autumn Begins in Martins Ferry, Ohio, 367

Badger, The, 193
Bait, The, 82
Bantams in Pine-Woods, 258
"Batter my heart, three-person'd God; for you," 88
Bavarian Gentians, 277
Beat! Beat! Drums! 216
Beautiful Changes, The, 347
Bee Meeting, The, 381
Bells for John Whiteside's Daughter, 299
BENEDIKT, MICHAEL, 391–392

BETHUNE, LEBERT, 391
Between the Porch and the Altar (selection: IV. At the Altar), 339
Binsey Poplars, 234
Blackberry Sweet, 337
BLAKE, WILLIAM, 135–141
Blow, Blow, Thou Winter Wind! 72
BLY, ROBERT, 365–366
Bonnie Broukit Bairn, The, 301
BRETON, ANDRÉ, 27–28
Bridge, The (selections: To Brooklyn Bridge and National Winter Garden), 318
Bright Star, 201
BROWNING, ELIZABETH BARRETT, 202
BROWNING, ROBERT, 207–211
Burning Babe, The, 68
BURNS, ROBERT, 141–146
BYRON, GEORGE GORDON, LORD, 173–186
By Way of Preface, 212
Byzantium, 246

CAMPION, THOMAS, 79–80
Canterbury Tales, The (selections from The Prologue), 45
Canto LXXXI (selection), 286
Care-Charmer Sleep, 69
CAREW, THOMAS, 97
CARROLL, LEWIS, 225–228
Cavalry Crossing a Ford, 217
CHAUCER, GEOFFREY, 45–48
Cherrylog Road, 353
Childe Harold's Pilgrimage (selection from Canto III), 175
Children's Rhymes, 320
Clare, John, 193–194
Clement Attlee, 391
Clerimont's Song, 88
CLIFTON, LUCILLE, 385–387
Clod and the Pebble, The, 138
Code, The, 252
COLERIDGE, SAMUEL TAYLOR, 155–173
Collar, The, 95
Composed upon Westminster Bridge, 150
Cornelia's Song, 90
CORSO, GREGORY, 371–374
Crabbed Age and Youth, 72
CRANE, HART, 314–320

Crazed Girl, A, 249
CREELEY, ROBERT, 363–364
Crowdieknowe, 301
Crow's First Lesson, 369
Crow's Last Stand, 370
Crystals Like Blood, 303
CUMMINGS, E. E., 308–312

Daddy, 379
DANIEL, SAMUEL, 69
Danny Deever, 240
Danse Russe, 263
Darkling Thrush, The, 229
DAVIDSON, JOHN, 237–239
December, 376
Definition of Love, The, 106
"De Gustibus——," 210
DEKKER, THOMAS, 80
Delight in Disorder, 91
Description of the Morning, A, 117
Design, 255
Desolation Row, 395
DE VREE, PAUL, 313
DICKEY, JAMES, 352–355
DICKINSON, EMILY, 221–225
Disabled, 306
Disillusionment of Ten O'Clock, 257
Dog, 299
DÖHL, REINHARD, 313
Dolor, 330
Do Not Go Gentle into That Good Night, 336
Don Juan (selection from Canto XI), 182
DONNE, JOHN, 15, 81–88
DOUGLAS, KEITH, 347
Dover Beach, 220
DRAYTON, MICHAEL, 69
Dream, The, 423
Dreams, 27
Drummer Hodge, 229
Drunkard Cannot Meet a Cork, A, 225
DRYDEN, JOHN, 18–19, 114–117
DUNCAN, ROBERT, 344–346
DYLAN, BOB, 395–397

Earth's Answer, 137
Easter 1916, 242
Ecstasy, The, 84
Edward, Edward, 53
Eleanor Rigby, 394
ELIOT, T. S., 288–299
Energetic Women, 276
Epistle to Dr. Arbuthnot, 118
Epithalamion, 56
Exposure, 305
Elegie 9   The Autumnal, 86
Elegy, 130
Elegy for Jane, 330

Fall of Rome, The, 327
"Farewell! thou art too dear for my possessing," 77
Farm Picture, A, 216
Fear No More, 74
February Evening in New York, 355
Felix Randal, 235
Fern Hill, 335
1st, The, 385
For the Marriage of Faustus and Helen, 314
For the Union Dead, 342
Force That Through the Green Fuse Drives the Flower, The, 334
"Frater Ave Atque Vale," 207
Frogs, 357
FROST, ROBERT, 251–255
Full Fathom Five, 75

Gallows, The, 255
Garden, The, 107
Gently Dip, 67
Gerontion, 293
Get the Gasworks, 338
Ghazals, 389
GINSBERG, ALLEN, 361–363
GIOVANNI, NIKKI, 397
Gold, 368
GOMRINGER, EUGEN, 412
Good-morrow, The, 81
Good Times, 385
GOOGE, BARNABE, 55–56
Grace for a Child, 92
GRAY, THOMAS, 130–133
Great Figure, The, 3
GUNN, THOM, 368–369

HALL, DONALD, 367–368
HARDY, THOMAS, 229–233
Hark, Now Everything Is Still, 90
Harlem, 322
HARRISON, JIM, 389–390
HARRISON, TONY, 392–393
Hay for the Horses, 375
HERBERT, GEORGE, 93–97
HERRICK, ROBERT, 91–92
Hibiscus on the Sleeping Shores, 257
"His golden locks time hath to silver turned," 68
Hollow Men, The, 295
Holy Sonnet 7: "At the round earth's imagin'd corners, blow," 87
Holy Sonnet 13: "What if this present were the world's last night?" 87
Holy Sonnet 14: "Batter my heart, three-person'd God; for you," 88
Holy Thursday (from Songs of Experience), 138
Holy Thursday (from Songs of Innocence), 136

Holy Willie's Prayer, 141
HOPKINS, GERARD MANLEY, 233–237
Horatian Ode, An, 109
HOUSMAN, A. E., 239–240
How Do I Love Thee? 202
How Soon Hath Time, 98
Howl (selections), 361
Hugh Selwyn Mauberley (selection), 278
HUGHES, LANGSTON, 320–323
HUGHES, TED, 369–371
Humming-bird, 273

I Haue a Yong Suster, 50
I Know a Man, 364
I Like a Look of Agony, 222
I Sing of a Maiden, 48
I Try to Waken and Greet the World Once Again, 367
Ice Eagle, The, 387
IGNATOW, DAVID, 338, 423–424
In Laughter, 369
In Mind, 356
Infant Sorrow, 140
Inner Part, The, 358
Insensibility, 303
Introduction (to Songs of Experience), 136
Introduction (to Songs of Innocence), 135
Invention of New Jersey, The, 383
Iris, 269
It Was a Lover, 73
It's No Good! 276

Jabberwocky, 227
January Morning, 263
JEFFERS, ROBINSON, 287–288
JOHNSON, SAMUEL, 128–130
JONES, LeROI, 382–383
JONSON, BEN, 88–89
Jubilate Agno (selection), 133
Juju of My Own, A, 391
JUSTICE, DONALD, 423

Kangaroo, 274
KAUFMAN, SHIRLEY, 423
KEATS, JOHN, 21–22, 194–201
Kind of Poetry I Want, The (selection), 301
KIPLING, RUDYARD, 240–241
Knoxville, Tennessee, 397
Kore, 364
Kubla Khan, 155

La Belle Dame sans Merci, 194
Lake Isle of Innisfree, The, 242
Lamb, The, 135
Lapis Lazuli, 248
LARKIN, PHILIP, 349–351

LAWRENCE, D. H., 273–277
LEAR, EDWARD, 212
LENNON, JOHN, 394
"Let me not to the marriage of true minds," 78
LEVERTOV, DENISE, 355–357
Likeness, A, 209
Lines Composed a Few Miles Above Tintern Abbey, 146
Listening to Foxhounds, 352
London, 139
Long-Legged Fly, 249
Looking At Pictures To Be Put Away, 378
Love Calls Us to the Things of This World, 348
Love Poem, 366
Love Song of J. Alfred Prufrock, The, 288
Love the Wild Swan, 287
LOVELACE, RICHARD, 104–105
Lover Showeth How He Is Forsaken of Such as He Sometime Enjoyed, The, 55
LOWELL, ROBERT, 339–344
Lycidas, 98
Lying in a Hammock at William Duffy's Farm in Pine Island, Minnesota, 366

Macavity: the Mystery Cat, 298
MacDIARMID, HUGH, 301–303
Magi, The, 23
Man He Killed, The, 230
Marches Now the War Is Over (selections), 218
Mariana, 203
MARLOWE, CHRISTOPHER, 70
Marriage, 371
MARVELL, ANDREW, 105–112
McCARTNEY, PAUL, 394
Medium IV Sights, The, 29
Meeting at Night, 208
Memories of West Street and Lepke, 341
Mending Wall, 251
Meru, 247
MILLS, NEIL, 438, 454
Milton: "And did those feet in ancient time," 140
Milton by Firelight, 374
MILTON, JOHN, 98–103
Mr. Bleaney, 350
Mr. Edwards and the Spider, 339
Mrs. Alfred Uruguay, 261
Morning Song, 378
Musée des Beaux Arts, 326
My Last Duchess, 207
"My mistress' eyes are nothing like the sun," 79
My Own Heart Let Me More Have Pity On, 236

My Papa's Waltz, 329
My Sad Captains, 368
my sweet old etcetera, 309

Name—of It—Is "Autumn," The, 224
Naming of Parts, 337
Nansen, 376
National Winter Garden, 319
Never Seek to Tell Thy Love, 140
New Mexican Mountain, 287
Night Funeral in Harlem, 321
Night Journey, 329
Night-Music, 350
No Worst, There Is None, 236

O Mistress Mine, 74
O, My Luve Is Like a Red, Red Rose, 145
O Whistle, and I'll Come to You, My Lad, 145
Ode on a Grecian Urn, 199
Ode on Melancholy, 21
Ode to a Nightingale, 197
Ode to Psyche, 196
Ode to the West Wind, 188
old age sticks, 311
On Forelands High in Heaven, 239
On His Blindness, 103
On the Beach, at Night, 219
On the Death of Dr. Robert Levet, 129
On This Island, 325
Order in the Streets, 423
Out of Sight, Out of Mind, 55
OWEN, WILFRED, 303–307

Passionate Shepherd to His Love, 70
Pattern Poem with an Elusive Intruder, 313
Paudeen, 242
PEELE, GEORGE, 67–68
Peter Quince at the Clavier, 258
Piazza di Spagna, Early Morning, 349
Pied Beauty, 234
ping pong, 412
Plain Sense of Things, The, 262
PLATH, SYLVIA, 378–382
POE, EDGAR ALLAN, 202
Poem, 268
Poem Against the British, 365
Poem, or Beauty Hurts Mr. Vinal, 308
Politics, 250
POPE, ALEXANDER, 118–128
Portrait, 308
POUND, EZRA, 25–26, 277–286
Prayer (1), 94
Preface to a Twenty Volume Suicide Note, 382
Preludes, 291
Prometheus, 173
Pulley, The, 96

RAKOSI, CARL, 29–30, 323–325
RALEGH, SIR WALTER, 56
RANDALL, DUDLEY, 337
RANSOM, JOHN CROWE, 299–300
Redemption, 93
REED, HENRY, 337–338
Resolution and Independence, 150
Retreat, The, 112
Rime of the Ancient Mariner, The, 156
Rising and Sinking, 423
River-Merchant's Wife: A Letter, The, 25
ROETHKE, THEODORE, 329–334
Rose, The, 331
Rose-Cheeked Laura, 79
Runner, The, 218

Safari West, 360
Sailing to Byzantium, 245
Same in Blues, 322
Schwiegermutterlieder, 392
Second Coming, The, 244
Send-Off, The, 305
SHAKESPEARE, WILLIAM, 13, 72–79
"Shall I compare thee to a summer's day," 75
She Walks in Beauty, 173
SHELLEY, PERCY BYSSHE, 186–193
Short Song of Congratulation, A, 128
Sick Rose, The, 138
SIDNEY, SIR PHILIP, 66–67
Similes for Two Political Characters of 1819, 187
Simplicity, 358
SIMPSON, LOUIS, 357–360
Since, 327
"Since brass, nor stone, nor earth, nor boundless sea," 76
Since There's No Help, 69
Sir Patrick Spens, 50
Slumber Did My Spirit Seal, A, 149
SMART, CHRISTOPHER, 133–135
SNYDER, GARY, 374–378
Solitary Reaper, The, 154
somewhere i have never travelled, gladly beyond, 310
Song, A: "Ask me no more where Jove bestows," 97
Song: "Go and catch a falling star," 81
Song: "Why so pale and wan, fond lover?" 103
Song for St. Cecilia's Day, A, 115
Song of a Man Who Has Come Through, The, 273
Song of Fixed Accord, 262
Song of Myself (selections), 214
Song to the Men of England, 186
Songs of Experience (selections), 136
Songs of Innocence (selections), 135

Sonnet, A: "His golden locks time hath to silver turned," 68

Sonnet 12: "When I do count the clock that tells the time," 75

Sonnet 18: "Shall I compare thee to a summer's day?" 75

Sonnet 30: "When to the sessions of sweet silent thought," 76

Sonnet 65: "Since brass, nor stone, nor earth, nor boundless sea," 76

Sonnet 66: "Tired with all these, for restful death I cry," 77

Sonnet 73: "That time of year thou mayst in me behold," 77

Sonnet 87: "Farewell! thou art too dear for my possessing," 77

Sonnet 94: "They that have power to hurt, and will do none," 78

Sonnet 116: "Let me not to the marriage of true minds," 78

Sonnet 129: "Th' expense of spirit in a waste of shame," 79

Sonnet 130: "My mistress' eyes are nothing like the sun," 79

Soul Selects Her Own Society, The, 222

SOUTHWELL, ROBERT, 68–69

Sparrow, The, 270

SPENSER, EDMUND, 56–66

Spring and Fall: To a Young Child, 235

Starlight Night, The, 233

Starting from Paumanok (selection), 214

STEVENS, WALLACE, 257–263

Still, 385

Stopping by Woods on a Snowy Evening, 254

Study in Aesthetics, The, 277

Study of Two Pears, 260

Success Is Counted Sweetest, 221

SUCKLING, SIR JOHN, 103–104

Sumer Is Icumen In, 49

Summer, 1960, Minnesota, 365

Sun Rising, The, 15

SWIFT, JONATHAN, 117–118

Swimmers, The, 312

SYMONS, ARTHUR, 241

Take, O! Take, 74

TATE, ALLEN, 312–314

Tears, Idle Tears, 206

TENNYSON, ALFRED, LORD, 203–207

"That time of year thou mayst in me behold," 77

That Women Are but Men's Shadows, 89

"Th' expense of spirit in a waste of shame," 79

There Was a Child Went Forth, 213

There's Been a Death, in the Opposite House, 223

They Are All Gone into the World of Light, 113

They Shut Me Up in Prose, 223

"They that have power to hurt, and will do none," 78

Thirty Bob a Week, 237

This Is Just To Say, 268

This Living Hand, 201

THOMAS, DYLAN, 334–337

THOMAS, EDWARD, 255–257

Thomas the Rhymer, 51

TICHBORNE, CHIDIOCK, 67

Tichborne's Elegy, 67

Tiger, The, 139

"Tired with all these, for restful death I cry," 77

To a Mouse, 144

To a Skylark, 190

To Althea, from Prison, 104

To Brooklyn Bridge, 318

To Daffodils, 92

To Elsie, 266

To Helen, 202

To His Coy Mistress, 105

To His Son, 56

To Lucasta, Going to the Wars, 104

To the Memory of Mr. Oldham, 114

To the Virgins, to Make Much of Time, 91

To Women, As Far As I'm Concerned, 276

Triumph of Charis, The, 88

Truth Kills Everybody, 371

Two Presentations, 344

Ulysses, 205

Under the Greenwood Tree, 72

Upon Julia's Clothes, 92

Valediction Forbidding Mourning, A, 83

VAUGHAN, HENRY, 112–114

Vergissmeinicht, 347

Volcanic Venus, 276

Waking, The, 331

Waking from Sleep, 365

Wakoski, Diane, 387–389

Way I Read a Letter's—This, The, 224

WEBSTER, JOHN, 90

"Western wind, when will thou blow?" 8

"What if this present were the world's last night," 87

"When I do count the clock that tells the time," 75

When I Set Out for Lyonnesse, 231

When Icicles Hang by the Wall, 13

"When to the sessions of sweet silent thought," 76

White Heliotrope, 241
White Knight's Song, The, 225
WHITMAN, WALT, 213–220
Who Wot Nowe That Ys Here, 49
"Why so pale and wan, fond lover?" 103
WILBUR, RICHARD, 347–349
Wild Oats, 351
WILLIAMS, JOHN A., 360–361
WILLIAMS, WILLIAM CARLOS, 3, 263–273
Willie B (2), 386
Windhover, The, 233

With How Sad Steps, 66
Within the Dream You Said, 349
WORDSWORTH, WILLIAM, 146–154
World Below the Brine, The, 219
WRIGHT, JAMES, 366–367
WYATT, SIR THOMAS, 55

YEATS, WILLIAM BUTLER, 23, 242–250
Young Couples Strolling By, 325

Zacoatl! 454
09 (zero nine), 438

6 7 8 9 10 11 12 13 14 15   88 87 86 85 84 83 82 81 80 79 78 77